Energy: Markets and Regulation

Energy: Markets and Regulation

Essays in Honor of M. A. Adelman

edited by
Richard L. Gordon,
Henry D. Jacoby, and
Martin B. Zimmerman

The MIT Press
Cambridge, Massachusetts
London, England

© 1987 by The Massachusetts Institute of Technology

All rights reserved. No part of this book may be reproduced in any form by any electronic or mechanical means (including photocopying, recording, or information storage and retrieval) without permission in writing from the publisher.

This book was set in Apollo by Asco Trade Typesetting Ltd., Hong Kong, and printed and bound by The Murray Printing Company in the United States of America.

Library of Congress Cataloging-in-Publication Data

Energy: markets and regulation.
  Bibliography: p.
  Includes index.
  1. Energy industries—Government policy—United States.   2. Energy industries—Government policy.   3. Adelman, Morris Albert.   I. Adelman, Morris Albert.   II. Gordon, Richard L., 1934–.   III. Jacoby, Henry D.   IV. Zimmerman, Martin B.
HD9502.U52E499   1987   333.79'0973   86-2927
ISBN 0-262-07103-7

Contents

List of Contributors

Ernst R. Berndt

Professor of Applied Economics, Sloan School of Management, Massachusetts Institute of Technology

Paul G. Bradley

Professor, Department of Economics, University of British Columbia, and Director, Mineral Revenues Inquiry, Government of Western Australia

Paul R. Carpenter

Vice President, Incentives Research, Inc.

Robert W. Crandall

Senior Fellow, The Brookings Institution

Paul Leo Eckbo

C.E.O., Marsoft Inc.

Richard L. Gordon

Professor of Mineral Economics, College of Earth and Mineral Sciences, The Pennsylvania State University

Henry D. Jacoby

Professor of Management, Sloan School of Management, Massachusetts Institute of Technology

Gordon M. Kaufman

Professor of Operations Research and Management, Sloan School of Management, Massachusetts Institute of Technology

Theodore E. Keeler

Professor, Department of Economics and Institute of Transportation Studies, University of California at Berkeley

Charles P. Kindleberger

Ford International Professor of Economics, Emeritus, Massachusetts Institute of Technology

Paul W. MacAvoy

Dean and Professor of Management, Graduate School of Management, and Professor of Economics, University of Rochester

Jeffrey K. MacKie-Mason

Assistant Professor of Economics, Department of Economics and Institute of Policy Studies, University of Michigan

Robert S. Pindyck

Professor of Applied Economics, Sloan School of Management, Massachusetts Institute of Technology

Philip K. Verleger, Jr.

Visiting Fellow, Institute for International Economics

G. Campbell Watkins

President, DataMetrics Limited, and Professor of Economics, University of Calgary

David O. Wood

Senior Lecturer, Sloan School of Management, Massachusetts Institute of Technology, and Associate Director, MIT Energy Laboratory

Arthur W. Wright

Professor of Economics, University of Connecticut

Zenon S. Zannetos

Professor of Management and Senior Associate Dean for Development, Sloan School of Management, Massachusetts Institute of Technology

Martin B. Zimmerman

Associate Professor of Business Economics and Public Policy, Graduate School of Business Administration, and Associate Professor of Economics, University of Michigan

Preface

Charles P. Kindleberger

I write about Morris Adelman as a friend, not as a professional economist. As I said in January, 1983,

I offer an opinion about oil with the greatest diffidence since the real experts differ so widely in the importance they attach to different facts .... Some economists like M. A. Adelman emphasize the low cost of finding and developing oil in Saudi Arabia and Kuwait. Others like Walter J. Levy the high cost of developing alternative sources and substitutes, and the vulnerability of Middle East supplies to Interruption ....[1]

On Morris Adelman, the friend, I am an expert, however. He and I came to MIT at the same time in the fall of 1948, and for the first year we shared an office in Building 1, near the Piranesi-like laboratories on stresses and strains that used to test the strength of lumber by breaking it in two. I was the Adelmans' first guest when Millie cooked dinner and embarked on her illustrious career as a gourmet cook. Morris and I read the *New York Times* together, and we helped grade 750 juniors' examinations in Ec 11, two men to a question that had to be graded 375 times. Morry has mellowed since those days when he, emerging from Harvard with a freshly minted PhD in economics, held to the highest standards of scholarship, not only for himself but also for juniors. For equity it was necessary to calibrate the two graders of a question, and to equalize their marks on average. Morry in those days would converge to a mean of 4.0 or 4.5 out of 10, whereas the oldest man in the department, and the most generous to students outside his own section whom he trained to a fine edge by low quiz grades, would weigh in with an average nearer 7.0 or 7.5.

How Morry got into economics in the first place is a story worth telling. Like many of the brilliant graduates of City College (as it was then) of New York, his ambition in the depressed thirties was to get a job in a New York high school teaching social science (or perhaps it was still then called "Civics"). He got the job and presumably was fixed for life. After Pearl Harbor, when he and his classmates were clearly destined for the armed forces, a friend with broadly the same background and ambition happened to get a job in Washington as a junior professional economist with only a BA degree. He told Morry that it was a useful, enjoyable, and not unrewarding way to put in time while waiting for greeting from Uncle Sam. Morry went to Washington and had his life changed. When he went into the Navy as an ensign on a landing craft in the Pacific, he took a stack of economics books two feet high—Marshall, Schumpeter, Keynes, Mitchell, etc.—and read these during the "wait" portions of the Navy's "hurry-up-and-wait" routine. When he emerged from the Navy—not without a marvelous story of how a petty-officer beach master frustrated the photographing of General Douglas MacArthur's return to the Philippines, striding purposefully from a landing craft through the waves up the shingle— he went to Harvard for graduate study in economics. New York City's high school loss was a gain for world economics.

During our year together in Building 1, I empathized as the doctoral dissertation on the A&P antitrust case was turned into the Wells Prize publication in the Harvard Economic Studies series. More, I absorbed the fundamental lesson of his antitrust teaching that much of the attack on bigness is in reality an attack on competition. Big may mean competition, and little may be beautiful but it may also signify local monopoly. It is a Schumpeterian message. But while the A&P dissertation was supervised by his friend and mine, Professor Edward S. Mason, Morry absorbed one of the most distinguished collections of anecdotes about Schumpeter I know.

When the economics department moved to Building 14—Course 14, as we are known at the Institute, in Building 14 confused some observers about the MIT systems of numbering both departments and buildings—Morry and I were graduated to separate offices. But we have kept in touch. One intimate professional association was his contribution of an essay to a symposium I edited on the international corporation[2] entitled "The Multinational Corporation in World Petroleum." It made the point that even if developing countries nationalize the producing fields, the corporations will still have a function in coordinating the production, transport, refining, and distribution of petroleum products. I recently found that I have referred to that piece three or four times in the last decade or more in my own writing. The success of the effort as impresario led me to invite him once again to hold forth at a symposium on multinational business in the Middlebury College Conference on Economic Issues held at that institution in the spring of 1982.[3]

Morris and I have also supervised a number of dissertations together over 35 years. Of them I especially recall those of Stephen Hymer, Richard Gordon, and Ching Chen. After his successful defense, Ching Chen gave us and our wives a marvelous dinner (of Pekin duck), a Swedish custom reinvented by a man of Chinese ancestry and Japanese upbringing. Ching Chen, I believe, also helped provide the entry that established Morry as the leading authority on oil in Asia. Of the details of his wide consulting on antitrust cases and problems in oil, I know little. I did, however, provide the Adelmans with the address of a delightful pension on the Rue Saint Romain in the 6th arrondissement in Paris where various Kindlebergers stayed in 1960 and 1961, and the Adelmans the next year.

The friendship of the Kindlebergers with the Adelmans has not been without a touch of envy on my part. I am chagrined that his French is better than mine after the same or probably even less exposure, and I am overwhelmed by his ability to quote Shakespeare, Samuel Johnson, Mark Twain and other pillars of Bartlett's *Familiar Quotations*, ten to my one-half. He is, moreover, if not a better, at least a more willing actor, as testified to by his performances in *Three Penny Opera* and *Guys and Dolls*.

I leave it to his students and other colleagues to sing Morry's praises as economist. I sing them as a human being.

Notes

1. C. P. Kindleberger, "The World Economic Slowdown since the 1970s," lecture to the Austrian Institute of Economic Research, January 1983.

2. M. A. Adelman, "The Multinational Corporation in World Petroleum," in C. P. Kindleberger, ed., *The International Corporation*, Cambridge, MA: MIT Press, 1970, pp. 227–241.

3. M. A. Adelman, "The Multinationals in the World Oil Market: The 1970s and 1980s," in C. P. Kindleberger and David B. Audretch, eds., *The Multinational Corporation in the 1980s*, Cambridge, MA: MIT Press, 1983, pp. 123–135.

Foreword

Richard L. Gordon
Henry D. Jacoby
Martin B. Zimmerman

Morry Adelman is the complete scholar. He was made major contributions to our understanding of industrial organization and antitrust policy, the economics of natural resource discovery, and (most recently) the world petroleum market. Time after time he has showed how simple economic theory can explain the most complicated of markets, and has relentlessly challenged resort to ad hoc "noneconomic" explanations of market behavior. By demonstrating its application he has increased our understanding of what that theory means. Moreover, through his ingenious and careful use of data he has inspired others to pay attention not only to technique, but also to the quality of information.

In nearly forty years of teaching he has armed his students with an ability to relate the tools of the discipline to activities in the real world. They in turn have carried his influence into other universities, the private sector, and into governments in many countries. Moreover, the number of Morry's students is not limited to those who were privileged to work directly under him at MIT. Throughout the fields of industrial organization and energy policy one finds people who have studied with him indirectly—as faculty colleagues or through his professional writings, public lectures, op-ed pieces, and testimony.

This volume is an attempt by some of these former students and current colleagues to honor Morry for his contributions, and to say a personal thank-you. Our way of going about the task has been to prepare a set of papers that reflect his career-long effort on market structure and behavior, and on the influence of government regulation. We have focused on the energy sector, which in recent years has drawn so much of his interest. The resulting collection falls into four rough categories: energy regulation, world energy markets, oil and gas supply, and energy demand.

Energy Regulation

Morry's best known early work was a book on the antitrust case against the A&P Company (Adelman, 1959). His analysis is still a standard for texts in industrial economics. Like much of his later research, it was concerned with the ambiguous roles of the government and the large corporation in influencing markets. He argued that A&P was prosecuted to a large extent for its success in undermining the monopoly pricing of products that the chain purchased and resold. This achievement he attributed more to the sophistication and capability of a large buyer than to monopsony power. Furthermore, as A&P faced substantial competition in its final market, many of the benefits of these efficiencies were passed on to consumers. The A&P study contributed importantly to our understanding of concentration, vertical integration, and large-buyer behavior, and also highlighted the misguided attempt by the Federal government to preserve a flawed notion of competition.

The vision of how A&P increased competition was transferred intact to Morry's analysis of world oil. He recognized that the integrated oil companies could play the same role in lowering energy prices as A&P played in retailing. He went on to develop analyses of how consuming country government policies prevented such an outcome.

Elsewhere Morry pointed out that vertical integration often was not an extension of monopoly power but a means of realizing technical economies (Adelman, 1949). Thus antitrust actions against vertical integration were often inappropriate—again, because they were based on an erroneous view of competition. In other words he identified cases in which the government itself restricted competition. Indeed, one of his first papers on the oil industry focused on the inefficiencies created by the prorationing scheme operated by the Texas Railroad Commission (Adelman, 1964). In many subsequent studies Morry has explored the intricacies of government influence on oil markets.

Probably the most Gordian of the regulatory tangles occurred in the US natural gas industry, and it is here that our volume begins. When Morry published his 1962 monograph on natural gas supply, the US Federal Power Commission had just begun regulating wellhead gas prices. In "Adapting to Change in Natural Gas Markets," Paul Carpenter, Henry Jacoby, and Arthur Wright trace the wrenching adjustments the industry has gone through since the price ceilings went into effect. A particular theme of their paper is the difficulties the industry has faced as an inflexible regulatory system encountered falling gas demand in the 1980s.

The Natural Gas Policy Act of 1978 created a crazy quilt of gas categories, each with a different controlled price, and some scheduled for deregulation in

1985. Interstate pipelines, under an obligation to maintain deliveries, bid up nonprice terms (e.g., take-or-pay clauses) in long-term contracts. Subsequently, falling oil prices and market-clearing gas prices made these contracts very costly to pipelines and their customers. A major task for the remainder of the 1980s is to undo the damage, and try to achieve a system that is more resilient in the face of market fluctuations.

Oil industry regulation is the subject of the contribution by Campbell Watkins, "Living under a Shadow: US Oil Policies and Canadian Oil Pricing." His concern is the import-control policy Morry wrote about and criticized at many points in his work on international trade in oil (for example, Adelman, 1972). Morry argued that the policy benefited small oil producers who were protected by the state prorationing programs. Watkins gives the view from the other side of the border and shows how US policies distorted policies and prices in Canada.

It is a fascinating analysis. From 1950 through the early 1970s, US policies in regard to oil imports and pricing were driven by domestic considerations— largely the protection of US suppliers. But the policy was wrapped in a cloak of national security, which made for very tricky dealings with Canada, a close and trusted neighbor. From the Canadian perspective, one is reminded of the old joke about where a gorilla sleeps: "Anywhere he wants to." It was not until deregulation of oil prices in the early 1980s that a normal commercial relationship developed in US-Canadian oil trade.

Morry has been a prescient observer of coal markets and the way they are affected by government regulation. In the mid-1960s he warned of the decline in US steam coal exports if rail rates for export coal did not come down (Adelman, 1966). High-priced coal could not compete with residual fuel oil in Europe. In another paper written about the same time and published first in Europe and Japan and then as an appendix in the petroleum market book (Adelman, 1972, pp. 265–275), he pointed out the costs involved in protecting European coal from competition with oil.

Richard Gordon, who first examined European coal industry policy in his MIT dissertation and has followed the coal industry ever since, analyzes coal policy in the major producing countries in his paper, "Coal Policy in Perspective." He argues that coal too often is an overrated fuel. It has reasonable prospects for electricity generation, but its other uses are unlikely to grow substantially. In countries with high-cost coal industries protectionism has retreated, but not completely disappeared. And among the relatively low-cost producers attempts to capture rents often have gone too far, possibly stunting the growth of the industry.

In the late 1960s and early 1970s it looked as if nuclear power would drive both coal and residual fuel oil out of the utility market. By the end of the 1970s it was clear this was not to be. In "The Evolution of Civilian Nuclear Power," Martin Zimmerman considers the odd history of nuclear power in the United States. How did an industry that was once so promising come to decline so rapidly? Zimmerman argues that government policy, particularly the indirect subsidy provided by the Price-Anderson Act, simply deferred the problems that nuclear power finally had to confront at the end of the 1970s. He also argues that state regulation of public utilities has compounded the difficulties of nuclear power development in the 1980s.

The response of the US economy to the oil price increases of the 1970s was importantly affected by simultaneous attempts to curb environmental pollution. Air pollution regulations increased the cost of burning fuel. Coal, because it is the dirtiest of the fuels, bore the brunt of the cost increases at the very time other government policies were trying to promote the substitution of coal for imported oil. While the costs of pollution control have been documented in a number of studies, little attempt has been made to measure the benefits realized in terms of reduced air pollution.

In his paper, "The Record of the Environmental Protection Agency in Controlling Industrial Air Pollution," Paul MacAvoy first uses a comparison of emissions before and after passage of the Clean Air Act to suggest that pollution control policies have had a relatively small impact on emission levels. This disturbing result then motivates an exhaustive search, using econometric techniques, to find out why so much effort and expenditure yielded such sad results. His answer lies in the regulatory system that we set up to undertake the cleanup task. The system includes a complex sharing of powers and responsibilities among a federal agency and 50 state agencies, and it apparently was designed to leave plenty of discretion to deal with "hardship" cases. As a result, in many instances the regulations on the oldest and worst sources of emissions have been the least restrictive. The paper contains important lessons for the future development of our laws and institutions in this area.

The automobile has also been the target of policies aimed at both controlling pollution and saving energy. Robert Crandall and Theodore Keeler discuss the effects of these policies, and of safety regulations as well, in a paper, "Public Policy and the Private Auto." They find that, while early pollution control measures were probably cost effective, those imposed since 1979 are not. As for fuel economy, their results suggest that corporate average fuel economy (CAFE) standards imposed in 1975 had little effect on the fuel economy of new cars. The observed increases in fuel economy of new cars can be explained as a normal industry response to higher gasoline prices and the consequent consumer demand for fuel efficient cars. In safety regulation, they find that most, but not all, of the efforts aimed at producing safer cars have been worthwhile. In general, they argue that we now need now selective relaxation in the regulation of this sector.

World Energy Markets

Morry's attention was drawn to the worldwide oil industry in the late 1950s. The industry was a rich field for research on industrial organization and issues of government regulation. Other scholars were working on the industry during this period, but when the oil crisis of 1973–1974 stimulated intense academic and public attention, it was Morry's massive work, *The World Petroleum Market* (Adelman, 1972), that any newcomer read first.[1]

Coming as it did in 1972, the book captured what must now be described as "the way it was in the old days." The industry was on the threshold of radical change—a transformation that continues even as this volume is being produced. Morry's book provided the foundation for efforts to map and understand that change, and no one has followed and interpreted the post-1973 events more energetically and productively than he.

There has been plenty of controversy: the price shocks of 1973–1974 and 1978–1979 produced some of the most heated economic and political debates of the decade. Morry has been in the thick of it, applying the time-tested lessons of industrial organization to the new situation (e.g., the inherent instability of a cartel and the risks of forecasting its course). As evidenced by the many pithy Adelman lines quoted by the authors of this volume, he has played the role with wit, and humor, and an unending supply of literary references.

Philip Verleger's contribution to this volume provides an analysis of oil market price trends that confirms a major and once controversial aspect of Adelman's evaluation. Through the years Morry has managed to irritate both the oil companies and their critics with his analysis of vertical integration. In typical Adelman fashion, he made an important empirical contribution to a long standing theoretical debate but refrained from inappropriate generalization. He noted that the widespread reliance on open market trading suggested that integration was not essential for the efficient coordination of supplies of crude oil to refineries.

But he also took the view that integration should be allowed. While few coordination benefits accrued from it, integration did expand the number of strong potential entrants. Moreover, at worst the effects were neutral, and it would be socially wasteful to devote resources to useless reorganizations.

In "The Evolution of Oil as a Commodity," Verleger studies the breakdown of vertical integration in the world oil industry as the producing countries have progressively reduced the role of the international majors by nationalizing resources and altering the terms of access to crude oil. He shows how the necessary institutions—organized spot and futures trading, and price reporting services—have emerged to create a well-functioning commodity market. Verleger also stresses that, to an ever greater degree, world oil prices are being formed in this market and not in OPEC deliberations. OPEC's influence is felt only from the output it makes available. Verleger makes clear that price erosion reflects the difficulties of restricting total output to the level salable at OPEC's target prices. He thus confirms another Adelman prediction: that as the OPEC countries shifted to more open market sales, control over price would be more difficult to maintain.

Many economists doubted that OPEC would hold together at all. Morry was careful on this score. He believed that OPEC could be broken if the right actions were taken, and correctly feared that they would not be. But he also indicated that, ultimately, traditional pressures would emerge. The way these market processes work is analyzed by Jeffrey MacKie-Mason and Robert Pindyck, who study cartelization in two nonfuel minerals—mercury and sulfur. The intent of their paper, "Cartel Theory and Cartel Experience in International Minerals Markets," is to provide contrasts to the OPEC experience to see what can be learned. After a useful summary of cartel theory, the authors proceed to analyze how, after years of success, both cartels collapsed largely through pressures from entry of new producers.

In "Worldwide Petroleum Taxation: The Pressure for Revision" Paul Eckbo analyzes tax developments in the world oil market. Following Adelman's lead in worrying about the allocative inefficiencies of typical mineral taxing schemes, Eckbo analyzes the problems faced by oil producing countries in devising sensible oil tax systems when cost and reservoir size vary so dramatically and oil prices can move over such a wide range. The paper is based on his wide experience as advisor on oil development and taxation, and it makes use of his special access to data and models of the various tax regimes.

Using Britain, the United States, Indonesia, and China as examples, Eckbo estimates the magnitude of the distortion to incentives because of differences in the different rent-capturing schemes. As a result, he is able to make some convincing predictions of changes to come in these systems.

At Morry's suggestion, Zenon Zannetos undertook in his doctoral dissertation to try to sort out some of the puzzles of the world tanker market. Zannetos succeeded in this. He made clear how vigorously competitive was the market and thus how unlikely it was that the oil companies could control it in the long run. He also helped clarify the curious way in which fluctuations in orders for new tankers respond to changes in oil market conditions.

In "Oil Tanker Markets: Continuity amidst Change," Zannetos analyzes how the tanker market has changed over the intervening 25 years. He looks at changes in scale economies, market structure, rate formation, and overall market behavior, and he finds the industry surprisingly little changed. He also looks at trends, particularly the move by exporting governments to integrate downstream and the changing structure of the majors, and ventures some predictions of how this market may evolve in the next few years.

Oil and Gas Supply

Morry has had a continuing interest in the nature of the supply function for natural resources and the way one ought to use the available data when formulating policy. He has been tireless in his efforts to eradicate confusion about "proved" reserves, explaining that they are a shelf inventory heavily influenced by economic incentives (as opposed to the popular perception that they reflect geological scarcity).

His early work on supply and price focused on natural gas and its joint production with oil (Adelman, 1962), and these issues played a major role in the larger work on the world petroleum market. During the 1970s he helped lead an NSF-sponsored project on the world oil market, carried out at MIT. Part of the project was the development of a model for forecasting supplies from various regions of the world (Adelman and Jacoby, 1979; Adelman and Ward, 1980). As is so often the case in Morry's work, the result was a framework that applied insights of mineral economics to make the best use of available data, while avoiding fancy tricks with little empirical substance.

Morry's knowledge of oil supply and cost has been well recognized within the industry. From 1966 to 1974 he served on the Coordinating Committee for Statistics and Economics of the American Petroleum Institute, which was the source of reserves data until the federal government took over the task (with unhappy results) in the 1970s. He also was the recipient in 1979 of the Mineral Economics Award of the American Institute of Mining, Metallurgical and Petroleum Engineers.

Much of this experience was collected in a book on resource supply written with several colleagues (Adelman et al., 1983). One of his coauthors, Gordon Kaufman, has been a pioneer in the effort to develop better ways of appraising the long-run supply of oil. In their joint book he contributed a lengthy review and analysis of the assorted efforts to estimate ultimate supplies of oil. He led the reader to the conclusion that each approach was flawed, often because those approaching the task from different disciplines failed to communicate with one another and that in any case data problems limited what could be done. In his essay for this volume, "Oil and Gas Resource and Supply Assessment," Kaufman has provided a shorter, more accessible version of his analysis of developments in the area.

The analysis of oil and gas supply is inherently difficult for two reasons. The first is the phenomenon of depletion—both the depletion of a deposit once found and the depletion of the stock of prospects to look for (so-called discovery depletion). The other is the extreme uncertainty, particularly in the analysis of undiscovered resources. Paul Bradley has been an active researcher on these problems, dating back at least to an early book with Morry on the discoveries in Alaska (Adelman, Bradley, and Norman, 1971). In his paper on "Cost and Output Analysis in Mineral and Petroleum Production," he develops a method for estimating supply functions that takes account of the incremental cost of development and the statistical characteristics of deposition and the exploratory process. The method is demonstrated by an application to gas deposits in Alberta.

The structure of Bradley's approach is inspired by a conception of the process that Morry laid out some years ago (Adelman, 1970). Thus the paper is an excellent example of the type of practical approach to analysis that Morry has fostered.

Energy Demand

As oil markets have developed since the 1973–1974 price shock, demand has played an ever more important role. The demand response was not anticipated by many analysts. Indeed, the performance of forecasters—and those who have tried to estimate the key parameters relating energy demand to measures of economic activity—has to be described as miserable. Something has been wrong with the way we conventionally model the relationship between energy and economic activity.

The failure of old models and methods has led to a radical rethinking of the relationship of energy to capital and other inputs in production, resurrecting old debates about the nature of capital. Ernst Berndt and David Wood have toiled mightily over the years in this complex and challenging area of economic research. In their paper, "Energy Price Shocks and Productivity Growth: A Survey," they cogently and wittily lead the reader through the competing ideas and the associated empirical work.

The paper also contains their own important insight: one cannot fully understand the relation of energy to economic activity without taking into account that different vintages of capital have different quality characteristics (such as energy efficiency). Thus one cannot even talk coherently about an economic measure of the capital stock without taking account of energy prices. Very likely these energy demand issues are the most important of all in this volume in terms of the future evolution of energy markets and the regulatory systems imposed on them.

The Larger Contribution

Finally, a word is needed about people who are part of this volume in spirit if not in pages of text. Several colleagues might have contributed to the volume but for matters of personal health or other exgencies, or because of limits to the length of the volume. Others—too many to name—offered whatever support and assistance we might need in putting the book together. So what the reader finds here is but the tip of the iceberg, a sample of the people Morry has influenced and helped to train in economics, and a partial view of the widespread respect and affection for him as a teacher, colleague, and friend.

Note

1. Although the book was a solitary achievement, Morry's list of acknowledgments is a Who's Who of energy economics at the time, and includes five of the authors in this Festschrift.

Energy: Markets and Regulation

1 Adapting to Change in Natural Gas Markets

Paul R. Carpenter
Henry D. Jacoby
Arthur W. Wright

With constant changes in supply, demand and technology, relative advantages must change, and some fuels or demands or sellers are under pressure to give ground to others. . . . An orderly retreat is, of all military manoeuvers, the hardest to carry out. (Adelman, 1962, pp. 112–113)

1 Introduction

In the early 1980s, the US natural gas industry first encountered the long-run demand curve, and it was ill prepared for the experience. For most of the industry's life, gas pipeline and distribution companies had not needed to worry about marketing their product. Sales expanded year in and year out as natural gas penetrated ever wider geographical markets and sectors of use. In this comfortable environment there evolved a set of institutional arrangements linking the vertical segments of the gas industry. Pipelines bought gas in the field under long-term, fixed-price contracts, and resold it to large industrial customers and local distribution companies (LDCs). Federal and state agencies regulated the tariffs and the entry/exit decisions of both pipelines and distributors. It was a tightly structured, deterministic set of arrangements.

Problems did arise in the late 1960s as federal ceilings on field prices began to bind, reducing the supply of new contracts to interstate pipelines and creating a seller's market. Pipelines lost some sales because they could not buy enough gas at the field to meet all the demands at end-use. But even with these difficulties, life in the gas industry was not all that hard. Marketing was no problem, and regulators assumed responsibility for managing the shortage.

Then came the dramatic events of the 1970s, which set off the current process of adjustment in the industry. The 1973–1974 oil shock further aggravated the interstate gas shortage. Increases in federal price ceilings could not prevent the situation from deteriorating even more. In 1977 the Carter administration proposed overhauling the whole system, and an 18-month legislative battle produced the Natural Gas Policy Act (NGPA) of 1978. This bill provided for the phased decontrol of prices for "new" gas, with removal of controls on 1 January 1985; perpetual control of "old" gas prices; and extension of federal price ceilings to intrastate field markets.

The NGPA decontrol process had only just begun when the second oil shock pitched the industry into the "market ordering problem"—renewed shortages, field prices ranging from $1.00 to $11.00 per thousand cubic feet (Mcf), and fears that a "fly-up" of new-gas prices on 1 January 1985 would create chaos. Contract terms responded to these confused conditions. Where permitted, higher gas prices were negotiated. When price ceilings bound, substitute terms (like "indefinite" price escalators and higher "take-or-pay" requirements) were introduced. Unfortunately, these changes rendered the industry even more vulnerable to the crunch that was coming.

And come it did, in the form of the Great Recession of 1981–1983 and the downward slide in oil prices that began in 1982. Slumping US manufacturing output and a warm winter in 1982–1983 added to the problems. The demand for natural gas fell sharply. But the gas industry lacked the flexibility to respond; instead of dropping to clear markets, prices continued to rise. Attempts to sell gas more competitively brought protests from other sellers whose markets were threatened. The gas industry had begun life on the demand curve, and an industry-wide crisis was at hand.

For the first time, gas pipelines and LDCs faced head-to-head price competition with coal, electricity, and especially oil. Since the early 1970s, oil prices have been volatile and appear likely to remain so. As oil prices change, the demand for gas will fluctuate, above and beyond shifts due to the business cycle. The sharp drop in gas demand in 1982 and 1983 was not a one-time phenomenon but a rude introduction to the new conditions of life in the gas business.

To prosper in this new market the industry will have to undergo substantial changes—in capital stock, technology, contracts, regulation, and corporate organization. The most important changes must occur in the terms of gas contracts and the associated federal and state regulation, because the gas surplus that underlies the current crisis is directly traceable to their inflexibility.

Change will not come easily. The particular prices and practices observed today are the product of a long history of political settlements involving economic rents. Any change will have immediate redistributive implications— among classes of customers, between pipelines and producers, and among regions of the country. Market conditions may change, but these political facts will remain. The quest for an institutional equilibrium cannot succeed if they are ignored.

2 How the Current System Evolved

2.1 The 1930s and the NGA

Our analysis begins with passage of the Natural Gas Act (NGA) of 1938, which first imposed federal regulation on interstate pipelines.[1] In the 1930s the natural gas industry operated in three distinct geographical markets: Appalachia, the Mid-Continent, and California. The West Coast was isolated from the rest of the country and had little influence on federal policy. Appalachia, where natural gas was first produced in the United States, served the metropolitan areas of New York and Philadelphia and the industrial centers of the eastern Great Lakes. Mid-Continent producing areas (Texas, Louisiana, Oklahoma, and Kansas) were distant from major markets, although already in the 1920s the new technology of long-distance pipelines had allowed limited service to St. Louis, Omaha, Chicago, and Minneapolis-St. Paul. Except for a single link from Missouri to Ohio, the gas systems of Appalachia and the Mid-Continent were separate.

Much of the impetus to regulation of interstate pipelines can be traced to differences in conditions between these two markets. Appalachian supply was declining: production peaked in 1916 and had dropped by 50% by the mid-1930s. In contrast, the Mid-Continent was awash in gas, most of it a by-product of oil production. Cutbacks in some areas while excess supplies were being flared in others were a source of frustration to interests in all areas.

In Appalachia, moreover, the process of adjustment to declining supply was distorted by state regulatory intervention. Most states regulated gas production, transportation, and distribution (including prices) within their own borders. As output declined, states sought to protect indigenous industries by allocating available supplies among users and in some cases by holding down prices. They could not, however, regulate gas transported across their borders in response to higher prices elsewhere. Between 1930 and 1934, the volume of Appalachian gas transported interstate increased by 36%, while total production in the region declined by 18% (Kitch, 1968). That interstate pipelines were able to divert economic rents from the states led producing-state interests to seek federal regulation of interstate trade.

The political atmosphere in the 1930s favored such a move. A case for federal regulation of gas pipelines was articulated by the US Federal Trade Commission (FTC) as part of a 96-volume study of public utility corporations commissioned by the Senate.[2] The FTC argued that natural gas pipelines should be regulated as common carriers.[3] Oil pipelines had been common carriers since the Hepburn Act of 1906, and virtually every other form of transportation had been regulated this way since the Interstate Commerce Act was passed in 1887 (gas pipelines were excluded at that time). In drafting Title III of the Public Utility Holding Company Act (PUHCA) of 1935, the FTC made gas pipelines common carriers. Congress, however, removed this title from the PUHCA and wrote a separate bill, the Natural Gas Act (NGA) of 1938.

The pipeline companies, originally started by town-gas distribution firms, had long owned most of the gas that flowed through their systems. Thus, they were traders as well as haulers of gas. Making them common carriers would have taken away their control over rights of access to pipeline capacity. Understandably, the interstate pipeline companies opposed replacing what is referred to as "purchase for resale" (PFR) with common carriage.

An additional technical argument against regulating gas pipelines as common carriers centered on their ability to handle seasonal and other variations in demand (Beard, 1941). In the 1930s gas storage located near the point of end-use was viewed as prohibitively expensive and dangerous. If the pipelines owned the gas, it was argued, they could operate more flexibly and adapt to changing conditions. As common carriers, in contrast, the pipelines could not achieve the requisite coordination.

Subsequently, of course, large-scale gas storage systems were developed, interruptible contracts came into use, and (recently) independent gas brokerage has emerged—all effectively negating the technical arguments against common carriage. But with the NGA the die was cast. Since the 1930s, pipelines have held rights to "bundles" of assets that include both gas reserves and transportation-and-storage systems. As will be shown below, current conditions may require the "unbundling" of these assets and associated services if the industry's ills are to be cured.

The NGA assigned responsibility for pipeline regulation to the Federal Power Commission (FPC), now called the Federal Energy Regulatory Commission (FERC). The essential features of FPC pipeline regulation were "certification" of facilities and a "tariff" governing rates and obligations to serve. This system has remained intact to this day.

The FPC set up procedures for certification of both new pipeline facilities and the modification or abandonment of old ones. To gain a "certificate of public necessity and convenience," pipelines had to enter into enough long-term purchase and sale contracts to demonstrate a 15- to 20-year supply of reserves and demand for gas. Certification also is required if a pipeline wishes to sell transportation services separately from its PFR commitments.

The pipeline "tariff" governs the terms of sale to local distribution companies (LDCs). The price terms of a tariff consist of "purchased gas costs" and transportation rates. Under PFR, a pipeline's weighted-average ("rolled-in") cost of buying gas is passed through to LDCs. Transportation rates are regulated in public utility fashion. The regulators try to design a structure of rates that is "nondiscriminatory" among different customer classes, and that allocates fixed and variable costs to "demand" and "commodity" charges so that the pipeline recovers its total costs inclusive of an allowed return on capital.[4]

In addition to price, the tariff agreement also obligates a pipeline to deliver natural gas to an LDC. The "service obligation" covers a range of volumes by type of service ("firm" or "interruptible"), delivered at the regulated transportation rates plus the cost of gas. More significant for present purposes, the obligation extends beyond any given term contract between the pipeline and the LDC.[5] The pipeline may not unilaterally alter the volumes in a tariff even after a contract expires. (To terminate or "abandon" service, of course, the pipeline would have to get a certificate.) For its part, the LDC frequently is obligated to make a minimum payment to the pipeline. This "minimum bill," as it is called, includes the demand-charge portion of the tariff rate plus a percentage of the contract demand volume valued at the commodity charge. Reflecting the perception that a pipeline company has bargaining power over the LDC, the service obligation is a stiffer requirement than the minimum bill.[6]

2.2 Chasing the Demand Curve: 1948–1965

Following World War II, the natural gas industry entered a boom period that lasted for more than two decades. The industry expanded so fast that it never experienced fluctuating volumes and prices from business cycles or the competition of close substitutes.

The comparative statics of these developments are illustrated in figure 1, which depicts a single market made up of the large end-users of the East and Upper Middle West. We abstract from the change in size of this "market" as the pipeline system expanded in the postwar period. Supply in the market is from the Mid-Continent fields—mainly Texas, Louisiana, and Oklahoma. The vertical axes show the average field price of gas, which is the average price to LDCs and large industrial customers less the cost of interstate transmission.

Market conditions from (say) 1948 through 1965 are depicted in panel (a). At the end of World War II, the short-run demand for natural gas was D_1—determined by the existing pipeline network and the stock of gas-using equipment. Short-run supply was S_1—relatively price-elastic compared to later years because of the backlog of reserves discovered in the 1930s but shut in until a market developed. The field price was P_1.

In the late 1940s the gas industry was far from long-run equilibrium. Long-

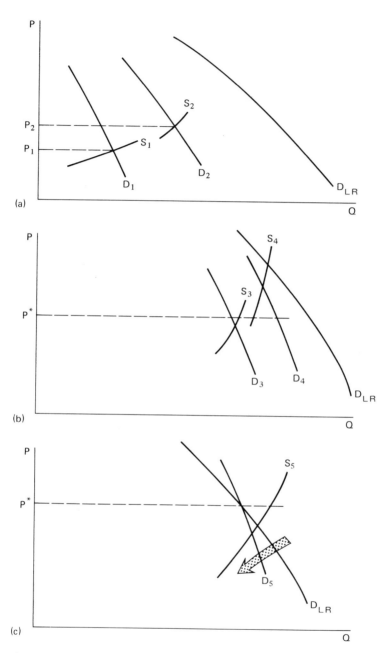

Figure 1
History of natural gas markets: (a) 1948–1965; (b) 1965–1981; (c) 1981–1983.

run demand would only be seen after the system had time to grow, with pipelines extended into all major markets and the energy-using capital stock adjusted to the relative price of delivered gas. This long-run demand is labeled D_{LR} in the figure. So long as D_{LR} remained a distant potential, the gas industry was shielded from demand fluctuations. System expansion and market penetration overwhelmed any offsetting business-cycle effects.

As the capital stock grew and adapted, short-run demand increased—say, to D_2. Indeed, between 1945 and 1960 total US pipeline capacity more than doubled. Supply also increased—say, to S_2. The net result was that prices increased somewhat, from P_1 to P_2. But demand was still far short of its long-term potential, and so the industry still was not exposed to interfuel competition and business cycles. Pipeline companies faced little volume risk, and (though prices were rising) there was as yet no evidence of demand instability.

A look at consumption growth rates confirms this story. Natural gas had a considerable price advantage over fuel oil, and the differential held for many years. Its effect shows up in figure 2 as a rapid and continuous growth in gas use from the end of World War II until the end of the 1960s. Other forms of energy, in contrast, show the effects of recessions—for example, in 1949, 1953–1954, and 1957–1958.

This was the setting in which the institutional arrangements of the gas industry evolved within the regulatory system set up under the NGA. One notable effect of that system was to reduce vertical integration in the industry. Instead of owning their own reserves, the pipelines preferred to purchase gas from others, because a pipeline's own production was subject to rate-of-return, cost-of-service regulation, while gas purchased from others was not.

The FPC also reinforced several practices that had emerged in the natural gas industry before federal regulation began. The agency formalized minimum reserve-to-production ratios and sinking funds tied to reserve life, which protected gas customers and bondholders against the "bleeding" of cash to pipeline shareholders while the reserve base behind service obligations and debt eroded. Further, the FPC was supportive of "take-or-pay" provisions in producer-pipeline contracts. Take-or-pay provisions, requiring pipelines to pay producers for minimum volumes even if less was actually taken, fostered stability in the industry in that they more or less matched the minimum-bill provisions in pipeline-distributor contracts. The burden of the "service obligation" was thereby distributed from wellhead to burner tip, at the same time that producers were assured a stable cash flow.

Thus the vertical market arrangements in the gas industry were closely determined and monitored by federal regulators. The resulting system was well-suited to the world for which it had been created—a world that, while

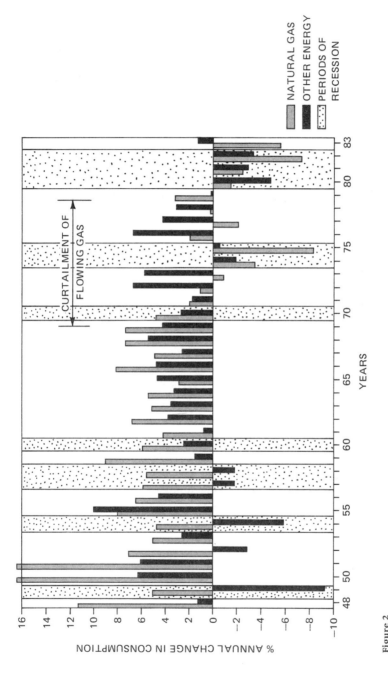

Figure 2
US growth rates for natural gas and other energy.

not static, was characterized by healthy growth and stable expectations about the future. The system was economical in terms of transaction costs, and at the time no one worried much about allocating risk.[7]

The other side of stability, of course, was inflexibility. The system would eventually prove ill-suited to a world of fluctuating demand and competition from other fuels. But the day of reckoning was postponed by yet another political settlement—this one dealing with gas prices in the field.

2.3 The Aftermath of the Phillips Decision: 1965–1981

The NGA was ambiguous on the regulation of field prices. Some clauses clearly excluded it, while others seemed to leave the door open. The rising field prices of the late 1940s and early 1950s brought "surprise and chagrin" that "made a lower gas price an end in itself, a Good Thing, and a clamorous political issue where the small voice of reason is drowned out" (Adelman, 1962, p. 43). The executive branch had always interpreted the law to say that field prices were to be left unregulated, but in a 1954 decision, *Phillips Petroleum Co.* v. *Wisconsin*, the Supreme Court ruled otherwise. As a result, the FPC commenced to regulate interstate field prices with ceilings based on historical production costs. As producers moved to higher-cost resources, the inevitable shortages appeared—in the mid-1960s in the market for reserves, and in the late 1960s and early 1970s in the market for flowing gas.[8]

The effects of the interstate price ceilings on the pipeline industry are illustrated in figure 1. Demand D_3 and supply S_3 represent the short-run conditions at the time of the Phillips decision and for a few years after: a price ceiling P^* had been set but was not yet binding. By the late 1960s it had begun to bind, however, as demand had shifted to D_4 but supply (to interstate markets) only to S_4. Interstate markets went into shortage, and the FPC had to create an elaborate set of "curtailment priorities" to determine which customers would be denied gas.

For interstate pipelines, the pertinent point is that the post-*Phillips* price controls were imposed in the midst of industry expansion. Thus, the industry never experienced long-run demand as a constraint; rather, it moved directly from a period of growth to one of sustained excess demand. Figure 2 illustrates what happened. During the period of curtailments, gas use dropped sharply while the use of other forms of energy was rising or (during the 1975–1976 recession) dropping only a bit.

As during the boom of 1948–1965, the interstate gas industry was insulated from the business cycle, but now it was shrinking instead of growing. In the seller's market created by the price ceilings, interstate pipelines had no difficulty marketing their gas; and the FPC curtailments protected the pipelines against legal repercussions from failing to deliver contractual volumes. Moreover, the wellhead price controls also obscured the view of both pipelines and regulators of what ultimate market demand might be in the future. The need to prepare for *downward* flexibility in volumes and prices received no attention.

The post-*Phillips* field price controls applied only to interstate shipments— gas sold across state boundaries. As these controls began to bind, separate *intra*state markets (free of controls) developed and prospered in the major producing states. Market-clearing intrastate prices exceeded the legal interstate ceilings, and so the trunk pipelines could not compete for new reserves with intrastate systems. Excess interstate demand spilled over into the intrastate markets, and industrial gas-using capacity migrated to Texas and Louisiana.

In an attempt to remedy the worsening shortage, the FPC boosted prices, first in 1971, and again in 1974. But the price differential only increased, as intrastate prices rose more rapidly than the FPC's interstate ceilings. By 1976 the average price of gas sold in intrastate markets was more than twice that of gas sold interstate.

The situation had become intolerable, and the Carter administration proposed legislation to fix it. The resulting Natural Gas Policy Act (NGPA) of 1978 was a marvel of complexity that laminated price increases (for efficiency's sake) to subtle distinctions between "vintages" of gas (for equity's sake). The bill had two main features: (1) a distinction between "new" and "old" gas, to reward efforts to increase supply but prevent transfers of economic rents to owners of preexisting capacity; and (2) the partial unification of the interstate and intrastate markets, designed to stanch the flow of gas and user capacity out of the interstate market.

The NGPA froze the prices of "old" gas—already flowing in April 1977 when the Carter energy package was first mooted—at the going ceilings, with escalation only for inflation. "New" gas prices were to phase up to putative market levels by the beginning of 1985. The target levels were calculated on the assumption that the real price of imported oil would remain at the then current figure of $15.00 per barrel (about $18.50 in 1984 dollars) during the phase-up. The price of "deep" gas (from wells deeper than 15,000 feet) was deregulated immediately. The interstate and intrastate markets were partially unified, not by decontrolling the former but by extending federal price controls to the latter.

The ink was hardly dry on the NGPA when the second oil shock (1979–1980) occurred. The price of imported oil soared to around $37 per barrel at its peak in 1981. The "market-ordering problem" created by this new shock is a tale in itself (see Jacoby and Wright, 1982, and Mitchell, 1983). What is important here is the effect these events had on contract arrangements.

The partial market unification under the NGPA took away much of the price-offer advantage of the intrastate pipelines, enabling interstates to begin signing up new reserves once again. But price ceilings were still below market-clearing levels, and so contract negotiators shifted to indirect forms of pricing. Suppliers won price-escalator clauses assuring them of the highest available prices, along with take-or-pay percentages that greatly reduced their volume risk (Broadman and Toman, 1983). The price escalators tied gas prices to residual or No. 2 fuel oil, and "most favored nation" clauses provided for the highest price among adjacent properties. The take-or-pay percentages were in the 80s and 90s—much higher than the previous range of 50 to 60.[9]

Even if the pipelines had wanted to hedge their bets, the intense competition for reserves would have made it difficult to get more flexible terms in new contracts. The excess demands coupled with the peculiar incentives of the NGPA led the pipelines to bargain away flexibility in return for rights to reserves. Arguably, they had little choice: they had contractual service obligations to their customers. Inflexible contract provisions were to be expected in a seller's market. But provisions were to prove ill-suited to different market conditions.

In mid-1981 the interstate pipelines held portfolios of gas contracts comprised of "old" gas at $1.00–$1.50 per Mcf; "new" and "stripper-well" gas at $2.25–$3.00 per Mcf and rising steadily; and high-priced gas (mainly "deep" gas and imported LNG) at $5.00–$11.00 per Mcf. Nationally, somewhat more than half of the interstate portfolio was old gas, just over a third was new, and the rest was high-priced gas. The pipelines "rolled in" these various sources to get a single, weighted-average cost of gas. The national average price to pipeline customers was in the neighborhood of $3.00 per Mcf. This average disguises considerable dispersion of end-use prices among pipelines, reflecting differences in their gas portfolios, but in a price-controlled seller's market such differences meant little. They were about to become very important, however, as price competition at end-use replaced the struggle to sign up new reserves.

3 The Interstates Meet the Demand Curve

3.1 Recession, Rising Prices, and Surplus

The 1979–1980 jump in oil prices could not be sustained. In 1981, the world economy went into the worst recession since the 1930s. Demands for oil and other energy goods, already declining in response to the price increases of the 1970s, now fell sharply. Augmented by price-induced increases in non-OPEC supply, a glut developed in the world oil market, and the price of oil imported into the United States dropped from a high of $37 per barrel in 1981 to less than $29 in 1984.

The 1981–1983 recession, combined with falling oil prices, radically reduced the demand for natural gas. With it came a price "break" of the kind that Morry Adelman had foretold in the early 1960s (1962, p. 690): "Even a tapering off in the rate of increase of demand for gas could cause a sharp decline in the demand for new reserves. When such a time comes, and come it will, one must be prepared for a reversal, perhaps even a break." As illustrated in panel (c) of figure 1, short- and long-run demand curves shifted sharply leftward. Between 1981 and 1983, total deliveries of natural gas dropped by more than 14%, as shown in table 1. Deliveries to industrial and electric utility customers fell even more, by around 21% each. The gas industry moved abruptly from shortage to surplus. In the trade vernacular, the industry had developed "excess deliverability" on an unprecedented scale.

The 1981–1983 recession would have been hard on the gas industry in any event, as it was on the rest of the US economy. But two factors made things worse for natural gas: virtually none of the actors in the industry was prepared for the reversal; and its system of pricing and allocation was rigid. Had the system been flexible, gas prices would have fallen as economic activity slowed and users switched to now-cheaper oil products. In fact, the opposite happened: prices continued to rise.

As table 2 shows, average US gas prices rose steadily through 1983 and even into 1984. For example, at $6.12/Mcf the 1984 residential gas price was slightly higher than the year before, and other prices either continued to rise or declined only slightly from their 1983 peak levels.

How this perverse result could come about is illustrated in table 3.[10] Like others, Unfortunate Pipeline Co. buys gas from an assortment of producers at one end, and resells the gas to large industrial customers and a local distribution company (LDC) at the other. The LDC in turn resells to residential and industrial customers. The interstate pipeline has a portfolio of gas-supply contracts, signed at different times and therefore carrying different prices and minimum "take" requirements. Only about half of Unfortunate's supplies under contract are "old" gas, selling at only $1.50 per Mcf and carrying only 60% minimum "takes." The rest is "new" or deregulated "deep" gas at much higher prices and minimum take rates. In the argot of the early 1980s, Unfortunate Pipeline has a relatively small "cushion" of old gas.

Before the fall of oil prices and the onset of the 1981–1982 recession,

Table 1
US natural gas deliveries by customer class

	Total delivery (bcf)[a]				Percent change				
	1982	1983	1984	1985	1981–1982	1982–1983	1983–1984	1984–1985	1981–1985
Residential	4,633	4,381	4,555	4,412	+1.9	−5.4	+6.1	−3.1	−2.9
Commercial	2,606	2,433	2,524	2,432	+3.4	−6.6	+5.2	−3.6	−3.5
Industrial	5,831	5,643	6,153	5,831	−18.2	−3.2	+2.0	−5.2	−18.2
Electric utilities	3,226	2,911	3,111	3,030	−11.4	−9.8	+6.9	−2.6	−16.8
Total deliveries	16,295	15,367	16,345	15,706	−8.6	−5.7	+6.4	−3.9	−11.9

Source: DOE/EIA, *Natural Gas Monthly* (Jan. 1986; published March 1986).

a. bcf = billions of cubic feet.

Table 2
Natural gas prices in the United States, 1973–1984 ($/Mcf)[a]

| Year | Wellhead | Major interstate pipelines | | | Bought by electric plants | Residential |
		Wellhead purchase	Industrial sales	Sales for resale		
1973	0.22	0.29	0.53	0.61	0.38	1.29
1975	0.45	0.41	0.73	0.83	0.77	1.71
1977	0.79	0.81	1.33	1.34	1.32	2.35
1978	0.91	0.83	1.54	1.46	1.48	2.56
1979	1.18	1.22	2.01	1.85	1.81	2.98
1980	1.59	1.63	2.53	2.52	2.27	3.68
1981	1.98	2.15	3.11	2.93	2.89	4.29
1982	2.46	2.72	3.73	3.72	3.48	5.17
1983	2.59	2.93	4.25	4.10	3.58	6.06
1984	2.66	2.91	4.13	3.99	3.72	6.12
1985	NA	2.82[b]	3.90[b]	3.95[b]	3.59[b]	6.13

Sources: DOE/EIA, *Monthly Energy Review* (January 1983); idem., *Natural Gas Monthly* (February 1985, December 1985).
a. 1973–1977 data are not strictly comparable with 1978–1983 data in all cases.
b. Through November.

Unfortunate buys and resells 100 units of gas. Its roll-in gas purchase cost is $2.95 per Mcf. At a volume of 100, its transportation rate adds another dollar to the price, so that large industrial ("direct") customers and the LDC pay $3.95 per Mcf. The LDC's rates, at a volume of 70 units, add $1.50 more, so that its customers (homeowners, small businesses, and firm industrial customers) were paying $5.45 per Mcf.

After the fall, Unfortunate Pipeline loses 40% of its load—15 units of it industrial, 25 units from the LDC. Taking only 60 units, the pipeline is 17 units below its minimum volume of 77. Shutting in both "old" and "new" gas supplies, the pipeline incurs a take-or-pay prepayment of $43.50, which is added to its rate base. (The prepayment would be larger, were relatively more "new" or "deep" gas shut in.) Now the pipeline's roll-in purchased-gas cost is higher—$3.425 per Mcf, nearly $.50 more than before—reflecting the greater weight of more expensive supplies in its smaller purchases. Moreover, the drop in volume raises the pipeline's transportation rate by $.68 per Mcf.

Thus the "wholesale" price of gas to large industrial customers and the LDC increases by $1.155 compared with before the fall. But the LDC's distribution rate also goes up by $.50/Mcf because of *its* own drop in volume. By the time the gas gets to small customers' burner tips, it costs a full $1.655 per Mcf (or 30%) more than before.

The adjustment mechanism is perverse: in the face of falling demand, gas

Table 3
Unfortunate Pipeline Co.

Before

	Old gas	+ New gas	+ Deep gas	= Total	= Deliveries
Volume	50	+ 40	+ 10	= 100	To LDCs = 70
					To firms = 30
Price	$1.50	$3.00	$10.00		
Purch. gas cost	$75.00	+ $120.00	+ $100.00	= $295	
Min. take rate	.60	.95	.90		
Min. volume	30	+ 38	+ 9	= 77	

	Weighted-average or roll-in price ($295/100)	=	$2.95 per Mcf
PLUS	Pipeline transportation rate[a]		+ $1.00
PLUS	Local distribution rate[b]		+ $1.50
EQUALS	Burner-tip gas prices:		
	Large firms		$3.95
	Small customers		$5.45

After

	Old gas	+ New gas	+ Deep gas	= Total	= Deliveries
Volume	25	+ 26	+ 9	= 60	To LDCs = 45
					To firms = 15
Price	$1.50	$3.00	$10.00		
Purch. gas cost	$37.50	+ $78.00	+ $90.00	= $205.50	
Take/pay prepayment	$7.50	$36.00	0	= $43.50	

	Weighted-average or roll-in price ($205.50/60)	=	$3.425 (+$.475)
PLUS	Pipeline transportation rate[c]		+ $1.68 (+$.68)
PLUS	Local distribution rate[d]		+ $2.00 (+$.50)
EQUALS	Burner-tip gas prices:		
	Large firms		$5.105 (+$1.155)
	Small customers		$7.105 (+$1.665)

a. Equals $Va + bK/V$, where V is pipeline volume ($= 100$ here); a is .002; b is 2.0; and K is rate-base capital cost ($= \$40$ here).

b. Equals $vc + dC/v$, where v is volume ($= 70$ here); c is .005; d is 8.05; and C is rate-base capital cost ($= 10$ here).

c. Assumes $K = 44.35$, including carrying charges on the take-or-pay prepayment. Volume is now 60, and a and b are as in note a.

d. Volume is now 45. The other variables are as in note b.

prices *go up*. The interstate pipeline and the LDC are unable to respond to falling demand by lowering prices. Both doubtless know of industrial users who have switched to oil because of price, and who would gladly switch back—if the price of gas were a little lower. But federal and state regulations limit the ability of pipelines and LDCs to price discriminate. Except for existing differences in price classes (allowing for distribution cost differentials or for "interruptible" versus "firm" service), the LDC must charge the same average price to all customers; otherwise, residential customers would (in the eyes of the state commission) be subsidizing industrial users.

At the field, shut-in gas supplies are available at prices competitive with oil on a delivered basis. (This is quite apart from producers' possible willingness to *cut* their prices in order to maintain volumes sold.) However, we have seen that the pipeline may prefer (or may be required) to shut in these sources and take higher-priced ones. And users (practically, the LDC or large industrial firms) cannot routinely get the cheaper gas delivered, even if they know how to go out and contract for it.

It is not easy to design a system in which everybody loses. But under recession and falling oil prices the institutional arrangements in the natural gas industry came close to just that. In our example, gas consumers burn higher-priced fuel than they might, and less of it than they would at lower prices. The LDC loses volume and is squeezed financially. The interstate pipeline is caught with sagging demand, high "take" requirements, and mounting "pay" liabilities. It is bearing a volume risk that is quite foreign to its previous experience. Many (though not all) producers at the field are losing revenues. The only clear winners are the lawyers, plus a handful of economists who testify in the judicial and administrative proceedings.

3.2 The System Tries to Cope

If the stresses are great enough, even the most rigid structure will bend, and that has happened in the past few years. The available legal options (such as "market-outs" in high-priced, deep gas contracts) have been exploited. And there have been attempts to stretch the definition of "legal"—for example, pipelines have sought to abrogate supply contracts on *force majeure* grounds (which would put market forces in a class with war, pestilence, and tornadoes). The resulting lawsuits are likely to go on for years.

Naturally there is talk of supply contracts being renegotiated to bring them more in line with market conditions.[11] But the pipelines often feel they can only renegotiate "on bended knee," and dispersed ownership rights to flowing gas in many large fields cause further difficulties. One state (Illinois) has tried to use the antitrust laws to force an interstate pipeline to alter the terms under which it will haul gas bought from off-system suppliers. Finally, reflecting uncertainty born of oil-market instability, the deliverability surplus, and doubts about what if anything Congress or the FERC will do, new long-term contracts have all but vanished.

In an industry which exhibits economies of scale, the efficient way to work off a surplus is to cut prices to your most price-sensitive customers—in a phrase, to price discriminate. Attempts at price discrimination by pipelines and LDCs have become commonplace in the gas industry in the last few years, just as they have in the railroad, airline, motor carrier, and telecommunications industries in the United States. In fact, one can argue that the central regulatory issue in all these industries is how best to promote efficient price discrimination.[12]

An inherent conflict arises, however, because of the dual role that regulatory agencies have assumed since the New Deal. On the one hand, regulators like FERC are required to protect the most vulnerable (read price-inelastic) customers from the potential abuses of monopoly power. On the other hand, since *FPC et al.* v. *Hope Natural Gas* (1944), regulators must also ensure that stockholders of regulated firms earn a rate of return commensurate with the risk they bear, and in general promote the financial and economic health of the industry. In a demand-constrained world, and for a declining-cost industry, these tasks require a dose of price discrimination.

This dual role of regulators explains both the origin and the fate of the FERC's efforts to cope with the gas surplus. It also accounts for the way its predecessor, the FPC, managed the shortage from the late 1960s until the mid-1970s: it adopted rules that allocated available gas among customer classes but also protected the economic rents that have traditionally accrued to the least price-sensitive customers. Unfortunately, allocating the surplus has been a much greater regulatory challenge for the FERC than was allocating a shortage. In the latter case, it merely had to rank the claims of various customers to the scarce supplies and assign its price-inelastic constituents top priority. The more price-elastic customers could switch to other fuels when "curtailed." The FERC could thus perform its dual roles through a single policy at tolerable political cost.

In handling the surplus, however, the FERC cannot restrict production (e.g., by setting production "allowables"). It must instead attempt to use the price system to encourage demand or sweep away the rigidities that are perpetuating the surplus. One way to accomplish this would be to step in and abrogate high-priced producer-pipeline contracts. Such a move would impose losses primarily on producers (particularly the independents) and engender litigation over the scope of FERC's authority to modify private contracts. A second approach would use the carrot instead of the stick: allow price discrimination to encourage the maximum increase in sales for each cent of price concession by producers. Unfortunately, this policy is opposed by price-inelastic customers and in fact has been challenged successfully in court as contrary to the FERC's consumer-protection role.

Much of the impetus to the surplus-management scheme that emerged in 1983–1984 came from the private sector itself. The interstate pipelines sought and obtained easier terms for "off-system" sales, and they were granted "blanket" certification to haul gas owned by others. In addition, a number of interstate pipelines and a few large producers received permission from the FERC to conduct Special Gas-Marketing Programs (SMPs). These programs attempted to use selective price cuts (again, price discrimination) to recover gas demand lost to oil, at the same time easing the pipelines' take-or-pay burdens. In many cases, producers absorbed the price cuts in the form of below-contract wellhead prices, but at least they were selling gas and avoiding legal costs required to force pipelines to pay contract prices on gas not sold. The added sales through the pipelines' SMPs went mainly to lower transportation rates rather than to increased pipeline profits or higher producer realizations.

In the typical pipeline SMP, a marketing-and-brokering service was offered in exchange for producer willingness to accept wellhead prices below contract levels.[13] The pipeline company informed its suppliers that it could not honor its minimum "take" obligations at contract prices. But it also offered to seek out potential users (e.g., industrial firms with dual-fuel capacity who had switched to oil) and ask for price quotes that would lure them back to gas. The producers received "netback" prices equal to the quoted prices less pipeline transportation costs. Any sales under the program were credited to the pipeline's take liabilities with the given producer.

When first proposed in 1982, the SMPs were touted as the basis for a restructured natural gas industry—one that could not only survive the surplus but undertake major new growth. At first glance, price cuts do seem an eminently sensible way of coping with market surplus. However, the SMPs suffered from a fundamental flaw: they had side effects that rendered them self-contradictory within the prevailing system. The purpose of the SMPs was to restore pipeline loads, but pipelines might be tempted also to "raid" other pipelines' markets. Market raiding would merely shift, not restore loads—and force higher transportation rates onto the remaining customers of raided pipelines.

To keep desirable market "retention" from degenerating into undesirable market "raiding," the FERC restricted each pipeline's SMP to its traditional service area or "core" market. In addition, the Commission wanted to prevent economic rents on price-controlled gas from leaking out through the SMPs to the most price-sensitive customers, as might have happened if an SMP were heavily loaded with price-controlled "old" gas. Normally, FERC would try to preserve this cheap gas for the least price-sensitive consumers who the FERC believes have the historical/political claim to the savings. The FERC at first required that prices charged under the SMPs be no lower than the pipelines' system average prices. When that provision dampened *end-user* interest in the programs, the FERC eased the minimum price rule but required pipelines to offer LDCs up to 10% of their regular contract volumes under the SMPs—which weakened *pipeline* interest in operating the programs.

The special gas-marketing programs seemed like a promising first step toward the "unbundling" of pipelines' brokerage and transportation functions, viewed by many as essential to providing greater flexibility in the trading of natural gas. But the regulatory restrictions necessary to make the SMPs compatible with existing public policy (and acceptable to its beneficiaries) rendered them insignificant and vulnerable to legal challenge. The whole experience with SMPs put into sharp relief the contradiction between bureaucratic and market institutions for allocating resources, and the familiar conflict between preservation of the existing distribution of economic rents and attempts to make the system more efficient. It also indicated that a true restructuring of the US natural gas industry would require major regulatory reform.

4 The Future

4.1 Market Flexibility and How to Get It

Current and expected future conditions in energy markets place a premium on flexibility in the way natural gas is traded. As we have seen, existing institutions are decidedly *not* flexible, but then they were designed for and conditioned by quite different circumstances. For many decades the main tasks were to promote growth, finance and build pipelines, economize on transaction costs, and (especially from the late 1960s on) control who could buy gas at below-market prices. These days, the main tasks are to maintain pipeline loads (to control costs and prevent bankruptcies) and allocate the new demand-side risks.

What changes, exactly, would more "flexible" institutions require?

1. Gas supply contracts should have flexible, not fixed-price terms.

2. Gas transportation tariffs need not include tightly structured rights and obligations, closely monitored and enforced by the FERC.

3. Pipelines need not act as intermediaries between production and end-use for reserves as well as for transportation.

Unfortunately, there are real obstacles to these changes. To achieve flexible prices in long-term contracts would require a reliable method of redetermining prices as market conditions change. Periodic redeterminations of price would help allocate systematic (nondiversifiable) market risks among the several actors, according to who was willing (for a price) to bear them. One would expect to see long-term contracts reemerge in the industry once things settled down, but such contracts would differ markedly from those of pre-1978 days.

On the second point, no matter how nimble the FERC might hope to become, its continued close involvement in workaday gas transactions would create rigidity and lags inimical to market flexibility. Moreover, close involvement would not be necessary: with the demise of field price controls, there would be fewer economic rents for regulators to appropriate and redistribute though their supervision of gas transactions. This assumes that both producers and end-users could find substitute means of assuring reliable gas supplies.

Finally, the conventional three-stage view of the gas industry—production, transmission, and end-use—is a product not of its physical layout but rather of the "purchase-for-resale" (PFR) system under which there must be two separate transactions involving the pipeline—one at the field and a second at resale to LDCs or large consumers. Different kinds of transactions can and do occur, involving direct contracts between end-users, producers, traders, and brokers (some of whom could, but need not be, trunk pipelines), with only a single side deal for transporting the gas. But such transactions have been rare, because (under PFR) the pipelines have controlled both transportation capacity and reserves—necessarily so, it is argued, if they are to meet contractual obligations to serve LDCs and their residential and commercial customers.

More flexible long-term contracting could emerge in conjunction with a liquid national spot market for natural gas. A liquid spot market would enable qualified participants to buy or sell gas at a reliable going spot price. If transactors were confident that these market prices were free of manipulation, then spot prices could serve as referent for redetermining prices in long-term contracts. Such spot prices would be superior to the oil-product prices, or indexes for "baskets of oils," that were inserted into the indefinite price escalator clauses of the late 1970s and early 1980s. Furthermore, a liquid spot market would provide reliability of gas demand or supply and permit some transactors to reduce the proportions of their business conducted under long-term contracts. The price risk inherent in spot trading could be allocated through organized futures trading, allowing transactors to speculate or to hedge price risks according to their wishes.[14]

Describing more flexible institutions is, however, only part of the task at hand. One must worry about how to get there from here. We do not have the luxury of starting from scratch, and the transition may well be path-dependent: how we proceed may significantly affect the eventual long run.

4.2 Do We Need to Do Anything?

The argument is made that we need not worry about the transition.[15] In this view, competitive pressures will overwhelm the rigid institutions we now have, and it is only a matter of time until flexible institutions emerge. Indeed, it is argued that the process is already well under way. Wellhead prices are effectively decontrolled, having reached market-clearing levels (on average) before the 1 January 1985 date for official decontrol of "new" gas. Proponents of this view note that flexible-price terms began to show up in long-term contracts after the NGPA was passed in 1978, and will appear again once long-term contracting resumes. Spot trading is already significant and growing. Interstate pipelines are shifting toward "contract" carriage and away from their brokering and trading roles. Soon, the interstate pipelines will, in their own interest, specialize in hauling gas and greatly reduce (if not give up) their now-dominant role as resellers. At that point, natural gas will have become a mere "commodity" like wheat, pork bellies, and gold.

We would be pleased if the optimistic view just outlined were to come true. But wishing will not make it so. The belief that we can do nothing and still get flexible institutions requires very strong assumptions about rights of access to trunk pipeline capacity and about the gas-policy making process itself. Given that gas can be transported economically only in pipelines, a liquid national spot market cannot develop until all potential transactors are able to get reliable access to pipeline capacity on uniform terms.[16] This is currently possible, however, only through *exceptions* to the present system. In the current glut, some pipelines are eager to haul gas for others, but (with their obligations to serve still in force) their motives are mainly to alleviate short-term supply-contract problems and increase system volumes. Thus, the current glut-inspired spot transactions (desirable though they be) appear to be merely stopgaps that will disappear once the surplus shrinks.

Moreover, one must assume not only that the FERC will move to adapt pipeline regulation, including rights of access to capacity, but also that the

Commission can accomplish this change. This assumption ignores 60 years of federal intervention in gas markets, and the way the policy process operates to protect established interests. That the system is not working well under new economic conditions does not imply that the political forces will realign themselves. Indeed, the very success of the optimists' economic scenario would likely engender political opposition to its further progress, unless the underlying institutional arrangements were changed to allocate gains and losses in a politically acceptable way.

A recent decision by the US Court of Appeals for the DC Circuit highlights these obstacles. In *Maryland People's Counsel* v. *FERC*, the court found that the FERC failed to consider adequately the possible anticompetitive features of the restrictions it placed on customer eligibility in the original SMP orders.[17] The court also vacated the "blanket" certificate transportation programs unless the FERC makes them explicitly nondiscriminatory with respect to customer eligibility. The DC Circuit Court seems to have ignored shareholders' interests.[18] The sole basis for the decision was the potential of the SMPs and blanket certificates to harm, through discrimination, "the consumers whom the Natural Gas Act (NGA) was designed 'to protect . . . against exploitation at the hands of the natural gas companies' (cite omitted)" (slip op. at 4).

The optimists had cited the SMP and "blanket certificate" programs as clear examples of what was needed to gain flexibility. It might be simplest, in their view, if the FERC could force pipelines to transport third-party gas, but absent this authority the antitrust laws could always be brought to bear against recalcitrant pipelines. We would point out an irony of the *Maryland People's Counsel* case: the same discrimination arguments that might be used against a recalcitrant pipeline were used against the only regulatory programs currently enabling flexible gas transportation. By legally stalemating the evolution of the gas regulatory system, this case may have done consumers more harm than good.

4.3 Recent FERC Attempts to Change the System

The cases brought by the Maryland People's Counsel, coupled with an almost complete change in Commission membership during 1985, prompted a radical rewriting of the rules by which the FERC would regulate interstate gas pipelines. On 1 November 1985 the FERC issued Order 436, which the Commission claims will both lay the groundwork for "flexible" regulation in the long run and provide a transition mechanism for realigning existing contractual arrangements in the short run. Order 436 has four parts, which the

FERC insists must be treated as a package:

1. *Blanket Certificates for Nondiscriminatory Third-Party Transportation*

A pipeline may obtain a blanket certificate to offer firm or interruptible transportation of gas for others, provided that it also offers the service to anyone who seeks it. LDC customers of a pipeline choosing blanket certification may reduce their tariff contract volumes by 15–25% per year over five years. The FERC will grant the abandonment certificates for the LDCs' reductions as "presumptively" in the public interest.

2. *Rate Treatment of Take-or-Pay "Buy-Outs"*

Any pipeline choosing part (1) may be permitted to include in its rates some portion of sums paid to producers to buy out of take-or-pay liabilities. However, whether permission will be granted and (if so) how the buy-outs will be incorporated into pipeline rates will be determined case by case. This leaves open the possibility of challenges over such matters as whether the original contracts were "prudent".

3. *Optional, Expedited Certification Procedures*

Simplified, accelerated certification will be available for any pipeline services, provided that the pipeline bears the entire economic risk of providing them and that the services are offered to all comers. To ensure the former, rates for these services will be set on a fully allocated, "volumetric" basis—that is, every unit shipped must recover its full share of fixed as well as variable costs, and no capacity-reservation fee (e.g., "minimum-bill" or "demand-charge") will be allowed.

4. *Block Billing instead of "Roll-In" Pricing*

This part of the new rules, which is still in the proposal stage, would create two pricing "blocks" for all interstate natural gas. As currently proposed, still-regulated "old" gas would be priced separately in Block 1. Entitlements to a pipeline's Block 1 gas would be assigned to customers based on their 1979–1984 purchases from the pipeline. The remaining, more expensive gas would go into Block 2.

The FERC's intention to make gas markets more flexible is readily apparent in Order 436. However, the new rules illustrate internal contradictions of the Commission's charge under current law. As we argued above, market flexibility will require that all parties have reliable access, on predictable terms, to interstate pipeline capacity. Making gas pipelines common carriers (along with all other major forms of transportation, including oil pipelines) would appear the simplest, most direct way to provide such access. But under the

NGA and the NGPA, the FERC may not promulgate regulations that make interstate gas pipelines common carriers.[19] The best it can do is to try to create conditions that will induce pipelines to offer third-party transportation services to anyone willing to pay for them. In Order 436, the FERC hopes to accomplish this by providing certain economic advantages to pipelines that commit to becoming nondiscriminatory transporters of natural gas for others.

When Order 436 was issued, interstate pipeline companies looked hard to find these economic advantages. What they found instead was that the FERC order allowed their least price-sensitive customers, the LDCs, to abrogate their purchase obligations (by reducing their contract volumes), but afforded little or no certain relief from problem producer contracts (e.g., those with high prices and no escape clauses) at the other end of the pipeline. In effect, Order 436 substantially increases the risks to pipelines of providing third-party transportation services. As a result, all but a few pipelines have thus far refused to seek the blanket certificates that are the linchpin of the FERC's order.

The transition mechanism in Order 436, parts (2) and (4), has also failed to elicit cheers from interstate pipelines. The rate treatment of take-or-pay buy-outs is old wine in new skins: it essentially continues existing FERC policy. As for block billing, its stated purpose is to create a "level playing field" for competing pipelines with different endowments of old gas: a pipeline with a large cushion of old gas under contract could no longer use it to competitive advantage against a rival with a small cushion.[20] But by segregating "old" from higher-priced gas, block billing will render much Block 2 gas unmarketable. If so, pipelines' financial losses could violate the NGA requirement that gas prices be "just and reasonable"—thereby undercutting the legal status of block billing.

The cool reception of Order 436 to date has raised serious questions about the FERC's ability to impart substantially greater flexibility to the gas market under existing law.[21] The course and eventual fate of the Order, particularly through mid-1986 or so, will provide a test of the proposition that the FERC can, under existing law, both institute long-term changes in gas regulation and provide a feasible path to get there from here. The requisite changes must reallocate economic rents (and assign some losses) and fundamentally alter the terms of access to interstate gas pipeline capacity. The early evidence indicates that the FERC's attempt through Order 436 will generate not only opposition but also a spate of litigation that will challenge whether the FERC has the legal authority to make such changes.

5 Conclusion

Writing about the US natural gas industry in the early 1960s, Morry Adelman observed (1962, p. 93),

"Speculation—in the strict economic sense of anticipating the future—will be rife, as buyers and sellers try to outguess and, inevitably, overreach. Contracts will be signed which may grievously disappoint and outrage one of the parties. It can only be hoped that enough flexibility will be built into the system to mitigate this." The hoped-for flexibility did not materialize. As a result, in the intervening quarter century we have been treated, first, to a regulation-induced shortage, then to a regulation-induced surplus. Both have been accompanied by market distortions and economic losses. That the regulation in the two cases was the product of one and the same system ought to tell us something: the system needs to change.

Our analysis suggests that the system will not—probably cannot—change on its own, at least not in the desired direction. A lasting improvement poses a real challenge of statecraft. We three lack the expertise to recommend detailed legislative language. But we can identify the essential features of a set of moves toward greater flexibility. The essential changes are five:

1. Deregulate the wellhead prices of "old gas"—or at least leave intact the de facto decontrol, on average, that now exists.[22] A windfall tax, of short duration, could make this particular change politically more palatable.

2. Reduce to "traditional" levels—from 90 + % to 50 or 60%—the take-or-pay percentages in the producer-pipeline supply contracts signed in the turmoil of the late 1970s.

3. Make interstate pipelines common carriers.

4. Remove the interstate pipelines' service obligations to local gas distribution companies.

5. Allow pipelines and LDCs to use rate structures based on Ramsey price discrimination.

The first two proposed changes are transitional. They would clear away a complex set of issues that will otherwise take years of negotiation, litigation, and lobbying to settle. The first one would sweeten the package for producers, the second one for pipelines.

We believe that a transition policy directed at the producer-end of the pipeline is vital. In implementing Order 436 the FERC believed that by focusing its policy at the distribution end of the pipeline (and increasing the risks borne by the pipelines) it would force the renegotiation of problem producer contracts without direct federal intervention in the process. Unfortunately, the large size of these obligations, and their wide distribution among pipelines and producers, ensure that this hands-off policy will not work. A one-time realignment of contracts would likely produce the least costly and most equitable transition (particularly if coupled with the decontrol of old gas prices).

The third and fourth proposals should also be viewed together. Making pipelines common carriers would unbundle rights to reserves from rights to pipeline capacity. The current system rolls the two together and confers them upon the interstate pipelines and their LDC customers. At the same time, the pipelines should be freed of their service obligations, if they are to be expected to offer capacity to all comers on uniform terms. Much of the pipeline companies opposition to common carriage grows out of the fear that the service obligation would remain in effect.[23]

Indeed, a variety of recent proposals referred to as "mandatory contract carriage" would add common carriage obligations to the *existing system*. Order 436 can be classified as one such proposal (now policy), with the exception that the FERC did not have the authority to make the contract carriage mandatory.[24] Mandatory contract carriage would make for *less*, not greater, flexibility. Pipelines would have even less freedom of movement than they do now, yet third-party shippers would not believe that they could readily arrange transportation for gas bought by themselves or through a broker. Order 436 attempted to open up pipeline capacity for transportation by allowing LDCs to unilaterally abrogate their existing purchase contracts with the pipelines. The one-sided nature of this approach is the chief reason why so few pipelines have chosen to participate in the Order 436 program.[25] Under true common carriage, in contrast, pipelines would be reconstituted as specialists in transportation. Even if they continued to broker or trade gas, common-carrier rights would guarantee third parties the requisite access to transportation without damaging the pipelines' financial status in the transition.

The fifth and last proposal would not be essential to achieving greater flexibility in natural gas markets. However, it would foster the rationalization of those markets. Now that the gas industry is operating on the demand curve, the ability to price discriminate—constrained by Ramsey conditions, which are required for efficient pricing under conditions of declining average cost— would enhance the pipelines' ability to compete as market conditions change.[26]

The unfortunate characteristic of this package is its requirement of congressional action. Most congressional observers view legislative reform as highly unlikely, particularly while the FERC continues to attempt reform through rule making. When legal stalemate results in further restrictions on the movement of natural gas and/or industry financial distress, and when it becomes apparent that the FERC does not have the authority or political flexibility to accomplish the required changes, then the impetus for Congress to pursue comprehensive reform may again arise. In the meantime one should expect the industry's "retreat" to be carried out in disarray as the forces of the market press their attacks on the industry.

Notes

1. For a longer analysis of the history, see Sanders (1981) and Carpenter, Jacoby, and Wright (1983).

2. US Senate (1936). As evidence of anticompetitive market structure, the FTC cited a high degree of concentration in the industry (the top four firms handled 79% of all interstate gas), together with widespread joint ownership of facilities and backward integration into gas production. The study also documented the territorial separation of markets and the lack of parallel competing pipelines. Much of the evidence was anecdotal, but it nonetheless painted a damaging picture of collusive activity.

3. A common carrier must provide service to any and all (qualified) comers at the going price (usually regulated). If capacity-constrained, the common carrier must offer all comers the same proportion of reduced service.

4. FPC and FERC rate-setting practice has followed the principles laid down in the Hope Natural Gas case: *Federal Power Commission et. al.* v. *Hope Natural Gas*, 320 US 591, 3 January 1944.

5. Thus, a pipeline tariff is an example of what Victor Goldberg (1976) has called an "administered contract."

6. In Order 380, Docket No. RM83-71-000 (1984) the FERC has further weakened the minimum bill by eliminating all variable costs from inclusion in the commodity charge portion of the minimum bill. Thus the pipelines are left holding the bag on fixed contractual commitments to purchase gas (US DOE, 1984a).

7. Williamson (1975, 1979) has stressed the importance of transaction costs in determining vertical institutional arrangements. Bohn (1982) and Carpenter (1984) on the other hand have argued that the need to allocate risk may override transaction-cost concerns.

8. Prices could not rise to market-clearing levels at end-use because (under PFR) pipelines' rates were based on roll-in or weighted-average costs of purchased gas. See Kalt and Stillman (1980, p. 13). For analysis of the field price regulations also see Breyer and MacAvoy (1974) and MacAvoy and Pindyck (1975a).

9. See US DOE/EIA (1984a) for details. Actually, the take or pay percentages began to rise during the period of natural gas shortage, but it was not until after the NGPA in 1978 that substantial numbers of new contracts were written for interstate sales.

10. The example is constructed to make the problem easy to see, but it is not out of line for the more troubled pipeline firms.

11. For those contracts renegotiated in 1984, the price was lowered by $0.05/Mcf. But the renegotiation activity was so small that the average domestic price was reduced by only $0.01/Mcf (INGAA, 1985).

12. The most frequently discussed system is "Ramsey pricing," where prices are set in an inverse relationship to elasticity of demand. See Baumol and Bradford (1970).

13. There is a parallel set of programs that have been initiated by producers, with much the same economic motivation. They involve lining up customers and transportation capacity for shut-in supplies, at lower prices than the producers were getting before the onset of surplus.

14. There seems to be little doubt that futures trading would be possible in natural gas. It is a homogeneous product whose characteristics are easy to measure accurately, and there are numerous geographic locations that (by dint of their numerous direct or indirect links to the broader national market) could serve as reference delivery points. Two contracts have already been submitted for approval to the federal Commodity Futures Trading Commission. One has been withdrawn as premature; the other would be limited to the Texas intrastate market. We are skeptical that futures trading would be viable in the interstate market under the existing institutions in the gas industry.

15. For a vigorous statement of this position, see Tussing and Barlow (1984).

16. This does not mean a single price, but rather a structure of prices based on relative costs and perhaps price elasticities of demand if Ramsey-type prices were in effect (see note 12 and accompanying text).

17. *Maryland People's Counsel* v. *FERC* 761 F. 2d 768, 780 (DC Circuit 1985). These two decisions have come to be known as MPC I and II. Recall that these restrictions were logical given FERC's dual role of protecting consumers from monopoly pricing and protecting the financial health of the gas industry (i.e., mediating the conflicts between ratepayers and shareholders).

18. "Shareholders' interests" are, of course, also "long-run consumers' interests." Failure of the regulatory system to compensate shareholders fully can lead to disinvestment in the pipeline industry and thus to lower-quality service and higher prices to consumers.

19. Proposed sections 303 and 304 of Title III of H.R. 5423 in 1935 would have imposed an affirmative duty on pipelines to transport. These sections were eliminated by the 74th Congress. Thus sections 4 and 5 of the NGA contain no affirmative duty to transport.

20. Incidentally, block billing would also restore the rents on "old" gas to end users, especially "firm" customers (those with the least price-elastic demands for gas). The NGPA dissipated these rents through the rolling in of old with higher-priced gas. One might interpret the proposed restoration of old-gas rents to firm customers as the political price of their acquiescence in Order 436.

21. Portions of Order 436, and particularly the block billing proposal, have come under vociferous criticism from nearly all segments of the gas business: producers, pipelines, distributors, state PUCs, and consumer representatives. For a preliminary analysis see Williams (1985).

22. Explicit deregulation would be preferable for two reasons. First, it would prevent another oil-price spike from reinflating the old-gas "cushion" and creating another "market-ordering problem." Second, it would open up efficiency gains from the redevelopment of old-gas reserves. (An indirect way to get the latter result would be to permit pipelines or other purchasers of reserve rights to finance the redevelopment work that is now unprofitable at the old-gas price ceilings.)

23. See the responses of the pipelines (and many distribution companies) to FERC's Notice of Inquiry on Interstate Transportation of Gas, Docket No. Rm. 85-1, February 1985.

24. As of spring 1986 the administration has drafted legislation that would impose mandatory contract carriage on the gas pipelines ("Natural Gas Transportation and Regulatory Reform Act of 1986"). In addition, the bill would decontrol old gas prices. Like Order 436, it contains no transition policy regarding problem producer contracts.

25. To date, the only major pipelines embracing Order 436 have done so on the condition that their LDC customers not exercise their contract demand reduction options.

26. We do not advocate deregulating the gas pipelines or local distribution companies. Unlike airlines, buses, and trucks, gas pipeline and distribution networks have scale economies and an immobility that are significant barriers to competitive entry. Unlike oil pipelines, natural gas pipelines do not face competition from rival modes of shipment.

Living under a Shadow:
US Oil Policies and
Canadian Oil Pricing

G. Campbell Watkins

In 1969, some ten years after the United States had instituted a mandatory program of oil import quotas, the US Senate Subcommittee on Antitrust and Monopoly held hearings on "Governmental Intervention in the Market Mechanism: The Petroleum Industry." Among economists invited to contribute was Morris Adelman. The following exchange was recorded.

Senator Hruska. Well, the act of 1954 as amended by the Extension Act of 1955 was the basis for the President's mandatory oil import program.

Dr. Adelman. Yes, sir.

Senator Hruska. And the thrust of those acts is national security.

Dr. Adelman. Those are the words.

Senator Hruska. Not individual investments, not individual industries, not even the economics of the thing. The thrust was national security. Now, do you mean to tell me that all of this legislation and all of these things taken on behalf of preserving our national security is not a serious discussion and debate and effort?

Dr. Adelman. The tone is a serious one, Senator, but the substance, I am afraid, was frivolous.

Senator Hruska. Was what?

Dr. Adelman. Frivolous, light-minded, not concerned with the basic facts, and I must say that reading—and I have spent many more hours than I like to recollect reading them—was like hearing the same scratchy records played over and over again.[1]

Not the least through Morry's efforts, the hearings revealed a lot of evidence on the oil import program. But one dimension not covered was the impact of US oil policy on other countries, and especially on the United States' closest and most important trading partner: Canada. This paper deals with that issue. The oil import program is fundamental to understanding Canadian oil price

---

An earlier version of parts of this paper was given to a policy seminar at the Center for Energy Policy Research at MIT, October 1981; see Watkins (1981). The paper also draws on material in Watkins and Bradley (1982) and Bradley and Watkins (1982).

formation in the 1960s.[2] The discussion also covers the Canadian-US interaction since 1973, when the US oil import program was dropped and world oil prices ascended. Section 1 looks at the way Canadian oil was treated within the US oil import program, while section 2 traces its implications for the Canadian oil industry. Section 3 comments on developments since 1973. Some concluding remarks are made in section 4.

By way of background, table 1 summarizes Canadian oil production and exports to the United States. At the time of the inception of formal import quotas (1959), about 20% of Canadian production was sent there. By 1973, when the program was terminated, that proportion had risen to 66%. But by the end of the 1970s it had fallen to levels not seen since 1955. At the time of writing, oil exports to the United States have recovered and now account for much the same share of Canadian production as when the United States imposed mandatory import controls in 1959. Figure 1 shows the location of the major Canadian crude oil pipelines serving United States markets— Interprovincial and Trans-Mountain; the Interprovincial extension from Toronto to Montreal was not completed until 1976.

1 Canada and the US Oil Import Program

Morry Adelman has reminded us that in the decade or so preceding the inception of mandatory oil controls in 1959 the US market was never in fact open. As he says (1972, p. 7), it was "a classic case of opposing escalation: growing economic pressure to import versus growing governmental counter-pressure." Inevitably the mandatory program became a protectionist device, allowing a divorce between US and world oil prices. During most of the period the program was in operation—1959 to 1973—world oil prices declined, while after 1965 or so the price of US domestic crude rose modestly. By and large, the program always gave special treatment to Canadian oil and therefore it is not surprising that such treatment was a significant determinant of Canadian oil policy, pricing, and output.

The discussion below proceeds by reviewing the origins and legal framework in which the mandatory program was grounded, since this history fundamentally affected the status accorded to Canadian oil. Then I turn to the treatment of Canadian imports under the Program.

1.1 Origins of the US Oil Import Program[3]

After World War II, the increasing use of foreign oil in the United States excited concern among several groups, especially domestic producers. As

Table 1
Canadian oil production and exports to the United States

	Canadian oil production (Mb/d)[a]	Canadian oil exports to the United States (Mb/d)	Exports as a proportion of production (%)
1950	79	0	—
1955	355	41	11.6
1960	520	116	22.3
1965	780	296	37.9
1970	1,240	660	53.2
1973	1,743	1,151	66.0
1975	1,382	719	52.0
1980	1,300	100[b]	7.7[b]
1984	1,435	311[b]	21.7[b]

Source: Canadian Petroleum Association, *Statistical Handbook*.
a. Mb/d = thousands of barrels per day.
b. Net of exchanges.

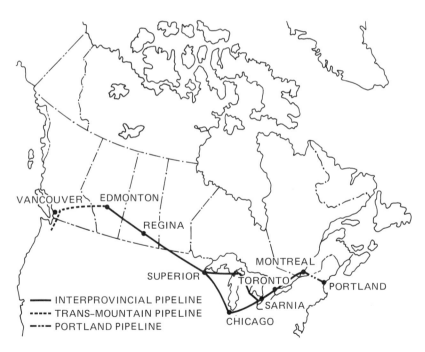

Figure 1
Major crude oil pipelines in Canada.

early as 1949, the National Petroleum Council (a federal advisory panel comprised mainly of industry representatives) advocated that foreign oil be assigned a solely supplementary role; the cited justification—national security—proved to be a pregnant one.

Congress in 1950 conducted hearings and commissioned studies to ascertain the effect of mounting oil imports on domestic oil and coal industries,[4] although shortly thereafter increasing freight rates resulting from the Korean War eased the situation, as did the Iranian crisis in 1952. However, already an important coalescence of interests—including domestic oil producers, natural gas and coal companies, the shipping industry, the National Petroleum Council, and the military—had began to favor what was tantamount to isolation of the US oil market.

A special Presidential Committee—the Advisory Committee on Energy Supplies and Resources Policy—was appointed in July 1954, and it suggested the United States restrict oil imports in 1955 to the same level as in 1954. The argument in favor of restriction saw impairment of domestic fuels as endangering orderly industrial growth, which in turn would undermine national defense. The recommendation was accepted and the first voluntary import program (VOIP1) emerged. The associated Presidential Proclamation (#3279) said, "In addition to serving our own direct security interests, the new program will also help prevent severe dislocations in our country as well as in oil industries elsewhere which also have an important bearing on our own security" (US Cabinet Task Force on Oil Import Control, 1970, p. 195). Meanwhile, Congress amended the Trade Agreements Extension Act—the so-called 1955 National Defense Amendment—to authorize the President to control imports of any article deemed to threaten national security. Under this amendment, the office of Defense Mobilization (ODM) was assigned the task of alerting the President if oil imports reached a critical level.

Initially under VOIP1 imports from all countries were restricted, but in October 1955 Canadian and Venezuelan imports were excluded, establishing an important precedent. At this time, the Deputy Director of the ODM said, "We consider production in the United States to be of first importance for defense. . . . For most intents and purposes, Canadian oil is considered in the same category. . . . Oil produced and refined in the Caribbean area will be for the United States a dependable source . . . " (Dagher, 1968, p. 363). In an October 1956 report, a Presidential Advisory Committee on Energy recommended the granting of preferences to hemispheric sources of supply, with Canadian oil excluded from quantitative restrictions, but suggested nevertheless that Canadian imports should "continue to be kept under close surveillance" (US Cabinet Task Force on Oil Import Control, 1970, p. 177).

The first voluntary program met with little success. The primary violators were newcomers to the import market, not the major companies. In August 1956 the Independent Petroleum Association of America (IPAA) requested limitation of imports under Section 7 of the Trade Agreements Extension Act of 1955.

The pressure from oil imports relented in the aftermath of the Suez crisis in 1957, but that crisis itself reinforced the security argument, and especially the relative security of Canadian supplies. Moreover, the closure of the Suez Canal alerted the average royalty owner in the United States to the additional revenue he would enjoy if imports were curtailed. As conditions returned to normal at the end of 1957, US government concern with oil imports revived, following advice from the ODM that oil imports were again threatening national security.

Accordingly, another committee, the Special Committee to Investigate Crude Oil Imports, was established. Its report established the second voluntary program (VOIP2), which recommended a variety of import controls. There were no exceptions by country of origin, but reference was made to a review of special consideration for Western Hemisphere countries, in line with a "joint interest in hemisphere defense" (Royal Commission on Energy, 1959, pp. 3–28). However, lack of special treatment for Canada in the 1957 VOIP2 reduced incentives to import Canadian oil. This was one of the adverse factors provoking a review of Canadian policy from which the Canadian National Oil Policy of 1961 eventually emerged (see below).

Dissatisfaction with the program was widespread, and eventually the system broke down as noncompliance spread. The number of newcomers into the oil import market—producers and refiners—had increased to some fifty by 1958. Their share of imports reached 55% (Shaffer, 1968, p. 22). In fact, the weight given to "historical" importers under the VOIP2 tended to provide an incentive for newcomers to torpedo the program, in the expectation that a reassessment might instigate more favorable treatment for them. The US government attempted to use suasion on the companies to implement the voluntary controls. And in March 1958, devotees of Orwellian Newspeak would have been enthused by insertion of the following clause in the Buy America Act: " . . . the contractor agrees that during the contract period he will comply in all respects with the voluntary Oil Import Program with respect to government contracts." [5]

Meanwhile, in 1958 a further amendment had been made to the Trade Extension Act to authorize the President to take action on imports if the national security were threatened. The criteria cited were quite broad, including the impact of imports on "domestic production needed for projected national defense requirements" and on the "capacity of the United States to meet national security requirements," as well as the "impact of foreign competition on the economic welfare of individual domestic industries" so as to determine "whether such weakening of our internal economy may [itself] impair the national security."[6]

It was under Section 8 of the Trade Agreements Extension Act of 1958 that in January 1959 the ODM was requested to review oil imports. The Director of ODM duly saw the national security as threatened. A Cabinet Special Committee then advised that the voluntary program should be superseded by a mandatory one. The Committee did not advocate preferential allowances for Canadian supply, but by recommending special quota allocations be made to refiners "not able to obtain sufficient quantities of domestic crude oil by ordinary and continuous means such as by barges, pipelines or tankers,"[7] some sort of preferential treatment was indicated for Canadian imports east of the Rockies.

Thus it was that the second voluntary program ended, and in March 1959 a mandatory quota program was instituted under the national security clause in the Reciprocal Trade Agreement Extension Act.[8] Restriction of imports was contrary to the general policy of trade liberalization the United States was advocating at that time. But justification on security grounds neatly avoided any breaching of GATT, while domestically the President could impose quotas without seeking additional Congressional authorization (Dam, 1971, p. 3).

National Security, then, was the main *legal* justification for the US Oil Import Program. In turn, the national security rationale implied special treatment for Canadian imports. But any open ended exemption potentially left a hole in the program, which could thwart its protectionist character. Thus, as discussed in more detail below, Canadian oil never enjoyed free access to US markets.

1.2 Treatment of Canadian Oil under the Program

1.2.1 The Initial Program
The 1959 version of the mandatory program bore a close resemblance to VOIP2. Importers were required to have a licence issued by the Secretary of the Interior. The issuance of licenses was to take the form of an " ... equitable distribution among persons having refinery capacity in these districts in relation to refinery inputs during an appropriate period ... in such manner as to avoid drastic reductions below the last allocations under the Voluntary Oil Import Program."[9]

The basic format of the program—control of imports by quotas allocated to individual refiners—continued until 1973, although there were numerous changes implemented by proclamations and executive orders. The major changes affecting Canada are outlined below, after a brief description of some technicalities of the program.

The system of quota allocations initially set imports at 9.6% of domestic demand east of the Rockies; west of the Rockies authorized imports were set at the difference between demand at the prevailing price and available domestic supply. Historical importers, defined as those companies importing oil under the VOIP2, were initially granted quotas equal to 80% of their last allocation under the voluntary program. The remaining authorized imports were divided among all other refineries in proportion to refinery inputs, according to a sliding scale: the smaller the refinery, the larger its proportionate share. Initially, about 75% of total imports were allocated to "historical" importers and 25% were allocated by the "sliding input scale"; the historical quotas were to decrease over time. However, "historical" importers were under no obligation to use the "historical" import quota. If the import allocation calculated on the basis of the sliding scale were larger, a company could elect to use it.

The original proclamation of March 1959 followed the policy of the second voluntary program in that no imports were exempt. But on 30 April 1959, Proclamation #3290[10] exempted overland oil imports; such imports from Canada and Mexico were not included in the maximum allowable imports into Districts I–IV or District V unless the resulting total level of imports were to increase to such an extent as to traduce seriously the intent of the policy.

No reason for the change in Canadian status was given in the announcement, but special treatment of Canadian oil was wholly consistent with earlier voluntary programs. Moreover, it harked back to the 1941 Hyde Park Agreement for collaboration on defense, trade, and resource development, including the removal of trade barriers, between the two countries. (Royal Commission on Energy, 1959, pp. 3–4). And in February 1959, the Canadian government had filed a strongly worded note with the US government (Dagher, 1968, p. 476) advising that

the Canadian government continues to believe that there is no justification on grounds of security (or, of that matter, on the other grounds) for U.S.A. Government restrictions on oil imports from Canada ... [restrictions] ... imposed in peacetime for security reasons, are not reconcilable with the need of Canada and the U.S.A. to pool their oil resources in time of common emergency. Any system of import restrictions applied against Canadian oil must have an adverse effect on Canada-U.S.A. relations; a system of mandatory controls on imports from Canada, related to security considerations, would be even more disturbing to Canada than would a system of voluntary controls of similar effect ....

Of course the national security justification of the import program itself suggested that Canada, and possibly other Western Hemisphere sources, should not be treated in the same way as other countries. And legal objections might have arisen in the event the program did not recognize this feature. The Korean, Iranian, and Suez crises had shown the dependability of Canadian sources, thereby buttressing arguments for distinguishing between offshore and overland imports. Also, the US government would not be unaware that, outside the northern border region, Canadian oil was not competitive with domestic production.[11]

On a broader basis, the US government would have appreciated that excess productive capacity in western Canada could induce Canada to extend the Interprovincial pipeline to Montreal, thereby displacing Venezuelan imports. This would have had serious political and economic repercussions for Venezuela because Canada was its second largest customer. The treatment of Venezuela under the import program was always a sensitive issue. The original import control proclamation made reference to special hemispheric interests involving both Canada and Venezuela, and Venezuela persistently lobbied about what it saw as unequal treatment.[12]

There is evidence of sympathy toward these Venezuelan views by US authorities. In 1965 Secretary of the Interior Udall wanted a reduction in the rate of growth of Canadian imports, while establishing some preferential treatment for Venezuelan over other foreign offshore imports.[13] On the other hand, the Canadian government saw the market provided for Venezuelan oil in eastern Canada in part as quid pro quo for favorable treatment in the United States.[14]

Given the April 1959 exemption under the mandatory import program, any refinery having access to Canadian crude could import it without a license in the quantities desired. This seemingly made Canadian crude a preferred input, always assuming its price were attractive. But refinery preferences were subtly affected by nuances that surrounded the award of offshore import quotas. As discussed, such quotas were allocated to refiners either on a sliding scale "eligible" input basis or on a historical basis (open to refineries traditionally dependent on imports). Refiners did not actually have to run offshore oil; while the quota itself could not be sold, the import "ticket" could be exchanged for US domestic oil. And the value of the "ticket" approximated the difference between the cost of domestic oil and offshore oil. Thus, in making feedstock decisions refiners would need to evaluate any effects Canadian oil might have on quotas under either allocative mechanism.

Specifically, refiners using the sliding input scale suffered a quota penalty in running Canadian crude. This was because the exempt crude could not count refinery inputs on which import quota "tickets" were awarded; only offshore and domestic crudes were eligible.

This implicit or clandestine tariff on Canadian oil for refiners on the sliding input scale was not trivial. For refiners on a quota to run ratio of 20% (a typical ratio for smaller refiners in 1967) and an import "ticket" value of, say, $1.50 per barrel, the implicit tariff would be 30¢ per barrel. But as long as the difference between the delivered price of Canadian oil and US domestic oil exceeded the quota penalty, the running of Canadian oil remained profitable.

The input decision for a refiner using a "historical" quota was more straightforward. He would exchange all his import quota for domestic oil, and Canadian oil at best would be a residual input—the difference between refinery runs and the historical quota—always assuming any delivered cost advantage enjoyed by Canadian oil were less than the value of the tradeable import "ticket" (which was normally the case).[15]

1.2.2 Program Changes and Developments

November 1962[16] saw several changes affecting Canada. One was a more rapid reduction of the historical allocations for those refineries using Canada crude under the overland exemption,[17] a process further accelerated in 1966. Overall, more rapid phasing out of historical offshore import quotas lowered an important entry barrier to Canadian oil by "freeing up" more refinery runs that might be devoted to Canadian crude, although in 1968 some minimum offshore quotas were set.[18]

Another change in November 1962 that affected Canada was an alteration in the basis for calculating the overall level of imports for Districts I–IV. The maximum level of imports for any six month period became 12.2% of total *production*, instead of 9.6% of total *demand*. Overseas imports were defined as a residual after deduction of the estimated volume of overland imports from total authorized imports. Under this mechanism, it was suggested that additional Canadian imports could directly displace offshore imports, thereby tightening supply and lessening competition in New England states.[19] Regardless of the merits of this concern, its significance lies in the perception of Canadian oil as a threat.

The combination of the imports of Middle East oil into eastern Canada and shipment of western Canadian crude to the United States was also viewed by some in the United States as a rather costly way of circumventing the import program, especially before the 1962 inclusion of "exempt" Canadian oil in the overall import umbrella. The argument was that oil imports into eastern Canada released western Canadian oil via the overland exemption for sale in the higher priced US market. According to this view, hemispheric security had not been improved, but Canada had effectively served as a conduit for offshore oil to access the US market at a higher price.[20] Again, the rationale for the argument is irrelevant; what it does do is demonstrate US concerns about Canadian imports.

Imports of Canadian oil by the Great Northern refinery at Clear Bend, Minnesota, illustrate the impact of the import quota control measures. At the inception of the Program, this refinery—which had been designed to process Saskatchewan crude—cut back on Canadian imports from sole reliance in 1959 to 67% by 1964, in order to participate in exchange agreements.[21] The reverse procedure accompanied the more rapid phasing out of historical quotas (fewer "tickets" to trade for domestic crude). Great Northern increased its Canadian feedstock to 77% of runs by 1966. But the 1968 decision to set a floor on historical allocations, which effectively guaranteed a minimum market via the exchange route for domestic crude, tended to offset the favorable effect of reduced historical quotas on Canadian crude imports.

During the 1960s, the Canadian and US governments were in frequent contact about Canadian oil exports, culminating in what was initially a secret agreement in 1967, around the time the Interprovincial Pipeline (IPL) was extended to Chicago to expand the marketing orbit for Canadian oil. The provisions of this agreement subsequently came to light; basically they sought to allay US concerns by limiting the growth in Canadian exports, and although the arrangement was only informal the US courts upheld its conditions.[22]

The 1960s also saw a change of emphasis in the US interpretation of the import policy, away from purely security of supply issues toward more overt protection of the domestic industry. In 1964 the Assistant Secretary to the Interior advocated restraint and patience in increasing imports of Canadian crude to the United States, noting that developments reacting adversely on the US domestic producing industry were not in US interests (*Oilweek*, Vol. 15, #7, March 30, 1964, pp. 12–14). More specifically, in 1965 Interior Secretary Udall said, "The limitation of petroleum imports rests upon a single premise: namely, that an excessive volume of such imports would discourage and limit the proper growth of the domestic oil industry . . . ."[23] In 1970, Canadian imports were apparently still seen to be a menace to the goals of the American program, because in March of that year the first mandatory ceiling on Canadian crude imports to the United States was imposed.[24]

As of 1 January 1971 the system of "historical" import quota allocations was officially ended. All refiners were to calculate their share of import tickets on the basis of the sliding input scale. In March 1973, special power was granted for additional allocations of imports to refiners, without regard to the maximum levels for the various Districts.

One month later needs overcame protection: April 1973 saw the abolition of the mandatory oil import quota system,[25] to be replaced by a system of six month license fees for oil imports. For the remainder of 1973, license fee exemption was granted to certain volumes of Canadian oil imports; the degree of exemption was to decline annually. But these provisions became academic after 1973 as Canada itself increasingly restricted exports of oil to the United States.

This discussion of the terms of access for Canadian oil under the USOIP makes two points very clear. First, Canadian oil occupied a special position. Second, although Canadian oil was given special treatment, its penetration was constrained in various ways. The reason for special treatment was simple. The legal justification for the Program was security, and Canadian oil transported overland to the United States was seen as more secure than overseas oil. Hence the decision to exempt Canadian oil from formal quotas. But Canadian oil never enjoyed unrestricted access. Various impedimenta emerged: hidden tariffs, exchange provisions, "jaw boning," secret agreements, intergovernmental discussions, and the like. Moreover, even in the proclamation under which Canadian oil was granted exemption there was a clear implication that if *total* imports threatened to impair the purpose of the program, further action would be necessary. Both within the administrative framework of the program, and by frequent consultation between the US and Canadian governments, volumes moving into the United States were kept under strict, mutual surveillance.

2 Implications of US Import Policy for the Pricing of Canadian Oil

2.1 Pricing of Canadian Oil—the Upper and Lower Boundaries

The Oil Import Program was the mechanism by which the price of US domestic crude became insulated from the world market. And this was a necessary condition for any corresponding departure for the price of Canadian traded crude. Whether higher-than-world prices for Canadian crude were acceptable in US markets depended on the terms of access. From mid-1959 to 1970 ostensibly Canadian oil was treated as US domestic crude, and in this sense whatever degree of penetration was desired for Canadian oil could be achieved by sufficient reductions in its price.

Given the exemption—real or apparent—one option would have been to price Canadian oil on a parity basis with US oil in the main markets served. But even if there were no hidden penalties, little incentive then would have existed to import Canadian oil except for those refiners unable to obtain sufficient domestic oil. And, as shown beforehand, hidden penalties did exist.

The input quota penalty was tantamount to a clandestine tariff on Canadian oil, over and above the actual duty of $10\frac{1}{2}$¢ per barrel payable on all oil imports; while for importers on "historical" quotas, the exchange provisions of the program favoured the use of domestic oil. These features, then dictated a laid-down cost of Canadian oil lower than any corresponding US price.

Such a competitive margin should not have been trivial, but neither should it have been too extensive. This is because too attractive a price for Canadian oil—say, world arms length price equivalence—would have stimulated strong pressures for more Canadian oil imports. But this development would have undermined the intention of the US government to avoid rapid growth from Canadian sources, notwithstanding exemption. Reference has already been made to the efforts of the US and Canadian governments to establish a framework that would allow only gradual increases in Canadian exports (the 1967 Agreement is the most obvious example).

Thus, any aggressive pricing of Canadian oil leading to strong growth of Canadian imports under exemption would almost certainly have provoked offsetting action by the US government and eroded support Canadian oil enjoyed from some interests in the United States.[26] But formal restrictions or discriminatory action on Canadian imports in turn would have embarrassed the apparent national security rationale of the oil import program; Canada would not want to have been seen as undermining controls under which it did after all enjoy special status.

The balance of influences thus favored a price for Canadian oil lower than the US price but nevertheless aligned more toward it than to world oil price equivalence. In this way, the pricing umbrella erected by the program not only provided a sheltered, albeit constrained, market for Canadian oil, but also *necessitated* that the price of Canadian exports to the United States depart from world levels.

It does not follow that the price for *all* Canadian production need have been predicated on the US market. The Canadian government could have let world prices in eastern Canada set western Canadian oil prices, and then placed an export tax on sales to the United States to absorb any differential. But this procedure probably would have evoked strong opposition in the United States. It was one thing for Canadian oil prices to be higher than world prices; it would be quite another for the Canadian government to be seen directly taxing exports to the United States, while enjoying world oil prices for domestic consumption. In this event, proposals would likely have emerged to eliminate the exempt status for Canadian oil, reducing it to the equivalent of offshore oil. Quite apart from that, imposition of an export tax by Canada may well have been contrary to GATT or other international trading agreements,[27] while practicing price discrimination toward the United States would not be an endearing posture towards Canada's largest trading partner.

The argument that the Import Program at least set lower and upper boundary values for the price of Canadian crude still leaves a fairly wide degree of latitude. How much lower than US domestic prices or higher than world prices might Canadian prices have been? What did happen to Canadian oil prices in the 1960s, and why?

Before attempting to answer these questions, I outline two key domestic policies under which the Canadian industry operated at that time. The first is prorationing in Alberta; the second is the 1961 National Oil Policy.

2.2 Prorationing in Alberta—Effects on Price Formation

The control of oil production by market demand prorationing is well known in the United States. Its inception in Alberta—the main Canadian producing region—in 1950 was in fact a legacy from US experience. Under Alberta prorationing, refiners are asked to "nominate" for oil they require *at the prevailing price*. All the nominations are added up, and the required level of total production allocated among wells by a quota scheme with the intention that each well owner would receive his "fair and equitable" production share.

Proration contributes to price stabilization by lending support to the going price, since competition between sources of supply within the prorated region is eliminated. Moreover, the dynamics of market penetration are constrained. Refiners can only nominate for oil production by the prorationing procedure and cannot contract directly with producers to negotiate both price and volumes, since any demand generated must be spread over all suppliers. The income of integrated firms from prorated production becomes largely independent of decisions they make as refiners, thereby reducing incentives for such firms to use more prorated crude if they have access to owned production not subject to proration.

Consequently, with proration price variations tend to be blunted and the degree of response to changing conditions becomes muted. If demand at the current price fell, supply was automatically curtailed. There was no easy way for the excess supply to find a buyer at a lower price, because refiners simply nominated at the going price. Discounting and price discrimination were ruled out as marketing techniques;[28] the Alberta Conservation Board stood between the purchasers and buyers and abjured any involvement in price setting. These circumstances opened the door for price leadership by those companies able to carry the industry with them, since some mechanism is required to make price changes.

The ability of the industry to compete is also determined by the way prorationing affects costs. There are two aspects to this, one inherent in the system, the other dependent on how the system is administered. With regard to the first, proration assumes the existence of spare capacity; that is, price will not fall to clear the market. Thus the existence of excess capacity, which entails an extra cost burden, is normal rather than exceptional.

Morry Adelman[29] made the first detailed assessment of the cost of prorationing in the United States, reminding us of the way that system nurtured the weeds (low productivity wells) at the expense of the flowers (high productivity wells). In the same vein, the Alberta system employed a prorationing formula, which, at least up to 1964 or so, had a marked effect on costs of production. Production quotas were set according to the number of wells drilled and were calculated to guarantee that well costs would be covered. Of course, this tended to stimulate well drilling and therefore led to higher costs of reservoir development.[30] Subsequently, changes made to the Alberta proration plan announced in 1964 tended to eliminate any incentives for "overdrilling" in a reservoir.

Thus prorationing tends to foist a higher cost structure on the industry, and the degree of cost increase is significantly affected by the manner in which production quotas are set. The industry is less able to compete against crude produced elsewhere and is more vulnerable and inclined to seek protection. Some of these features became critical when the Canadian industry faced adversity, as it did in the latter part of the 1950s, the genesis of the Canadian National Oil Policy.

2.3 Canada's National Oil Policy, 1961–1973

In 1957, only about half of Alberta's oil productive capacity was being utilized, while the United States was moving toward mandatory import controls. Canadian habits suggested a Royal Commission examine such problems, and one—the Borden Commission—was duly set up. It reported in 1959. The main point of controversy was a proposed pipeline linking Montreal to the western oil fields. A Montreal pipeline was championed by the "independent" oil producers, but was strongly opposed by the Montreal refiners, primarily major oil companies. The root problem was that when Canadian crude coming east met the price of US crude in Sarnia, Ontario (see figure 1), it implicitly enjoyed the higher-priced US market. To put Canadian crude the rest of the way into Montreal meant meeting world competition, implying an immediate price cut for western producers. Furthermore, past pipeline expansion had involved guarantees by users to maintain agreed-upon levels of throughput.

With alternative overseas suppliers, the Montreal refiners were certainly not prepared to offer guarantees of this sort.

One of the majors—Imperial, an Exxon affiliate—suggested market expansion be pursued by securing the entire Ontario market for Canadian crude while concurrently expanding exports to the United States. The Montreal market would be set aside. By and large, the Borden Commission followed Imperial's "line" and in turn in 1961 the Canadian government accepted the main Borden proposals.

The measures selected to secure designated markets for Canadian Oil became known collectively as the National Oil Policy (NOP). Target 1963 levels of production were set to be reached both by substituting Canadian crude for both foreign crude and products in Ontario and by additional exports to markets served by established pipelines. The National Energy Board (NEB) was to exercise surveillance over progress of the program. Mention was made of the program being "... wholly consistent with the growth of sales of Canadian oil contemplated when exemption from United States oil import controls was established ...," while "... progressive displacement of imported crudes and products in the Ontario market is considered to be fully consistent with the public announcement of the Government of Venezuela that it considers its oil should not reach these markets in the interior of Canada. The United States Government has been made aware of the Canadian Government's plans in view of the close connections between the oil economies of the two countries."[31] Subsequently, the United States indicated acceptability of the general level of exports contemplated in the Hees announcement.[32] The policy relied on a voluntary mechanism, although regulation always loomed, especially the possible imposition of Canadian import quotas.

As mentioned before, throughout the 1960s the question of Canadian oil exports involved constant consultation with the US government. Also, underlying Canadian policy there seems to have been a general presumption that displacement of Venezuelan oil by Canadian oil in Montreal would provoke restriction of shipments of Canadian oil to the United States.[33] And in 1967 the Canadian government indicated increased exports to the United States were more desirable than building a Montreal pipeline.[34]

Thus, the main feature of the National Oil Policy, 1961–1973, was the protection from offshore oil given to Canadian oil in markets west of the Ottawa Valley. However, protection was not complete. Products refined from offshore oil and minor amounts of offshore crude could enter the Ontario market, although sizable quantities would have provoked formal controls. In the latter half of the 1960s, a growing cost advantage for imported products in the Ontario market increased incentives to transgress the NOP, and by 1970 protection for Ontario refiners became overt with the imposition of import controls on gasoline.

2.4 The Evolution of Canadian Oil Prices

In the 1950s prices paid by eastern Canadian refineries with access to alternative supplies were decisive in establishing the price of all western output. Alberta prices evolved to meet competition from alternative supplies in the most distant market or "competitive interface" in a way that nicely illustrated Adelman's diagram of oil price formulation in his seminal book.[35] The interface became Sarnia, Ontario, where Illinois crude provided a competitive yardstick. However, by the end of the 1950s, Canadian oil prices no longer equated with US crude at Sarnia; a price reduction in 1959 to reflect world oil prices was not triggered by reductions in US prices, the first time Canadian price adjustments reflecting market conditions did not mirror what was happening in the United States. In 1961, the devaluation of the Canadian dollar to a pegged rate resulted in an Alberta (Redwater) wellhead price of $2.62 per barrel. This price held until 1970.

The *structure* of Canadian prices in 1960 was consistent with what would have occurred in competitive markets—one price was quoted at Edmonton for a particular grade of crude regardless of its destination or origin—but the *level* was not necessarily so. Certainly, the buyers' discretion to raise price was limited by the presence of alternative suppliers in the most distant market. And in the 1950s a downward trend in prices had taken place as a prerequisite to continued extension of the market area. However, the downward pressure on prices was never severe enough to force demand to be met from lowest cost sources. Instead, excess capacity both fueled and controlled by prorationing was always present. Price changes reflected the objective of increasing industry output through orderly market expansion. But the overriding constraint on the evolution of Canadian crude oil prices during the 1950s had been the Alberta Oil and Gas Conservation Act and nascent protectionism in the US market.

Under the National Oil Policy (NOP), Canada in the 1960s developed a curious position, combining under one roof a protected domain and an open one. Ontario and the West were to be supplied by western Canadian crude, while Quebec and the Maritimes were open to world trade. With the NOP, the industry had to harmonize operations to meet a prescribed balance between domestic and imported crude supplies and satisfy access conditions under the US Oil Import Policy.

What is notable is that after 1961 the field prices of Canadian crude were

Table 2
United States, Alberta, and world oil prices, 1960–1969

	(1) Mid-Continent (wellhead) (36°) ($US/barrel)	(2) Persian Gulf ($US/barrel)	(3) Redwater at Edmonton (35°) ($Can/barrel)
1960	2.97	1.50	2.42
1961	2.97	1.50	2.62
1962	2.97	1.61	2.62
1963	2.97	1.59	2.62
1964	2.93	1.29	2.62
1965	2.92	1.17	2.62
1966	2.98	1.27	2.62
1967	3.03	1.23	2.62
1968	3.10	1.83	2.62
1969	3.23	1.27	2.62

Sources: column (1), Midcontinent (Oklahoma-Kansas 36° gravity) crude, *Twentieth Century Petroleum Statistics*, Degolyer-MacNaughton, 1980, p. 97; column (2), Adelman (1972, tables VI-3 and VI-6)—these prices are based on Rotterdam composite product prices less refinery margins and tanker costs; column (3), Alberta Energy Resources Conservation Board.

frozen for the rest of the decade. I have already suggested that Canadian prices would be set within limits prescribed by world and US domestic prices. But during the 1960s the world price was falling while US prices rose modestly in the latter half (see table 2). So ostensibly there was scope for both upward and downward movement in Canadian prices. Why, then, their inertia?

Let me deal first with upward movements. One element is the exchange rate. The Canadian dollar was pegged at 92.5¢ United States during the 1960s, so adjustments to Canadian prices were not required on this account. With US prices creeping up, and with Canadian pipeline tariffs falling (see table 3) there would seem to have been room for a modest upward movement in Canadian prices to have been tolerated in US markets without a marked impact on market penetration. A comprehensive time series on laid down costs of crudes in US markets is elusive, but the numbers in table 4 for Detroit show a trend of widening differentials in laid down cost between Alberta and US crudes in US markets in the 1960s. At the same time, the hidden penalties on the use of Canadian crude tended to increase, for two reasons.[36] First, the decline in ''historical'' quotas meant a larger proportion of imports were allocated on the input scale. Second, the rising spread between world prices and US domestic prices tended to increase the value of the import ticket. There is no precise relationship between the increasing laid down cost differential shown in table

Table 3
Pipeline tariffs, Edmonton, Alberta, and Cromer, Saskatchewan, to Detroit/Toledo ($Can/barrel)[a]

	Edmonton, Alberta, to Detroit/Toledo	Cromer, Saskatchewan, to Detroit/Toledo
1959	0.61	0.48
1960	0.55	0.435
1963	0.53	0.423
1971	0.52	0.409

Source: Interprovincial Pipeline, *Annual Reports*, 1960, 1963, and 1971.
a. Transportation system, IPL and Buckeye pipelines.

Table 4
Laid down costs: US and Alberta crudes at Detroit, selected years ($US/barrel)

	Wyoming sour (36°–36.9°)	Alberta redwater (35°)	Difference
1961	3.444[a]	3.182	0.262
1965	3.449	3.123	0.326
1967	3.475	3.104	0.371
1969	3.725	3.104	0.621

Source: Alberta Energy Resources Conservation Board.
a. Wyoming sweet.

4 and the rise in hidden penalties; nevertheless the compensating trends at least help to explain any reluctance to increase Canadian prices.

But a more compelling explanation is the political tension any increase in prices would have created in Canada, and perhaps in the United States. The prices of oil imported in eastern Canada were falling, albeit with some lag in relation to world arms length prices.[37] Any increase in prices west of the Ottawa Valley would simply have made the pricing disparities—which had hitherto seemed modest—more visible and politically unpalatable. Thus there were sound reasons for the Canadian industry price leader—Imperial Oil— not to initiate any upward movement in prices of Canadian crude.

What of erosion in the price of Canadian crude? Certainly this would have served to avoid aggravating pricing tension between the unprotected and protected parts of the Canadian market. But it would have increased pressures exerted by Canadian oil in the US market. There was already excess demand for Canadian oil, only held in check by intergovernmental agreements. In- creasing the attraction of Canadian oil would have been provocative, leading in all likelihood to controls of a more formal nature, which in turn would have made the legerdemain of the apparent exemption for Canadian oil under the US program more obvious. In other words, a lower price structure for imports of Canadian oil would have tended to create more problems for US administrators than keeping the status quo.

These conflicting factors within the framework of government policy appear sufficient to explain why inertia in Canadian oil prices made sense during the 1960s: as price leader, Imperial Oil's adherence to $2.62 per barrel at Edmonton may have seemed an infatuation, but it was also astute. Keeping Canadian crude oil prices where they were caused fewer problems than varying them up or down. However, once world oil prices started to increase in 1971, inertia was no longer attractive.

3 Pricing Policies in the 1970s and 1980s

I have argued that the US import program, which ended in 1973, was a fundamental determinant of Canadian oil price formation in the 1960s. What of developments since that time? Have US policies continued to cast a shadow over the Canadian scene, or has Canadian oil pricing become solely a function of Canadian federal and provincial government policy?

First I summarize pertinent policy developments in the United States and Canada during this period; then I discuss the issue of whether US oil policies have conferred a further legacy on Canadian oil pricing policy.

3.1 US Policy[38]

In February 1970 the US Cabinet Task Force on Oil Import Control had recommended the replacement of quotas with tariffs, but with Canadian oil admitted essentially tariff-free on an unrestricted basis. All the Task Force recommendations were ignored. Instead, a month later the US government unilaterally imposed import quotas on Canadian oil, a development one observer called one of the great bone-headed plays in the history of US energy policy (McKie, 1975, p. 722). As an example of misplaced timing, it ranks high—because it was precisely at this point that Canadian oil production peaked.

The system of license fees for oil imports that replaced the Mandatory Oil Import Program in April 1973 granted exemption to certain volumes of Canadian oil. In July 1973 US policy turned turtle with the statement that it would freeze the level of fee-free oil from Canada unless Canadian oil exports to the United States increased. Again this timing was bizarre, because it coincided with the imposition by Canada of oil export controls.

With the elimination of controls on quantities, US regulatory activity shifted to the pricing arena. The initial essay here was the ninety day Phase I price freeze of August 1971, imposed under the "Economic Stabilization Act" (ESA) of 1970. During Phases I and II of the program, which lasted to the end of 1972, price increases were held to 3% annually, and the gap between domestic and import oil prices widened as world oil prices rose.

When the less restrictive Phase III regulations were issued in January 1973, prices of petroleum products increased rapidly. In March 1973, the Cost of Living Council issued "Special Rule 1" specifically applying to the petroleum industry. This imposed mandatory price controls on crude oil and other refined products. As a price restraint device, "Special Rule 1" failed; gasoline and fuel oil prices rose by more than 30% during the six months it was in place.[39] In June 1973, under the authority of ESA a further sixty day freeze on prices was instituted.

The passage of the Emergency Petroleum Allocation Act (EPAA) in November 1973 established a general form of price controls on crude oil. A major provision of the EPAA was the introduction of a two-tier pricing system for domestically produced crude oil, distinguishing between "new" oil and "old" oil.[40] "Old" oil was defined as the quantity of crude oil produced in the corresponding month of 1972. Output over and above 1972 monthly production levels and from new wells not producing in 1972 was defined as "new" oil. Moreover, for each barrel of "new oil production above the base level of "old" oil, a producer was permitted to release a barrel of "old" oil from the "old" classification. This transmogrification was called "released" oil. Finally, "stripper" oil was defined as output from wells producing less than ten barrels per day. Imported, "new," "released," and "stripper" oils were exempt from price controls and permitted to sell at world equivalent prices.

Under this two-tier system, nearly 40% of domestic oil in the United States was deregulated. The "uncontrolled" oil prices were about double the "old" oil price. In the absence of some cost equalization program, a two-tier pricing system for oil could result in substantial differences in crude feedstock costs for refiners. To eliminate such cost disparities, the Federal Energy Administration adopted an "Entitlements" program in December 1974. Thus it is that regulation doth breed upon itself!

It is not necessary to get into the labyrinth of the entitlement program. Suffice it to say that by purchase and sale of entitlements, the average cost of crude to each US refiner would be roughly equalized, although as usual with this kind of program all sorts of exceptions were built into it.

The crude oil pricing regulations of EPAA were superseded in February 1976 by the Energy Policy Conservation Act (EPCA) of 1975, which added another tier to the pricing program. The vintage oil pricing system was buried in April

1980, to be replaced by vintage oil taxing. Under the new rules domestic oil would sell at prices roughly equivalent to world prices; the federal government would receive a percentage of the difference between the selling price and the base price, with five tax rates levied on different types of oil and three base prices set on which these varying tax rates were imposed.

The complex entitlement system was ended January 1981 when the United States decontrolled all prices on crude oil and products. Two years earlier Adelman had called for decontrol, averring that it would lower the cost of oil to the US economy (Adelman, 1979). Happily, his prescience has been fulfilled to date.

3.2 Canadian Policy

There are some important parallels between Canadian pricing policy developments and those in the United States following the world oil price shock of 1973–1974. Both governments sought to cushion consumers from spiraling world prices, involving increasingly extensive regulation of both the upstream and downstream oil sectors to an extent that has been described as making Trivial Pursuit seem a productive enterprise (Waverman and Watkins, 1985, p. (ii)).

The year 1973 saw the formal control of oil prices pass from industry to government, where until just before the time of writing it continued to reside. Such control started with a freeze on Alberta wellhead oil prices at $3.80 per barrel in August 1973. Ominously, in March of that year Section 87 of the National Energy Board Act was invoked and controls on the export of Canadian crude to the United States began. In June of 1973 the export controls were extended to oil products. And in October 1973, export taxes were levied on Canadian oil shipments to the United States.

The National Oil Policy was formally terminated in December 1973. The policy that replaced it provided for a single, subsidized oil price in Canada (with adjustments for transportation differentials), establishment of a national oil company, and extension of the Interprovincial oil pipeline to Montreal. To achieve the single price, an oil import compensation program to subsidize importers of foreign oil became effective on 1 January 1974.

Price increases were set by intergovernmental agreement in March 1974 and at regular intervals thereafter until 1980, when the arrangements between Alberta and the federal government expired. The Alberta government then acted alone until the September 1981 pricing accord. In general, over this period the gap between world oil prices and domestic Canadian oil prices widened, notwithstanding federal intentions, announced in 1976, that

Canadian prices would reach international levels within four years (Canada EMR, 1976, p. 126). Correspondingly, the tax on oil exports to the United States increased to absorb the growing differential between prices of oil imports and Canadian domestic oil prices, although the volume of crude oil exports declined to modest levels under the export formula adopted by the National Energy Board in 1974.[41]

The United States' move to deregulation in 1981 did not find a sympathetic response in Canada, where more rather than less regulation of oil prices was in vogue. In fact the National Energy Program (NEP) of October 1980 viewed world oil prices as "arbitrary and artificial" (Canada EMR, 1980, p. 27), something from which any right minded country should "dissociate itself" (Canada EMR, 1980, p. 7). Hence the emergence of a "made-in-Canada" oil pricing regime involving "vintage" pricing—a US legacy?—and scheduled price increases to lag behind a presumed ever rising trajectory of world oil prices. But OPEC was not a signatory to the NEP and the subsequent pricing agreements, and by the summer of 1984 while "old" oil prices were held below world levels, both they and "new" oil prices—and it was surprising how much "old" oil was increasingly found to be "new" oil—were directly treated as a function of world oil prices.

With a change in federal government in September 1984, deregulation became de rigeur, and on 1 June 1985 deregulation became fact. At present, Canadian and US oil prices are in harmony for the first time in thirty years.

3.3 US and Canadian Pricing Policies—Cross Breeding?

Did US policy in the 1970s and 1980s continue to constrain Canadian oil pricing in the way I have suggested it did in the 1960s? The short answer to that question is no. Canada embarked on an independent course, charging the United States world equivalent prices for exports of Canadian oil, subsidizing imports, and holding down prices on domestic oil. Ostensibly, US actions were irrelevant. Yet it is hard to resist the conclusion that the United States' decision to continue to insulate itself from the world oil market certainly predisposed Canadian authorities to do likewise. This "demonstration effect" on the part of Canada's closest trading partner certainly added conviction to Canadian government pricing policies of a similar ilk.

If the United States had moved quickly to deregulate oil prices in the 1970s, the policies pursued by Canada would have stood in more stark relief and the hand of those who for efficiency reasons sought to see Canada move away from oil price subsidization would have been strengthened. But all this is mere speculation. What does seem plausible is that US policies for grappling with

OPEC pricing in the 1970s and early 1980s did find an echo in Canada. Moreover, ownership of oil by Canadian provinces created tension and confrontation between the federal and provincial governments, with price controls emerging in part as a clumsy solution to disputes about rent sharing.

One might also argue that deregulation in the United States of oil (and gas) pricing since 1981 has cast a benign shadow in Canada, easing the path of dismantling controls by demonstrating the truth of Morry Adelman's remark that "decontrol will lessen the damage to our economy" (Adelman, 1979, p. 40).

4 Summary and Concluding Remarks

This paper has dealt with the repercussions of US policies on the pricing of Canadian oil both during the fourteen year period, 1959–1973, that the Mandatory Oil Import Program held sway, and from 1973 to the present.

The combination of the three sets of government policies reviewed beforehand—two Canadian (Alberta prorationing and the National Oil Policy) and one American (the United States Oil Import Policy)—defined the arena within which the Canadian industry performed in the 1960s. And it was quite a restricted arena. Market demand prorationing curtailed competition between different sources of supply and constrained pricing dynamics that would otherwise have determined market growth. Excess capacity, which both induced proration and was sustained by it, was burdensome. The cost structure of the industry was inflated. Restraints on the ability to adjust imposed by proration and associated regulatory features contributed toward the depressed circumstances in the late 1950s that precipitated formulation of the Canadian National Oil Policy (NOP). The latter erected a protective barrier around the western Canadian industry by reserving markets west of Quebec for Canadian oil.

But the protective character of the NOP coincided with and was even necessitated by an even more pervasive protective policy—the US Oil Import Quota program. Under this umbrella, US domestic prices increasingly departed from world levels. By virtue of the legal security rationale for the US import quotas, Canadian oil enjoyed special access. But any rapid growth of exports of Canadian oil to the United States would have provoked retaliation. Accordingly, Canadian oil prices were bounded from above by US domestic prices and from below by world prices. Canadian oil output was governed by gradual increases in exports, in part negotiated between the respective federal governments, and the growth in domestic markets west of Quebec.

Once the impact of US policy on Canadian pricing was recognized, meeting competition from world oil at Montreal was no longer a viable option, unless overt price discrimination were practiced on exports. The latter was never feasible, because it would have required export taxes or other mechanisms which would have tended again to annoy the United States.

Thus, in the 1960s paradoxically the US import policy effectively "protected" the Montreal market from penetration by western Canadian oil, since the necessary price reductions would have created pricing distortions on Canadian exports. In this way, acceptance by Canada of special treatment under the program placed corresponding restrictions on Canadian policy. Price inertia for Canadian oil in the 1960s was consistent with the desired gradual penetration of US markets while at the same time avoiding too embarrassing a pricing disparity within Canada east and west of Ottawa. In short, US policy is the key to Canadian oil pricing in the 1960s.

How different the 1970s and early 1980s have been. Import controls in the United States were abolished. US domestic prices became lower, not higher, than world prices. Canadian imports would have been welcome, not restrained, but the Canadian government imposed export controls and diverted production to serve the Montreal market. Canadian crude prices were set lower, not higher, than world prices. Prorationing in Alberta became largely irrelevant as production approached or met capacity. Ostensibly, Canadian oil output and pricing became solely a function of Canadian and provincial government policy. But although US policies after 1973 have only had an intangible impact on Canadian oil price formation, nevertheless both their nature and style contributed to the "ambiance" that governed pricing decisions in Canada.

I cannot in this paper get into an overall assessment of whether the pricing regime pursued by Canadian authorities was a "good thing" for the country. But let me make the following point. As a broad generalization, Canadian and US policies in both the pre- and post-OPEC pricing eras thwarted impulses transmitted by the price mechanism. Foreign oil was both cheap and readily available in the 1960s, which should have encouraged increased reliance on it. Instead protectionist barriers were erected. In turn these barriers accelerated absorption of domestic resources that would otherwise have been available when foreign oil became dear after 1973. Yet during the 1970s both the US and Canadian governments continued to frustrate price signals. These policy responses to both declining and rising world prices may have been perverse, but they were consistent!

Several years ago, the American writer Clarence Day said,

When eras die their legacies
Are left to strange police
Professors in New England guard
The Glory that was Greece.[42]

If for "Greece" we read "Washington," it is doubtful that one New England professor would have sought to sustain the US oil regulatory apparatus over the past three decades. Morry Adelman's work tells us that Government Policy that seeks to suppress rather than promote adjustment is seldom worthwhile.

Notes

1. US Senate (1969), p. 31.

2. This contradicts the conclusions of a recent Canadian Combines Investigation; see R. J. Bertrand (1981), Vol. 1, p. 78.

3. For a resume of the US import policy, also see Adelman (1972), pp. 150–155.

4. US Congress, House Select Committee on Small Business (1950).

5. 23 *Federal Register* 2067, "Government Purchases of Crude Petroleum Products."

6. As amended, these statutory provisions were incorporated without substantive change into the Trade Expansion Act of 1962, as Section 232; US Cabinet Task Force or Oil Import Control (1970), pp. 159–160.

7. Report of Special Committee to Investigate Crude Oil Imports, Washington: 6 March 1959, p. 8. Reproduced in US Cabinet Task Force or Oil Import Control (1970).

8. Proclamation #3279; 24 *Federal Register* 1781.

9. 24 *Federal Register*, 1781, p. 12.

10. The Cabinet Special Committee that recommended mandatory control did not advocate preferential treatment for Canada, but did recommend special allocations for refiners unable to obtain sufficient domestic oil, thereby implying preferential treatment for "northern tier" refineries; see J. H. Dagher (1968), p. 388.

11. Indeed, support was given in 1957 to Canadian imports by the Texas legislature and the Independent Petroleum Association of America (IPAA) precisely because competition from Canada was limited; see Dagher (1968), p. 574.

12. See US Senate (1969), p. 118. Also, see Betancourt (1979), pp. 384–403. On 20 March 1965, the Venezuelan Chamber of Deputies unanimously approved a motion calling US import controls on Venezuelan crude exports "unjust and discriminatory and contrary to the treatment given to imports from other countries" (*Platt's Oilgram*, 22 March 1965, p. 4).

13. As reported in *Oilweek*, 20 September 1965, p. 45.

14. The Hon. Jean-Luc Pepin, Minister of Energy, Mines and Resources, *Address to the*

Canadian Institute of Mining and Metallurgy, 19 October 1966. See *Platt's Oilgram*, Vol. 44, No. 203, p. 1.

15. For more details on refinery economics under the program, see Watkins (1981), Appendix.

16. Proclamation #3509, 27 *Federal Register* 11985.

17. For details, see Shaffer (1968), table 22.

18. See Proclamation #3823, *Federal Register* 1171.

19. See *Hearings* (1969), p. 260.

20. *Hearings* (1969), p. 261.

21. See Shaffer (1968), p. 162.

22. Litigation arose in a case where Clark Oil wished to import Canadian oil into the Chicago area in 1969. Its application was turned down on the basis that the agreements were a pact that "bears the dignity similar to that of a treaty"; see *Oilweek*, 22 September 1969, p. 19.

23. See *Platt's Oilgram*, Vol. 43, No. 48, 12 March 1965, p. 1.

24. Proclamation #3969; see 35 *Federal Register* 4321.

25. Proclamation #4210; see 38 *Federal Register* 4645.

26. See earlier reference in note 11.

27. After 1973, Canada levied export taxes on oil going to the United States, but that situation was quite different. Canadian oil was subsidized, so the purpose of the export tax was to avoid passing on a subsidy to US buyers.

28. "Common purchaser" legislation was important, whereby each common purchaser "shall purchase oil ... without discrimination in favour of one purchaser or owner ... in the same pool ... (or) ... between pools ... and shall not discriminate in favour of his own production." See "The Oil and Gas Conservation Act: Oil and Gas Conservation Regulation," Office Consolidation, Energy Resources Conservation Board, Alberta, p. A-23.

29. Adelman (1964).

30. For estimates of economic waste induced by Alberta prorationing in the 1950s and early 1960s, see Watkins (1977).

31. Speech by Hon. G. Hees, *Hansard*, 1 February 1961, p. 1642.

32. See R. D. Howland, *Address to the Annual Meeting of the Canadian Institute of Mining and Metallurgy*, Quebec City, April 1966. Note also that Interior Secretary Udall said in 1961 that "... if the Canadian plan has a marked and abrupt adverse effect on our petroleum industry, such action would undoubtedly furnish the basis for a review of the United States treatment of Canadian imports" (cited in Dagher, 1968, p. 634).

33. See Hon. Jean-Luc Pepin, op. cit.

34. See Hon. Jean-Luc Pepin, *Hansard*, 31 January 1967, p. 12454,

35. See Adelman (1972), p. 133.

36. Recall that the quota "penalty" from using Canadian oil was the product of the marginal quota to refinery input ratio and the import ticket value.

37. The desirability of preserving the balance between eastern and western markets in Canada tended to undermine incentives the major oil companies would have to seek lower crude prices for the Quebec and Maritime regions—but that is another story.

38. For a general reference, see Kalt (1981).

39. This was mainly because US domestic regulations could not control the world price of crude oil: OPEC had the temerity to ignore them.

40. The two-tier system was intended to permit increased domestic crude oil production by raising prices at the margin while allowing the lower average price of crude to determine refined product prices.

41. See National Energy Board, *In the Matter of the Exportation of Oil*, October 1974, pp. 4–8. The NEB formula provided for a gradual phase out of exports, unless productive capacity grew strongly. In 1976, the formula was relaxed to permit additional exports of heavy oil, where surplus capacity had become endemic.

42. Clarence Day, "Thoughts Without Words."

3   Coal Policy in Perspective

                               Richard L. Gordon

Overoptimism about coal is endemic. Impending exhaustion of oil and gas supplies (perhaps reenforced by efforts of Middle East oil producers to rig world oil prices) is expected inevitably to restore coal to its pre-World War I position as a dominant multipurpose source of energy. The restoration, moreover, is supposed to benefit coal producers everywhere.

Rising oil prices of the 1970s were taken by many as confirmation of these contentions. The advocates of a coal revival ignored the basic economic principles of energy decision making. Among the most important failures was to overlook three critical conclusions in Morry Adelman's research on energy economics—that exhaustion would not be a problem, that ineptitude among consuming country governments had made the world vulnerable to cartelization, and that nevertheless limits existed to how high oil prices profitably could be pushed.

A critical element of the last error was underrating Morry's post-price-rise observation that one of the profitable long-term responses to higher prices would be investments in energy-saving equipment.

Competition from coal industries in other countries and from nuclear power created additional problems for some coal industries, particularly those in western Europe. These industries proved incapable of withstanding competition. Rising oil prices proved no relief. Thus, the protectionist programs instituted during the era of failing oil prices have persisted.

However, in some parts of the world, stronger coal industries effectively competed in the market for electric-utility fuel and benefited from fueling growing electric power output. The critical countries in this group are the

---

In the long period between the completion of a first draft and this version, I undertook and completed the manuscript of a short book on coal around the world (referred to in the notes as the World Coal manuscript). In the process, I cannibalized and improved many parts of the draft. In rewriting, I have deleted much material better left for the book and brought the remainder up to date.

United States, South Africa, and Australia. These countries and Canada also secured export markets for coking coal. Overoptimism about coal has had the perverse effect that the successes of these countries are often denigrated because they fell short of expectations.

Several distinct coal situations prevail internationally (and intranationally). The coal industries of different regions range from the stably growing to the dying. Thus, those of Australia, South Africa, western Canada, and the western United States largely became established since World War II. Those of western Europe, Japan, and eastern Canada have endured protracted contractions.

Public policy excessively perpetuated these last industries instead of efficiently easing the pains of a rapid contraction. Various intermediate cases arise, such as the eastern United States. The coal industry east of the Mississippi enjoyed growth in the 1960s. Performance in the 1970s and into the 1980s has been more uneven. Output has fluctuated without showing much growth. China has grown to become the number two producer. The long period of growth of Soviet Union coal output ceased in the late 1970s.

This experience with coal is interesting both in its own right and because of what it demonstrates about such problems as policymaking, mineral-resource scarcity, and adaptation to economic change. While the ends of coal policies have differed with national conditions, the universal problem of poor policymaking has prevailed.

As background, a summary discussion of coal economics is presented. The effort is to suggest the analytic failures that contributed to bad policies.

1 Coal Industry Performance

Worldwide coal production has grown modestly and irregularly over both the whole twentieth century and the post-World War II period (see table 1).[1] As noted, the interesting developments relate to differences among and even within countries. The distribution of production among countries has shifted greatly.

Throughout the world, coal has lost markets. Oil and gas have displaced coal as fuels for use by manufacturing industries, commercial buildings, and residences. Coal can compete best in the electric sector and in providing coke for pig iron manufacture. The market for coal then depends on the state of the steel and electric power industries.

The steel industry has been a less attractive coal market than electric power. While electric power output has grown, steel has had slow growth and more recently decline. In addition, steel industry technology has changed so that

Table 1

Twentieth-century coal production in selected countries and years (millions of metric tons)

A. Selected leading hard coal producers

Year	World	US	USSR	China	Austra-lia	Poland	South Africa	India	Canada
1900	701.0	244.7	16.2	N/A	6.5	29.6	0.9	6.2	5.2
1913	1,216.0	517.1	30.0	16.1	12.6	49.0	8.0	16.5	13.4
1920	1,191.8	595.3	7.2	22.9	13.0	35.9	10.4	18.3	12.0
1929	1,325.4	549.7	36.9	25.4	10.5	74.2	13.0	23.8	12.3
1938	1,203.6	355.3	113.0	31.0	11.9	69.4	16.3	28.8	12.0
1946	1,214.7	536.8	139.0	11.5	14.1	47.3	23.2	30.2	11.7
1947	1,368.6	621.4	154.0	14.1	15.1	59.1	23.0	30.6	10.0
1948	1,405.4	592.9	170.0	8.7	15.0	70.3	24.0	30.6	12.4
1958	1,815.4	389.4	353.0	270.0	20.1	95.0	37.1	46.1	7.0
1960	1,983.2	391.5	374.9	420.0	21.9	104.4	38.2	52.7	6.6
1970	2,179.1	550.4	474.0	360.0	45.4	140.1	54.6	73.7	8.0
1978	2,599.6	574.2	557.5	593.0	71.8	192.6	90.4	101.5	17.1
1983	2,919.4	662.6	557.7	687.6	98.7	191.1	145.8	136.2	22.6
1984	3,018.1	742.5	555.0	740.0	113.5	191.5	162.0	145.0	32.0

B. Selected Western European hard coal producers

Year	Britain	Germany	France	Spain	Belgium	Nether-lands	Italy
1900	228.8	73.0	33.4	2.7	23.5	0.3	0.0
1913	292.0	131.9	43.8	4.0	22.8	1.9	0.0
1920	233.2	100.7	24.3	5.4	22.4	3.9	0.2
1929	262.0	144.7	53.8	7.1	26.9	11.6	0.2
1938	230.6	151.3	46.5	5.7	29.6	13.5	1.5
1946	193.1	61.8	47.2	10.7	22.9	8.3	1.2
1947	200.6	81.6	45.2	10.5	24.4	10.1	1.4
1948	212.7	99.5	43.3	10.4	26.7	11.0	1.0
1958	219.3	148.8	57.7	14.4	27.1	11.9	0.7
1960	196.7	142.3	56.0	13.8	22.5	12.5	0.7
1970	144.6	117.0	37.4	10.8	11.4	4.5	0.3
1978	121.7	90.1	19.7	12.0	6.6	0.0	0.0
1983	116.4	89.6	17.0	15.3	6.1	0.0	0.0
1984	49.3	84.9	16.6	15.0	6.3	0.0	0.0

Table 1 (continued)

C. Leading lignite producers

Year	World	West Germany	East Germany	Czecho-slovakia	USSR	US
1938	261.9	68.3	119.6	16.0	19.0	2.7
1946	241.5	51.6	109.8	19.5	49.8	2.4
1947	267.5	58.7	101.7	22.4	51.0	2.6
1948	293.7	64.9	110.9	23.6	58.2	2.8
1958	619.0	93.7	215.0	56.8	143.0	2.2
1960	643.7	96.1	225.5	58.4	134.7	2.5
1970	796.2	107.8	260.6	81.8	144.7	5.4
1978	952.4	123.6	253.3	95.3	162.9	35.3
1983	1,087.7	124.3	278.0	102.4	158.3	46.7
1984	1,131.0	126.7	295.0	104.5	157.0	54.2

Sources: for all countries and all coal types, 1900, 1913, 1920, 1929, 1946, 1947, 1948, Unternehmensverband Ruhrbergbau; 1961, *Die Koklenwirtschaft der Welt in Zahlen*; 1937 and 1958 and later years, Statistik der Kohlenwirtschaft, *Zahlen zur Kohlenwirtschaft*, various issues (except Australian data from Joint Coal Board, *Black Coal in Australia*).

the input of coke per ton of steel products fabricated has fallen.[2] Coke use per ton of pig iron declined due to technical advances, greater preparation of ores, and use of other fuels. Pig iron output per ton of raw steel has dropped because of greater scrap use. Raw steel per ton of fabricated steel has lessened because of technologies that reduce conversion loses (mainly by fabricating molten steel).

Considerable interregional and intertemporal variation prevails in the ability of coal to compete in the electric power market. These are major influences on the differences among countries already noted in the behavior of coal production and consumption.

2 Coal and the Economics of Mineral Resource Development[3]

The basic considerations about coal economics are those that Morry Adelman (especially 1970, 1972; see also Adelman et al., 1983) has stressed about mineral supply. He has shown that many options always exist for increasing mineral supply. We do not need to search frantically for resources. The combination of developing known resources, improving technology, and a well directed exploration effort combine to prevent rapid rises in extraction costs. The persistent fears of massive cost rises arise from ignorance about the underlying economics.

Morry's work has stressed that, in particular, considerable potential exists for preventing oil and gas price rises over the next several decades. As he also suggests, this is sufficient information for basic planning. It is too soon to know about and plan for later periods.

The problem is, not pending exhaustion, but the ability of certain oil-producing countries to exercise monopoly power to restrict output and raise prices. Given the limits to price increases imposed by both alternative supplies and considerable opportunities to adopt energy-saving technologies, price rises due to monopoly cannot proceed unabated.

Falling oil prices indicate that those restricting oil supplies had adopted unsustainably large output reductions. At the very least, the minimum output goals of individual OPEC members summed to levels too high to be salable at 1980 prices. It is less clear, but quite likely, that even if OPEC were a more cohesive cartel, it would have found it desirable to have allowed prices to fall from their 1980 levels to prevent severe losses from rising output by nonmembers and reduced energy consumption.[4]

By early 1986, oil prices weakened far more than I previously dared to hope. The forecast often issued by government and energy industry sources that price rises will reappear seems based mainly on continued belief that oil resources are severely limited. However, the germane concern, as Morry long has warned us, is that another political crisis will create an opportunity for the OPEC countries to raise prices.

Coal optimism is primarily oil and gas pessimism—expectations of rapidly rising oil and gas costs. Thus, the inevitable result of accepting Morry's analysis is to be less optimistic about coal. Moreover, rising energy prices have encouraged efforts to substitute other inputs for energy. This alternative to coal is another brake on coal expansion.

Thus, the concept of a plethora of coal resources reflects bad economics. Economic plenty relates to cheapness in final use. Coal is more expensive to transport and use than are oil and gas. Only those coals cheap enough to produce to overcome these other cost disadvantages can compete. In practice, the cost problems and thus the ability to use coal differ with user size (see below). As a result, only a portion of coal resources is presently competitive with oil and gas. Large physical quantities prove economically irrelevant. This irrelevance could persist forever. By the time oil and gas costs actually rise sharply, other cheaper alternatives to coal use may have arisen.

3 The Sources of Competitive Problems for Coal

Coal is a heterogeneous mixture of fuel and waste that must be torn from the earth and is difficult to process into a more satisfactory form. Oil and gas, in contrast, flow out of the ground and through the processing system with far greater ease. Moreover, oil and gas, particularly the former, can be more readily and thus more cheaply transformed into more valuable specialized fuels and chemicals.

A coal-burning boiler must be larger than one to burn oil and gas to overcome the more difficult combusion problems associated with coal. A coal-fired plant also requires more complex receipt and handling facilities than in those burning oil or gas. As concern over air pollution has mounted, coal use has become increasingly unattractive. It tends to contain more pollutants than do oil and gas and, more critically, pollution control is much more expensive for coal than for oil and gas.

The principal impact of these disadvantages is on the price at which coal can compete at the point of use. To overcome the extra costs of using coal, final consumers will employ coal only if its delivered price is sufficiently lower on a per unit of heat basis to overcome the extra nonfuel costs incurred. Thus, the critical requirement for coal to compete is to be minable and transportable at costs low enough to offset the higher costs of using it. Customers are best found near cheap-to-mine deposits.

However, economies of scale exist in the special facilities needed for transportation, handling, burning, and pollution control of coal. Thus, the extent to which nonfuel costs of coal burning exceed those for oil and gas narrows as the size of facilities increases. For sufficiently large users, coal consumption may be economic. Oil and gas prices may exceed coal prices by so wide a margin that it pays to endure the extra costs of employing coal.

The most clear-cut example is electric plants. It is possible in the United States to lower fuel cost by \$2–\$4 per million Btu by using coal instead of oil in an electric utility plant. The extra nonfuel costs of burning coal instead of oil must be less than the price premium because US utilities have stopped ordering oil- or gas-fired plants while continuing to order coal-fired plants.

For an existing facility, the cost disadvantage of coal consumption necessarily is greater than for a new plant because the required special facilities are more expensive when added on instead of being integrated from the start.

Conversions to coal have occurred when little or no additional investment was needed. This is possible when the plant was originally designed to burn coal, still possesses the special facilities needed to use coal, and is not subject to environmental regulations that require addition of expensive control facilities. Boiler-size requirements for coal use largely obviate conversion of any but boilers designed to use coal. Efforts, however, have been made to effect coal use in smaller boilers by diluting it with oil or water, but this approach remains experimental.

Thus, Virginia Electric and Power, Florida Power, New England Electric, and Northeast Utilities have undertaken major conversions back to coal because the key conditions have been met. Others, notably Consolidated Edison of New York, have been unable to act because of severe environmental problems.[5]

An offset to the advantage of coal over oil and gas in new electric power plants is the possibility that nuclear power would be even cheaper. Zimmerman's review in this book of US policy indicates that the nuclear option is no longer relevant for newly initiated plants, but this is not true in many other countries, particularly France and Japan (see Evans and Hope, 1984, for a review of worldwide nuclear prospects).

The US Energy Information Administration (EIA) and several private coal-forecasting services regularly argue that rises in world-oil prices would cause the next largest type of fuel user—large manufacturing plants—also to find coal preferable to oil and gas in new facilities.

However, few signs of this change have emerged. The problem seems to be that the forecasters underestimated the nonfuel costs of burning coal at the manufacturing-plant scale and overestimated future oil and gas prices. The key cost underestimate appears to be that of environmental controls. The fundamental error about oil and gas prices was in taking the 1980 level as a base for further increases instead of a peak to which prices would not return for many years.[6]

These cost disadvantages have proved sufficiently important to limit severely the substitution of coal for oil and gas in nonutility markets. Therefore, actual prevailing economic forces have led to an increasing tendency of electric-power use to dominate coal markets.

4 A Tale of Three Policies—Protectionism, Caution, and Control

Government intervention in supposedly capitalistic markets has always been significant and has greatly increased since World War II. Energy, including coal, has been one of the principal areas in which this expanded control has arisen.

Three distinct coal policy patterns can be distinguished. First, those countries with weak coal industries have tried to retard, to various degrees, the decline of these industries. Second, the United States since the late 1960s has been devoted to imposing numerous regulations on coal production and use. These controls have been justified by concerns over environmental problems, worker health and safety, alleged emerging energy monopoly, and prospects for windfall profits.

A third approach has been that of such countries as South Africa, Australia, Canada, and now Colombia of designing export policies. Their concerns are the simplest to treat and are disposed of first.

Canada represents an interesting hybrid. It possesses significant coal resources in the West that are economic to export to Japan and use near the producing areas but cannot compete with US coal or Canadian nuclear reactors in the critical Ontario market. High cost coal mines exist in the East and receive protection. Thus, Canada is simultaneously an exporter worried that this activity will cause long-run harm, an importer worried about dependence on one supplying country,[7] and the protector of a small weak coal industry in the East.

5 Export Policy Issues

Fear of export is the least interesting case in theory and practice. The stated rationale for preventing exports is a simple inversion of standard fallacious protectionist arguments and can be answered by recourse to the standard economic counterargument of comparative advantage.

The real concern of the exporters is whether exports are sufficiently profitable. The argument typically is submerged in ruminations about how export sales mortgage the national patrimony. The only sensible meaning of such statements is that various market imperfections make coal exports inadequately remunerative. At least two concepts of inadequate payments could be defined—(1) that while exporting is more socially profitable than not selling the coal now, the market gives inadequate returns, or (2) that saving the coal for future domestic use is more profitable than export.

The first argument does have some substance. Demand for coals from these export-oriented countries is reduced by protectionist policies, discussed below, in countries, notably those in western Europe, that the exports could best serve. The exporting countries and those imposing protection would be better off if protection were ended. (The United States seems to have a perverse reaction to this situation. Objections are rarely raised about European protectionism. When special circumstances cause unexpected, usually temporary surges in export demands for US coal, the industry tends to blame itself for not being prepared.)

More usually, the mutterings about inadequate profits are standard complaints about the rigors of competition. Similarly, the future patrimony contention is the previously criticized point that energy exhaustion is around the corner.

6 South Africa[8]

Fortunately, the alleged fears of exporting appear to have had little practical impact. This is best illustrated by South Africa, which has the most systematic effort to limit exports. Starting in the early 1970s, as the possibility of developing an export market emerged, the government has set export quotas supposedly to restrict volumes.

In practice, the government has regularly maintained limits at levels equal or above the amounts industry planned to export. The quotas jumped from 10 million metric tons in the early 1970s to 80 million tons by 1982. South African sources suggest that the present political consensus would allow raising the quotas to 100 million but not more. However, these sources also believe that it is doubtful that the present 80-million-ton allocation can be produced and marketed before the 1990s and that the 100-million-ton level is unlikely to be economically feasible before the twenty-first century. By then, the political climate for exports (and possibly everything else) may change radically.

The more interesting aspect of the quotas is the policy employed to assign export rights. The first quotas went to the associations (principally the Transvaal Coal Owners Association) that jointly market coal for the large producers. Subsequent grants have gone to individual actual and potential producers. Initially, the quota holders consisted of both the large mining firms that dominate the coal industry (and much of the rest of the South African economy) and several international oil companies. (Shell, British Petroleum, and Compagnie Française des Petroles were the initial beneficiaries. In 1982, a subsidiary of Italy's state-owned Ente Nazionale Idrocarburi—ENI—was added to the list.)

South African coal industry sources described the allocations as rewards for being faithful suppliers. Presumably, this refers to a continued willingness to market in South Africa. Clearly, the operations of these companies in South Africa and the continued flow of oil make clear that sanctions on supply are ineffective.

The 1982 allocations produced complaints about including many small firms—some getting quotas in the 15,000–50,000-ton range. The large firms argued that these small suppliers with small quotas could not compete efficiently.

Such firms certainly could not efficiently participate independently in the present arrangements at the Richards Bay terminal through which large scale exports move. The procedures involve bulk rail shipments and handling while keeping the coal from each supplier separate. The quotas are clearly too small to allow independent participation by each quota holder. This might be overcome by joint ventures among the holders of small quotas, and the question is whether this would be profitable.

However true this argument, the analytically most interesting question about the quota system is the socially optimal way to transfer the rights. The allocations are best interpreted as the classic process in quota allocation of providing marketable rights as a means of off-budget subsidy. Such grants are widely criticized because no satisfactory rules exist to decide how to assign quotas. The policy question then is whether it is better to distribute the gains widely by making the quotas marketable or to limit the benefits to actual exporters. If the quotas are truly nonbinding and thus of no value, the allocation seems pointless. Conversely, quotas are widely condemned as unsatisfactory policies because of the problems just noted of deciding how to allocate them.

7 Australia

In Australia, the industry expresses discontent similar to that prevailing in the United States. Concern exists over producers in Australia and its competitors expanding to meet greater demands than have materialized. Customers, particularly Japanese steelmakers, are recognized as exploiting fully these conditions.

Both the industry and its supporters in government see the need to alter practices adopted when optimism was rife. The extensive efforts of federal and state governments to tax the industry heavily are particularly stressed. The primary complaint is that the railroads owned by the states of New South Wales and Queensland set charges far above costs in a deliberate effort to tax coal mining rents. Here as elsewhere, major differences exist between the two main coal producing states—Queensland and New South Wales.

Australian coal output started expanding markedly in the 1960s. Output of coal (net of cleaning losses) had gone from about 17 million metric tons in 1950 to 22 in 1960; by 1970, the level was 45 million. By the coal year ending June 1985, 118 million was produced. Initially, New South Wales was a far larger producer than Queensland—the respective levels were 13 and 2 million in 1950; 17 and 3 in 1960; and 32 and 10 in 1970. Queensland has since greatly reduced the disparity; the 1984–1985 coal year levels were 58 and 54 million (Joint Coal Board, 1985).

More critically, the Queensland mines include highly productive surface mines well located to serve export markets. Typically, the rail spurs were especially built for newly established mines. Thus, the actual costs of rail service can be calculated with considerable accuracy. It is readily established that rates far exceed the cost (including return on investment) of rail service.

In contrast, coal mines in New South Wales use a congested existing network. Moreover, the railroad has a problem, absent in Queensland, of maintaining service for a large city (Sydney). Thus, it is difficult to determine the degree to which rail charges reflect taxation or high costs. The situation is aggravated by strong trade union pressures in coal mining and railroads and probably also by a weaker intrinsic economic situation relative to Queensland. Concern over these problems has inspired efforts at the federal and state levels to improve the economic climate. Efforts have been made to stabilize railroad rates and to encourage labor-management efforts to agree on ways to improve the competitive position of the industry.

8 European Protectionism[9]

European coal policy involves a long history of seeking vainly but expensively to preserve the coal industry. The roots of the problem and the first governmental actions date to the World War *I*. The war led to disruption of coal production; the peace settlement involved transfer of coal producing regions from Germany to France and the newly created Polish state. The adjustment process was hindered by the great depression and another war. Although government policy studies were undertaken previously, extensive intervention began after World War II.

The policy process had two phases—up to 1958 and afterward. It initially was hoped that prior ravages could be reversed and coal could resume its historic role.

The sharp recovery of oil supplies after the termination of the 1956 Suez crisis created awareness that tough oil competition was here to stay. Policy emphasis shifted to damage control. Things proved so bad that not even the oil price rises of the 1970s could alleviate the problem.

Post-World War II planning in Britain, France, and West Germany involved major efforts to restructure the coal industry. The first two countries decided that government ownership was the answer and nationalized the bulk of their coal industries.

A different force—the pressures to destroy industrial combines— dominated initial postwar West German actions affecting coal. The principal change was the breakup of Vereinigte Stahlwerke into several steel companies. Each steel company retained ownership of coal mines. In addition, an independent coal mining firm was created to own the remaining mines formerly in Vereinigte Stahlwerke.[10]

Moreover, the legacy of concern over monopoly in West German coal persisted into the 1960s. This illustrates a common defect in analysis of competition—the neglect of import competition. The discussions proceeded with apparent disregard of the severe import competition that had developed.

Eventually, recognition of import competition became unavoidable, and the approach to competition in the Ruhr became more realistic but no wiser. In 1968, the West German government encouraged the combination of management of the Ruhr mines in a single company (not all the companies actually joined). This corporation, in which the old owners held shares, became effectively a major instrument through which government aid was channeled.

In the early 1950s, advocates of political unification of Europe decided that the sensible starting point would be an organization devoted to a few critical areas. Therefore, creation of a European Coal and Steel Community (ECSC) was proposed as the first step. It was established in 1952. This proved sufficiently successful that an Economic Community and an Atomic Energy Community were begun in 1957. Subsequently, the administration of the three Communities merged, and other countries—most notably the United Kingdom—joined. However, even the Communities' greatest admirers must recognize that its achievements were far different from a United States of Europe. Instead, stress was upon increased economic cooperation. Press reports regularly indicate that the cooperation has fallen far short of eliminating all undesirable barriers to trade. Criticism is widespread of the expensive farm subsidy program that has arisen. Nevertheless, economic and political conditions have improved in Europe, and the Communities probably contributed to this.[11]

The key consideration here is the wisdom of initially choosing coal and steel as the focus. Subsequent experience showed that the premises behind this choice were invalid. Coal and steel were neither keys to prosperity nor areas in which policy accords could easily be reached. However, the original members of ECSC believed otherwise and were willing to take the step. Fortunately for the cause of integration, ECSC had a few years of successes that encouraged creating the more broadly focused Economic Community before coal and steel problems might have chilled willingness to continue.

The critical concern here is the implication for coal of the persistence of nationalism. One key effect has been persistence of protectionist policies, of which aid to coal has been only one small element.

These policies could survive because the penalties for nationalism proved less dire than advocates of integration predicted. Peace and prosperity could be maintained despite the retention of protectionism. Politicians often do not consider increased economic efficiency desirable enough to risk removing aid to the inefficient. The policies were justified by the short-run problems of adjusting to changed market conditions. The warnings Morry Adelman (see, e.g., Adelman, 1972) has often given of the dangers of such policies have gone unheeded. As he predicted, many resources were freshly committed to the industry. A cycle of perpetual aid was launched.

The start of the newer European Communities coincided with the reevaluation of energy prospects necessitated by reappraisal of the oil situation.

The Europeans struggled through much of the 1960s trying to effect a systematic response to this challenge. Many proposals for coordinated energy policies were issued, and many efforts were made to support the proposals with projections of world energy developments.

However, goals differed radically among members of the Communities. The interests of countries with large coal industries conflicted with those who had small coal industries and were large energy importers. The protectionism-minded countries were allowed to undertake independent policies of assistance to the coal industry.

The Communities assumed a passive role. The precrisis program of subsidizing adjustments of the coal and steel industries to economic hardship continued. A new Community program of subsidies of coking coal was instituted. National subsidy programs were subject to review by the Communities. However, the review is perfunctory. The member states directly provide the bulk of the aid. The standard the Communities are supposed to use to judge aid is whether it distorts competition among Community coal industries. Year after year, the annual reviews of subsidies aver that every grant meets this standard.

The aid provided to coal industries at different times and places has encompassed practically all the protective devices known to policymakers. The assistance included trade restrictions—largely consisting of nontariff barriers, subsidies to production, sales, and worker readjustment, and measures to force coal use. The form and substance of the programs naturally were affected by differences in national situations and attitudes. On the latter, the West Germans proved the most resistant to contraction. The British have a somewhat lesser, but still strong, commitment to preserving coal output. The other members ultimately allowed a large proportion of their coal industry to close.

Another consideration was differences among the institutional arrangements in each country. The nationalized industries of Britain and France could and did receive aid in many forms. Financing at the governments' cost of capital was provided and when even this could not be repaid, write-offs were allowed. In West Germany, the nominally privately owned Ruhrkohle benefits from similar assistance. Aid was channeled through the companies to assist in adaptation to disruption.

The French approach to coal-import limitation was the most explicit, but most definitely not the most restrictive. Only a government-controlled purchasing agency was allowed to import coal. (Its freedom is further limited because its main customers are two other government bodies—Electricité de France and Charbonnages de France, which imports coals for blending purposes.) Britain and West Germany used more informal, but much more restrictive, methods of restriction. Administrative barriers were imposed to limit coal imports. Imports in to Britain have been virtually nonexistent; those into West Germany, carefully restricted.

Another component in the coal-support program was the use of subsidization, taxation, and fiat to ensure greater use of European coal in coking and electricity generation.

Two major elements—particularly critical in West Germany—are devices to increase use of European coal in coking and electricity generation. Coking coal subsidies are heaviest in West Germany. The aid guarantees that all domestic coking coal sales are of West German coal and that significant exports can be made, mainly to France and Italy. A portion of the extra cost of using West German coal for power generation is financed by a tax on electricity sales. However, most sales occur under 1980 contracts between the utilities and coal companies to purchase West German coal at costs above those of imported coal. The government forced these accords.

Another major problem was a substantial commitment to pensions and other social benefits. The industry had followed the mode adopted by the US social security system of making payments out of current income instead of funding them actuarially. The pressures of competition made maintenance of the payments onerous. Government takeover of the burden was a major element in the assistance programs.

According to a Community report (EEC Commission, 1985), direct aid in 1984 was planned to be about $8 per ton in West Germany, $13 in Britain, and $24 in Belgium and France. The burdens of past pensions amounted to $2 billion in West Germany, $1 billion in France, $600 million in Belgium, and $70 million in Britain.[12]

The programs have produced billions of dollars in outlays and coal industries that appear highly uncompetitive. The best estimates are that only the British industry might be able to stay close to its present size. About 40–60 million metric tons of low cost capacity appears to exist. Optimistic interpretations of the data (United Kingdom Monopolies and Merger Commission, 1983) on costs at extant mines suggest that overall 60–90 million tons could survive (see Turner, 1984, and Robinson, 1984). Very little capacity elsewhere is competitive.

In any case, the assistance effort succeeded only in limiting output declines. The 12 million metric tons per year of the Dutch and the 1 million metric tons per year of the Italian industries have been allowed to vanish. Belgian output went from around 30 million metric tons in the 1950s to around 6 million in 1984; France, from 55 million to 17 million. British output fell from 220 million to 115 million (in 1983); West German, from 150 million to 84 million in 1984 (recall table 1).

The effort has occurred with rising output per worker so that employment has fallen even more. British National Coal Board annual reports show a peak total employment of 775,000 in 1958; the 1983 level was 245,000. West German data (Statistik der Kohlenwirtschaft) show employment of laborers went from 607,000 in 1957 to 169,000 in 1984. Total labor forces in both countries are about 25 million.

9 From Neglect to Roadblocks in the United States

Coal has been a far less-favored fuel in the United States than in Europe. In fact, few promotional policies have been undertaken. The critical policy impacts have resulted from decisions made for concerns other than the role of coal in energy consumption. Through the mid-1960s, the coal industry was the incidental beneficiary of protection accorded the US oil industry under various oil-import-control programs. Nevertheless, coal use declined sharply from 1947 to 1960.

Since the middle 1960s, US policy has imposed numerous impediments to coal development. First and most justifiably, the oil-import program was changed in a fashion particularly unfavorable to coal. In 1966, quotas on the import on the East Coast of the heavy fuel oil that is the principal competition for coal were increased to levels comfortably in excess of prevailing demands at world oil prices. The result was a massive shift of East Coast utilities from coal to oil.

Moreover, substantial parts of the response to the low oil prices involved actions that hindered reconversion to coal when oil prices rose. Not only did many utilities stop building plants with the capabilities to burn coal, but facilities to receive and use coal were removed from some old plants and the land was dedicated to other facilities.

10 Coal and the Environment

Numerous new regulatory programs have adversely affected the coal industry. The first were environmental. Two major problems developed—response to rules attempting to control air pollution resulting from coal use and compliance with controls on the land damage resulting from surface mining of coal. Both policies proved burdensome.

Out of concern over urban smog grew an ever more complicated set of air-pollution control regulations. In particular, several critical pollutants were singled out for action, and control of one of these—sulfur oxides—had a significant impact on coal markets.

Air-pollution regulations, particularly those directed at sulfur oxides, discouraged coal use by electric utilities. Regulations propounded in 1971 among other things severely limited the amount of sulfur oxides that could be emitted from *new* large-scale fuel-burning facilities. Thus, the eastern coal that would normally have been burned in such new plants could not be used without reducing emissions.

Three alternatives existed—finding a naturally lower sulfur fuel, removing the sulfur before combustion, or employing devices to remove the pollutants after combustion but before discharge to the atmosphere. Suggestions were widespread that scrubbers, the devices for removing sulfur oxides, had been perfected and were a cheap, reliable control option. Thus, policymakers and some in the coal industry expected that compliance would occur quickly with the rapid installation of scrubbers. In fact, scrubbers proved harder to develop and more expensive than optimists proclaimed.

The results were some shifts to oil by eastern electric utilities, shifts to low-sulfur western coal by many utilities in the East–North Central states and Minnesota, moves to low-sulfur eastern coal in other states, and a growing conviction among utilities that nuclear power was the preferable long-run alternative. The shift to western coal produced severe political repercussions. It created what has been described (by, e.g., Navarro, 1980, and by Ackerman and Hassler, 1981) as an unholy alliance. Environmentalists secured the cooperation of eastern coal interests and the union representing eastern workers. Their efforts secured passage in 1977 major changes in air-pollution law.

Among the numerous provisions was the requirement that pollution abatement involve the use of best-available control technology (BACT). The intent was to tilt the compliance choice more toward scrubbers and less toward western coal. In practice, problems arose in interpreting the law. Totally forcing scrubbing was neither clearly required nor desirable since to shift to scrubbing without increasing pollution could be very expensive, if not impossible.

Scrubbers cannot remove all the sulfur; the residual pollution from use of a very high-sulfur coal could exceed the emissions from unscrubbed use of a low-sulfur coal. Thus, implementation had to include modest recognition of the economic and air-pollution impacts of making coal sulfur content as well as scrubber performance an element in policy.

Other aspects of the revisions included a provision that allowed prohibition of the use of nonlocal coal in existing plants if the local economy were damaged. To date, the closest thing to a use of the provision was the loosening of the air-pollution standards in Ohio to stave off application of the local-coal provision. Political pressures by state agencies have been more effective in restraining shifts from local coal.

Still other clauses divided the country into two parts—nonattainment areas in which air pollution standards were not met and prevention of significant deterioration (PSD) areas where they were. In nonattainment areas, expansion of industry was severely limited by requirements that no new facility that produced pollution could be opened unless an offsetting reduction in pollution occurred elsewhere.

In PSD areas, limits were set to the allowable *increases* in pollution. The law, moreover, established three levels of allowable increases—the most limited applicable to areas, such as National Parks, where air quality preservation was considered particularly critical. More liberal increases were allowed where the concern was less severe.

Most criticisms of the rules have stressed the role of PSD in preventing extensive moves of industry from industrialized areas and downplayed the pressures on such areas of the nonattainment rules. It seems more accurate to describe the policy as potentially discouraging economic expansion everywhere.

Just what effect these changes in environmental regulations have had on coal consumption is uncertain. The only clear conclusion is that the EPA chose to adopt a definition of visibility that limited concern to a few critical scenic areas. A slowdown in the growth of electricity output caused cutbacks in expansion plans that delayed facing PSD constraints and lessened the number of plants subject to BACT. The EPA did not issue BACT rules for nonutility boilers until mid-1986. No systematic evidence seems available about whether the threat of BACT or the uncertainty about what the rules will be was a major reason why so few industrial boilers have converted to coal.

11 Regulation of Mining

The National Environmental Policy Act of 1969 (NEPA) produced federal involvement in regulating surface mining. NEPA added a requirement that major federal actions must be accompanied by a statement showing that environmental damages had been taken into account in planning the project.

The federal government controls about 70% of western coal reserves. Under the very broad definitions of major actions set by the courts interpreting NEPA, leasing coal was deemed important enough an action to require environmental impact statements. Thus, the Act necessitated federal action on surface disturbances when its coal was exploited. An additional step was taken in 1977 when Congress rejected the view that the prior state efforts at control were adequate and passed a federal bill. This bill specified in great detail rules for reclamation (see Gordon, 1978a, 1978b). Its enforcement is yet another area in coal policy of great disputation and inadequate analysis.

A 1969 mining disaster inspired Congress severely to tighten coal-mine safety regulation and introduce controls of impacts on worker health. Here, too, questions exist about the wisdom of the action. Again, questions arise about the heavy-handedness of the intervention. A more fundamental question is what market failure justifies the intervention. In principle, collective bargaining could lead to accord on optimal health and safety practices. No clear evidence exists that this principle is invalid in practice.[13]

12 Assessing Environmental Policies

Given the extensive criticism these policies have received, a summary view suffices (see, e.g., Kneese and Schultze, 1975, Mills, 1978, or Portney, 1978). This literature almost uniformly attacks environmental legislation for adopting unduly complex approaches to attaining the goals. The basic complaint is that the government is overly specific in selecting the means to attaining the objectives rather than allowing the regulated industries to use their superior knowledge of the costs of alternatives to select the cheapest way to meet the goals.

However, these economic arguments have thus far received low priority in policy formulation and press discussion. The political preference for more cumbersome laws may be explained by the prevailing climate. Such laws may be needed to form alliances strong enough to secure legislation. The lack of journalistic criticism is more difficult to explain. Environmentalism apparently is considered so noble a cause that it is immune from criticism.

A further consideration is that the critiques may be too timid. The stress is on the excess cost of meeting accepted goals. The wisdom of the goals has received less challenge. To cite a critical example, much evidence exists that the estimates of the health effects of air pollution used to justify present policy were far too high (see Ramsay, 1979). Moreover, given that several pollutants occur together, the estimates cannot determine which one or combination is the culprit (see especially Wilson et al., 1980).

The problem of achieving rational discussion is dramatized by the acid precipitation debate of the 1980s. Instead of reducing controls in response to evidence that the damage is less severe than first argued, a campaign is being conducted to strengthen the rules. Initial stress was on possible harm to some lakes and forests. However, the costs of proposed abatement measures far exceed the readily measured benefits of preserving these lakes and forests. Attention has turned to arguments that the policies are needed to deal with inadequate control of previously recognized problems such as health damages (see US Congress, OTA, 1984).

13 Coal Leasing Issues

Another problem is continuing debate over coal leasing policy. Fears of giveaways during the heavy leasing of the 1960s and the rising pressure of environmental concerns produced in 1971 a decade-long coal leasing moratorium (see Nelson, 1983).

During the moratorium, the OPEC oil-price rises occurred. This increased long-standing worries about windfall profits due to either monopoly or the failure to tax the economic rents earned by higher quality mineral deposits. US energy leasing policy generally moved toward tighter controls on producer profits. One aspect of this was a 1976 law amending the rules for leasing federal coal. Severe restrictions were set on the conditions under which coal could be leased.

The law imposed the requirement, generally favored by natural-resource economists, that coal be sold by competitive bidding. This was offset by numerous less attractive features. First, to assure higher receipts, a 12.5% royalty requirement was imposed on surface-mined federal coal. The production-reducing aspects of a royalty were deemed less important than their rent-collection prowess (on these issues, see McDonald, 1979, or Tyner and Kalter, 1978).

A variety of ancillary provisions were imposed including stringent requirements for extensive land-use planning before offering land (provisions extended by subsequent acts devoted to surface-mine reclamation and overall plans for the use of federal lands), limits on the size of individual leases and of total company holdings, and diligence requirements that leases be forfeited if not put into production in a timely fashion.

The net effect is an overly complex program riddled with unwise requirements. Diligence requirements, for example, may cause premature development of a mine when it is cheaper to endure losses from early development than to lose the lease or make payments to keep it long. The risks of losing the lease before it can be developed make bidding less attractive (see Gordon, 1981b and 1985a). The rules also make it impossible for those who wish to prevent mining to secure permanent rights to the land by outbidding potential producers.

Leasing did not resume until 1981, after the peak of enthusiasm about coal. Bids on leases were much lower than expected. Controversy ensued. Evidence of inadequate planning of the leasing process and inept explanations of what had been done aggravated the situation. A Study Commission was appointed. The Commission endorsed continued leasing but with a scaling back of the administration's prior plans (US Commission of Fair Market Policy for Federal Coal Leasing, 1984). The Commission's support of leasing was unanimous. The suggestion for decreased leasing goals was supported for various reasons. Some members seemed to share congressional fears that high leasing undesirably reduces revenues. Others were making concessions to political pressures. In fact, the only valid argument is that such political pressures necessitate a slowdown in leasing until the administration of the policy becomes less blatantly open to attack.

The starting point of the case for high leasing is that, from the viewpoint of private efficiency, one can underlease but never overlease. Nonleasing can prevent a good property from being developed in time, but competition will prevent the premature development of an extant lease. This argument is not necessarily altered by the existence of environmental side effects of mining. We can and do impose separate laws to control the side effects of coal mining. To the extent that these laws make all mine operators liable for the side effects they impose, socially efficient operation will occur on all leases. (This follows directly from the definition of social efficiency—namely, that all costs are considered.) If such surface mining laws are defective, it is doubtful that a secondary review will be any more successful.

Nevertheless, coal leasing law unwisely requires that leasing policy serve as a supplemental screen for environmental damages and ensure that better private uses are not neglected. Planners are supposed to select the socially most desirable tracts for leasing; to make matters worse, the law seems to stress side effects over the market benefits and thus ignore the trade-offs among them. Any need to adjudicate among private uses arises from a serious flaw in the law; the limited duration of leases hinders those seeking alternative uses from buying out the mining rights. Heavy leasing then affects environmental quality only to the extent that the haste causes poorer screening, which leads to the use of inferior resources.

Similarly, the *direct* effect of higher leasing levels on receipt of fair market value can only be socially beneficial. So long as the supply of leases and the market for coal are competitive, the market for coal determines the fair market value (which is best interpreted as the competitive market price). The only possible change in the value comes from reducing leasing below competitive levels—government use of its monopoly power. (Those, not including me, who believe that the social cost of capital is less than the private cost would qualify the argument by noting the need to delay leasing because of the higher cost of private holding compared to public holding. The major problem in trying to optimize the timing of leases is the impossibility of knowing when it is most appropriate to do so.) Diligence requirements artificially lower the value by creating risks of nondevelopment.

Institutional peculiarities in landholding patterns, mostly in the form of existing large holdings close to unleased tracts, often give one party, the lessee of the adjoining land, a marked advantage in exploiting that tract. This is widely seen as weakening the competition for tracts and causing them to sell for less than their fair market value. This view probably is invalid since the threat of bidding by others should force the firm with an advantageous position to offer the full fair market value. Whatever the reality, again leasing levels are only incidental. The inadequacy of competition is independent of leasing levels. At most, lower leasing might facilitate effort to efforts to ensure payments closer to fair market value.

These results occur because leasing, like all investment decisions, is guided by plans to employ the asset optimally. Fears of overleasing arise from inappropriate analogies. Comparisons are made to flooding the market with goods that must be consumed immediately (or at least are expensive to store). Prices of such goods will fall because of the inability to delay use. However, not only is delay possible, but its anticipation is built into the price of assets.

The bulk of the Coal Leasing Commission's recommendations concerned ways to improve leasing management by correcting the many failures to design the program to meet congressional desires for vigorous efforts to secure fair market value. Efforts at all levels seemed inadequate both in conducting the best possible prelease evaluation of tract economics and in adopting policies to increase competition for tracts. Many issues, such as the wisdom of most of the law, had to be neglected due to pressures of time and political resistance to a broader inquiry. As suggested, ample evidence exists that many of the provisions of the law are unwise. Moreover, production efficiency may be excessively restricted by the concern for government revenues. Considerable changes in coal leasing laws seem desirable.

Surface mine reclamation and leasing policies are further examples of unholy alliances. The environmentalists have supported vigorous efforts to ensure receipt of fair market value as an indirect way of restricting federal coal output. (Their testimony before the commission suggested that impossibly stringent standards were being proposed.) They have been joined by rival western business interests, such as ranchers, and by supporters of eastern coal. Those for whom fair market value is the true concern find themselves working with those who want to make coal more expensive to an undesirable extent.

14 The Effects of US Policy

As should be expected, all these policies lowered greatly the attractiveness of coal as a fuel. To be sure, two offsets occurred. World oil prices rose massively. Nuclear power in the United States vanished as a satisfactory alternative. Bitter debate exists on the causes. Electric-utility executives insist that in a world of rational regulations, nuclear power would be preferable to coal in most of the country. The irrationality of regulation makes new nuclear projects undesirable (see Zimmerman's chapter in this book).

Critics of nuclear power assert that the problem is excessive costs. Costs are uncompetitive. The question is the extent to which cost rise was due to regulation, mismanagement, or market developments.

The coal industry, however, may have gained less from these offsets than it has lost from the impact of higher energy costs on the growth of energy consumption. To what extent this outcome is desirable also depends upon how much of the cost increases was attributable to sound policy and market developments beyond the control of the US government and how much was due to unsound policies.

15 Conclusions

The dominant theme of Morry Adelman's work has been the relevance of economic principles. He has always insisted that a complete economic analysis be undertaken before judgments are made. He correctly has believed that all too often analysts prematurely gave up on applying economics and too glibly sought alternative explanations. He has also been (perhaps less explicitly) an advocate of the view that economic efficiency should be a major consideration in policies affecting individual markets. He has frequently shown that intervention often has been inequitable as well as inefficient.

His work has been one of the major inspirations of the substantial general extensions of economic analysis that have produced both better analyses of the market sector and trenchant appraisals of the economics that guide nonmarket decisions. More specifically, he has led the way in deflating the belief that energy and other minerals obey radically different laws from those for other marketed commodities.

Here an effort was made to show how these propositions apply to the coal industry. It was first argued that economic principles clearly allow us both to explain past coal industry behavior and more accurately to predict at least the basic pattern of future developments. Then, an effort was made to show the complexities of policies affecting coal.

These policies reflect the basic confusions over coal. To various extents, coal producing countries simultaneously respond to both the myth of great immediate desirability and the reality of the problems of coal. The Europeans rationalize avoiding adjustment by clinging to slogans about the future need for coal. Whether this is self-delusion or cosmetics is not clear. Moreover, Europe, no less than other countries, has been forced to face the environmental problems associated with coal use. The main impact on the United States, South Africa, and Australia of belief in the great need for coal has been the efforts to tax or regulate profits in the industry. These countries too have had to deal with the problems of environmental impacts. Thus, the misunderstandings about coal evaluated here have among other things produced more examples of the defects of government intervention.

Considerable temptation exists to generalize from these and the widespread additional examples of defective intervention that have by now inspired an economic literature far too large to review adequately here.[14]

Here too we can learn from Morry's example. Wisely, he has always let the facts speak for themselves. He has carefully shunned the perils of overgeneralization. This has created a desirable tradition in energy economics of rigorous analysis uncontaminated by preconceptions.

Perhaps, he has generalized too little. Despite his work and many similar analyses by others, popular recognition of the shortcomings of intervention remains deficient. Too many post-1945 writings on economics have tended to underrate the dangers of intervention. The attacks on intervention have been left to strident ideologues. It would be preferable if someone could make clear how widespread skepticism concerning intervention is among economists of many different ideologies.[15]

Notes

1. West German sources proved the best place to secure data on world coal production.

2. My World Coal manuscript discusses this further. Examination of data for many countries shows movements away from coal. The process has gone further in OECD countries than in the Communist bloc.

3. A much revised version of the original of this section appeared as a portion of my World Coal manuscript. A shorter presentation of the essentials now seems preferable to repeating that version. A preliminary discussion appears in Gordon (1985b).

4. Morry's view that the exercise of monopoly power best explains such developments seem the most plausible. See Deacon and Mead (1985) for a statement of other views.

5. In the Con Ed case, it was not until 1983 that a request made in the late 1970s was evaluated. The decision was to require a degree of pollution control that, Con Ed argues, would make conversion prohibitive for at least one of the two plants being considered.

6. Detailed criticism of such pieces (e.g., Alm and Curham, 1984) is not feasible here.

7. See the chapter in this book by Watkins for a discussion of the even greater problems Canada has had of dealing with world oil suppliers and the problems of the United States as one oil and gas importer.

8. The material in this section was obtained during 1983 and 1984 visits to the Rand Afrikaans University in Johannesburg and Macquarie University in New South Wales. Much comes from interviews with industry and government officials.

9. This section was drafted prior to a summer 1985 visit to Western Europe. Only modest updating was made here. The World Coal manuscript devotes a chapter to the situation.

10. Lister (1960) provided a good summary of this.

11. Lister (1960) and Diebold (1959) provided two good, only slightly overlapping studies of the creation and early years of the European Coal and Steel Community.

12. The report uses a Community measure of value called a European Currency Unit (a weighted average of currency values), and shows the value of each member country currency in terms of that unit. These imply a worth of the unit of from 70¢ to 75¢ US at 1985 exchange rates. A 70¢ value was used here.

13. The literature on this subject is too diffuse to treat adequately here, but see Julian (1982) for one effort at appraisal.

14. The problem areas range broadly. My research, for example, has led to concerns with electric power regulation (Gordon, 1982) and public land policy (Gordon, 1985a).

15. The complaints are directed at both a long series of popularized books in economics and many popular textbooks. The best available discussion still is Schumpeter (1950). He cleverly builds suspicion of intervention by conceding as much as possible to the interventionists and letting the reader deduce that even so a highly regulated economy is less attractive than one heavily reliant on free markets.

4 The Evolution of Civilian Nuclear Power

Martin B. Zimmerman

1 Introduction

The nuclear industry began the 1970s with high hopes. In 1973, 212 megawatts of nuclear reactors were under construction, on order, or announced. Expectations were that nuclear power would, by the end of the decade, play a large role in the provision of electricity in the United States and the rest of the industrialized world. Nuclear power was seen as a low cost and environmentally acceptable means of generating electric power. By the end of the 1970s it was clear these expectations would not be realized. Even the oil price increases of 1979 and 1980 could not stem the decline of nuclear power in the United States.

There are several points of view about why the competitive position of nuclear power declined. Some suggest that the economics of the technology were misunderstood (Bupp and Derian, 1981). Government and private consumers were overly optimistic, and the decision to build large scale plants was made when experience was limited to demonstration plants. Others contend that the public reaction to the new technology was the key cause of cost increases (Komonoff, 1981). And still others (Gordon, 1982) stress the effects of a regulatory process that got out of hand. In all explanations, government policy plays an important role.

This paper examines the evolution of the industry and how that evolution was affected by government policy. The government set out to speed civilian adoption of nuclear technology. Did it succeed? Would the shape of the nuclear industry have been different had the government not intervened? Would costs have risen less had the government acted differently? The sections that follow examine the effect of government policy in three distinct periods—the demonstration and commercialization phase in the late 1950s and early 1960s, the heyday of nuclear power in the mid-1960s to the mid-1970s, and the period of decline in the late 1970s and early 1980s.

The experience of nuclear power is relevant to a broader policy debate conducted in the United States during the period of oil price increases in the 1970s. Government policymakers set a goal of reducing oil imports. To this end, the development of substitutes such as oil shale and coal gasification was advocated. It was claimed that the private market would not develop these technologies fast enough. The construction and operation of a plant would teach not only the firm responsible for the plant, but the whole industry, what the true costs were and how to produce energy more cheaply. This meant, according to the proponents of government action, that firms, left alone, would underinvest. Each firm would find it cheaper to wait for another firm to invest and costlessly learn from another's experience. With all firms reasoning like this, the proponents concluded, technology development required government investment.

It was also maintained that if the public feared that the technology would cause environmental damage, the technologies could not be built successfully. It was argued that the government should take the first risks to learn how the public reaction would affect the costs of the technology.

The review of the US nuclear industry provides insight into a subject that has been a recurrent theme in Morry Adelman's work—the effects of government policies in the energy sector. In an attempt to promote a technology, government action might well have worked to limit US reliance on nuclear power.

2 The Early Years

2.1 The Demonstration Phase[1]

The civilian nuclear reactor was the outgrowth of naval research on nuclear propulsion systems for submarines and aircraft carriers. The dominant reactor technology now in civilian use, the light water reactor, emerged as the Navy's choice, not because of its theoretical superiority, but because it was the option closest to being operational. Admiral, then Captain, Rickover decided that the light water reactor design would allow him to meet his goal for nuclear submarine development in five years, that is by 1 January 1955.

At the time, competing reactor types were the gas cooled graphite moderated reactor and the breeder. The former uses sodium to cool the reactor and graphite to moderate the neutrons to maintain the nuclear reaction. The breeder reactor would produce more fuel in the form of plutonium than it consumed in the form of uranium, which would lower long-run needs for uranium.

In the early 1950s the federal government took steps to promote the civilian use of the technology. The Eisenhower administration felt that development of a civilian reactor would demonstrate the country's resolve in the peaceful use of nuclear power and demonstrate the technological superiority of our atomic power program. Again, priority was placed upon a design that would be workable relatively quickly and again the choice was the pressurized water reactor. The military experience gave that technology a head start.

In December 1953, the Atomic Energy Commission (AEC) invited proposals from private firms to join in a partnership to develop a demonstration power reactor based on the pressurized water technology (PWR). The most attractive proposal submitted was that of the Duquesne Light Company of Pittsburgh, Pennsylvania. The company contributed over $300 million toward the construction and operation of a 600 MW (PWR) plant at Shippingport, Pennsylvania, that began generating electricity in 1957.

While construction proceeded on the Shippingport reactor, the AEC began the Power Reactor Demonstration Program (PRDP), which went through several phases over the period 1955–1963. The objective was to involve the private sector in the development of nuclear power reactors. Alternative reactor types were also to be considered. In the first round, begun in January 1955, the AEC offered aid to firms in several forms. Fuel use charges were to be waived for seven years, a negotiated percentage of R&D was to be done by the government at its own laboratories, and the R&D aspects of plant operation were to be subsidized. The remainder of the costs, the construction and operation of the reactor itself and the risks associated with construction and operation, were to be borne by the private firms. The evident philosophy was to subsidize R&D somewhat but leave a large portion of the risks to the private sector.

The AEC approved three of the four proposals submitted in the first round of the PRDP. One, the Fermi fast breeder reactor, suffered severe problems during construction and operation. Another, the Hallam sodium graphite reactor, also was an unsuccessful project. But the third, the Yankee PWR, was a great success, taking advantage of the early military experience.

The fourth proposal, submitted by a Commonwealth Edison-led utility consortium, proposed a boiling water reactor (BWR) of 175 MW, a size much larger than had yet been built. In a few months the consortium dropped its subsidy request and undertook the project alone. The project resulted in the 200 MW Dresden plant, which began operation in 1959. This privately financed project succeeded in demonstrating the BWR technology as a feasible design for large scale electric generation.

The second round of the PRDP had two goals. It aimed to involve small rural electric cooperatives and to develop new reactor concepts. According to Allen (1977), the combination of small firms and experimental designs was not successful. Apparently, new designs required R&D input that these small firms were unable to provide.

The third round and the so-called modified third round of the PRDP moved back toward large utilities and larger reactors of proven design. Two third round reactors, the 375 MW San Onofre unit of the Southern California Edison Company, ordered in 1963, and the 490 MW Haddam Neck plant of the Connecticut Yankee Atomic Power Company, ordered in 1962, used PWR technology. These orders were particularly important because their size was substantially larger than all projects then underway. The government thus went beyond the demonstration of the feasibility of technology. In this round of the PRDP, the AEC actively promoted commercialization through direct and indirect subsidy.[2]

In summary, the development of the power reactor concept and the emergence of the light water reactor owe a great deal to decisions and to programs of the government. The attempts to involve private industry, through the PRDP if nothing else, sparked interest in the technology among the electric utilities. The reactor concept itself was a product of military research, and it took changes in the law to allow civilian participation in the nuclear industry.[3]

2.2 The Commercialization Phase: Direct Subsidy of Large Scale Plants

While government involvement was important to reactor development, it appears that government subsidy was unnecessary to induce private firms to build the large scale commercial reactors. The Commonwealth Edison consortium built a large PWR on its own without subsidy. Consolidated Edison of New York also decided to build the Indian Point 1 plant, a 265 MW reactor, without government money. In December 1963 The Jersey Central Power and Light Company, without government subsidy, ordered a 515 MW reactor from General Electric.[4] Thus, before any experience was gained on the San Onofre and Haddam Neck plants, private investment in nuclear power was taking place. Clearly, by this time government efforts were not essential to the development of the nuclear power industry. We cannot dismiss the importance of the government's early efforts at technology demonstration, but their efforts to promote the large scale reactors, in retrospect, seem redundant.

Even if some private firms were willing to undertake investment in nuclear power without subsidy, the possibility remains that by helping build two more units, the government accelerated the development of nuclear power.

These two reactors might have provided experience that lowered costs for everyone and thus encouraged other utilities to build nuclear power plants. Research has examined the extent of learning associated with nuclear power plant construction. Mooz (1978), in a study of the factors affecting the costs of nuclear power plants, examined the influence of the experience of the architect-engineering firm on the costs of construction. He found that construction time and costs declined with the number of plants built by the architect-engineering firm.[5] But the advantages of this learning accrued to these private architect-engineering firms.

Zimmerman (1982) examined the effects of experience on several types of learning. Not only did construction costs decline with experience, as Mooz had found, but more experienced firms more accurately forecast costs. Furthermore, some of this learning was external to the firm. Zimmerman found that costs declined and forecasts became more accurate as cumulative industry experience, measured by total plants completed by the industry, increased. Apparently, individual firms did learn from the experience of others. However, while learning was present, the value of the external learning was small in the case of nuclear power—estimated in this study at less than the cost of a plant in the 1960s.[6] In short, the effect of direct federal government participation in the commercialization phase of nuclear power appears to have been minor.

2.3 Commercialization: Indirect Subsidy through the Price-Anderson Act

The direct subsidy of commercial scale plants was only one method used by the government to promote nuclear power. Another aid to commercialization was provided by passage in 1957 of the Price-Anderson Act. The early commercialization efforts of the AEC showed an underlying belief that government had to help the market along, but not ignore market judgments. Ironically, this view led the promoters of nuclear power to favor the Price-Anderson Act as a means of removing an obstacle to the private development of nuclear power.

This act limited liability to $560 million in offsite damage in case of nuclear accident. Firms were to acquire $60 million of insurance from private insurance companies. The remaining $500 million of indemnity was provided by the government. Since passage, several modifications of the act have occurred. The modification in 1975 established that in case of a nuclear accident, each licensed nuclear reactor is assessed $5 million to form an additional pool of available funds. This eliminated government financial responsibility for the $500 million of insurance. As of July 1985, taking into account privately available insurance and the reactor assessment, the total liability limit amounts to $635 million. This represents an increase in liability since 1957 of 13% although prices have doubled over that period. This amount increases by $5 million for each newly licensed reactor.[7]

The rationale for the Price-Anderson Act was presumably that the private market did not understand the risks associated with nuclear power.[8] If the technology was safer than private firms believed, the price charged by private firms for insurance would be too high. In addition, the Price-Anderson Act established a strict liability standard, making recovery of damages up to $560 million easier for plaintiffs than if they had to prove negligence.

Several questions arise about the effects of the Price-Anderson Act. First, what effect did it have upon incentives to provide safe reactors? Second, would nuclear power have developed commercially in the absence of the act? Finally, in what way would the development of the commercial nuclear industry have been different in the absence of this act? Even with the act there are strong incentives for operating safe reactors. The accident at Three Mile Island caused substantial financial damage to General Public Utilities. Any firm facing similar costs of an accident would take care to operate in a safe manner.

While potential private costs will induce investments in safety, firms will still consider the cost-effective level of safety measures. There is evidence (Wood, 1983) that trade-offs are made between increased cost and increased safety. Statements in the record of the investigation of the accident at Three Mile Island indicate that managers were aware of the costs involved in taking extra precautions to increase safety and rejected those actions precisely because of their cost. For example, the utility at Three Mile Island would have learned about similar problems at other reactors had they read Nuclear Regulatory Commission (NRC) reports, but management felt such a review would not be cost-effective.[9] While demonstrating that there is a trade-off between safety and cost, this does not indicate that existing private incentives for safety were insufficient at Three Mile Island. Such a review might have had little effect on safety and might not have been worth the cost, regardless of the potential liability. The limited liability provided by Price-Anderson might not have influenced this particular outcome.

There is a case, however, in which incentives for safety are likely to be considerably lessened in the presence of the liability limits imposed by the Price-Anderson Act. In case of an accident, offsite costs could be substantially higher than the limits provided in the act. Without the liability limit, a firm would have purchased more insurance and the premium would have varied with the potential costs of an accident. The offsite costs of an accident rise substantially, the closer a reactor is to populated areas (Joskow and Yellin, 1980) and insurance premiums as well, in a private market, would rise. A utility will weigh the increased transmission costs associated with remote locations against the increased insurance costs that come with a less remote location. In limiting liability, the government lowered the private costs of less remote locations and tipped the scales toward siting reactors closer to population centers.

If we assume that without the liability limit reactors would have been more remotely located, we can bound the effect the Price-Anderson Act had on the early development of nuclear power. Joskow and Yellin (1980) have estimated both the reduced accident consequences and the increased transmission costs associated with remotely located nuclear reactors. They calculate that prompt fatalities associated with a major release of radioactivity would be eliminated by siting reactors at least 25 miles from urban areas. Siting reactors 150 miles from urban centers would substantially reduce the incidence of latent diseases caused by radiation release. According to their calculations, an increase of 50 miles in the transmission distance adds approximately .6–.9 mills per kilowatt-hour (kWh) (in 1977 dollars). Comparable calculations for 150 miles yields a range of 1.2–1.7 mills per kWh.[10] The maximum possible cost occurs if, in the absence of the Price-Anderson Act, utilities react to their increased liability and higher insurance premiums by siting reactors an additional 150 miles from the urban center, thus raising costs in a range of 1.2–1.7 mills per kWh.

Table 1 presents the costs of nuclear power and of coal power in the mid-1960s in the Midwest as estimated by various sources.[11] The advantage of nuclear power was small, on the order of .3–.8 mills per kWh. This advantage must be compared to the cost increase due to remote siting of .7–.9 mills (in 1966 dollars). Increasing transmission distances by 150 miles would thus have eliminated, on average, the perceived advantage of nuclear power in the Midwest.

However, without Price-Anderson, nuclear power with remote locations would still have remained a competitor in the electric generation market. The removal to 150 miles from an urban center is an extreme assumption. The reaction of utilities would have been an intermediate one. Second, the nuclear power costs in table 1 are area averages and site-specific factors would have led some to choose nuclear power. For example, those plants situated farther away from the coal fields than the average Midwestern plant would have found it advantageous to build nuclear power plants. Finally, in areas such as New England and the South, nuclear power would have maintained an advantage.

To get an idea of how adversely nuclear power would have been impacted

Table 1

Comparative expected costs of coal and nuclear power in the Midwest, 1965–1968 (mills per kWh)

	Coal costs				Nuclear costs			
Year	Capital[a]	Operation and maintenance[b]	Fuel[c]	Total	Capital[a]	Operation and maintenance[b]	Fuel[c]	Total
1965	1.60	.3	2.4	4.30	1.76	.4	1.58	3.74
1966	1.63	.2	2.4	4.23	1.87	.2	1.38	3.45
1967	1.67	.4	2.4	4.47	2.07	.7	1.38	4.15
1968	2.04	.4	2.5	4.94	2.48	.7	1.46	4.64

Source: Table is from Zimmerman (1982).

a. Plant capital costs, including interest during construction, are taken from the sources listed below. Where a range of capital costs is available, we use the midpoint of the range. 1965, Hoehn (1967); 1966, Hoehn (1967), Sporn (1968); 1967, Hoehn (1967); 1968, interpolated between 1967 and 1969; 1969, Sporn (1970). We assume an 80% operating rate, which was the expected operating rate in those years, and a 10% annual capital charge rate. Cost in mills per kWh is [capital cost per kW × .10]/[(8,760 × .8)].

b. Operation and maintenance costs as well as nuclear fuel costs are from the same sources as above.

c. Coal prices are average as-burned cost for Illinois as reported by the National Coal Association. The heat rate, or Btu/kWh, is assumed to be 10,000.

without Price-Anderson, we use a model (Ellis and Zimmerman, 1983) that estimates the probability that an electric utility would choose nuclear power over coal as a function of the relative costs of capital, fuel, and operations and maintenance. These items represent the generation costs easily observed by the analyst. However, site-specific factors unobserved by the modeler will also affect utility decisions. For any given set of observed costs, there is some probability that the utility would have chosen nuclear power. Using the probability model, one can estimate the impact of remote location on nuclear orders. The remote location can be treated as the equivalent of higher observed nuclear capital costs. The results suggest that orders would have declined by about 4–7% in the years 1965–1968, years in which 62,620 MW of reactors were ordered.[12] Of course, this analysis assumes that enough remote sites were available, and that transmission lines could have been constructed.

Without Price-Anderson, fewer plants would have been built initially, and they would have been farther away from population centers. The Price-Anderson Act might also have increased the public reaction against nuclear power. The public was being asked to bear more of the costs of nuclear power. One can interpret attempts to intervene in the licensing process as attempts to force an internalization of the external costs. It is possible that Price-Anderson made regulatory intervention greater than it otherwise would have been and undermined the industry in the long run.

Without the Price-Anderson Act, the purely private provision of the optimal level of safety would still have been problematic. The liability of the firm was ultimately limited by bankruptcy (Wood, 1983). To some extent, therefore, the costs of an accident would be borne by the public.[13] The public, under the circumstances, would demand that either utilities provide a high degree of insurance or some degree of safety regulation. With the Price-Anderson Act this effect was attenuated, although to exactly what extent we do not know.

In summary, nuclear power emerged as a commercial technology shaped by government intervention. The development and choice of the light water reactor technology was an outgrowth of decisions made by the Navy and the AEC. Direct subsidy of commercialization, on the other hand, had a small effect. As to the effects of the indirect subsidy of the Price-Anderson Act we can only speculate. Had liability for offsite damages not been limited, it is likely more remote locations would have been chosen, the rate of development of the industry would have been slowed somewhat, and the public reaction to nuclear power would have been different.

3 The Middle Years

3.1 Cost Developments

The 1970s saw the decline of nuclear power as a viable technology for new power plants in the United States. As table 2 (US DOE/EIA, 1983a) shows, the last orders for nuclear power plants in the United States came in 1978. The costs of nuclear power increased more rapidly than those for coal, and nuclear power was ultimately priced out of the market.[14] Expectations about cost proved to be overly optimistic. Several factors contributed to this cost increase, and again government regulation was an important influence.

3.2 The Facts

The real costs of nuclear power plants, after netting out inflation, rose at a prodigious rate. Mooz (1978) found that for completed plants costs had risen, holding all other things constant, by $140 per kW (1976 dollars) per year. That is, plants granted a construction permit in 1971 cost $700 per kW more than plants granted a permit in 1966, holding other plant characteristics constant. The average cost of a plant in his sample (plants completed by 1978) was $629 per kW. The consulting firm Energy System Research Group (ESRG) found somewhat smaller increases in a later study: "All other things equal, a plant

Table 2
Nuclear units ordered and cancelled in each year, 1972–1982

Year	Orders placed		Cancellations		Cumulative orders	
	Number	MWe	Number	MWe	Number	MWe
Pre-1972	131	109,392	0	—	131	109,392
1972	38	41,315	7	6,117	162	144,590
1973	41	46,791	0	0	203	191,381
1974	28	33,263	7	7,216	224	217,428
1975	4	4,148	13	14,699	215	206,877
1976	3	3,804	1	1,150	217	209,531
1977	4	5,040	10	10,814	211	203,757
1978	2	2,240	14	14,487	199	191,510
1979	0	0	8	9,552	191	181,958
1980	0	0	16	18,001	175	163,957
1981	0	0	6	5,781	169	158,176
1982	0	0	18	21,937	151	136,239
Total	251	245,993	100	109,754		

Source: Table is from US DOE/EIA (1983).
US Department of Energy, Energy Information Administration, *U.S. Commercial Nuclear Power*, DOE/EIA-0315, Washington, DC: March 1982; Atomic Industrial Forum, "Historical Profile of U.S. Nuclear Power Development," *AIF Background Info*, 31 December 1981, and "Nuclear Power Plants in the United States," *AIF Info*, 1 January 1983.

licensed at the start of the data base period (March 1967) cost about $600/kW [1980 dollars] less than one licensed at the end (February 1973)." This lower rate most likely reflects differences between the samples used in the two studies. Other studies generally confirm these high rates of increase. Zimmerman (1982) found an annual rate of real cost increase of between 11% and 18% and Ellis and Zimmerman (1983) reported an 18% annual rate of increase. Coal plants too experienced a high rate of cost increase, although not as high as for nuclear plants. Estimates for coal plants range from an annual increase of 6% (Joskow and Rose, 1984) to 14% per year (Ellis and Zimmerman, 1983).

3.3 The Causes

There are many competing hypotheses about what caused the real cost to increase. Construction costs in general were increasing in the 1970s. But, the deterioration in nuclear power's position relative to coal suggests more was behind the cost increase than general factor price increases and construction productivity decline. Some suggestive evidence appears in a report completed by the Energy Information Agency (EIA) of the Department of Energy (US DOE/EIA, 1982) (see figure 1). The figure shows that materials input for a

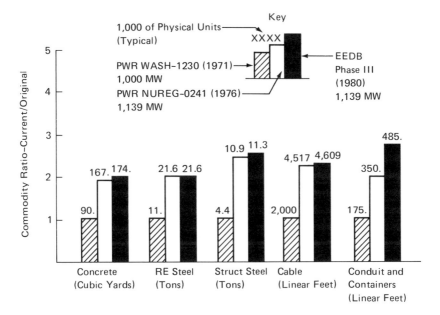

Figure 1
Changes in basic commodities for nuclear power plants, 1971–1980. Figure is from US DOE/ EIA (1982). Source: United Engineers and Constructors, "Energy Economic Data Base (EEDB) Program," US Department of Energy, Vol. I, Contract No. DE-AC02-78ET3202 (Washington, DC), April 1981.

typical plant measured in physical units greatly increased over the 1970s. In response to requirements for greater safety, thicker, stronger vessels and containment structures were constructed. Greater "redundancy and separation of mechanical and electrical systems" was required, and seismic standards were tightened.[15]

Figure 2, from the same report, shows estimates of man-hours required to design and construct nuclear plants. Part of the increase in cost displayed in figure 2 is due to declining productivity, holding regulations constant. Part was due to greater design complexity and quality assurance, but the data do not permit us to separate out these components. It seems clear, however, from the figures that the nature of nuclear plants was changing in response to requirements for greater safety.

Another factor regarded as a major contributor to cost increases is the increased delay experienced in licensing and constructing a power plant. Table 3 shows how the time to license and construct a reactor increased over the late 1960s and 1970s. Regulation is often cited for this increase in delays. If delays were important contributors, and if they were due to regulation, in

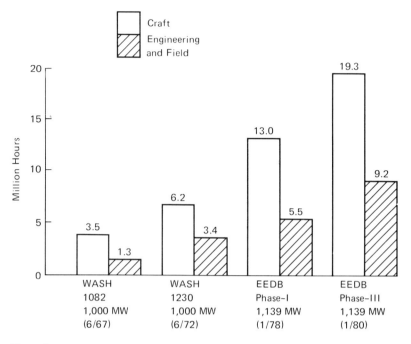

Figure 2
Changes in craft, engineering, and field service requirements for nuclear power plants, 1967–1980 (million hours). Figure is from US DOE/EIA (1982). Source: United Engineers and Constructors, "Energy Economic Data Base (EEDB) Program," US Department of Energy, Vol. I, Contract No. DE-AC02-78ET3202 (Washington, DC), April 1981.

theory the regulation could be improved and the cost increases could be moderated or even reversed.

We turn first to the question of the effect of delays on costs. Again, the main evidence comes from regression analysis of costs where delays are included as one of the explanatory variables. Mooz (1978) found that the effect of the delay between filing for and receiving a construction permit had a small effect on the direct costs of constructing a nuclear reactor. This is to be expected since at this stage most costs are prospective—little has been purchased or constructed. Mooz found project delay costs to be $3.00 per kW per month, a large, but statistically insignificant, effect.

Other studies have shown a more statistically significant effect of delay on costs. Zimmerman (1982) found that a doubling of construction period, holding all other things constant, would double the real costs of a reactor. Ellis and Zimmerman (1983) found that had the expected construction period not increased over the 1970s from about 7 years to 13 years at the end of the

Table 3
Average reactor licensing and total lead times, 1956–1979

Calendar year	Number of construction permits issued	Average megawatts	Average construction permit review time[a] (in months)	Number of reactors completed as of 12/79	Average total lead time[b] (in months)
1956	3	165	12	3	78
1957	1	175	16	1	49
1958	—	—	—	—	—
1959	1	22	9	1	44
1960	7	45	12	7	48
1961	—	—	—	—	—
1962	1	40	19	1	68
1963	1	50	5	1	57
1964	3	552	10	3	53
1965	1	610	14	1	54
1966	5	722	7	5	62
1967	14	764	10	14	70
1968	23	814	14	21	82
1969	7	910	19	7	99
1970	14	764	20	14	72
1971	4	963	21	3	80
1972	14	815	35	3	1
1973	14	1,076	34	—	—
1974	19	1,069	31	—	—
1975	9	1,166	26	—	—
1976	9	1,136	25	—	—
1977	15	1,065	39	—	—
1978	13	1,123	—	—	—
1979	2	1,150	—	—	—

Source: Table is from US DOE/EIA (1980). Department of Energy, US Central Station Nuclear Electric Generating Units: Significant Milestone, September, 1979.
a. As measured from date of construction permit application to date of construction permit issuance.
b. As measured from date of construction permit application to date of initial fuel loading.

decade, the relative economics of nuclear power would not have deteriorated so strongly. Using a probabilistic choice model, they estimate that rather than the probability of choosing a nuclear power plant in 1978 being zero, a 7 year construction lag would have raised that probability to about $\frac{1}{3}$. Energy System Research Group (ESRG, 1982) also found in its work that delays exerted a powerful influence on cost, each year of construction time raising costs by \$39 per kW.

If delays were important in increasing costs, why were they important? The most obvious effect is the interest cost of money outstanding during construction (IDC), an item that has come to account for a large fraction of the costs of nuclear plants. Delays, coupled with the higher interest rates of the 1970s, clearly led to higher costs. However, the studies by Mooz, ESRG, and Zimmerman used typical expenditure profiles for nuclear power plant construction to calculate the IDC component and eliminate it from their analyses. Thus, delays were associated as well with increases in the direct costs of constructing a plant.

It cannot be inferred from these regressions that delays caused cost increases. The results make clear that high cost plants were associated with longer construction periods. But the construction period can serve as a proxy for nonregulatory difficulties of all kinds, such as strikes, nondeliverability of components, and contractor error. If the delay is due to these problems, increasing the speed of the regulatory process will have little effect on costs.

A number of studies have examined causes of delays. A study by the NRC in 1977 (US DOE/EIA, 1980) examined licensing delays experienced by 24 reactors licensed between 1 July 1975 and 31 December 1977 (see table 4). The study strongly suggests that the licensing delays were overwhelmingly caused by the regulatory agency, and most of these delays revolved around safety determinations. However, since at the construction permit stage delays are likely to be the least costly one, more revealing is table 5, also from a 1977 study of the NRC (US DOE/EIA, 1980). Strikes and materials deliveries accounted for a relatively small fraction of total delays. Financing, management, and NRC regulatory action each accounted for 18–19% of total delay time. This suggests that regulation is responsible for only a small portion of the more costly construction delays. However, the interaction between delay-causing factors is bound to be large. Other authors have referred to this as a "ripple" effect. For example, delays and cost increases incurred because of retrofit requirements or court decisions will undoubtedly create management difficulties and affect the ability to finance a project. A more recent study (Radlauer, Bauman, and Chapel, 1985) found that 53% of all delays resulted from redesign or rework problems that were "overwhelmingly in-

Table 4

Source of delays in the licensing phase of reactor projects issued construction permits, 1 July 1975–31 December 1977

Source of delay	Number of cases
Public sector delays	
Substantive issues	
Safety	
Basic reactor design changes[a]	8
Radiological containment	6
External accidents	2
Environmental	
Geology/seismology	7
Meteorology/hydrology	3
Site characteristics	2
Other	
Corporate financial/managerial capability	3
Antitrust	1
Redundancy/inefficiency	
Bureaucratic delay/data transmission	5
Other government organizations	3
Public participation	6
Private sector delays	
Reconsideration of need for power	1
Total number of reactor projects	24

Source: Table is from US DOE/EIA (1980). Nuclear Regulator Commission, *Reactor Licensing Schedule Performance Critique*, 1977.
a. Including ECCS (emergency core cooling system).

stigated by the direct or ripple effects of existing or new regulations. Thus the majority of new delays were outside the scope of normal estimating procedures."[16]

To summarize, longer delays were strongly associated with higher cost plants. Case studies suggest that safety regulation, either directly or indirectly, caused a large fraction of the delays. This says nothing, of course, about whether the cost of the regulations was worth the benefits. All that one can conclude from these studies is that the technology was continually changing and as a consequence costs rose. Furthermore, had the changes in technology been anticipated at the design phase, the technology could have been brought into conformance at a lower cost. The positive association between delays and cost and the studies of causation of delays suggests that retrofit of construction in progress added importantly to the cost of nuclear reactors.

There is further evidence that the problems of nuclear power were related to the change in the nature of the technology. Since the introduction of commer-

Table 5

Average amount and sources of delays in construction phase of reactors currently in progress

Source of delay	Average amount of delay (in months)	Total amount of delay (in months)	Source of delay as percent of total delay
Private sector			
Labor (strikes, low productivity)	1.02	84.42	3.86
Materials (late or incorrect delivery)	.97	81.66	3.73
Financing (inability of capital markets to generate funds, or failure of internal financing)	4.97	417.50	19.07
Management			
Project delays (problems encountered during construction)	4.72	396.67	18.12
Demand delays (reconsideration of entire project in view of changing demand projections)	7.11	597.42	27.29
Public sector (NRC regulatory delay, forced retrofits; court and referenda decisions outside NRC)	4.95	415.75	18.99
Unknown (delay occurred before data collection commenced)	2.33	196.00	8.95
Total	26.06	2,189.42	100.01

Source: Table is from US DOE/EIA (1980). Nuclear Power Plant Licensing: Opportunities for Improvement, NUREG-0292, June 1977.

cial scale reactors, no case has occurred in which costs were overestimated. A study (Zimmerman, 1982) of the divergence between expected and actual costs found that the average cost forecast for newly ordered plants was low by a factor of two compared with the ultimately realized constant dollar cost. What explains this dismal forecasting record? It has been argued that experience was with small demonstration reactors and firms poorly understood the economics of scale (Bupp and Derian, 1981). The evidence is consistent with this view. Zimmerman's study regressed both actual cost and expected cost on plant size and other variables. The results suggested that realized economies of scale were half as great as were expected by industry cost estimators.[17]

The time pattern of errors in cost estimation provides further insight into what went wrong. Recall from the earlier discussion that actual costs rose at approximately 11% per year. Forecasted costs also were found to rise at 11% per year (Zimmerman, 1982). Apparently, forecasters observed what had happened over time and took account of these developments in their forecasts for new plants. However, while delays were associated with higher actual costs, regressions on expected costs show no relation between anticipated project length and expected cost. The forecasters updated their predictions each year based on past cost increases, but did not assume similar increases would continue into the future. If they had expected continuing annual cost increases due to rising factor prices and more stringent regulatory requirements, they would have expected the construction lag to be positively associated with cost. Their error was not in misunderstanding what had taken place, but rather in failing to anticipate that increased factor prices, new regulatory requirements, and the consequent retrofitting would continue to affect nuclear power plant construction.

The analysis of Joskow and Yellin (1980) and the previous discussion of the Price-Anderson Act suggest that remote siting might well have been a cheaper way to provide safety than the constant changing of standards. But limited liability reduced private incentives for remote locations. Furthermore, while the Atomic Energy Commission and its successor agency could have required remote location, regulatory procedures favored siting preferences of the utilities (Joskow and Yellin, 1980).

There is evidence suggesting that other safety standards were established in an inefficient manner. One study found that measures taken to control iodine-131 implies a value of life of $100 million (Cohen, 1980).[18] Since other safety measures taken by the NRC are worthwhile at a much lower value of life, redirecting resources away from iodine-131 control toward other safety measures would improve safety at the same overall cost.

Whether cost effective or not, regulations and consequent developments, by 1978, had dramatically altered the competitive position of nuclear power in the electric utility industry. Of course, by 1978 many plants had already been successfully completed and were producing power at reasonable costs. Yet in 1979 another surprise occurred: the accident at the Three Mile Island station of Metropolitan Edison. This event directly affected already operating reactors and brought into question the advisability of completing reactors then under construction.

4 The Accident at Three Mile Island

On 29 March 1979, a "transient" occurred at the Three Mile Island station. Through a combination of design fault and human error, a loss of coolant led to substantial damage to the reactor. The accident at TMI probably did not alter near term orders for new nuclear plants since previous studies suggest that by the end of 1978 the probability of a new nuclear order was already minuscule (Ellis and Zimmerman, 1983). Rather, research suggests that the main effects of the incident lie with operating reactors and, most important, with plants under construction.[19]

After the incident a number of commissions were established to extract lessons from the events at TMI.[20] The NRC made 200 recommendations to rectify problems uncovered in the staff investigation, including both improved training for personnel and changes in reactor design. The cost of meeting these requirements is in dispute. The DOE/EIA (1982) estimates the costs, including engineering and design, to be between $24 and $83 million per reactor. These estimates, as pointed out by the Atomic Industrial Forum (AIF), exclude the cost of replacement power during shutdown for repair. The AIF estimates that all the costs incurred could be as low as $24 million but could be as high as $700 million for older reactors requiring lengthy shutdowns.[21]

More subtle and more difficult to measure is the impact of the accident on the value of nuclear power to electric utility companies. As long as the costs of retrofitting an operating reactor or a reactor under construction are recoverable, little harm is done to the utility company by new TMI-induced safety requirements. The company will ask for and receive higher rates to cover those costs. For plants under construction, upon completion the plant will enter the rate base, including the additional expenditures on safety equipment. As long as the rate of return granted the utility by the regulators reflects the cost of capital, the utility suffers little financial damage. If, on the other hand, because of the accident utilities are unable to get new reactors in the rate base, there is a potential financial loss. Furthermore, if the accident at TMI caused investors to believe that other plants were at risk of similar accidents, the owners of these plants would also suffer financial loss. Therefore, differences are possible in the impact of TMI on individual electric utilities.

A number of authors have examined the change in equity value of utility companies after the accident at TMI. The studies use the abnormal returns methodology pioneered by Fama et al. (1969). This methodology estimates the normal variation of a firm's equity value and the value of the stock market as a whole. The relationship is then used to predict how a firm's stock price should have performed, given the actual performance of the market as a whole. On the day of an event, such as TMI, the deviation of stock price performance from the normal relation is taken as a measure of the impact of the event.[22] Several researchers found that right after the transient at TMI, utility companies with substantial amounts of nuclear capacity experienced a large and significant decline in equity value. Laslavic (1981) and Hill and Schneeweis (1983) found that negative abnormal returns persisted for a period of about two months after the accident. Both studies divided the sample into nuclear and nonnuclear portfolios and found that the nuclear portfolio lost value relative to the nonnuclear utilities. It is impossible, however, to surmise from these studies exactly why the market perceived nuclear power had lost value. It could have been fear either that all reactors faced risk of similar accidents or that utilities would not be successful in licensing new nuclear plants and would be unable to recover past investment.

To sort through these alternative explanations, Zimmerman (1983) examined the pattern of abnormal returns in more detail. He regressed the loss in value on the amount of nuclear, coal, oil, and gas generating capacity for each utility. Each type of capacity was further broken down into currently operating capacity and capacity under construction. Finally, to account for the influence of state regulation, allowance was made for capacity under construction in states where construction work in progress (CWIP) was allowed and states where it was not. CWIP refers to the practice of placing expenditures on construction in progress in the rate base as the expenditures are made. The alternative procedure is to cumulate expenditures and interest on those expenditures and place the entire sum in the rate base upon plant completion. The former practice yields revenue to the firm sooner. In theory, if the interest rate allowed on expenditures equals the cost of capital, a firm should be indifferent between getting the revenue now or later. The problem is that not granting CWIP means that the firm has only a promise it will receive the present value of its expenditures after completion of the project. If something intervenes to prevent completion, the firm will not receive the present value of all it has expended.

Zimmerman found, as did the other researchers, that after the accident at TMI all nuclear utilities lost value. However, over a period extending out 12 months from the accident, most of the loss in value was recovered.[23] The only persistent loss was on nuclear capacity under construction in states where CWIP was not allowed. For plants under construction but in the rate base, and therefore generating revenues, no financial loss was suffered. The fact that operating capacity did not suffer persistent losses suggests that fears of other TMI-type accidents did not increase among investors. It also suggests that investors expected that whatever cost would be incurred in response to new requirements either would be small or, more likely, would be recovered by the firms through higher rates. What TMI appears to have put in doubt was the ultimate recovery of revenue from reactors under construction not yet in the rate base.[24] This suggests the market's main fear was over the regulatory response to the accident. TMI put in greater doubt when and to what extent new nuclear plant expenditures would be recovered. Again, response to perceived safety issues appears to be the main factor affecting the valuation of nuclear power.

5 The Current State of Nuclear Power

Cancellations of nuclear power plants have been numerous in recent years. Columns in table 2 show how cancellations have increased in the late 1970s and early 1980s. Since 1982, utilities have cancelled plants in which they invested billions of dollars. There are many reasons why cancellations have taken place (US DOE/EIA, 1983). The major factors cited by utilities for cancellation were lower forecasted load growth, financial conditions, regulatory changes, and uncertainty and reversal of economic advantage.[25] These factors are not mutually independent. As studies of the effects of TMI indicate, financing difficulties depend heavily upon regulatory uncertainty. Low demand growth can lead to a reversal of economic advantage. The independent contribution of each of these factors to cancellation decisions is therefore not known. From a public policy perspective, the important issue now, however, is whether the cancellations are efficient.

A recent study (Zimmerman, 1985) suggests that the treatment by state public utility commissions of abandoned property has contributed to the cancellation of plants, particularly plants in which a great deal of money has been invested. The study suggests that incentives created by regulatory rules might be leading to cancellations of plants that should be completed.

Ratepayers' and utilities' incentives depend upon how rates are set by regulators. In general, rates are set to allow a utility to earn a given rate of return. Regulators determine what the appropriate rate of return is and they determine what investments are properly recovered by the firm. For example, imprudent investments or cost increases due to incompetent management will be excluded from the rate base. But any prudent investment that is "used and useful" will normally be allowed in the rate base.[26]

When a prudent investment must later be abandoned, the firm usually is able to recover its expenditures but is not allowed a rate of return on that investment. If $100 million was spent before abandonment, the regulators raise rates over a period, usually ten years, so as to return $100 million.[27] Over a ten year period, rates would be higher by $10 million per year. Clearly, the higher the interest rate, the lower the value returned to the firm. At nominal interest rates of 2%, this amounts to a recovery of 90¢ on the dollar. At 15%, the recovery is only 50¢ on the dollar. The fact that only part of the sunk cost is returned to the firm establishes incentives for firms and for ratepayers that can diverge markedly.

The problem is that consumers can walk away from an investment for only 50¢ on the dollar in today's economic environment. Consumers will sometimes see that it is cheaper for them to cancel a plant and pay for substitute power rather than complete the plant. If half the sunk cost plus the cost of the alternative is less than the full sunk cost plus the incremental cost of completing the plant, consumers will seek cancellation. The firm, of course, loses by cancellation and will be reluctant to abandon the investment.

Efficient decision making would ignore sunk cost. But these costs are not sunk to the consumer until the plant is finished and enters the rate base. To the consumer, only one-half of the costs are sunk. Regulators could, in theory, solve this problem. They could prohibit cancellation of efficient plants. In practice this is unlikely since regulators are responsive to consumer interests, quite apart from efficiency. This phenomenon was probably at work in the decision to cancel the Midland plant of the Consumers Power Company of Michigan (Zimmerman, 1985). In sum, the extent to which nuclear power plants are being abandoned may be inefficient. Consumers have a powerful incentive to get plants cancelled, an incentive much stronger than that provided by a social efficiency criterion.

While these incentives operate, it is not clear how strong they are, or how many of the most recent cancellations were due to such regulatory induced incentives. A case-by-case analysis is the only way to answer this question, a task far beyond the purpose of this survey. What this discussion does point out, however, is the difficulty in disentangling the various factors affecting cancellation, and the difficulty in determining the social efficiency of the retreat from nuclear power. Low demand growth, for example, need not justify a cancellation. If the completed plant will substitute for higher cost oil plants, the completion of the plant might be desirable. However, consumers desiring cancellation for the reasons outlined above will seize upon low demand forecasts as an argument for cancellation.[28] Uncertainty created by long regulatory proceedings to litigate this issue will create financing difficulties that further contribute to cancellation decisions. In sum, we cannot separate the individual factors, and we do not know whether what is occurring is efficient. As in the past, the impact of government regulation in this industry is still not completely understood.

6 Summary and Conclusions

This survey of the development of the nuclear power industry puts particular emphasis on the role of the federal government in promoting and regulating the technology. Several points that are relevant to the general question of the role of the government in technology adoption emerge from this analysis.

The technology of nuclear power generation and its initial civilian demonstration were the result of government policy beginning with the naval research and development directed by Admiral Rickover. The Shippingport reactor, which demonstrated the civilian potential of the technology, was also a government initiative. The subsequent steps in the commercialization of the technology, however, were accomplished with relatively little direct subsidy. The large number of orders for nuclear power plants in the 1960s, what some have called the great "bandwagon" (Bupp and Derian, 1981), came about because private firms thought that the technology was the low cost way of generating electricity. Even the indirect subsidy, through the Price-Anderson Act, seems to have had a relatively small effect on the number of reactors ordered in the early days of civilian nuclear power. Commercialization was basically a private sector phenomenon.

An unresolved issue that emerges from this survey, however, is whether the government was wise to override market perceptions of safety. What we saw over time was organized pressure for safer technology. By passing the Price-Anderson Act, the issue of the optimal level of safety provision was transferred from the private to the public sector.

The industry would have developed differently without the limited liability provided by the act. Analyses of the costs of remote locations suggest that such locations would have been a way to provide safety at lower cost than the continuing process of new regulations and retrofit of reactors. The perceived advantage of nuclear power in the early years would have been lessened, and the rate of growth would have been slowed by a different location policy. But the public demand for safety as manifested in increasingly stringent regulations of the NRC might have been lessened, and the ultimate viability of the technology might have been increased.

The experience of nuclear power suggests lessons for future government actions aimed at promoting new technology. Substituting government for market judgment, even in highly technical areas, is a perilous process. Market "obstacles" are not simply something to be overcome. True externalities can justify government action, but the nuclear case suggests that establishing whether such an externality exists is often difficult. Was the inability to insure power plants in the absence of the Price-Anderson Act a market failure? Furthermore, if such an externality exists, policies should be tailored to correct that market imperfection and no more. In the case under review here, limiting liability through the Price-Anderson Act was a poor choice for dealing with an insurance market that, arguably, was not functioning correctly.

Notes

1. The discussion of this section relies heavily on Allen (1977).

2. There were other subsidies of fuel enrichment that we do not discuss here.

3. The Atomic Energy Act of 1954 allowed civilian ownership of nuclear materials.

4. This was a turnkey project. General Electric agreed to deliver the plant at a fixed price.

5. In 1976 dollars, increasing the number of plants from 10 to 20 reduced costs, *ceteris paribus*, by $55 per kWe. The average cost per kW for plants in the sample was $629.

6. There is some irony here. The estimates suggest that what was learned from experience was that it was more costly than originally anticipated to construct nuclear power plants. Therefore the information provided by the government plants actually led to fewer plants ultimately being built.

7. American Enterprise Institute (1985), pp. 5–7. As of this writing, Congress is considering reauthorization of the act, and changes in liability limits are likely.

8. See Wood (1981) for an argument that perhaps the private market had a better estimate.

9. Wood (1983, p. 18).

10. Joskow and Yellin (1980, p. 55). This is for a four-unit site.

11. Zimmerman (1982).

12. A nuclear plant will be chosen if it is lower cost, or if

$$Z_n \gamma_n - Z_c \gamma_c < \varepsilon_c - \varepsilon_n,$$

where c and n refer to coal and nuclear, respectively, and the Z_i are vectors of observable fuel, capital, and operation costs and the ε_i represent nonobservable cost factors. The γ_i are parameters that reflect expectations about cost increases, discount rates, etc. If ε_c and ε_n are randomly and normally distributed, and $X = Z_n \gamma_n - Z_c \gamma_c$, then $P(N) = 1 - \Phi(X)$, where Φ is the cumulative standard normal distribution and X is a matrix of capital, operations, and fuel costs for nuclear and coal plants and estimated weighting parameters. The midpoint, .8 mills/kWh, was converted to an equivalent capital cost per kW using the assumptions of Joskow and Yellin (1980) about captial charge rate and capacity factor. The parameters of $\Phi(X)$ are from Ellis and Zimmerman (1983) and the values of the observed costs are from Zimmerman (1982). The increased cost of remote location was then converted into a reduced probability of choosing nuclear power.

13. Of course, utilities would not expect to recover costs of accidents due to imprudent behavior. Also, there is always ambiguity as to who bears the costs of large accidents, since regulatory precedents have been known to change.

14. Ellis and Zimmerman (1983).

15. US DOE/EIA (1982, p. 30).

16. Radlauer, Bauman, and Chapel (1985, p. 50).

17. The scale coefficient was expected to be .35, that is costs were expected to follow the following relationships: cost per $kW = (size)^{.35}$ but the actual relationship was cost per $kW = (size)^{.17}$, holding other plant characteristics constant.

18. Study cited in Wood (1983, p. 58).

19. There are other important issues that affect plants that are completed and enter the rate base. Rate setting based on historical cost leads, in these instances, to "rate shock." We ignore this issue here.

20. Among these commissions were one established by presidential order, the Kemeny Commission. The Nuclear Regulatory Commission also established a study commission under the direction of Mitchell Rogovin.

21. These numbers are cited in US DOE (1980, p. 175).

22. This technique assumes that the stock market is efficient in the sense that movement in stock prices is an unbiased estimate of the effect of new information on the value of a company. This assumption has been supported by a number of studies.

23. Zimmerman (1983) found that by March 1980 the value of operating reactors had returned to its pre-TMI value. Hill and Schneeweis found that for their nuclear portfolio as a whole, equity values did not recover. However, other factors could have affected the portfolio value over that time period, and it is difficult to ascribe to TMI a permanent loss in value. See Hill and Schneeweis (1983, p. 1291).

24. It could also have been the fear of longer time to completion because of new regulatory proceedings. This too reduces the economic value of nuclear plants to a firm since it puts the plant at risk for a longer period. For a discussion of this phenomenon, see Zimmerman (1985).

25. The other factor cited a number of times was denial of state certification.

26. There have been recent decisions in state courts that change this rule. Recently, for example, the Montana Public Utility Commission (PUC) ruled that a completed coal plant that is being used represented excess capacity and denied rate base treatment. The interpretation of "used and useful" varies from state to state.

27. Ten years is the modal value. There is, however, variation from state to state and even within states over time. See Zimmerman (1985).

28. Consumers will attempt to present the worst case for completing the plant. Firms, on the other hand, will be reluctant to cancel and will present the best case, citing those forecasts that predict the greatest rate of growth in demand.

5 The Record of the Environmental Protection Agency in Controlling Industrial Air Pollution

Paul W. MacAvoy

The revision of the Clean Air Act completed by Congress in 1970 set out both a highly ambitious new federal environmental control policy and a regulatory system for achieving the results from that policy. The goal was to eliminate those levels of particulate matter and of the sulfur, carbon, and nitrogen oxides that caused illness for the most sensitive members of the general population.[1] This was to be achieved through an innovative control system in which a new federal agency set pollution standards, and the state environmental regulatory agencies then in place were to set out implementation plans subject to federal review of plan performance against the standards. The critical element in this joint federal-state system was the new federal agency, the Environmental Protection Agency (EPA), with the power to set nationwide compulsory health-based standards for air quality, and to require the state agencies to control emissions from industrial plants at levels consistent with achieving these standards. Once state controls were in place, enforcement actions were to be taken against violators first by state officers, then by the EPA, and, upon EPA referral, finally by the US Department of Justice.

This chapter of the Adelman Festschrift describes the results. After setting out the methods of regulation, hypotheses as to what should have taken place

The research reported here has been funded by the J.M. Foundation, the General Electric Foundation, and the Olin Foundation. Olin Fellows Jeffrey Adler, Mark Austin, Scott Cantor, Harin de Silva, James Giesel, Precious McLane, Denise McMillan, Michael Miles, and Jennifer Urich provided assistance in data gathering and analysis. Important critical comments have been provided by Robert Crandall of the Brookings Institution. George Eads of the University of Maryland produced an exceptionally helpful line-by-line critique of an earlier manuscript version. The comments and criticisms of Jerry Zimmerman and George Benston of the University of Rochester, Martin Zimmerman of the University of Michigan, Richard Gordon of Pennsylvania State University, and Henry Jacoby of MIT were very helpful. Michael Levin, Chief of the Regulatory Reform Staff at EPA, commented extensively on the manuscript, and his clarifications of details of EPA operations were very useful. This chapter itself was a project in the Center for Research in Government Policy and Business in the Graduate School of Management at the University of Rochester.

are compared to the limited improvements in air quality that were in fact realized. The concluding paragraphs seek to explain the gap between goals and results by specifying the extreme limitations of the control process by which this was to be done.

1 Methods of Regulation

The new EPA was to take its initial step by setting nationwide air quality standards. Guidelines for these standards were provided in the Agency's statute: Congress took the position in the 1970 revision of the Clean Air Act that legal maximum pollutant levels were to be formulated solely on the basis of health considerations. Senator Edmund S. Muskie, a principal architect of the 1970 amendments, stated that "the first responsibility of Congress is not the making of technological or economic judgements or even [to determine] what is or appears to be technologically or economically feasible. Our responsibility is to establish what the public requires to protect the health of persons."[2] National Ambient Air Quality Standards (NAAQS) were to be set "to protect the public health ... allowing an adequate margin of safety for those particularly sensitive citizens such as bronchial asthmatics."[3] They in fact turned out to be a set of specified maximum air content levels derived from scientists' judgments as to "safety margins" for particulate matter, sulfur oxides, nitrogen oxides, photochemical oxidants, hydrocarbons, and carbon monoxide. Their implementation generally would have required reductions in factory and plant emissions by more than one-third of the levels realized in the late 1960s.[4]

Given such standards, the state agencies were to respond with State Implementation Plans (SIP). The SIPs would require such reductions in individual plant emissions that local air quality would conform. Each state was to have its Plan in place and approved by the EPA by 1975, so as to achieve NAAQS air quality levels in that year. Otherwise that state would have controls imposed directly on local plants by the Environmental Protection Agency.

Yet, to the contrary, the majority of states did not even have preliminary SIP submissions to the EPA by 1975. Wyoming had its SIP accepted by EPA in 1971;[5] but, the EPA had approved only sixteen state Plans by 1982. The Agency was in the process of reviewing seven others that year, but was faced with the fact that the remaining Plans had been provided only in preliminary form or not at all by the appropriate state agencies.[6] There were no alternative EPA Plans imposed on laggard or recalcitrant states. At the same time EPA's initial management system was itself not functioning by 1975. The Agency was required by the 1970 Clean Air Act to set emissions levels directly for all new plants, wherever located, separate from the SIP process. But it established "new source" performance standards (NSPS) over the decade of the 1970s for only three of fifty-nine emission source categories.[7]

The state Plans and the "new source" standards that were set in practice turned out to be specifications for pollution treatment equipment. This routinely followed from the states using EPA guidelines for "effective" control equipment as state plant-to-plant requirements in SIP. Arguably, the equipment would limit individual plant emissions, so that total discharges into the air shed would be reduced to levels specified in the NAAQS. But for this to occur, the required equipment had to be not only in place but also operated according to design standards, and the SIP did not generally extend to regulating operations directly.

More important, these equipment requirements were not uniform or comprehensive. The states using the EPA guidelines specified installation of "reasonably available" control equipment (RACT), which was widely used second or third generation stack precipitators with known performance. The EPA imposed more stringent specifications in NSPS when new plants "contributed significantly to air pollution which causes ... the endangerment of public health or welfare."[8] These new source performance standards were best available control technology (BACT) that the administrator determined had been demonstrated.[9] Thus the state agencies were less demanding in their requirements for cleansing equipment to be placed on old plants than the EPA was for that to be put on new plants.[10]

Not only were the less stringent RACT standards used as the basis for SIP specifications, but, as important, there were extensive variations and even exemptions from the minimum RACT requirements. Older plants in financial difficulty were allowed to conform by switching to low-pollutant fuels without installing control equipment. Power plants were allowed to conform by building higher stacks to spread pollutants over wider areas. In the extreme, existing plants were grandfathered into the Plan with existing high levels of emissions that were in excess of average NAAQS levels. At the same time other plants in the same industry or at similar locations were required to install RACT equipment on schedule.

This pattern was not random, but rather was the result of adjusting the stringent, health-based federal standards to local political and economic conditions. The SIP specifications, even though presumed on EPA approval to be consistent with the health goals in the NAAQS, realistically were set by the state agencies with the necessity in mind to keep local plants in operation. The result was to require emissions equipment that was not so costly that the plant would have to shut down in the process of conforming to the plan. The rule of thumb was "that ninety percent of sources subject to such a [control technology requirement] must be able financially to comply."[11] The 90% included many of the most polluting sources, since as the larger plants they had the most severe adverse impact on the community if otherwise forced to close. The states in practice made RACT exceptions for major chemicals and steel making plants in order to prevent shutdowns that would have caused substantial unemployment.

Regulation practiced in this way had to encounter problems, ultimately, of effectiveness. Even if and when all Plans were completed and in operation, there would be wide variations in emissions. The state Plans, with many exceptions for the individual plant, turned away from those consistently applied limits on emissions necessary to attain higher levels of air quality.

2 Pollutant Emissions Levels

While the new regulatory process was going into place, however slowly and incompletely, emissions from plants and factories continued to change from year to year in accordance with previous trends. Particulate emissions began to decline during the 1950s, and continued to do so, with the decline rate accelerating slightly in 1970–1973 before the new regulations were installed (as in table 1). Sulfur oxides emissions were more variant, however. While they declined by 1 percentage point a year in the 1950s, they increased by more than 3% per annum in the 1960s (a rate still 2% less than industrial production growth). Sulfur emissions were roughly constant in the 1970–1973 period before the beginning of EPA regulation. Nitrogen oxides, which were increasing from 1948 to 1970, at 2 to 4 percentage points per annum, continued at that rate during the inception of the new regulation.

From 1973 to 1983, with regulation more or less in full operation, emissions of all the major pollutants were reduced. Particulates fell the most and nitrogen oxides the least. But these declines continued to bear the same relationship to the rate of growth of industrial production as established in previous decades. Particulates increased at a rate 6 to 7 points less than industrial production and sulfur oxides increased at a rate 5 points less than industrial production, just as before the advent of this EPA system of controls (as in comparing columns 1 and 2 with column 4 in table 1). Thus it is not evident from an examination of annual emission rates whether the emissions declines of the last decade were related to regulation or to the business cycle.[12]

Further, however, there was considerable variation in the growth of emissions from industry to industry throughout the 1970s that cannot be explained by regulation. The largest volumes of particulate matter, sulfur oxides, and

Table 1
Annual percent changes in pollutant emissions,[a] 1948–1983

Years[b]	(1) PM	(2) SOX	(3) NOX	(4) Industrial activity[c]
1948–1960[d]	−2.03	−0.85	2.58	4.05
1960–1970	−1.48	3.50	3.53	5.00
1970–1973	−8.26	0.59	3.73	6.39
1973–1979	−7.34	−2.60	0.73	2.72
1979–1981	−6.46	−4.60	−1.43	−0.49
1981–1983	−5.34	−3.42	−2.72	−1.10

Source: US EPA, Office of Air, Noise and Radiation, Office of Air Quality Planning and Standards, *National Air Pollutant Emission Estimates, 1940–1983*, EPA-450/4-89-028 December 1984: 2. All percentages are calculated as $[(y_1/y_t)^{1/t} - 1]$ for a period of t years.
a. Emissions are measured in teragrams per year; this includes emissions from both stationary and mobile sources. PM = particulate matter; SOX = sulfur oxides, NOX = nitrogen oxides. Values of PM, SOX, and NOX are annual percentage changes.
b. Years chosen are National Bureau of Economic Research business cycle peaks except for 1960, which is a year after the 1959 peak. Data for 1959 pollutant levels are not available.
c. Industrial production index is from US Executive Office of the President, *Economic Report of the President* (March 1984).
d. 1948 emission estimates are interpolated from 1940 and 1950 emission estimates based on rates of coal consumption.

nitrogen oxides in the atmosphere were the result of emissions from electric power plants and from boilers in manufacturing facilities. More than three-quarters of nationwide sulfur oxides and almost half of nitrogen oxides emissions came from these sources (as shown in table 2, for a representative year, 1978). At the same time, 16% of nationwide particulate emissions were from power plant and factory boilers (also shown in table 2). This was because of the concentration in these plants of coal as the fuel source (67% of sulfur oxides emissions and 12% of particulate emissions in 1980 were from coal utilization).[13] As regulation was installed in the middle 1970s, sulfur oxides emissions from chemical plants were reduced, but those from petroleum and electric power plants held constant, and emissions from mineral products facilities increased. Nitrogen oxides emissions declined in chemicals, metals, and in fuel combustion in commercial and industrial facilities, but increased in electric utilities, mineral products, and petroleum refining.[14] Particulate emissions declined in chemicals, metals, and mineral products, but they increased in petroleum refining. Such a pattern contradicted across-the-board application of the new SIPs and were more in keeping with the new growth and product changes specific to an industry but not to regulation.

Even with such industry-to-industry variation, the nationwide reductions

Table 2
Percentage of national emissions by major industrial category for 1978[a]

Industrial category	PM	SOX	NOX
Stationary source boiler use			
Electric utilities	11.6	64.9	29.8
Industrial	4.7	10.5	16.7
Industrial processes			
Metallic ore mining	4.5	—	—
Coal mining	2.9	—	—
Natural gas production	—	0.5	—
Mineral mining	8.0	—	—
Pulp mills	1.3	0.3	0.1
Chemicals	1.7	1.1	1.0
Petroleum refining	0.7	3.1	1.6
Asphalt paving/roofing	1.6	—	—
Mineral production	14.0	2.8	0.7
Metal production	8.1	9.6	0.2
Grain elevators	5.8	—	—

Source: US EPA, Office of Air, Noise and Radiation, Office of Air Quality Planning and Standards, *National Air Pollutant Emission Estimates, 1940–1980*, EPA-450/4-82-001 (January 1982).
a. Includes emissions from both stationary and mobile sources. PM = particulate matter; SOX = sulfur oxides; NOX = nitrogen oxides.

in emissions after 1973 should have resulted in improvements in air quality. To be sure, it is not likely that improvements in air quality would have followed immediately from reduced emissions since fugitive emissions from natural sources could increase at the same time. In fact, during the 1970s, air quality was improving, but at a rate lower then earlier (as shown in table 3). Sulfur content would appear to have gone down by roughly 15% over the 1973–1979 period, as indicated by two different sets of data from the EPA monitoring system (in table 3). Particulate content went down by only 7% between 1973 and 1979, while nitrogen content increased by 12% over that part of the same period for which estimates are available. These rates are lower than the 20% reductions in the 1960s.

These changes in air quality indicate limited overall improvement in ambient conditions. Moreover, they cannot easily be associated with the introduction of the new EPA plant and factory regulations. The variations in air quality across industries show rapid emissions growth in some sectors just at the time of the new regulations from the 1970 Clean Air Act. They had the effect of causing disparity in air content across regions when the new regulation should have achieved about the same level of air quality in all regions. Particulate content of the air decreased more in the Northeast and South, where initial content was already lower, than in other parts of the country (see table 4). The

Table 3
National composite average air quality, 1960–1979

| Year | PM (mg/cm^3) | Ambient air quality | |
		SO_2 (mg/cm^3)	NO_2 $(10^6$ metric tons/year)
1960	88	—	—
1961	84	—	—
1962	82	—	—
1963	84	—	—
1964	86	55	—
1965	84	51	—
1966	80	54	—
1967	74	50	—
1968	74	45	—
1969	69	43	—
1970	72	32	—
1971	68	25	—
1972[a]	64	23	—
1973	63	22	—
1974	61	21 (38)[b]	56
1975	59	20 (37)	55
1976	60	20 (37)	58
1977	59	19 (33)	59
1978	58	— (32)	64
1979	59	— (33)	63

Source: US EPA, Office of Air Quality Planning and Standards, *1980 Ambient Assessment—Air Portion*, EPA-45014-81-014 (February 1981): Appendix A.

a. Increase in monitoring sites produces a break in data series for this and subsequent years.

b. Second series, from 188 continuous monitors only.

sulfur content of the air either increased uniformly across all four regions of the country (on the one-hour tests, as in table 4),[15] or decreased in the Northeast and Northwest while increasing in the Southeast (according to the annual averages in table 5). These variations are difficult to explain,[16] but are not very likely the result of systematic and uniform application of the EPA air quality standards by all the state agencies.

Most basic, such quality improvements were not sufficient to achieve the goals set for the regulators by the 1970 Clean Air Act. The National Ambient Air Quality Standards had not been attained across the country by the late 1970s given that particulate, sulfur, and nitrogen oxides levels were excessive, particularly in urban areas with populations greater than half a million. Of some 45 such highly populated areas of the country, 33 had annual average levels of particulate content of the air that were higher than the National Ambient Air Quality Standards.[17] Slightly more than one-half of the major

Table 4
Comparison of air quality measures, 1972 and 1979

Region	1972		1979	
	Mean ambient content level[a] ($\mu g/m^3$)	Number of air quality control regions ($\mu g/m^3$)	Mean ambient content level[a] ($\mu g/m^3$)	Number of air quality control regions ($\mu g/m^3$)
PM: arithmetic mean; 24-hour tests				
Midwest	77.1	76	70.7	105
West	85.3	24	77.8	34
Northeast	70.1	53	54.9	55
South	73.7	71	57.2	84
SOX: arithmetic mean; 1-hour tests				
Midwest	19.5	41	30.2	30
West	11.7	8	22.4	13
Northeast	22.5	38	34.2	32
South	11.9	49	23.4	11

Sources: US EPA, Office of Air Noise and Radiation, Office of Air Quality Planning and Standards, *Air Quality Data—1979 Annual Statistics*, EPA 450-4-80-014 (September 1980); US EPA, Office of Air, Noise and Radiation, Office of Air Quality Planning and Standards, *Air Quality Data—1972 Annual Statistics*, EPA 450-2-74-001 (March 1974).
a. Weighted average of observations from monitoring sites in each region. These numbers are indicators of air quality calculated for purposes of comparison, although not used by EPA as determinants for attainment. Definitions of regions: Midwest = EPA Regions 5, 7, 8; West = EPA Regions 9, 10; Northeast = EPA Regions 1, 2, 3; South = EPA Regions 4, 6.

Table 5
Ambient air quality SO_2 trend, 1974–1979

EPA Region	Area	Sites	Estimated annual arithmetic mean ($\mu g/m^3$)					
			1974	1975	1976	1977	1978	1979
1	New England	8	33.6	32.9	30.4	31.7	34.3	31.7
2	NY & NJ	46	44.6	36.9	37.0	38.6	36.9	34.6
3	Mid-Atlantic	16	58.9	42.1	54.1	52.6	50.9	45.7
4	Southeast	39	20.7	23.7	26.3	20.7	20.3	30.9
5 & 7	Midwest	40	46.0	40.4	40.0	35.9	34.5	37.2
6	South-Central	5	23.3	18.8	12.6	15.6	17.0	21.9
8	West-Central	6	14.1	15.9	16.5	14.2	17.2	16.9
9	Southwest	22	22.7	30.1	26.1	21.4	22.7	18.6
10	Northwest	6	101.6	147.0	133.3	82.5	46.7	38.3
	Nation	188	38.4	36.7	37.1	33.2	31.5	32.6

Source: US EPA, Office of Air, Noise, and Radiation, Office of Air Quality Planning and Standards, *Appendices A and B to the 1980 Ambient Assessment Air Portion* (February 1981).

urban areas were either on or over NAAQS levels in sulfur content, with most of them showing no substantial reduction in content levels over the last half of the decade.[18] The nitrogen oxide content in 1979 was so high that 40 of the 45 areas were either barely matching or failing the NAAQS standard.[19] Thus, emissions reductions by industry in the 1970s were too limited to achieve the air quality goals underlying the new EPA regulations.[20]

There are any number of possible explanations for these conditions. Plant pollutant emissions were on the decline, if not for regulatory reasons. As implied in the business cycle reference points in table 1, during the middle 1970s the economy was in the process of experiencing a sharp recession, so that industrial production and consequently emissions declined from year to year. At the same time, materials recycling and recovery were reducing waste materials and thus emissions systematically. Another development during that period was the 1974–1975 fourfold increase in oil prices, which caused reductions in fuel use relative to other inputs in the production process. Since both particulates and sulfur oxides are residuals of fuel combustion, the relative cutback in energy use caused these pollutant emissions to decline. Again, however, there were complications—while factor substitution away from energy and reduced output caused pollutant emissions to decrease, the substitution of cheaper coal containing more sulfur and soot for relatively higher priced fuel oil with less pollutants caused pollutants to increase.

Given these various and sometimes conflicting economic factors, did EPA regulation by itself have a significant impact on emissions and thus on air quality? With various sets of determinants, economic and regulatory, operating at the same time, the answer is not evident. To account for specific regulatory impact requires an analysis, similar to that in the next section, of each of the factors affecting emissions at the industry level.

3 The Determinants of Industry-by-Industry Emissions

In most general terms, the relationship between manufacturing and emissions can be characterized by a simple production function $Q = f(x_i; e)$ for goods production Q and emissions e, based on input factors x_i including labor, materials, and capital. The level of utilization of each input factor $x_i = f(x_j, P_i, P)$ is chosen so that the cost of an additional unit used in production (the factor price P_i) is equal to the value of its marginal product as determined by quantities of other inputs x_j and output price P. Pollutant emissions e can also be considered to be a variable in the production function, because they too incur costs that can be justified only in terms of increasing the value of final products. These costs consist of the myriad expenses for waste disposal, and they have the potential for varying over a wide range, based on different levels of energy use per unit of output. Thus the level of emissions actually chosen by the company would be based on output price, pollution control cost, and technical limits on use rates of fuel and materials in operating plants and factories. That is, each company can set emissions so as to make its costs of the pollutant equal at the margin to the value of goods and services made possible by the additional discharge.

Thus it is presumed in the most general case that emissions levels depend positively on the utilization rate of input factors, such as raw materials and fuel, positively on the price of goods output, and negatively on the disposal costs of the pollutants.[21] These propositions can be formulated for testing at the industry level so that emissions ($QEMIT$) depend on industry plant and equipment investment ($INVEST$), fuel use ($COALTON$), output price ($PRIC$), and the level of disposal costs ($RCOST$).

In logarithmic form, so that causal variables are additive,

$$\log(QEMIT) = B_1 + B_2 \log(INVEST) + B_3 \log(COALTON)$$

$$+ B_4 \log(PRIC) + B_5(RCOST).$$

Taking the right-hand-side variables in order, $INVEST$ is specific industry capital outlay on production plant and equipment (but not pollution control equipment). The larger the investment, the greater the plant efficiency, with consequent reductions in fuel use and emissions.[22] The second variable, $COALTON$, measures annual coal utilization by industry, and the higher the utilization rate of this fuel, the greater should be $QEMIT$ emissions.[23] And the higher the sales price $PRIC$ of final goods and services in that industry, the more will be produced and thus the greater the pollutant discharge.[24] But the greater the outlays on equipment to increase pollution disposal ($RCOST$), the lower should be the level of emissions. Altogether, three economic factors can be said to have an impact on emissions—investment $INVEST$, coal utilization $COALTON$, and output price $PRIC$. At the same time, pollution control policies should reduce emissions by increasing pollution disposal costs $RCOST$ in the state Plan process of adopting plant to plant equipment requirements.

The EPA regulatory processes enter into the industry-level determinants of emissions by dominating $RCOST$ in the 1970s. In response to EPA ambient standards, as promulgated in the state Plans, industry outlays for pollution control equipment had to be substantially increased and these are included in measured "$RCOST$." Of course, expenditures on control equipment were made before EPA began operations in order to meet local zoning and state regulatory requirements. But multiplicative year-to-year increases in outlays on such pollution control equipment in the middle 1970s were required for the implementation of those SIPs certified by EPA (as in note 20).

In order to test this simple model of economic and regulatory effects, a data set at the industry level has been compiled, as described in table 6. While most variables in that set come from known and reliable sources, the *QEMIT* series is sufficiently different to require extended discussion.

Measures of emissions levels *QEMIT* by industry have been obtained from the *National Air Pollutant Emission Estimates, 1940–1983* or Trends Reports of EPA. The emissions levels in this source are calculated, rather than estimated, by EPA using the following procedure. An "emissions factor" is computed for each industrial process by multiplying the stipulated emissions rate per unit of fuel for that process times the observed fuel utilization rate. If the stipulated emissions factors are equal to the average estimated emission rates per Btu actually experienced in recent years, then the EPA calculated emissions are reliable surrogates of total emissions. The EPA states,

The preparation/revision of each factor involves, first of all, locating and obtaining all the known written information on that source category from such sources as available literature ... and the National Emissions Data System point source file ... the process descriptions, process flow sheets, and other background portions of the section are prepared ... representative emission factors are developed for each pollutant emitted by each point source of the process category....

[T]he factors generally will not permit the calculation of accurate emissions for an individual installation. Only an on-site source test can provide data sufficiently accurate and precise to use in such undertakings as design and purchase of control equipment or initiation of a legal action. Factors are more valid when applied to a large number of processes, as, for example, when emission inventories are conducted as part of community or area-wide air pollution studies.[25]

Because the stipulated factors have been frequently revised with more operating information, the calculated emissions estimates are not comparable from one EPA report to the next. However, each year's report updates the estimates by industry from previous years to make them consistent within that year's report. Through use of the latest publication, a consistent data base for earlier years has been obtained. From that data base, annual emissions for seven industries have been regressed on industry investment expenditures, prices, coal tonnage use rates, and that industry's outlays on required pollution control equipment.[26]

The fitted relationship for 1973–1980 for particulate emissions is shown in table 6. The estimated coefficients B_1 to B_4 have signs as expected from the general economic arguments. *QEMIT* in the equation declines when invest-

Table 6

Regression analysis of particulate emissions by industry, 1973–1981[a]

Coefficient	Estimate of coefficient	t-value of coefficient	Statistical significance
B_1	-1.546	-1.559	Not significant
B_2	-1.076	-4.721	Significant
B_3	$+0.377$	$+7.153$	Significant
B_4	-0.390	-0.722	Not significant
B_5	$+0.989$	$+3.469$	Not significant

Sources:

QEMIT: National Air Pollutant Emission Estimates, 1940–1983; US EPA, Office of Air, Noise and Radiation, Office of Air Quality Planning and Standards, EPA 450/4-84-028 (December 1984);

COALTON: "Fuels and Electric Energy Consumed: Industry Groups and Industries," *Annual Survey of Manufactures*; US Department of Commerce (various years); *Annual Energy Review*, 1983; Energy Information Administration, Office of Energy Markets and End Use Department of Energy;

INVEST and *RCOST:* Gary L. Rutledge and Betsy D. O'Connor, "Plant and Equipment Expenditures by Business for Pollution Abatement, 1973–80, and Planned 1981"; *Survey of Current Business*, Bureau of Economic Analysis (June 1981, 1983);

PRIC: Statistical Abstract of the United States, 1956–1982 (various volumes); table, Producer Price Indexes, by commodities, 1965–1982.

a. $\log(QEMIT) = B_1 + B_2 \log(INVEST)(-1) + B_3 \log(COALTON) + B_4 \log(PRIC) + B_5 \log(RCOST)(-1)$. Instrumental variable: *TIME TREND*. Mean of $\log(QEMIT) = -1.088$. R-squared $= 0.693$. Sum of squared residuals $= 17.618$. Standard error of regression $= 0.588$. F-statistic $(4,51) = 28.73$. Number of observations $= 56$.

Variable identification:

QEMIT = Emissions measured in teragrams by industry and by year. The industries are Electric Utilities, Chemicals, Petroleum Refineries, Metals, Mineral Production, and Pulp Mills. For Chemicals, Petroleum Refineries, Metals, Mineral Production, and Pulp Mills, *QEMIT* is for emission from the Industrial Process only. All boiler emissions from those industries are aggregated as "industrial fuel combustion."

INVEST = Investment, billions of real (1972) dollars of capital expenditures, net of new plant and equipment expenditures for air pollution abatement, by industry and by year.

RCOST = New plant and equipment expenditures for air pollution abatement, in billions of real (1972) dollars, by industry per year.

SUMRCOST = Cumulative new plant and equipment expenditures for air pollution abatement, in billions of real (1972) dollars, by industry and by year.

COALTON = Thousands of tons of coal consumed by industry and by year. 1972 and 1973 coal data are interpolated for industrial processes. Petroleum refineries coal consumption estimated.

TIME = Trend, 1970 = 1.

PRIC = Producer price index, by industry and year, divided by the economy-wide price index.

Observations are measured for a given industry in a given year, for each of seven industries and eight years, for a total of 56 observations. For industrial fuel combustion, a set of observations not specific for one industry, matching data for investment and coal tonnage are for total manufacturing. Coal tonnage for industrial fuel combustion is defined as total industrial coal consumption net of coal used in industrial resource.

ment ($INVEST$) increases, given that B_2 is negative and statistically significant. $QEMIT$ increases as the tonnage of coal ($COALTON$) increases over the decade, as indicated by the positive and significant coefficient B_3 in the estimated equation. But for these industries, $QEMIT$ was not affected by prices ($PRIC$) since calculated B_4 is negative, and not significant. Most important, $QEMIT$ increased as regulation-determined pollution equipment outlays $RCOST$ increased over the period; that is, the coefficient B_5 for control expenditures is positive. Nearly 70% of the variance in emissions is explained by the independent variables in the regression equation as indicated by the value of the coefficient of determination (R-squared).

This fitted equation indicates that the major determinants of particulate emissions by industry in the 1970s were investment and coal use rates. Neither factor had a direct relationship with EPA regulation. There are further indications, moreover, that EPA regulation did not have the intended effect. Particulate emissions were positively related to expenditures on air pollution control equipment, rather than negatively related to such expenditures as hypothesized.[27]

One possible explanation for such results is that regulatory impact has occurred with a substantial lag, as the effectiveness of the new equipment in reducing pollution discharge has been established over some years. But substantial delayed impact from the new pollution control equipment required by EPA regulation would be observable as a pattern of differences between equation-estimated and actual levels of $QEMIT$. In fact, particulate residuals show no such pattern of serially correlated residuals at the end of the decade. Petroleum refining actually experienced a sharp emissions reduction in 1974, below levels expected from the equation, but this residual was made up in large unexpected increases in subsequent years. Chemicals and metals also had sharp reductions in one year, 1978, but chemicals at least recovered so rapidly as to have the largest excess of actual emissions over equation-predicted $QEMIT$ by 1980. In general, the differences between equation-predicted and actual emissions seem to be declining over the middle and late part of the decade, which is the opposite of the result from reductions in emissions caused by intensive utilization of recently acquired pollution control equipment.

Alternatively, it could be hypothesized that the required $RCOST$ had another impact, that of bringing about across-the-board emissions reductions soon after all such equipment in an area or air shed was in place. In that case, because no such process is ever discontinuous, emissions reductions over time would be associated with cumulative expenditures on control equipment. To test this possible association, the equation $QEMIT$ was reformulated with $SUMRCOST$, for cumulative expenditures on control equipment, replacing

Table 7
Alternative regression equations for particulate emissions by industry, 1973–1981[a]

Equation number	Particulate emissions			
	1	2	3	4
B_1	−1.033	−6.240	−1.017	−3.985
	(−1.481)	(−5.625)*	(−1.477)	(−6.538)*
B_2	−1.189	+0.290	−1.202	−0.350
	(−7.086)*	(−0.832)	(−7.895)*	(−3.224)*
B_3	+0.381	+0.535	0.366	+0.468
	(+7.269)*	(+5.429)*	(+7.288)*	(+7.290)*
B_4	−0.081	+1.791	−0.522	+0.980
	(−0.146)	(+1.614)	(−1.031)	(+1.469)
B_5	+1.224[1]	−0.935[1]	+1.159	—
	(+5.794)	(−2.000)*	(+6.778)	
B_6	−0.292	—	—	−0.127
	(−6.316)*			(−2.718)*
R-squared[2]	0.749	0.428	0.747	0.580
Standard error of regression	0.586	1.020	0.582	0.750
F-statistic	29.83	9.54	37.70	17.64
	(5,50)	(4,51)	(4,51)	(4,51)

Source: Data sources and formulation as described in the notes to table 6.
a. $\log(QEMIT) = B_1 + B_2 \log(INVEST)(-1) + B_3 \log(COALTON) + B_4 \log(PRIC) + B_5 \log(RCOST)(-1) + B_6(TIME)$. *, statistically significant; [1], substitutes variable $SUMRCOST$ for $RCOST$; [2], unadjusted.

year-to-year expenditures in the variable RCOST. Again, the coefficient B_5 should be negative and significant if the stock of new control equipment had an impact on emissions at the industry level.

Further along those lines, it is possible to consider other plausible formulations of the equation. An additional variable for "time trend" could be included on the presumption that in the basic equation federal regulatory effects are confounded with the gradual reduction in emissions due to long term technical improvements. To separate regulation and technical growth, both RCOST and TIME should be in the equation.

Such alternative formulations are used to produce the fitted equations in table 7. The first equation contains an additional variable for time trend, while both the first and second equations include summed equipment outlays SUMRCOST rather than one year outlays RCOST.[28] The first, third, and fourth equations provide alternative results based on estimation by ordinary least squares, on the assumption that the instrumental variable in two stage least squares, while plausible, has no significant impact. The four equations

Table 8
Alternative regression analyses of sulfur oxides emissions by industry, 1973–1981

Equation number	1	2	3	4	5
B_1	−1.386	−0.787	−7.796	−0.452	−4.716
	(−1.229)	(−0.933)	(−5.391)*	(−0.586)	(−6.141)*
B_2	−0.663	−0.787	+1.203	(−0.885)	+0.328
	(−2.556)*	(−3.881)*	(+2.642)	(−5.181)*	(+2.398)
B_3	+0.425	+0.433	+0.641	+0.407	+0.550
	(+7.095)*	(+6.838)*	(+4.990)*	(+7.209)*	(+6.794)*
B_4	+2.775)	+3.234	+5.753	+2.542	+4.646
	(+4.512)*	(+4.837)*	(+3.977)*	(+4.476)*	(+5.526)*
B_5	+1.350	+1.629[1]	−1.277[1]	+1.650	—
	(+4.165)	(+6.373)	(−2.094)*	(+8.604)	
B_6	—	−0.394	—	—	−0.173
		(−7.025)*			(−2.945)*
R-squared	0.791	0.809	0.489	0.835	0.654
Standard error of regression	0.668	0.709	1.329	0.653	0.945
F-statistic	48.25	42.43	12.20	64.52	24.13
	(4,51)	(5,50)	(4,51)	(4,51)	(4,51)

Source: Data sources and formulation as described in the notes to table 6.
a. $\log(QEMIT) = B_1 + B_2 \log(INVEST)(-1) + B_3 \log(COALTON) + B_4 \log(PRIC) + B_5 \log(RCOST)(-1) + B_6(TIME)$. *, statistically significant; [1], substitutes variable SUMRCOST for RCOST; [2], unadjusted.

indicate very limited sensitivity of calculated emissions to these alternative formulations. Final goods prices are still not significant determinants of emissions, although technology seems to have some effect.[29] The determinants of particulate emissions are consistently investments in new plant and equipment and coal use.[30] The plausible regulatory determinants are not significant and do not even create a pattern of negative impacts on pollutant emission level.[31]

Similar equations have been formulated to explain sulfur oxides emissions. Sulfur discharges QEMIT are the log linear sum of investment (INVEST), fuel use (COALTON), product prices (PRIC), and regulatory related discharge costs (RCOST). Equation 1 in table 8 indicates that the coefficient for investment is negative and significant, and that for fuel use is positive and statistically significant. The coefficients for product price and regulatory cost both are positive, the first as expected, but the second indicating that emissions of sulfur oxides increased with regulation-determined expenditures on pollution control equipment.[32] This finding is the opposite of what would result from regulation because EPA requirements for the installation of control equipment

Table 9
Regression analysis of nitrogen oxides emissions, 1973–1981

Coefficient	Estimate of coefficient	t-value of coefficient	Statistical significance
B_1	−4.528	−3.360	Significant
B_2	+0.168	+0.542	Not significant
B_3	+0.439	+6.126	Significant
B_4	+1.947	+2.650	Significant
B_5	+1.048	+2.705	Not significant

Source: As in table 6.
a. $\log(QEMIT) = B_1 + B_2 \log(INVEST)(-1) + B_3 \log(COALTON) + B_4 \log(PRIC) + B_5 \log(RCOST)(-1)$. Instrumental variable: $TIME\ TREND$. Mean of $\log(QEMIT) = -1.126$. R-squared = 0.831. Sum of squared residuals = 32.521. Standard error of regression = 0.799. F-statistic $(4,51) = 62.86$. Number of observations = 56.

should reduce sulfur emissions.[33] For all seven industries, as well, the residuals of actual emissions from those expected from the equation value of $QEMIT$ seem to show no cumulative effects from regulation. That is, if regulation gradually pushed down emission levels, without regard to values of the other variables, then equation-estimated $QEMIT$ should be higher than actual emissions levels in the last half of the decade. In fact, industry emissions for all except chemicals were higher than equation-estimated emissions over the last half of the decade. Only minerals in 1975, and metals in 1980, experienced one year downturns in realized emissions below the regression [calculation] of $QEMIT$.

Different formulations of this equation, as shown in table 8, produce generally similar results. Substitution of the variable $SUMRCOST$ for $RCOST$ results in an insignificant coefficient for regulatory costs in equation 2, but a marginally significant coefficient in equation 3. Equations 2, 4, and 5 using ordinary least squares provide an indication of the effects from economic and regulatory variables quite similar to that indicated from two stage least squares equations. Investment, coal use, and output prices have the predicted effects on emissions, but larger regulatory expenditures for pollution control equipment have the surprising result of being associated generally with increased emissions.[34]

The most striking pattern of economic and regulatory effects is found in the regressions for nitrogen oxides emissions. The equation coefficients shown in table 9 indicate that fuel use and product price were significant positive determinants of year-to-year nitrogen emissions but that investment was an insignificant determinant. Regulatory determinants as measured by effluent control equipment expenditures also had a positive but insignificant effect on emissions. Altogether, changes in NOX emissions appear to have been the result of fuel use, as expected, but not of investment in either direct production equipment or regulation-related pollution control equipment.[35]

The conclusion from these equations for all three pollutants is that the factors determining changes in emissions from manufacturing plants in the 1970s were economic and not regulatory. Fuel use rates, and less frequently investment rates and product prices, were significant determinants. Investment in pollution control equipment related to regulation had no systematic effect on emissions levels at the industry level. There was no pattern of reduced emissions that can be attributed to the introduction of the state SIP and the national NSPS regulatory processes.

4 Factors Determining Regulatory Effectiveness

The lack of regulatory impact can be explained two different ways. The 1970s new regulatory process was not sufficiently complete to have an impact; and even where installed, this process was characterized by malfunctions that prevented any direct results. Whether the fault was with the lack of presence, or the regulatory process itself, can be determined at least in general.

This can be done by comparing the emissions at locations where firms were in SIP compliance with emissions at other locations where compliance had not yet been established.[36] "Compliance" in this comparison constitutes the operation of a state Plan approved by EPA with designated factories and plants carrying out required programs to install emissions equipment. The comparison of emissions from any one industry in state A in compliance with those from the same industry in state B not yet in compliance should indicate regulatory effects, where other determinants of discharge such as fuel use level and fuel type are held constant. For the equation

$$QEMIT = B_1 COMP + (B_2 + B_3 COMP)COAL$$

$$+ (B_4 + B_5 COMP)OIL + B_{6i}INDUSTRY,$$

the variable $COMP$ takes a value of one for that subsample of industries in that state in compliance, and a value of zero for the counterpart subsample in another state not in compliance. The quantity emitted $QEMIT$ in a state should be less when that state is in compliance, so that the coefficient B_1 for $COMP$ should be negative. Emissions $QEMIT$ should be greater the more fuel utilized, so that both coefficients B_2 for coal and B_4 for oil should be positive.[37] But emissions should be less where fuel is used in states in compliance so that both the coefficients B_3 and B_5 for fuel specific $COMP$ should be negative. Finally, as a matter of course, emissions levels differ from industry to industry, because of differences in technology, so that the coefficients B_{6i} can be greater than or less than zero depending on the designated industry.

Table 10 reports estimated values of these coefficients with respect to sulfur oxides emissions at the state level, based on a 1979 sample for six industries in 50 states. There is no difference in the level of emissions between states in compliance and those not in compliance, given that the coefficient B_1, for COMP, while negative, is insignificant. The compliance coefficient COMP on coal use B_3 is negative, but on oil use B_5 is positive, and neither is statistically significant. The coefficient for the coal utilization rate B_2 is positive and significant, indicating that SOX emissions variations from state to state have primarily been the result of the levels of coal use actually experienced that year.

There has been more effect from compliance with respect to particulate emissions, however. As shown in table 11, for particulate QEMT the coefficient B_3 for compliance COMP on coal utilization is negative and statistically significant, as is the coefficient on B_5 for COMP on oil utilization. But the effect of compliance on the average level of emissions, as shown by B_1, is positive and statistically significant. These estimates B_3, B_5, and B_1 together indicate that plants located in compliance states at low fuel use rates have equal or higher particulate emissions than those in out of compliance states. Overall, the most important determinants of sulfur discharge have been coal and oil utilization rates, given that standardized coefficients for these variables (the average value of the variable times the coefficient) account for most of the level of emissions.

With respect to nitrogen oxides emissions, only one of the coefficients is statistically significant, that for coal utilization, and it is positive as expected (also as shown in table 11). Comparing the state subsamples in and out of compliance by industry indicates that compliance makes no overall difference, since the coefficient B_1 is positive but statistically insignificant, and given that compliance does not significantly reduce emissions per unit of fuel since B_3 and B_5 are insignificant. Similar analyses completed for hydrocarbon and carbon monoxide emissions, the least important of the pollutants from manufacturing, show no effect from compliance. Emissions of both pollutants are determined only by the levels of fuel utilization and not by the compliance variables.[38]

The general pattern implied by these results suggests that emissions depend only to a limited extent on the state-to-state compliance status of plants. For sulfur oxides, particulate, and nitrogen oxides pollutants, the major determinant of emissions has been the coal utilization rate at the plant. Except for

Table 10

The effects of state plan compliance on factory emissions of sulfur oxides

B_1	−4005.16
	(−.2504)
B_2	.0364
	(11.5601)
B_3	−.0034
	(−.9410)
B_4	.0487
	(.1318)
B_5	.0758
	(.2042)
INDUSTRY coefficients B_{6i}	
Chemicals	7070.77
	(.3724)
Petroleum Refining	−20603.5
	(−.4810)
Minerals	2234.41
	(.1210)
Ferrous Metals	768.056
	(.0401)
Nonferrous Metals	5617.86
	(.2158)
Electric Utilities	−2127.75
	(−.1221)

Source: "Emissions by SCC Reports," unpublished data from National Emissions Data System, US EPA, 1982.

a. $QEMIT = B_1 COMP + (B_2 + B_3 COMP)COAL + (B_4 + B_5 COMP)OIL + B_{6i}INDUSTRY_i$. Mean of $QEMIT = 69591$. R-squared $= 0.7487$. Sum of squared residuals $= 9.27E + 13$. Regression standard error $= 80227.5$. F-statistic $(11, 144) = 53.228$; Sig Level $= 0.0\%$. Number of observations $= 155$. t-statistics are shown in parentheses. Variable identification:

$QEMIT =$ Emissions measured in tons per state and year, 1979.

$COAL =$ Tons of coal burned.

$OIL =$ Thousands of gallons burned.

$COMP =$ Dummy variable if equal to one if that industry in that state was in compliance.

$INDUSTRY =$ Dummy variables for the following industries: Chemicals, Petroleum Refining, Minerals, Ferrous Metals, Nonferrous Metals, and Electric Utilities.

Each observation represents the pollution emissions for a given state, industry, and compliance-value (in or out). Originally, there were 600 observations:

600 observations $= 50$ states $\times 6$ industries $\times 2$ compliance-values.

From this data set, a subsample of 155 observations was used in the regression. This subsample consists of the pollution emissions for each compliance-value and industry of every state in which there was coal combustion.

Table 11

The effects of state plan compliance on factory emissions of particulates and nitrogen oxides

Coefficients	Particulates		Nitrogen oxides	
	Estimate	(t-statistic)	Estimate	(t-statistic)
B_1	3772.70	(1.9583)	2831.24	(0.6718)
B_2	0.0041	(10.8979)	0.0117	(14.1470)
B_3	-0.0030	(-6.9209)	-0.0015	(-1.5823)
B_4	0.1197	(2.6895)	0.1509	(1.5499)
B_5	-0.1087	(-2.4311)	-0.0958	(-0.9793)
INDUSTRY coefficients B_{6i}				
Chemicals	3954.36	(1.7290)	-1544.63	(-0.3087)
Petroleum Refining	360.598	(0.0699)	-8417.84	(-0.7459)
Minerals	5792.21	(2.6058)	-1763.70	(-0.3626)
Ferrous Metals	-271.139	(-0.1175)	-1849.05	(-0.3664)
Nonferrous Metals	-1531.71	(-0.4885)	-522.503	(-0.0762)
Electric Utilities	-2642.53	(-1.2595)	5758.33	(1.2547)

	Particulates	Nitrogen oxides
Mean of *QEMIT*	8246.8	26560
R-squared	0.4947	0.8363
Sum of squared residuals	1.34E+12	6.43E+10
Regression standard error	9662.37	21136.5
F-statistic (11, 144)	24.878	94.677
Number of Observations	155	155

Source: "Emissions by SCC Reports," unpublished data from National Emissions Data System, US EPA, 1982.

a. $QEMIT = B_1 COMP + (B_2 + B_3 COMP)COAL + (B_4 + B_5 COMP)OIL + B_{6i}INDUSTRY_i$. Sig Level $= 0.0\%$. Variable identification and sample size as in table 10.

particulates, the level of emissions per unit of fuel used has not been reduced by that state's factories being in compliance. For particulate emissions, compliance seems to have reduced emissions per unit of fuel, but the effects of this reduction on overall emissions has been cancelled by higher average emissions rates in the in-compliance states. Only in the states with the heaviest fuel utilization have particulate emissions overall been reduced by compliance with SIP regulation.

Such limited regulatory impact on emissions raises fundamental questions about the methods of determining and enforcing emissions reductions. As has been indicated, these requirements have been set based in part on what equipment was economically feasible for industry to install to cut pollution. As a result of substantial variability in such economic conditions, actual emissions controls for different coal burning power plants have differed substantially. As an example of the wide range of regulatory limits, table 12 details such requirements for certain adjacent states. The Indiana SIP stated that operating power plants were in compliance when using coal with 3.7 pounds of sulfur per mm Btu of fuel, which essentially was what was already being achieved before regulation. But the Ohio SIP everywhere required less than 3.0 pounds, and in some locations allowed only 1.1 pounds. This simple example suggests that, while some states have been stringent, there has not been any systematic limit placed on emissions by the overall system of SIPs.[39]

The lack of systematic regulatory requirements has not been the only contributing factor to this record, however. Also of great importance is the general practice that compliance with the Plan has been determined without monitoring and controlling actual plant emissions after stack equipment has been installed. The EPA and state agency regulatory agencies have relied mostly if not solely upon initial licensing of installed equipment in order to achieve certified regulation. To be sure, this should be effective, given that SIP licenses anticipate that the required equipment when operated reduces emissions. But the experience has been to the contrary. Licensed plants with particulate and sulfur emissions control equipment have in many cases operated to reduce emissions only part of the time. Particulate control equipment has been prone to corrosion caused by the scrubbing water, which contains sulfuric acid, hydrochloric acid, and nitric acid,[40] and the costs of prevention or reduction of such corrosion have been substantial. Given that such corrosion reduces equipment effectiveness, the operators of in-compliance plants do not always generate emissions consistent with theoretical design operation of the equipment.

The difference between actual and theoretical emissions in plants with SIP equipment has in fact been substantial. In a 1979 study covering plants in nine

Table 12
Compliance requirements for sulphur dioxide emissions as outlined in SIPs

State	Limit (lb SO_2/mm Btu)	Comments
Illinois[1]	6.0	Where air quality 45 mcg/m^3
	1.9	Chicago, Peoria, St. Louis SMSAs
	1.8	Where air quality 45 mcg/m^3
Indiana[1]	3.7	
Kentucky[3]		
Class I (Jefferson, McCracken)	1.8	Industries w/heat input of 100 mm Btu/hr[4]
	1.2	Industries w/heat input of 250 mm Btu/hr
Class II (Bell, Clark, Woodford)	3.0	Industries w/heat input of 100 mm Btu/hr
	2.3	Industries w/heat input of 250 mm Btu/hr
Class III (Pulaski)	4.1	Industries w/heat input of 100 mm Btu/hr
	3.3	Industries w/heat input of 250 mm Btu/hr
Class IV (Muhlenburg, Webster, Hancock)	5.9	Industries w/heat input of 100 mm Btu/hr
	5.2	Industries w/heat input of 250 mm Btu/hr
Class V (All Other Counties)	6.7	Industries w/heat input of 100 mm Btu/hr
	6.0	Industries w/heat input of 250 mm Btu/hr
Michigan[1]	2.4	Industries w/heat input of 500 mm Btu/hr
	1.6	Industries w/heat input of 500+ mm Btu/hr
Ohio[2]	1.1	Where air quality 100 mcg/m^3
	1.6	Where air quality 60–100 mcg/m^3
	3.0	Where air quality 60 mcg/m^3

Pennsylvania[5]	
SE Penn. air basin	0.9
Allentown, Bethlehem, Easton, Reading, Johnstown and	
Upper Beaver Valley air basins	2.8
All other air basins	3.7
West Virginia[1]	2.3
	3.1

Industries at maximum capacity
Industries at 75% capacity

Sources: [1], Ohio EPA compilation of SIP requirements from neighboring states. [2], Regulations of the Ohio Air Pollution Control Board, Ohio Department of Health. [3], 401 KAR 61:015; existing indirect heat exchangers; Kentucky Department of Natural Resources and Environmental Protection; the class into which a county is placed "has been determined by mathematical atmospheric diffusion models and other methods which evaluate those factors which necessitate limits on sulfur dioxide emissions." [4], The two categories of heat input listed for each class are taken from a total of six categories per class, ranging from less than 10 to 1500 mm Btu/hr. [5], Title 25; State of Pennsylvania Department of Environmental Resources, *Rules and Regulations Part I; Subpart C: Protection of Natural Resources Article III* (Air Resources Chapter 123, Standards for Contaminants pp. 123.5–123.10).

states, EPA monitored operations of 180 plants over a two-to-three-year period. Of these plants 70% had intermittent downtime with emissions levels substantially greater than operations according to the Plan. Individual plants had an average of thirteen breakdowns each year in emissions control equipment, of three days' duration, in which emissions were 25% or more greater than expected for licensed operations. In the extreme, a small number of plants emitted from ten to twenty times the design level of emissions and were continuously beyond emissions limits implied by their compliance status.[41] Extrapolating from this study is not a straightforward exercise, but this sample behavior raises the question as to whether significant numbers of plants "in compliance" operate control equipment with emission results similar to those in plants not covered by the regulation.[42] To that extent regulation has lost track of the presumptive relationship between equipment standards and pollutant emissions.

5 Regulation and Resulting Air Quality

The new regulatory system sought to establish a relationship between plant equipment requirements and national air quality. This relationship cannot now be determined and quantified for equipment and emissions. The state agencies have established equipment controls at RACT levels that apparently do not require widespread and significant emissions reductions. Furthermore, those improvements in air quality that were realized in the 1970s cannot be directly associated with plant emissions variations during that period.

This more startling conclusion follows from a regression analysis of the variations in levels of air quality from location to location. For each air shed in the country in 1979, data have been compiled for the mean ambient density of the major pollutants, and for total plant and other source emissions of these pollutants. The equation

$$\log AQ = B_1 + B_2 \log(EMIT) + B_3 \log(AREA)$$

fitted to these data on air quality AQ, on region emissions levels $EMIT$, and on the size $AREA$ of the air quality control region provides a measure of the impact of emissions levels on air quality. This measure consists of a determination as to whether B_2 equals one, so that it can be inferred that $EMIT$ reductions are associated with proportionate increases in AQ, or B_2 equals zero, so that there is no $EMIT$ and AQ association.

As shown in table 13, for the largest regions, variations in $EMIT$ and $AREA$ together explain only 5% of the variation in particulate content AQ of the air from region to region (i.e., R^2 equals 0.049 for equation 1).[43] For smaller

Table 13
The effect of emissions on air quality in 1979

Equation	B_1	B_2	B_3	R^2
(1) Particulates in large AQCRs	5.528	−0.006	−0.121	0.049
	(7.527)*	(−0.151)	(−1.867)	
(2) Particulates in medium AQCRs	−2.670	0.091	0.659	0.084
	(−0.587)	(1.183)	(1.468)	
(3) Particulates in small AQCRs	3.885	0.101	0.002	0.114
	(6.845)	(3.450)	(0.019)	
(4) Particulates in metropolitan AQCRs	5.105	0.099	−0.152	0.276
	(9.574)	(2.820)	(−2.357)	
(5) SOX in large AQCRs	4.073	0.189	−0.146	0.174
	(1.102)	(1.612)	−(0.432)	
(6) SOX in medium AQCRs	−7.792	0.144	1.041	0.064
	(−0.531)	(1.096)	(0.719)	
(7) SOX in small AQCRs	5.084	0.254	−0.284	0.278
	(2.405)	(3.910)	(−1.280)	
(8) SOX in metropolitan AQCRs	1.653	0.206	0.143	0.325
	(1.571)	(3.464)	(1.129)	

Sources: US EPA, Office of Air, Noise and Radiation, Air Quality Planning and Standards, *Air Quality Data—1979 Annual Statistics* EPA 450-4-80-014 (September 1980); US EPA, National Emissions Data System, *1979 National Emissions Report* EPA 450-4-81-029 (August 1981).
a. $\log AQ = B_1 + B_2 \log(EMIT) + B_3 \log(AREA)$, where AQ = mean ambient concentration of pollutant in that air quality control region in AQCR 1979, $EMIT$ = total emissions of that pollutant in that AQCR in 1979, and $AREA$ = the area of that air quality control region AQCR.

regions these two variables $EMIT$ and $AREA$ explain from 8% to 28% of the variance in particulate air quality (as indicated by R^2 for equations 2, 3, and 4). Much the same result obtains for air quality as measured by sulfur content, except that the percentage of explained variation is roughly six points higher (equations 5–8). The percentage change in air quality with respect to a 1% change in emissions levels for both pollutants, as shown by B_2, is between zero and 0.25 points even in the smallest regions. Both sets of equations indicate that region-to-region variations in air quality during 1979 cannot be explained by emissions levels. Since there has been no direct connection between emissions and controls initiated by the Environmental Protection Agency, regulation could scarcely have had an impact on air quality.

6 The Limits of Regulation

The process of regulation by which the EPA has set air quality standards, and the states have implemented plant-by-plant controls to attain these standards, has been subject to a decade of trial. It has produced volumes of data that generally indicate little or no marked impact of that plant-by-plant regulation on the pollutant content of the air.[44] The sulfur and nitrogen oxides content of the air associated with manufacturing and power plant emissions has not been substantially scaled back as a consequence of the new regulatory controls. Variations in emissions, due to the business cycle and investment-driven technological change, were as evident before as after the new EPA regulatory system was installed. Since then, where regulation has brought plants into compliance, emissions have not been reduced to levels lower than those in comparable out-of-compliance plants elsewhere. Even where changes in emissions have been most marked, air quality has not been much affected. Thus where the particulate content of the air has decreased, due to economic or regulatory factors, there has been no clear association between that reduction and the critical air quality benchmarks put in place as the foundation of EPA regulation.

The explanation for such conclusions can be found in the mode of operation of the regulatory system. The statute requirement for federal air quality standards, to be attained from state-determined fully specified emissions controls at the plant level, made a decentralized system of regulation necessary. The federal contribution was to establish highly stringent air quality standards to be achieved by state agency implementation plans. But the state programs had to adjust to limits on what each plant could invest, and with the heaviest pollutors the least financially able to comply, the state Plans became a patchwork of exceptions to those general emissions limits that would meet uniform national quality standards.

Is it possible to improve on this system to achieve substantial impact on air quality? To establish the linkage between on-site plant regulations and national air quality would require fundamental changes in the existing regulatory scheme. Emissions levels would have to be set the same across all sources to achieve an air quality impact. Such a radical change in procedure would conflict with the myriad of installed equipment standards by which the state agencies accommodate local plant operations. These local regulatory agencies would have to change in ways contrary to the interests of the state governments of which they are part. Thus conflicting policies inherent in the current regulatory scheme prevent achieving results consistent with air quality goals.

Notes

1. There was as much if not more concern with pollutants from automobiles. But such policies for dealing with automotive emissions are not the focus of evaluation here.

2. Cf. Bureau of National Affairs (1975)

3. US Congress, Congressional Budget Office (1982, section 109 (b)).

4. They were to be followed by even more restrictive secondary standards, which were "to protect the public welfare" on dimensions beyond health to include aesthetics and recreation. Since most secondary standards were not developed in the period under study here, these effects are subsumed with those from the primary NAAQS.

5. National Commission on Air Quality (1981, 3.4–13).

6. US General Accounting Office, Report by the Comptroller General (1982).

7. National Commission on Air Quality (1981, 3.7–5).

8. Congressional Budget Office (1982, section 111 (b) (1) (A)).

9. US Congress, Congressional Budget Office (1982, section 111 (a) (1)).

10. As a further variant, for states both without an SIP and experiencing air quality below NAAQS standards, the EPA regulated new plant operations most stringently of all, by requiring Lowest Achievable Emissions Rate (LAER) levels of any pollution control equipment specifically at those locations.

11. Michael H. Levin, Chief of the Regulatory Reform Staff, Office of Policy and Resource Management, EPA, in letter to Marvin Kosters of the American Enterprise Institute, dated 2 May 1983, p. 2.

12. Earlier versions of table 1 also contained percentage changes for volatile organic compounds and carbon monoxide. Cf. University of Rochester CRGPB working paper PPS 83–7. Since volatile organic compounds (VOC) and carbon monoxide (CO) were the results in great part of highway use of automobiles, they have been deleted to meet space constraints. Cf. US EPA, Office of Air Quality Planning and Standards (1978a).

13. US EPA, Office of Air, Noise and Radiation, Office of Air Quality Planning and Standards (1982).

14. US EPA, Office of Quality Planning and Standards (1978a, 1981b).

15. Robert W. Crandall of the Brookings Institution in correspondence has questioned whether the air quality data in table 5 are accurate. The number of sources for these measures is small and varies from year to year. For example, the number of AQCRs involved in measures in 1972 differs significantly from the corresponding number for 1979. Given substantial differences in readings across sites in a given region, the SOX readings from 49 sites in the South in 1972 are not necessarily comparable to the SOX readings from 11 sites in 1979. It is possible that if the sampling errors were known, no inferences at all would be drawn from the observed trends.

16. Martin Zimmerman has suggested, however, that the application of NAAQS standards could have been similar to setting pollution limits, so as to increase air quality in regions previously breaching the guidelines and reduce quality in other regions previously doing better than the guidelines. Thus he infers that regulations should have produced greater uniformity in the levels of pollution, and table 5 suggests that this happened in the middle 1970s. But see the next paragraph of the text.

17. Cf. US EPA, Office of Air Quality Planning and Standards, (1981b, pp. 2–4).

18. Cf. US EPA, Office of Air Quality Planning and Standards (1981b, pp. 2–8).

19. Cf. US EPA, Office of Air Quality Planning and Standards (1981b, pp. 2–14).

20. At the same time there were substantial expenditures on pollution control equipment. Compliance with the sulfur dioxide emissions limits set directly by EPA cost the electric utility industry $1.4 billion annually. Cf. US EPA, Office of Air Quality Planning and Standards (1979). The primary metals, petroleum refining, and chemical industries each spent more than $1 billion per year. Cf. McGraw-Hill Publications Company (1981). During the middle and late 1970s, outlays for pollution abatement by manufacturing, industrial, and other stationary sources of pollution increased from $15 billion to more than $25 billion per annum. While large in aggregate dollar terms, it cannot be determined whether if spent another way these amounts would have been sufficient.

21. Here R is the emissions equivalent of the input price of capital or fuel. Over time, as new technologies are introduced, fuel use should decline, and emissions should decline. Cf. the Berndt and Wood chapter in this volume on the general presumption that new equipment is energy saving and thus pollution-reducing.

22. The position is that the latest vintage capital when installed should be fuel saving, particularly in decades when fuel prices are rising relative to other input prices. Cf. the Berndt and Wood chapter below. But if, as implied by Jorgenson's findings, (reported by Berndt and Wood) new technology is fuel using, then the sign of B_2 would be positive rather than negative. For purposes here of measuring EPA regulatory impact, the sign of B_2 does not matter.

23. The pollutant content of coal dominates that of other fuels to such an extent that the volume of other fuels is not included in the equation.

24. Henry Jacoby in commenting on this relationship raised doubts as to whether price is exogenous, particularly in an industry set dominated by electric power. It has not been possible within the confines of this paper to test multiequation models in which feedback from QEMIT to PRIC has been explicitly recognized.

25. US EPA, Office of Air and Waste Management (1977), 1–2.

26. The two stage least squares equations are as follows,

$RCOST = f(PRIC, INVEST, COALTON, TIME)$,

$QEMIT = f(PRIC, INVEST, RCOST, COALTON)$,

with the variables as previously described except for the seven year trend variable TIME. The rationale for the two stage approach is that the right-hand-side variables in the first equation account for all determinants including both market factors and EPA regulation for expenditures on control equipment. Thus, the fitted values of RCOST from that equation account for regulation in the second equation. Also, the two stage procedure and use of constant dollar measures in investment remove trend-related effects from the second equation that might possibly be attributed to regulation so as to confound the effects with those measured by RCOST. The fitted coefficients for the first equation of the two stage least squares analysis are not shown here to save space.

27. The coefficient B_5 is concluded to be statistically insignificant, even with t greater

than 2.0, because we cannot reject the hypothesis that B_5 is equal to zero rather than negative.

28. This new variable takes on values equal to the sum of all outlays from 1970 to the year of each observation on the alternative presumption that the full impact of the expenditures on such control equipment associated with EPA regulation comes from the cumulative outlays.

29. Only two of the four coefficients have the correct sign on B_4 for PRIC. The coefficients for time have the predicted negative sign and significance to the extent that they serve as surrogates for technical change processes.

30. An F-test with the null hypothesis that the coefficients of investment (INVEST), coal use (COAL), and sales activity (PRIC) are zero for the formulations in tables 7 and 8 is rejected at any level of significance.

31. To the contrary, it should be noted that SUMRCOST does have a negative coefficient, in equation 2, when TSLS is used with time as the instrumental variable. This coefficient is marginally significant, and the only one departing from the general pattern.

32. The coefficient B_5 is statistically insignificant, because we cannot reject the null hypotheses that B_5 is greater than or equal to zero at the 95% confidence level.

33. Martin Zimmerman suggests that this could be a cross-section effect, given that the high pollution industries were installing the most equipment. But dummy variables for each industry did not result in an equation in which B_5 was then negative, as could be expected if interindustry differences were the determinant of the wrong sign for B_5.

34. The only finding to the contrary is in the last coefficient in equation 2. The insertion of a time trend in emissions produces a statistically significant coefficient for RCOST. That is, separate from investment and coal use determinants of emissions, the emissions were significantly lower over the period of large cumulative outlays on control equipment. This is a single finding, however, that disappears when time trend is accounted for separately (in equation 2).

35. Here again there are no substantial unexplained reductions in emissions, as would be indicated by a series of successive negative QEMIT residuals, that could be credited to the new EPA regulatory process. To be sure, minerals industry emissions residuals fell sharply in 1976, but these residuals increased again in 1979–1980. Chemicals emissions residuals fell below equation values in 1978, but were above equation values in 1979, and metals emissions residuals were low only in 1980. The other emission residuals in some years were above the line, while in other years below the line, with no discernible pattern. Also, equations similar to those for sulfur, as in (2)–(5) of table 8, were not different from that shown in table 9.

36. Emissions estimates used in this analysis were obtained from the National Emissions Data System (NEDS) of EPA. In this source, emissions by manufacturing are aggregated on three levels: the air quality control region, state, and nation. It is important to note that the national levels of emissions shown in this report may not be the same as those given in the Trends Report underlying the previous set of regressions. The NEDS Report includes only those larger point sources that emit more than 100 tons per year of

any one pollutant, and show "measured" emissions. The Trends Report includes all sources in its estimates but show "calculated" emissions.

37. Earlier analyses along this line also contained a variable for gas utilization, but the low pollutant content of gas resulted in zero or insignificant positive coefficients so that the variable was excluded in the results shown in table 11.

38. The equations are not shown to save space, but B_1, B_3, and B_5 are all statistically insignificant.

39. The "new source" exception to the SIP process has produced demanding regulatory requirements that in turn may have contributed to these overall weak results. The New Source Performance Standards (NSPS) on power plants, set directly by the Environmental Protection Agency, could have been met in the early 1970s by burning low sulfur coal without SIPS-specific emissions treatment equipment. But an alliance between environmental interest groups and producers of high sulfur Eastern coal successfully added a provision to the 1977 Clean Air Act amendments requiring in-stack treatment of all emissions from new sources regardless of coal sulfur content. The amended Act called for reductions in the sulfur content of coal by 70% in plants using fuel containing 0.6 lb SO_2/mm Btu, and 90% in plants utilizing fuel containing 1.2 lb SO_2/mm Btu. These equipment-requiring limitations have probably led to a slowdown in the construction of new plant capacity. Although no estimates of the extent of such a slowdown can be made at this time, the NSPS results in old plants in under less demanding SIP mandates staying in operations longer.

40. Cf. US EPA, Office of Enforcement (1981).

41. Vickery, Cohen, and Cummins (1980).

42. Staff in the EPA informally estimate that 30% of all sources listed as in compliance in 1980 were operating with excess emissions. These conditions have not been substantiated by source testing procedures used in the EPA.

43. Separate equations have been fitted for three sizes of air shed, because "fugitive" emissions, not subject to regulatory jurisdiction, play a larger role in determining air quality in larger regions.

44. To be sure, those pollutants associated with automotive operations probably have been reduced as a result of direct EPA control of auto emissions. Cf. L. White (1982).

6 Public Policy and the Private Auto

Robert W. Crandall
Theodore E. Keeler

The American public has always been of two minds regarding the private automobile. The accessibility, convenience, mobility, and privacy afforded by the car have made it a valued possession to most Americans. On the other hand, from the earliest years, the automobile was also thought to represent a safety hazard and an environmental danger to the communities through which it passed. During the past two decades, the perceived negative effects of the automobile have become strong enough to bring about new legislation controlling the private automobile more than it was controlled at just about any other time during its history.

This control has taken on both indirect and direct forms. Indirect controls have come from efforts to promote use of substitutes for auto travel, most especially in urban transportation, in the form of increased federal, state, and local aid to mass transit (bus and rail), and from a considerable slowdown in the construction of urban highways.[1] Direct controls on the automobile have come in the form of direct regulations on the emissions, safety, and fuel economy of new cars sold in the United States (most regulation in this area is federal, but the State of California has also played a strong role in emissions control in that state).

The purpose of this paper is to survey and evaluate the evidence available on the need for and efficacy of these efforts to control the undesired side effects of private auto transportation in the United States. The first section briefly examines the growth of the auto as a transportation mode and the corresponding effects on safety, pollution, and energy consumption. The second section provides evidence on the prospects for reducing the undesired

This research was supported by grants from the Institute of Transportation Studies of the University of California, the National Science Foundation, the Alfred P. Sloan Foundation, the Ford Foundation, the Alex C. Walker Educational and Charitable Foundation, and the Andrew F. Mellon Foundation. The opinions expressed here, however, are solely those of the authors and not of the granting agencies

Table 1
Automobile ownership and vehicle-miles traveled

Year	Auto-miles traveled (billions)	Registrations (millions)
1940	250	28
1950	364	40
1960	588	61
1965	709	75
1970	891	89
1971	939	93
1972	986	97
1973	1,017	102
1974	996	105
1975	1,028	107
1976	1,075	110
1977	1,119	114
1978	1,171	117
1979	1,141	119
1980	1,112	122
1981	1,114	124
1982	1,180	124
1983	1,222	127

Source: US Federal Highway Administration, *Highway Statistics (various years)*.

side effects of auto transportation (to the extent that they are found to exist) through substitution of other modes of transportation for the private auto. The third section summarizes the evidence from a recent Brookings Institution study (in which the present coauthors were participants) of the effects of direct regulation of the private auto by the US federal government, including controls on safety, emissions, and fuel economy. The final section sums up our evidence and provides an overall evaluation of the success of public policies on the private auto over the past two decades.

1 The Growth of Automobile Travel

The pattern of growth in the use of the automobile is shown by the data in table 1. The evidence suggests strong growth, not only in the early years, when the market penetration of the auto was relatively weak, but even in more recent years, when the market was regarded as a mature one and the cost of owning and operating a car was rising rather rapidly. During the entire period since 1940, even through the fuel shortages and recessions, the stock of automobiles has risen steadily. Total automobile miles have been more sensitive to the ups and downs of the economy and to fuel availability problems,

Table 2
Costs of owning and operating a full-sized sedan (cents/mile)

Model year	Current prices	1972 prices using PCE deflator
1956	7.14	10.9
1960	9.14	12.7
1965	9.26	13.0
1970	11.07	12.0
1971	11.48	11.9
1973	12.03	11.4
1974	15.47	13.3
1975	16.08	12.9
1977	15.97	11.5
1978	16.80	11.3
1979	18.61	11.5
1980	22.31	12.4
1981	26.30	13.5
1982	28.69	14.0

Sources: American Automobile Association, *The Cost of Owning and Operating an Automobile* (annual issues); US Department of Commerce.

but even total mileage evidenced a rising trend through the mid-1970s. Since 1977, however, the high cost of driving, low fares from airline deregulation, and severe recession have caused automobile use to stagnate. (The effects of airline deregulation are evident from table 13, which summarizes intercity passenger-miles by mode, and shows that air passenger-miles indeed grew relative to automobile miles in the late 1970s.) Even here, however, the trend has once again been upward since the 1980 recession (and through the severe recession of 1981–1982).

The nominal cost of owning and operating a car more than doubled from 1956 through 1974 (see table 2). In real terms, however, these costs have risen much less than is widely believed. By 1981, real operating costs were about the same as in 1965 despite two oil shocks in the 1970s. Although it is difficult to estimate a stable demand function for auto ownership and use from such aggregate time series data, it should be clear enough that there has generally been a strong secular upward trend in the demand for auto services. This growth, which has slowed somewhat in recent years, has had obvious implications for pollution, highway fatalities, and fuel consumption.

Safety   In the United States, transportation by means of the private auto is a major source of deaths, ranking alongside some of the most common major illnesses (National Safety Council, 1982). Accidents also contribute substantially to the total cost of owning and operating a car: until the mid-1970s,

Table 3
Fatality rates from auto accidents, 1975–1980

Country	Fatalities per 100 million vehicle-miles	
	1975	1980
Australia	5.9	4.9
Belgium	12.1	8.6
Canada	5.6	4.3
Denmark	5.4	4.1
Finland	9.0	3.6
France	10.1	7.3
Germany	9.2	6.7
Italy	7.9	6.6
Japan	8.0	4.8
Netherlands	7.1	5.3
Norway	6.1	3.0
Spain	13.4	12.1
United Kingdom	4.5	3.7
United States	3.5	3.5

Source: Motor Vehicle Manufacturers' Association, *Motor Vehicle Facts and Figures, 1983*, p. 92.

accident and insurance costs represented a greater expense than the costs of fuel (Keeler, Small, and Associates, 1975)—about 3¢ per mile as of the early 1970s. With the decline in gasoline prices since 1981, the costs of motor vehicle accidents are once again about equal to fuel costs. Despite the fact that per capita auto ownership in the United States is very high by world standards (creating the potential for accidents through more crowding and congestion of the roads), the US fatality rate is consistently among the lowest in the world, as indicated in the international comparison provided in table 3. Furthermore, there has been a long-term, secular trend in the United States toward greater auto safety. As table 4 indicates, the fatality rate from auto travel in the United States fell from a rate of 18.2 million vehicle-miles traveled in 1923–1927 to 5.16 in 1961.

This trend toward improved auto safety was the result of many factors, including better highways, better driver training, better law enforcement, and better vehicles. Had this trend continued, automobile safety might not have become a major federal issue in the 1960s any more than it had been for the previous forty years. But, in the early 1960s, a change occurred, one that caused auto safety to come to the forefront as an important policy issue. As table 4 indicates, the auto fatality rate began to increase in 1962, reversing a long downward trend. This change, combined with some well-publicized arguments against the safety of certain auto models (Nader, 1965), brought much attention to the problem in the late 1960s. As a result, pressure mounted,

Table 4
US motor vehicle fatality rates, 1923–1982 (deaths per hundred million vehicle-miles)

Year	Fatality rate
1923–1927 (average)	18.2
1928–1931 (average)	15.6
1933–1934 (average)	15.6
1938–1942 (average)	11.5
1942–1947 (average)	10.5
1950	1.6
1955	6.3
1960	5.3
1961	5.2
1962	5.3
1963	5.4
1964	5.6
1965	5.5
1966	5.7
1967	5.5
1968	5.4
1969	5.2
1970	4.9
1971	4.6
1972	4.4
1973	4.2
1974	3.6
1975	3.5
1976	3.3
1977	3.4
1978	3.4
1979	3.5
1980	3.5
1981	3.3
1982	2.9
1983	2.7

Source: Motor Vehicle Manufacturers' Association, *Motor Vehicle Facts* (various years).

Table 5
Estimated emissions of three automobile-related pollutants, 1950–1970 (teragrams per year)

	Volatile organics (hydrocarbons)		Nitrogen oxides		Carbon monoxide	
	Total	From motor vehicles	Total	From motor vehicles	Total	From motor vehicles
1950	17.5	7.1	9.3	3.4	82.8	46.2
1960	21.6	10.2	12.7	4.6	90.8	63.4
1970	27.1	12.1	18.5	7.5	110.9	86.6

Source: US EPA, *National Air Pollutant Emission Estimates,* January 1982.

in Congress and elsewhere, for the federal government to take a more active role in encouraging and enforcing a higher degree of safety on the nation's roads.

Pollution   In early 1960s it became clear that the internal combustion engine used in automobiles was an important contributor to atmospheric pollution. The emissions of hydrocarbons and nitrogen oxides combine, in the presence of sunlight, to form photochemical oxidants (or "smog") that are a potential threat to human health and to agriculture. In addition, carbon monoxide (CO) emissions were identified as a potential contributor to cardiovascular problems.

Until the 1950s, no one believed that the air pollution caused by automobile exhaust represented a serious enough problem to justify any special public policies. By the 1960s, however, the State of California began to require that all autos sold in the state have emissions control devices. This was the nation's first regulation of auto emissions. By the late 1960s, more and more people were advocating federally mandated emissions controls for all new cars sold in the United States because of the perception that the photochemical smog problem was worsening. There were very few data on the severity of the pollution problem, but subsequent theoretical calculations demonstrate why the smog problem may have been growing (table 5). Emissions of hydrocarbons increased by 23% between 1950 and 1960, while emissions of nitrogen oxides increased by 37%. At the same time, CO emissions were also increasing by 10%, but motor vehicle emissions of CO were increasing by 37%. While these data are at best crude ex post estimates of the growth of the pollution problem in the 1960s, they provide some evidence that the public demand for emissions controls in the 1968–1981 period may well have been justified.

Energy   As long as the United States produced most of its petroleum domestically, and as long as this petroleum was inexpensive, energy consumption was

Table 6
US oil production, oil imports, and gasoline consumption 1950–1973 (million barrels per year)

Year	Domestic oil production (all oils)	Imports (including products)	Gasoline consumption
1950	2,153	309	1,109
1960	2,909	666	1,531
1965	3,290	901	1,676
1970	4,123	1,255	2,131
1973	3,995	2,275	2,452

Source: US Bureau of Mines, *Minerals Yearbook* (annual issues).

not viewed as a problem in the United States. Indeed, prior to the 1970s, US autos were quite inefficient in their energy consumption relative to the cars of other countries, which had higher gasoline prices.

In the early 1970s, however, US energy consumption increased, domestic petroleum production decreased, and the United States found itself importing more and more petroleum (table 6). Gasoline consumption accounted for an increasing share of the total demand for petroleum products throughout the 1960s and 1970s. By 1973, motor vehicles consumed nearly 40% of all petroleum consumed in the United States, an important share of that scarce commodity (Kulp and Holcomb, 1977).

Given the extreme discomforts caused by the oil supply disruptions in 1973–1974, as well as the political risks of being overly dependent on OPEC members for oil supply, it is not surprising that in 1974 automobile energy consumption became a policy concern of the US government. By 1975, Congress had legislated mandatory fuel economy standards for new automobiles and a reduced speed limit for all states receiving federal highway funds. Unfortunately, Congress had also legislated a notoriously inefficient system of crude-oil and refined-product price controls that seriously inhibited the adjustment of the US economy to a world of higher-priced energy by keeping fuel prices below market levels (Kalt, 1981).

2 Reducing Auto Use as a Means of Controlling Its Externality Costs

One alternative for controlling the externalities caused by automobiles is simply to reduce the use of the car. The private automobile is simply a form of transportation, and if people can be induced to use other modes of transportation, these externalities can be reduced. This argument depends, of course, on the assumption that alternative modes of transport impose significantly fewer externality costs than does the private auto—an assumption to be examined below. When most planners talk about "getting people out of their cars," they

Table 7
Deaths of passengers in transportation, 1980

Mode	Passenger-miles (billions) (1980)	Deaths (1980)	Deaths (millions), 1980	Rate per 100 passenger-miles average, 1978–1980
Autos	2,200.0	29,050	1.32	1.30
Buses	85.8	130	0.15	0.15
Urban, school	39.7	107	0.37	N. A.
Intercity	17.3	23	0.13	0.05
Intercity rail	11.0	4	0.04	0.07
Scheduled air	221.2	11	0.01	0.04

Source: National Safety Council (1982), p. 73.

are usually referring to inducing people to substitute urban mass transit (rail or bus) for the private automobile. At the federal, state, and local levels, the most popular approach to this has been through the subsidization of transit, in the hopes that if transit were cheaper, faster, or more comfortable, more people would use it (especially for commutation) rather than their private cars.

The federal government became an important participant in the subsidization of mass transit with the Urban Mass Transit Act of 1964, administered by Urban Mass Transit Administration (UMTA).[2] This program restricted federal support to local transit authorities to capital grants, and provided for the federal government to match state expenditures with $2 of federal support for every $1 of state and local support made available (grants were, however, subject to the approval of UMTA, both in terms of the practicality of the project and UMTA's budget constraints). In the 1970s it became possible for UMTA to provide subsidies for operating expenses, as well as capital outlays.

Subsidizing mass transit would seem to be an appealing way of improving safety, because there is good evidence that public transportation (rail, bus, or air) has a better safety record than the private auto, as vividly demonstrated by table 7. However, as table 8 indicates, public transit has less of an advantage over the automobile in urban transportation than in intercity transportation. Even though public transit appears to be safer than the private automobile, once injuries to nonpassengers are included, its advantage over the private auto disappears. And, as Altschuler has argued, the accident rate for autos is even lower for urban rush hour travel than for urban auto travel as a whole (Altschuler, 1979, p. 225).

There is at least some reason to believe that another serious externality, pollution, could be reduced substantially by a shift away from auto transportation. Table 9 shows that with reasonably full loads, public transportation

Table 8

Urban fatality rates by mode (per 100 million passenger-miles)

Group experiencing fatalities	Mode		
	Auto, truck	Bus	Rail transit
Passengers	0.53	0.07	0.25
Nonoccupants (excludes motocycles)	0.42	0.51	1.65
Overall	0.94	0.58	1.90

Source: Altschuler (1979), table 7.8.

Table 9

Air pollution costs of various transport modes (in 1974 cents)

Mode	Cost per vehicle-mile		United States outside California	Cost per passenger-mile (US)
	United States	California		
Auto				
pre-1961	.36	1.05	.20	.24
1969	.33	.96	.18	.22
1974 (new)	.20	.57	.11	.13
1975 (5 years old)	.35	.74	.14	.17
1974 (composite)	.28	.81	.15	.19
Motorcycle	.07	.21	.04	.07
Diesel bus (50 seats)	.96	2.78	.53	.03
Diesel train (4 cars, 320 seats)	24.46	70.94	13.45	.13
Air (per takeoff, landing; 150 passenger plane) (per passenger-mile)	6.49	18.83	3.57	.0001

Source: Kenneth A. Small, "Estimating the Air Pollution Costs of Transport Modes," *Journal of Transport Economics and Policy* (May 1977), pp. 109–132, table 5. The assumptions about passengers per vehicle for calculating the last column: auto, 1.5 occupants/vehicle; motorcycle, 1 occupant/vehicle; public transportation modes, 60% of seats filled.

Table 10
Energy intensity of transportation modes, 1980

Mode	Energy intensity (1,000 Btu per passenger-mile)
Rail transit	2.6
Commuter rail	2.5
Amtrak	3.2
Air carriers	6.0
General aviation	14.0
Transit buses	2.7
Intercity buses	1.0
Auto	4.4
Motorcycle	3.5

Source: G. Kulp and M. C. Holcomb, *Transportation Energy Data Book*, Park Ridge, NJ: Noyes Data Corp., 1982, p. 20.

generated substantially less pollution than the private auto prior to the imposition of pollution controls in the late 1960s. But by 1974, emissions controls on autos were closing the gap. By 1981, tighter controls on autos made the automobile even more attractive from the standpoint of pollution. In any event, it should be evident from table 9 that pollution costs are a small part of the costs of any mode of passenger transportation. The relative social costs of the various modes (and hence the desirability of using them) are likely to be relatively insensitive to pollution costs.

It is also doubtful that public transportation has a substantial advantage over the private automobile in energy efficiency. Urban buses, operated at average loads, may indeed have some advantage in energy consumption over the private automobile, operated at a typical load of 1–2 passengers (see table 10). However, as Altschuler has argued, if the number of people using urban bus transportation is to be expanded substantially, it is not the average fuel economy of bus transportation that matters, but rather the fuel economy achievable for marginal, extra passengers on newly expanded bus systems (Altschuler, 1979, pp. 155–179).

Moreover, the fuel economy per passenger trip handled on such bus lines tends to be well below the fuel economy achievable with the private automobile. The reason is, of course, that while a full bus is an energy-efficient mode of transportation, a near-empty bus is a highly fuel-inefficient mode. Expansion of bus service into new or marginal neighborhoods more often than not generates near-empty buses.

Prospects for fuel savings through substitution of urban rail transportation for the automobile are even less attractive than for buses because of the energy required to build rail systems (Lave, 1976). Furthermore, with prospective

Table 11
Vehicle-miles traveled in the United States, 1981 (billions)

Vehicle type	Road type		
	Rural	Urban	Total
Autos	456.5	675.8	1,132.3
Buses	3.0	3.4	6.4
Trucks	227.3	184.2	411.5
Total	686.9	863.4	1,550.3

Source: US Federal Highway Administration, *Highway Statistics, 1983.*

improvements in automobile fuel economy likely to occur in the 1980s, rail transit will no longer have an energy advantage over the automobile even for operating costs (Altschuler, 1979, p. 159).

Even if rail and bus transit modes were more socially desirable than the auto from the viewpoint of safety, energy efficiency, and pollution, it is nevertheless far from clear that a substantial number of people can be induced to reduce the use of their cars, even for urban transportation. The only type of urban trip for which public transportation is usually thought to be a viable alternative is for urban work trips in relatively large metropolitan areas. Yet urban vehicle-miles are only half the total, and vehicle-miles by urban autos are less than that, as shown in table 11. Furthermore, urban work trips are themselves well below half the total number of urban vehicle-miles. It is unlikely that many more than half again of those vehicle-miles are in metropolitan areas large enough to support substantial mass transportation activity. Therefore, it is difficult to believe that more than 10–15% of the nation's automobile miles might possibly qualify for replacement by urban mass transit.

Even for those urban areas where mass transit is a potential alternative, commuters may find it an unattractive substitute for private automobiles. With a realistic allowance for the value of most travelers' time, public transportation is often not cost competitive with the private automobile, even with allowances for the costs of publicly provided highways, congestion, and the externalities discussed above. Fixed rail transit would seem to have the greatest disadvantage here: evidence from a study for the San Francisco Bay Area indicates that fixed rail transit is at a cost disadvantage relative to the private auto, even with very high corridor densities, such as a peak-hour flow of 20,000–30,000 passengers.[3] On the other hand, buses with a density of 2,000–5,000 passengers per peak hour have a social cost advantage over the private auto. Unfortunately, only the higher-density urban areas have many corridors that fit this specification. Moreover, for those users with higher-than-average time values, buses may be uneconomical at even these densities.

The above discussion indicates that while there is some hope that an economic rationalization of urban transportation modal choices might increase the share devoted to bus transportation, the reduction in automobile vehicle-miles in the country is likely to be quite small. This is particularly true because urban work trips in large metropolitan areas, the only trips for which urban mass transportation has some hope of replacing the private automobile, are a relatively small proportion of total US vehicle-miles traveled. Transit's higher travel time costs reinforce this conclusion, offsetting the environmental, safety, and energy cost advantages that public transit (especially bus) may enjoy.

2.1 The Role of the Private Auto in Intercity Passenger Transportation

The data presented earlier in this paper suggest that air transportation enjoys an advantage over the private automobile in the areas of safety and pollution, if not necessarily in energy consumption. Furthermore, as air transportation has been deregulated and fares have fallen (especially for discretionary, auto-oriented travelers), it would appear that air transportation has increased market share at the expense of the private auto (see table 13). As incomes rise, air transportation will probably play a greater role in intercity travel in the future, further enhancing safety and environmental quality.

Similarly, it is possible that intercity rail and bus transportation could increase their market shares relative to the private auto. However, given that intercity bus travel is an inferior good (i.e., one that travelers prefer not to use as their incomes rise), and given that intercity rail passenger service is less cost-efficient than air, bus, or auto travel in all but a few high-density corridors (Keeler, 1971), it would seem that the gains to be made in these areas are relatively small.

2.2 Summary

This survey of the evidence on the policy alternatives to the private auto suggests that while there may be a few circumstances under which it would be socially efficient for passengers to replace auto transportation with other modes (most particularly intercity air and perhaps urban bus transportation), the opportunites for increased economic efficiency on the part of society as a whole are quite limited and account for relatively few vehicle-miles traveled. Even if user charges are applied as Pigovian taxes for all the automobile's externalities, they are not likely to lead to a wave of substitution against the private auto.

In other words, the private auto is a highly useful and desired means of transportation to most people. The most promising way to control its adverse effects is not to try artificially to reduce its use, but to "civilize" it—that is, to reduce, either through incentives or direct regulation, its undesirable external effects.

3 The Current Regulatory Framework

The major pieces of regulatory legislation controlling externalities from vehicle use are the Clean Air Act Amendments of 1970 and 1977 (pollution), the National Traffic and Motor Vehicle Safety Act of 1966 (safety), the National Traffic and Motor Vehicle Information and Cost Savings Act of 1972 (safety), and the Energy Policy and Conservation Act of 1975 (fuel economy). The Environmental Protection Agency (EPA) administers the Clean Air Act provisions, while the National Highway Traffic Safety Administration administers safety standards and the Secretary of Transportation is responsible for fuel economy standards.

Air pollution   Unlike most social regulation, emissions standards for automobiles are set by Congress, rather than by an executive-branch agency. The 1970 Clean Air Act Amendments originally set very ambitious goals for the reduction of hydrocarbons (HC), carbon monoxide (CO), and oxides of nitrogen (NO_x). Each was to be reduced by 90 or 95% of average levels in 1970 automobiles. The CO and HC standards were to be 3.4 and .41 gram per mile, respectively, by 1975, while the NO_x standard was to be .4 gram per mile by 1976. These standards were not achieved, as vehicle manufacturers successfully persuaded first EPA and then Congress to delay their implementation.

In the 1977 Clean Air Act Amendments, Congress modified the emissions standards. The original HC and CO standards were put off until the 1980 model year and the NO_x standard was raised to 1 gram per mile for 1981 and beyond. The .4 gram NO_x standard was relegated to a "research" goal. In addition, EPA has the responsibility for making sure that the pollution control systems installed to meet these standards do not degrade rapidly in use. These systems must be certified to work for 50,000 miles, and EPA may require (in nonattainment areas) the implementation of a program for periodic inspection and maintenance.

Safety   Unlike the emissions standards, safety standards are set by an executive-branch agency–the National Highway Traffic Safety Administration. NHTSA promulgates vehicle safety standards and is empowered to order recalls for vehicle defects that create serious safety problems. Most of NHTSA's standards are performance standards, which require that vehicles meet some minimum safety standard under various operating conditions.

Others are less related to occupant safety than to an attempt to reduce repair bills resulting from collisions. Perhaps the most important and best known of these is a requirement that the bumpers of all cars sold in the United States after 1974 should be able to withstand a 5 mile per hour collision with no damage to the cars. This standard, however, was relaxed by the Reagan administration in 1982, though there has been some controversy since that time as to whether it should be reinstated.

Among the most controversial issues before NHTSA is the passive restraint rule, which has been before the Agency and the courts for sixteen years. All told, there are more than 50 separate standards in existence for passenger vehicles.

Fuel economy   In 1975, Congress included in the Energy Policy and Conservation Act a set of "corporate average fuel economy" (CAFE) standards for new cars produced in the United States. These standards require vehicle manufacturers to achieve a sales-weighted fleet average fuel economy of 27.5 miles per gallon in the 1985 model year. The Secretary of Transportation set interim standards of 22 miles per gallon for 1981, 24 miles per gallon for 1982, 26 miles per gallon for 1983, and 27 miles per gallon for 1984. Only cars manufactured in the United States may be used in computing the corporate-wide fuel economy for American-based producers. The Secretary has reduced the standard for the 1986 model year to 26 miles per gallon.

In addition to CAFE standards, the Department of Transportation is ordered to police the requirement that the states enforce 55 mile per hour speed limits by cutting off federal highway funds to states with lax enforcement programs. This sanction has never been used despite considerable evidence of frequent violations. Finally, Congress has enacted gas-guzzler taxes to be imposed as manufacturers' excise taxes on those automobiles falling short of a minimum level of fuel efficiency.

4 The Costs and Benefits of Auto Regulation

The results presented here are based on a much longer and more detailed Brookings Institution study (Crandall et al., 1986), in which the present authors were participants. Readers seeking more detailed analysis and documentation are referred to that study. Although the various regulations do have interactive effects (discussed below), it is nevertheless convenient to discuss the costs and benefits of the various forms of regulation separately.

4.1 The Effects of Safety Regulation

To estimate the costs of safety regulation, we used two alternative approaches, one based on engineering evidence on the cost of each component added to the auto as a result of the regulations, and one based on econometric evidence, relating the regulations to the estimated cost of owning and operating various auto models over a 25-year period. The results of the two studies were reasonably consistent with each other, and they also suggested that the auto manufacturers pass on very nearly the full costs of the regulations, albeit perhaps after a lag of up to a year.

Estimates of benefits of the regulations are based on a detailed econometric analysis of the automobile fatality rate before and during various stages of regulation. The analysis controls for various nonregulatory effects on that fatality rate, including the age of the nation's licensed drivers, alcohol consumption, and other relevant factors. It also takes account of a potentially important offsetting effect first analyzed by Peltzman (1975), which suggests that improved accident protection in a vehicle will induce drivers to take more risks, thereby partially offsetting the effect of the regulation, and also increasing accident risk for pedestrians.

In addition to these empirical results, our benefit-cost analysis of safety regulation requires assumptions regarding the value of early death from accident fatalities. We have chosen a range from $300,000 per fatality avoided (1981 prices) as a lower bound to $1 million as a still-conservative upper bound.

Table 12 summarizes the results of our study. Even at a $300,000 estimate of the cost of a premature death, these estimates produce annual benefits of $10.5 billion. We estimate that the annual costs of safety regulation range between $671 and $981 per car produced, or, at an annual production rate of 10.5 million cars per year, the total costs are $7.0–$10.3 billion. Without the standards requiring bumpers to keep the car intact in a 5 mile per hour collision, the cost is only $4.9–$6.9 billion. Only the most pessimistic of assumptions concerning the effect of safety regulation and the value of reducing premature death will provide an unfavorable ratio of life-and-injury saving benefits to costs. But there are other benefits, and some of the costs should not properly be attributed to saving lives or reducing injuries.

Based on evidence from the National Highway Traffic Safety Administration (1983), $40 billion of the $57 billion in annual motor vehicle accident costs are not associated with life and limb. Medical costs are only $3.3 billion

Table 12
Estimates of the benefits and costs of automobile safety regulation (billions of 1981 dollars)

Benefits (injury and fatality reductions only)

Assumption	Reductions in premature deaths	Reductions in deaths and injuries, $(1) \times 1.50$	@$1 million/ fatality avoided (Estimated value)	@$300,000/ fatality avoided (Estimated value)
Optimistic	23,400	35,100	35.10	10.53
Pessimistic	13,000	19,500	19.50	5.85

Costs	Cost per car ($ per car)	Annual cost, 10.5 million cars		Annual costs less costs of bumpers with 10.5 million cars
Optimistic	671	7.0		4.9
Pessimistic	981	10.3		6.9

Source: See Crandall et al. (1986).

of the $57 billion, while property damage is $21 billion. Moreover, other costs, such as insurance administration, legal, and court costs, and public sector emergency-service costs add $18.7 billion to the total costs of motor vehicle accidents. It is difficult to know how a reduction in the fatality-injury rate affects these various cost components, but it clearly must reduce many of them. For instance, the $18.7 billion in insurance administration and public sector costs must certainly be affected by the extent and severity of accidents. Even if these have only been reduced by 10% as a result of improved crashworthiness of passenger cars, the annual savings would be enough to make even the pessimistic estimate of benefits greater than the gross cost of safety regulation. In short, there is considerable evidence that the benefits from safer passenger cars are at least as great as the costs and perhaps substantially greater. Whether these improvements in safety are solely the result of regulation or not, they have been worth it.

On the other hand, the evidence supporting the now-rescinded 5 mile per hour bumper standard is much weaker. It suggests that if the standard is justified, people should be willing to pay for it, trading off the savings from lower insurance rates afforded by it. It is difficult to find an economic rationale for imposing it on motorists.

4.2 The Effects of Emissions Regulation

Once again, we used a combination of econometric and engineering methods to analyze the costs of emissions regulation. The evidence indicates that as of the

1979 model year, the cost was about $560 per car, or $5.9 billion overall. But the more onerous 1981 model year standards raised this total to as much as $16.2 billion. It is possible that our methods have overestimated these costs; nevertheless, the annual costs of the current automobile emissions program are certainly in excess of $10 billion per year for an annual output of 10.5 million cars.

Benefits of auto emissions regulation are difficult to estimate for several reasons. First, the relationship between emissions and ambient levels of pollutants is a complicated one, controlled by climate, topography, and interaction with stationary emissions sources. Second, to the extent that there is a relationship between ambient pollutant levels and human health, the relationship is not well-understood, and many researchers question whether it exists at all. Third, the aesthetic benefits of clear visibility and lack of discomfort from smog are difficult to quantify in dollar terms. Fourth, while emissions regulation does indeed have an effect on the emissions of cars, the program does not appear to be working as well as some of its advocates had hoped in controlling emissions. This is because of violations of the rules (disconnecting of equipment or use of leaded gasoline), failures of the emissions-control equipment, and a tendency to keep older, uncontrolled vehicles longer as a result of regulation (to avoid the higher prices and reduced performance of controlled cars).

It is likely that emissions regulation has gone far past the point where the incremental benefits equal the incremental costs. This can be documented by noting that there are far less expensive ways of achieving the same aggregate pollution rates, simply by controlling stationary sources more and autos less.[4]

Based on the evidence we have surveyed, stopping with the 1979 federal standards would have been a far more cost-effective approach to emissions controls than the program as it has developed. Such a change would save the nation over $5 billion per year (in 1981 prices), with little additional environmental degradation.

4.3 Effects of Fuel Economy Regulation

To analyze the effects of fuel economy regulation, we first attempted to predict the fuel economy that would likely have been achieved without it. This was accomplished by examining the trade-off between the cost of building a car to save fuel and the cost of the fuel itself. The results show that the automobile producers' increase in fuel economy through the 1981 model year is about what one should have expected given the rise in gasoline prices since 1973. CAFE appears to have provided little but nuisance value until recently. As gasoline prices have fallen in real terms since 1981, the CAFE standards have become a binding constraint upon producers attempting to satisfy the demand for larger cars.

Should the CAFE program be continued? At the present time, one finds it very difficult to argue that automobile drivers should not respond to market prices of energy in the same fashion as commercial, industrial, or residential users of liquid hydrocarbons. If there is a societal case for increasing conservation efforts (and it appears rather weak as of 1986, with oil prices at $12 per barrel), the appropriate mechanism is (as suggested by Adelman, 1971, chapters 7 and 8 and others) a federal tax on the use of all liquid and gaseous hydrocarbons, not a set of technological standards applied to new cars. The CAFE standards only encourage higher large-car prices and the postponement of replacement decisions. This postponement is counterproductive with respect to the policy of reducing emissions, vehicle deaths, and fuel consumption.

4.4 Comparison with Results of Other Studies

It is natural to ask how the results shown here compare with those of other studies of the benefits and costs of auto regulation. Any systematic comparison is difficult if not impossible, because (at least to our knowledge), no other study has attempted a systematic look at all aspects of auto safety, emissions, and fuel economy regulation. Nevertheless, previous studies have considered some of the same individual issues in auto regulation as are considered here.

In the area of emissions regulation, our results are generally consistent with those of White (1982; see Crandall et al., 1986). Indeed, for one set of calculations, we used his estimates as the basis for ours (our results on the costs of emissions regulation were further substantiated by a separate econometric study, as mentioned above). White's estimates (and hence our own) lie in between those of two earlier studies, one by the Environmental Protection Agency, and another by Schwing and associates at General Motors Research Laboratories.[5] Thus, for 1979, our results (as previously mentioned) suggest a cost for emissions regulations of $560 per car produced. Converting the estimates from the other studies to 1981 prices would suggest values for them of about $300 per car for the EPA and $800–$1,000 per car for GM Labs (both are based on engineering estimation techniques that are impossible to replicate). As White argued previously, the EPA may have an incentive to understate the costs of regulation, and, if anything, GM has an incentive to overstate it,. so that in lying between these two bounds, our estimates are at least plausible.

Concerning the effects of safety regulation, again, there are no readily available numerical results directly comparable with our own. Indeed, concerning the costs of safety regulation, our study attempts to achieve at least a rough consistency with estimates for varying years done by the General Accounting Office, the Bureau of Labor Statistics, and NHTSA.[6] Regarding the benefits of safety regulation, our conclusions are more sanguine than those of Peltzman (1975), who found that safety regulation had different effects upon occupants and pedestrians (because safer cars induce drivers to take more risks, thereby causing more fatalities to both motorists and pedestrians). While our results take account of the effect hypothesized by Peltzman, we nevertheless find positive overall benefits. Although the equation we used to estimate these benefits is similar to that of Peltzman in some ways, it is dissimilar in that it is estimated over a longer period of time than is Peltzman's equation, and it is also specified somewhat differently, with a direct measure of the safety of the automobile stock included.

4.5 Conflicting Goals of Regulation

As this brief summary of evidence from a larger study suggests, the individual regulatory programs affecting the automobile industry have a mixed track record. Safety regulation appears to have worked tolerably well, emissions regulation may have served to reduce air pollution, although at a very high cost to society since 1981, and fuel-economy regulation appears to have been largely an irrelevancy until the recent decrease in gasoline prices.

But how well have these regulatory programs been coordinated to achieve maximum impact for the lowest cost? The simple answer is "Not at all," since each program was developed and is administered separately from the others. Furthermore, the full story is even more complicated, for the very structure of these programs has been counterproductive to the rapid achievement of clean air, safe highways, and reduced gasoline consumption. For example, the large regulatory costs have reduced the replacement rate for automobiles. Therefore, Congress and the regulators have (at least in the shorter run) served to exacerbate the very problems that they thought they were curing.

The most straightforward of these conflicts are the ones between fuel economy on the one hand and the extra weight and fuel consumption caused by emissions and safety regulations on the other. Our analysis, together with that by White (1982), suggests that safety and emissions regulations combined have reduced the fuel efficiency of the new vehicle fleet by around 10.5%. As we have already argued, however, some of these regulations are likely to be cost-effective. If, however, 1977–1979 emissions standards (which are far more likely to be cost-effective than the present ones) were held and never exceeded, the new car fleet would have been 4% more fuel efficient *and* total vehicle emissions of CO and HC would have been lower for the first years of the 1980s (this is true because with lower emissions standards, newer vehicles would be cheaper and more attractive, and more people would buy them). A decision not to impose the 5 mile per hour bumper standard in the late 1970s and early 1980s would have added another 2 percentage points to the fuel efficiency of the new car fleet.

4.6 Conflicts Involving Indirect and Feedback Effects

A second, but often neglected conflict in auto fuel economy regulation has been overall energy policy. Kalt (1981) has estimated that the entitlements policy may have kept gasoline prices as much as 8% below world market clearing levels. Surely this encouraged inefficient use of fuel in transportation, including personal autos.

Because they applied only to new cars, another effect of the auto regulations was to encourage people to keep older cars longer than they otherwise would have done. This has had the already mentioned undesirable effects on safety and emissions, but in addition to that, it has caused higher fuel consumption, because older cars have tended to be less fuel efficient.

Another important adverse feedback of auto regulatory policies has been in the area of output, employment, and profits in the US auto industry. Had the regulations not existed, auto prices would have been lower, and industry output and employment would have been higher. This, as well, is clearly a policy concern of the US government, as evidenced by its recent policies of restricting Japanese imports to protect US industry. By our estimates, had the bumper regulations never been implemented, and had emissions controls stayed at 1979 levels, each car produced in 1981 would have been $621 cheaper than it actually was, and new car sales would been higher by 800,000 or more. This would obviously have had a strong positive economic effect on Detroit. By our estimates, for example, as of 1981, the US auto industry would have enjoyed a 5.7% higher level of employment and 22.9% greater net cash flow. While these numbers are only suggestive, they do indicate that more cost-effective regulatory policies would have had a highly beneficial effect on American auto producers and American auto employment.

Yet another effect of auto regulation has been on product quality. There is evidence that American cars have indeed suffered more severe reliability problems during the 1972–1974 and 1978–1982 periods, and each of these periods has been one of sharply tighter emissions requirements. The problems occurring in 1978–1982 are especially unfortunate, given that Detroit was required to make substantial changes in its vehicles simply to stay competitive with the Japanese, and the additional changes required by the sharp tightening of emissions standards during that period may have made this task more difficult, reducing the reliability of Detroit's cars.

5 Conclusions

The record of US policy toward the private automobile is a mixed one. On the positive side, there has been very little attempt to limit the use of the car by subsidizing its substitutes. Indeed, the declining budget of the Urban Mass Transit Administration (UMTA) is an indication of a movement away from this approach, as is the decision in 1983 substantially to increase expenditures on highway improvement. In addition, the Air Deregulation Act of 1978 would appear to have had a favorable effect on externalities from autos, because the lower plane fares resulting from it have encouraged intercity travelers to substitute air travel for auto travel, with concurrent reductions in the pollution and safety costs of auto use (see table 13).

Furthermore, there is evidence that safety regulation has been quite cost effective, with the possible exception of the 5 mile per hour bumper standard. And through 1979, the evidence is that the emissions standards were also reasonably cost effective, although this assumes considerable value for the aesthetic improvements from reducing smog.

On the other hand, US policy toward the private auto has also had some significant failures. Most important, the emissions controls imposed since 1979 are quite expensive and difficult to justify on the basis of cost effectiveness. Furthermore, these recent emissions regulations have had undesirable indirect effects in the form of substantially higher energy consumption, lower employment and profits in Detroit, lower reliability of new cars, and even higher levels of pollution in the short term, because of their effect upon the cost of producing automobiles. These higher costs have led to higher new-car prices that have caused postponement of auto replacement decisions, causing older, less fuel efficient and more polluting vehicles to stay in the fleet.

What are the implications of these results for future policies? Moving emissions controls back to 1979 levels would clearly have a salutary effect, although it would not be as effective as a policy that never implemented the tighter emissions controls (many of the costs involved in getting 1981 emissions levels are already sunk and cannot be recovered). Similarly, it would appear most reasonable not to reinstitute the 5 mile per hour bumper standard. The public could well vote for this standard through the marketplace, but it

Table 13
Autos and other modes in intercity travel (billions of passenger-miles)

Year	Auto	Bus	Rail	Air	Total
1960	706	19	22	34	781
1965	818	24	18	58	917
1970	1,026	25	11	119	1,181
1975	1,171	25	10	148	1,355
1976	1,260	25	11	164	1,460
1977	1,316	26	10	177	1,529
1978	1,362	26	11	203	1,601
1979	1,322	28	12	228	1,590
1980	1,300	27	11	219	1,558
1981	1,344	27	12	216	1,599
1982	1,345	27	11	227	1,609
1983	1,400	26	11	245	1,682
Percentage shares					
1960	90.4%	2.4%	2.8%	4.4%	
1965	89.2%	2.6%	1.9%	6.3%	
1970	86.9%	2.1%	0.9%	10.0%	
1975	86.4%	1.9%	0.7%	10.9%	
1976	86.3%	1.7%	0.7%	11.3%	
1977	86.1%	1.7%	0.7%	11.6%	
1978	85.1%	1.6%	0.7%	12.7%	
1979	83.2%	1.7%	0.7%	14.4%	
1980	83.4%	1.8%	0.7%	14.1%	
1981	84.1%	1.7%	0.7%	13.5%	
1982	83.6%	1.7%	0.7%	14.1%	
1983	83.2%	1.6%	0.6%	14.6%	

Source: Motor Vehicle Manufacturers' Association, *Motor Vehicle Facts, 1984.*

should not be enforced by the government. If people want the insurance cost savings afforded by this standard, they should stand ready to pay for them.

In the area of safety, there is currently some degree of controversy surrounding the issue of passive restraints. In a world in which consumer sovereignty were respected, there would be no reason for mandatory air bags or passive restraints, because the existing seat belt or shoulder harness is in fact safer than either option. The reason for these regulations stems from the fact that current seat belts and shoulder harnesses are used by only 10–15% of US drivers and passengers, and either passive belts or air bags could achieve a higher rate of protection for front-seat occupants. Passive belts have the strong advantage of low cost, but the disadvantage that they are easily disabled. On the other hand, motorists have little incentive to disable air bags, but they are expensive (adding $300–$400 to the price of a new car in 1981 prices) and may be unreliable.

A mandatory seat belt use law—if it were enforceable—would be a cheaper alternative, as would an insurance system that refused to compensate for casualties resulting from the failure to use seat belts. If, on the other hand, these policies do not appear to be politically feasible, and if a paternalistic concern for the value of human life overrides concerns for consumer sovereignty, it is possible that air bags are justified on a benefit-cost basis.[7] Our estimates show that they can indeed be justified for a value of early deaths of $500,000 or more per person. But even this argument must be qualified by noting that this calculation does not account for the fact that the higher cost of cars resulting from this regulation will cause some motorists to postpone the purchase of new cars, with adverse effects on the pollution, safety, and fuel economy of the fleet in use.

Another potential reform is in the area of fuel economy regulation. To the extent that it is believed that the marketplace does not provide adequate fuel conservation incentives (and we question that this is a problem in 1986), a tax on all fuel consumption would be a much more efficient way to conserve energy. Moreover, the CAFE standards, penalizing larger cars as they do, make Detroit's battle against foreign competition more difficult. All these considerations suggest that the most appropriate reform of the CAFE regulations would be to eliminate them.

Overall, then, our results suggest that most changes in public policy toward the private auto should entail a reduction in regulation, rather than an increase. This is especially true in the areas of emissions and fuel economy.

Notes

1. A summary of these policies and programs may be found in Meyer and Gomez-Ibanez (1981).

2. More detailed discussion of this history can be found in Meyer and Gomez-Ibanez (1981), chapter 1.

3. Keeler, Small, and Associates (1975). See also Meyer, Kain, and Wohl (1965).

4. See Crandall et al. (1986); Lave (1976), chapter 5; White (1982).

5. US Environmental Protection Agency (1979); Schwing and others (1980); US Bureau of Labor Statistics (1980).

6. US Comptroller General (1976); US Bureau of Labor Statistics (1980); unpublished NHTSA studies of the costs of meeting various safety regulations.

7. The paternalism inherent in a decision for mandatory air bags could be justified by noting that our health insurance and welfare system already provide such paternalistic protection for those injured in auto accidents and their families; our health care system

subsidizes needy people injured in auto accidents, and our welfare system supports those families whose primary earners are killed or injured in auto accidents. It can thus be argued that given our society's decision to support these groups, a "paternalistic" policy of mandatory air bags could reduce the total burden on taxpayers and motorists. But more evidence is needed before such arguments can be accepted.

7   The Evolution of Oil as a Commodity

Philip K. Verleger, Jr.

Shortly after the *World Petroleum Market* was published in 1972, the late macro economist Otto Eckstein asked the question, "What is the price of oil?" This question was asked again and again as prices (whatever they were) tripled. Through this period of time it was difficult to answer the question because tax regimes and royalty arrangements were so complicated. After much hemming and hawing invariably one would guess that price should be about x. This answer was usually followed by a second question, "How do you know that the price of oil is x?" Here the answer never changed. It was simply, "I am following Adelman."

Morry Adelman's volume provided economists of the early 1970s with a basis by which they could determine the value of oil. The study laid bare the mechanism by which economic value could and should be attached to the feedstocks awaiting export from the Persian Gulf. Although complicated, the message emerging from the study was the irrelevance of posted crude prices except as to determine the allocation of rents between the resource owner and oil company. The distinction made by Morry in 1972 was necessary because trade in oil in the 1960s and 1970s was extremely light.

Twelve years after the publication of the *World Petroleum Market* few of the vestiges of market contracts remain. Commercial trading has come to dominate the oil business. The change was noticed recently by Niering (1984), who stated that "up to 40–50 percent of world oil trade now takes place in the spot market."

The evolution of the oil market may be noted from the explosion of daily petroleum publications. In 1972 *Platt's Oil Price Survey*, one of the two major price publications relied upon in Morry's work, contained little or no discussion of spot prices in crude markets. The focus was on posted prices and on assessment of spot product prices in the two major product markets: Rotterdam and New York. *Petroleum Intelligence Weekly* (*PIW*), the other primary source of market data in Professor Adelman's work, carried even fewer references. Today the situation has changed: *PIW* carries detailed monthly assessments of spot crude prices and conditions in spot markets. These reports are updated in every issue. Further, coverage has been extended to the eastern market in Singapore, where a third center of world trade has developed. *Platt's* has also changed. Spot crude prices are reported daily and roughly one-quarter of the analysis is devoted to conditions on spot crude markets.

Moreover, *Platts* and *PIW* are no longer the only major sources of data on spot crude and product prices. Both publications face intense competition from vendors of instantaneous reports via electronic media including Reuters and Telerate. The competition has become so intense that the publishers of *Platts* have augmented the basic price reports with daily telexes on market conditions and instantaneous reports via computers. The expansion of the electronic market was symptomatic of the transformation of oil from the relatively controlled conditions that existed in 1973 to a true commodity market.

The evolution of the petroleum market can be traced to a number of forces. Among these are

• the nationalization of the producing interests of multinational oil companies,

• the failure of exporting countries to manage production in a manner which stabilized prices,

• creation of new outlets for crude oil by exporting countries,

• the entry of exporting countries into downstream product markets,

• the drastic decline in consumption of petroleum (and resulting surplus in refinery capacity),

• the change in character of petroleum demand,

• the adoption of rigid price control regimes in some consuming countries,

• the adoption of punitive tax systems on resource production, and

• the development of North Sea production and the abandonment of traditional markets by major integrated oil companies in favor of secure, "rationalized," and defendable market areas.

Oil has become a commodity because the oil exporting countries failed to maintain an environment in which the multinational companies could continue to operate profitably. These firms have elected to cut back or withdraw from regions, restricting their activities to those areas, such as the United States, Canada, and the United Kingdom, where they have a reasonably good chance of remaining profitable. The withdrawals have, however, created opportunities for new independent marketers and traders to enter the market, and for new institutions to develop.

Most of these changes have occurred during the "OPEC decade," and their effect has been to make the oil market more competitive. Had these changes occurred ten years earlier many of the detailed calculations given in the 25 detailed numerical appendixes in *The World Petroleum Market* would have been unnecessary. Thus the effect of the "OPEC decade" has been to lift the veil that concealed the details of trade in oil until 1972. Morry was one of the few outsiders to pierce the veil for everyone before the industry was transformed.

This paper explores the evolution of the petroleum market. It is argued that oil has become more like other widely traded commodities, such as corn, wheat, copper, and silver. In a word, oil has been "commoditized."

To understand the nature and importance of the change we begin by describing the characteristics of commonly traded commodities and attempt to note the manner in which oil has taken on the attributes of these commodities. We then seek to identify the changes in industry structure that can be credited (blamed) for causing the metamorphosis of oil. Finally, we attempt to assess the status of the evolution of oil toward a true commodity.

1 General Characteristics of Traded Commodities

The theoretical and empirical behavior of commodity markets has been the subject of countless economic treatises. The list of distinguished economists who have written on the subject includes Keynes, Hicks, Houthakker, and Samuelson. Generally economists have been fascinated with the impact of price volatility, the role of inventories, as well as the parts played by the principal protagonists, hedgers, and speculators. Much of the applied literature has been written in the context of description and analysis of futures markets and the relationship between futures markets and cash markets. However, many of the conclusions apply to those commodity markets that exist without a parallel futures market.

An examination of the research on commodity markets leads one to the conclusion that widely and successfully traded commodities enjoy three or four basic characteristics. Hieronymus (1982, p. 21) lists three characteristics common to successfully traded commodities. "First, they are all bulk commodities that can be described and the separate lots of which are more or less interchangable. Second, none of the commodities has been processed or manufactured to the point of being a product identified with the processes of a particular firm; in general they are bulk commodities but are not, in a strict sense, raw materials. Third, prices are variable and relatively competitively determined."

The US Commodity Futures Trading Commission (the US Government's regulator of the commodity industry) has adopted a longer and more precise list of six criteria to define a commodity that may be eligible for futures trading, a list that actually dates to Baer and Saxon (1948). These criteria require that a commodity meet the following conditions:

First, the commodity must be sold in homogeneous units. A trader buys or sells a commodity according to established grades, not specific lots or identifiable units.

Second, the commodity obviously must be susceptible to standardization. Trade in a commodity cannot take place unless units can be standardized and grades established so that units can be made interchangable.

Third, the supply and demand must be large. Hieronymus notes that trading in small markets is often unsuccessful because speculators with large financial resources may gain control of either supply or demand so that the market "ceases to be natural and free" and becomes instead "merely a battleground for contending speculative factions." (Hieronymus, 1982, p. 20.)

Fourth, the supply of the commodity "should flow naturally to the market" unimpaired by artificial restraint imposed by governments or private organizations.

Fifth, supply and demand must be uncertain. Baer and Saxon suggest that prices may be readily adjusted without the intervention of market machinery if supply and demand are known with certainty. A market is required, however, where supply and demand are both large, uncertain, and subject to wide variations from year to year.

Sixth, the commodity must be storable so that forward and futures contracting can take place.

Since trade exists in some commodities that do not satisfy all of these criteria, one must conclude that these conditions do not represent necessary and sufficient conditions for the existence of markets. For instance, trade in grains is large and well established despite significant government intervention. Daily trade in foreign currencies, currently estimated to be in the range of hundreds of billions, takes place despite periodic central bank intervention. Further, trade in eggs, broilers, and live hogs is well established despite the obviously perishable nature of the commodity. Thus these criteria provide only a framework for evaluating the comparability between various markets.

In this context they provide a useful basis for assessing the evolution of the oil market.

In this connection it may be noted that most texts and studies of futures markets written in the 1960s and 1970s include grains and live stocks, lumber, industrial metals, precious metals, and financial instruments as items where trade can and will take place. Crude oil and petroleum products were notable by their exclusion. By 1985, however, crude oil and petroleum products could be found on many of the standard lists signifying its emergence as a true commodity.

The World Petroleum Market and the well publicized events occurring subsequent to its publication provide a clear explanation for the emergence of oil as another commodity. When Morry finished this seminal work international trade in crude oil was controlled by seven companies while production in the United States was managed by five state regulatory authorities. Increases in demand were relatively predictable and stable. Further, there was little variance in prices. The conditions for a successful commodity markets were not fulfilled.[1]

2 The Factors That Contributed to the Evolution of the Petroleum Market

The evolution of this market from the controlled environment of the period prior to 1973 into the relatively free market of the 1970s can be traced to a number of factors. Changes experienced in the 1970s appeared to

- affect the flow of the oil to the market,
- make the level of supply and demand uncertain, and
- contribute to an increase in price volatility.

The nationalization of the producing interests belonging to the multinational companies, together with changes in the process by which crude prices were set, caused multinational oil companies to reduce their activity as distributors of crude oil and created the opportunity for entry by other firms, such as Japanese trading companies. The variation in the level of supply and demand increased simultaneously with the nationalizations. During the 1970s and 1980s, year-to-year variation in consumption rose as a consequence of more erratic economic activity, higher real prices of oil, and vacillating regulations relating to fuel choice. At the same time, new sources of supply from the North Sea, Mexico, Alaska, Malaysia, and other countries were put on the market.

Volatility in prices increased due to the revision of tax regimes in consuming countries (principally the introduction of the Windfall Tax in the United States and the Petroleum Revenue Tax in the United Kingdom) and the creation of a crude oil futures market. The introduction of trading in crude oil futures increased volatility in prices by drastically cutting the cost and risks of speculation.

2.1 Changes in the Flow of Oil to the Market

Changes in both the pattern by which oil is moved from the well to the market and the economic incentives affecting oil production have represented a major force in the evolution of oil as a commodity. These changes have included alterations in traditional relationships between producing countries and the multinational oil companies, discoveries and developments in other lands, and changes in economic incentives to lift oil. In the 1960s and early 1970s the multinational oil companies were joined in an implicit (or perhaps explicit) partnership with the producing nations under which they shared any increase or decrease in revenues due to fluctuations in price or volume. This partnership had become a distant memory by the 1980s.

2.1.1 The Replacement of the Majors as the Agents of the Producing Countries
Adelman made a detailed examination of concentration and integration in *The World Petroleum Market*. The ultimate purpose of the study was "to explain and predict price behavior" (Adelman, 1972, p. 78). He noted "the fewer sellers in any given market, the better chance of cooperative action" (Adelman, 1972, p. 78). To this end he examined both the concentration of total Free World production controlled by the majors and joint production agreements between companies. The first concept provided a classical measure of concentration in the industry. The measure of joint production or joint venture offered a more subtle measure of market control. He noted, "Since the heart of the problem is the control of output, we need to ask what a joint venture does about bringing the production plans of its members into line. Can each partner order out as much as he likes without being penalized for it, and regardless of the others' opinion that he may be spoiling the market?" (Adelman, 1972, p. 83).

Morry's calculations led him to conclude that the market was concentrated in 1972, and that joint agreements had an impact on supply. He noted, "Each (firm) can be assured that nothing is contemplated to threaten an excess of supply and a threat to price" (Adelman, 1972, p. 88). By 1984 the multinationals' share of oil moved to the market had declined dramatically. Further, joint agreements had become a thing of the past.

Table 1

OPEC nations' share of Free World oil production, excluding North America and eight company share[a] of the market (%)

Year	OPEC share (%)	Eight Company share of OPEC sales (%)
1950	NG[b]	100
1957	NG[b]	92
1966	90	84
1969 (first half)	87	81

Source: Adelman (1972), p. 81.

a. The eight companies were Esso, B.P., C.F.P., Gulf, Mobil, Standard Oil of California, Shell, and Texaco.

b. NG = not given.

2.1.1.1 The Decline in Market Shares   The seven major multinationals accounted for the most oil sold in international trade until 1979. Adelman noted the high concentration of supply in table III.1 of the *World Petroleum Market*. His calculations are summarized in table 1.

The companies covered by Morry include the traditional seven majors (Esso, B.P., Gulf, Mobil, Standard of California, Shell, and Texaco) along with C.F.P (Companie Françoise Petroleum). According to Adelman, C.F.P. accounted for 4.7% of the liftings from OPEC, leaving the seven majors with 76.1% of the 1969 market.

In his calculations, Morry segregated the world market by separating the North American market from the rest of the Free World. While this distinction may seem arbitrary, his choice makes sense because the United States had become an economically isolated market by 1958. Imports were limited by a mandatory quota while domestic production was tightly controlled by various state regulatory agencies.

Vernon (1983) has recently updated Adelman's calculations to 1979. In that year his calculations indicate that the seven major oil companies distributed only 24% of OPEC production, while the share of oil distributed directly by producing country exporting companies had increased to 69% from zero in the same time period. In the same year calculations made by this author from *PIW* data indicate that OPEC accounted for 84% of the oil distributed to the Free World market excluding North America.

By 1983 the share of the market controlled by the seven majors further decreased as had OPEC's share. Rough estimates of market shares indicate that the equity production controlled by the seven majors accounted for approximately 14% of OPEC production and 14% of non-OPEC, non-North American output. In addition, the majors appeared to have purchased another 11% of

OPEC controlled production. At the same time, OPEC's share of Free World production outside of North America had declined to 59%.

Thus, in sixteen years OPEC's share of the market had declined from 87% to 60%, while the seven majors' share had declined from 75.7% to a mere 18%. The majors had been replaced by a large number of medium sized oil companies, producing country oil companies, consuming country oil companies, and traders.

2.1.1.2 The Demise of Joint Agreements   The loss of market share incurred by the major oil companies was accompanied by the demise in joint producing agreements. The joint arrangements that were of concern to Adelman in 1972 seemed to have become a thing of the past by 1984. The change in the industry may be noted from tables 2 and 3. Table 2, taken from *The World Petroleum Market*, displays the distribution of crude production in 1969 by exporting countries distributed by major producing companies. Adelman notes, "In the tables, the eight large companies are arranged as much as possible according to their important joint ventures" (Adelman, 1972, p. 81). Table 3 presents the author's attempt to make the same calculation for 1984. It may be noted that the problem of joint production agreements had mostly become an historical artifact.

The demise of joint producing agreements has undoubtedly increased the competitive pressure between exporting countries. In the 1960s and 1970s exporting countries experienced great difficulties when they attempted to increase their share of the market because the operators (usually working under a joint agreement) would actively discourage or refuse to increase liftings. (The experience of Iran in 1952 provides a classic example of this phenomenon.) By 1984 the situation had changed. In many cases the country was the sole operator and could vary production as it wished, effectively reducing constraints on the volume of oil moved to the market.

2.1.2 Increase in Non-OPEC Production

The expansion of production in new areas of the world represents the second factor that contributed to an increase in the flow of uncontrolled oil to the market. As table 4 indicates, OPEC accounted for almost 90% of non-North American Free World production in 1973 but less than 65% of this output in 1983. The primary increase in output had come from Egypt, Mexico, Norway, and the United Kingdom. Each of these countries has followed vigorous market efforts to make sure that the maximum possible volume of oil was produced and sold every year. Further, the role of the majors was considerably circum-

Table 2
Production of principal crude oil companies and producing countries in the world oil market, 1969: first half (thousand barrels per day)

	Esso	Mobil	SoCal	Texaco	B.P.	Gulf	Shell	C.F.P.	Others	Total
Persian Gulf										
Iran	208	208	208	208	1,192	298	417	178	394	3,223
Iraq	181	181			361		361	361	76	1,520
Qatar	23	23			45		203	45	9	348
Abu Dhabi	49	49			236		99	167	21	620
Kuwait					1,254	1,254				2,508
Saudi Arabia	870	289	870	870						2,898
Oman							256		45	301
Other										
Subtotal	1,331	750	1,073	1,073	3,087	1,462	1,335	751	999	11,871
Africa										
Libya	683	126	181	181	155		119		1,561	3,006
Algeria							85	249	602	936
Nigeria					168	200	168			536
Other						36	63		406	505
Indonesia[a]	25	25	285	285			138		90	848
Venezuela	1,472	112	56	171		383	916		424	3,534
Total	3,511	1,013	1,600	1,692	3,433	2,081	2,824	1,000	4,082	21,236

Source: Adelman (1972) pp. 80–81.
a. Includes Brunei and Sarawak.

Table 3

Production of principal crude oil companies and producing countries in the world oil market, 1984: first half[a]

	Esso	Mobil	SoCal	Texaco	B.P.	Gulf	Shell	C.F.P.	Others	National oil companies	Total
Persian Gulf											
Iran										2,164	2,164
Iraq										1,152	1,152
Qatar	7	7			15		15	15	107	250	416
Abu Dhabi	15	15			36		36	36	183	482	803
Kuwait										983	983
Saudi Arabia										4,951	4,951
Oman									1	403	403
Other				35					724	839	1,598
Subtotal	22	22		35	41		41	41	1,015	11,224	12,470
Africa											
Libya									686	481	1,167
Algeria										617	617
Nigeria		176	28	28		173	715		252		1,372
Other				10		182	16	11	538		756
Indonesia[b]		95	305	305			173		815		1,693
Malaysia	246						216				462
Venezuela										1,820	1,820
Ecuador				216					27	4	247
Total	268	292	333	594	41	355	1,161	52	3,043	14,146	20,604

Source: *Oil and Gas Journal* 82:53 (31 December 1984).

a. Adelman notes, "There are numerous small discrepancies among all these sources and it is impossible to reconcile them fully." The same comment applies here. Volumes of production are assigned to companies listed in the Oil and Gas Journal Worldwide Report. In some cases the production is shared between two or more companies. In other cases, the production is shared with the government. In this table these distinctions have been ignored except in the case of the well known production sharing agreements. Data published in company annual reports will differ from the totals shown here because companies include only the share of production that is actually owned by a company.

b. Includes Brunei and Sarawak.

Table 4

Relative share of Free World, non-North America production by OPEC and other producing countries, 1973 and 1983 (thousand barrels per day)

Area	1973		1983	
	Production	Share (%)	Production	Share (%)
OPEC	31,600	69.6	18,700	63.2
Mexico	550	1.6	2,950	10.0
United Kingdom	—	—	2,360	8.0
Egypt	225	0.6	775	2.6
Norway	35	0.1	625	2.1
Argentina	420	1.2	490	1.7
Others	2,040	6.9	3,370	12.4

Source: *British Petroleum Statistical Year Book, 1984.*

scribed in these new producing countries although they have played a major role in developing fields in the United Kingdom and Norway.

2.1.3 The Change in Economic Incentives

The decline in the share of crude moved by the multinational oil companies is generally attributed to the nationalization of the concessions by exporting countries. However, the loss of ownership need not have caused an almost total withdrawal by the majors from marketing crude produced in lands where they were formally active. Indeed, the companies remained several years after nationalization. As late as 1978 the seven majors were marketing approximately 4 million barrels per day to third party buyers according to *Petroleum Intelligence Weekly.*[2] Thus the seven majors still accounted for 46% of the market outside of the United States if their sales to third parties are added to the 13 million barrels per day of product these companies reported distributing.[3] However, during 1979 most of the crude sales to third parties were dropped because such sales had become unprofitable.

The major impetus to the termination of third party sales was the financial loss incurred by the majors during 1977 and 1978, followed by restrictive conditions imposed at the peak of the 1979, which prevented sellers from profiting during the tight market. *PIW* described the problems experienced by the majors at that time (*PIW* 18(19): 1, 7 May 1979):

The oil companies now charging price premiums are extremely sensitive about the subject but make no apologies for action they defend as 'eminently reasonable.' Otherwise they see no point in third-party sales when their traditional base of low-cost equity oil supply is shrinking. 'Buying crude at the

Table 5
Sources of crude oil to Japan (million barrels per day)

Source	1976–1978	Percent Share[a] (%)	1980–1981	Percent Share[a] (%)
Japanese oil companies				
Traditional contracts	1.50	50	0.25	8
Producer nation contracts	0.85	28	1.45	45
Spot type purchases	0.25	8	1.10	34
Overseas production	0.40	13	0.40	13
Subtotal	3.00	100	3.20	100
Foreign oil companies				
Interaffiliate purchases	1.80		1.70	
Total	4.80		4.90	

Source: *Petroleum Intelligence Weekly*, 19:4 (25 February 1980).
a. Percent shares refer to distribution of supply of oil to Japanese oil companies.

official price and reselling to third parties at no profit is utter nonsense. It just guarantees a profit for my customers,' says one supply executive. Oil companies point out they absorbed substantial losses in 1977 and 1978 when they were forced to sell crude to contract buyers at substantial discounts off official prices. 'We can't eat the losses when markets are weak and then be expected to make no reasonable profit when the markets are strong,' the marketers argue.

Special surcharges adopted by exporting nations on incremental production provided a further incentive to terminate third party sales. First Saudi Arabia and then other exporters imposed higher prices and shorter credit terms on incremental crude liftings by contract buyers. Some of these buyers passed these premiums onto their customers on a proportionate basis, while other firms offered their customers the option of accepting lower volumes with no premiums or full volumes with the premiums (*PIW*, 19 March 1979). Through much of 1979 these companies were forced to pay larger and larger premiums for incremental supplies and yet found that they could, at best, pass on the increase in their average cost of crude oil to their third party buyers.

This type of incremental economics made no sense. The majors withdrew from the market and left their former customers to deal with the OPEC producing companies on their own. The wisdom of these actions was confirmed in late 1982 and early 1983 when Saudi Arabia forced its former partners in Aramco to lift crude at postings of $34.00 per barrel when the oil was worth less than $28.00 per barrel.

The effect of the end of third party sales is demonstrated by table 5, which describes the change in crude oil supply to Japan between 1976 and 1980. Historically, the Japanese oil companies had acquired roughly 50% of their crude supplies through contracts with the major oil companies, with the other half coming from a mix of spot type purchases (8%) and purchases from state oil companies. However, by 1980 *PIW* indicates that only 8% of the oil supply came from traditional sources, while 45% came through purchases from producer nations.

The multinational companies withdrew from the distribution of OPEC crude because it was no longer profitable to act as a middle man. This change need not have occurred. The exporting countries could have offered the multinationals an incentive to continue lifting crude under long term contractual arrangements. However, such arrangements would have required that the exporting countries offer a financial incentive to those companies acquiring crude under contract.

Instead, the exporting countries adopted a strategy that was at best neutral and, at its worst, biased against the long term buyer. Under this approach term prices were adjusted to market conditions with a long lag.[4] Since the process appears to be symmetric, the contractual buyer gains no advantage but suffers no loss as compared to the spot purchaser. However, the balance was shifted in favor of the spot purchaser by sales policies that forced contractual customers to purchase their full quotas when markets were soft but then denied these buyers their full entitlements at times of tight markets, such as 1979.[5] Given these sales practices the multinationals found that it was no longer in their best interest to be the conduit through which most of the crude oil supply flowed.

2.1.4 The Increase in Volatility of Supply and Demand

The increase in the variance of consumption represents the second change in the structure of the market. (Hieronymous points out that no organized market machinery was required if supply and demand for a commodity were both certain, as noted above.) In the case of the oil market the variance in consumption and sources of supply have increased after 1973 and particularly after 1979.

The increased volatility in the level of consumption may be noted in several ways, the most obvious of which may be by simple trend analyses. From 1960 to 1973 both US and total Free World consumption were highly correlated with a simple time trend. The standard error of the fitted trend line was 400 Mb/d (thousand barrels per day) for the United States and 1,160 for the Free World. This relationship collapsed after 1973 for obvious reasons. From 1974 to 1983 the correlation coefficients drop from the mid-90s to zero, no trend is exhibited, and the standard errors triple to 1,248 Mb/d for the United States and 3,515 for the Free World.

A second indicator of the increased uncertainty as to supply and demand

Table 6
Projections of Free World oil consumption for 1985 (million barrels per day)

Forecast	Year of forecast					
	1977	1978	1979	1980	1981	1982
CIA	70					
IEA	64	65	56		53	
CRS	69					
DOE	66	66	48	48	49	51
WAES	61					
EPRI		66				
Exxon		65				
Shell		64	56		53	
Chevron			59	54	49	48
Texaco				58	52	

Source: US Department of Energy, *Annual Review of Energy* (various issues), company publications, and the *Oil and Gas Journal*.

may be noted from the errors made in projecting future petroleum consumption. Presumably, if future levels of supply and demand are certain, then forecasting errors should be small. However, a comparison of projected levels of consumption with actual realizations illustrates the degree to which forecasters have missed the mark, and by implication, the uncertainty present in today's oil market. The period of transition again appears to be between 1979 and 1982.

The period of transition may be noted by examining two groups of forecasts. The first group of forecasts represents a collection of projections of Free World consumption in 1985 made between 1977 and 1982. The 1977 and 1978 forecasts are clustered in a range from 61 to 70 million barrels per day (MMb/d) while the later projections fall in a range between 48 and 51 MMb/d (see table 6).

The great adjustment in forecasts was made in the years between 1980 and 1982. One may note, for instance, that the IEA's forecast has been cut from 65 MMb/d to 53 MMb/d between 1978 and 1981 (and to 47 MMb/d by the end of 1984), and that half of the cut had been made in 1979 and 1980. Chevron made a similar cut of 10 MMb/d in its forecast between 1979 and 1981, while Shell cut its forecast in one year.

Part of the explanation for the large changes in forecasts may lie in the errors experienced in short term forecasts made between 1979 and 1982. These errors may be observed by examining errors made in projections of US petroleum consumption submitted to the Texas Railroad Commission by companies operating in Texas.[6] Table 7 presents data on the forecasts for the years from

Table 7
Summary of forecasts of US petroleum consumption submitted to the Texas Railroad
Commission

Year	(1) Mean projected increase (%)	(2) Actual increase (%)	Forecast error percentage points	Mean squared percent error	Projections that exceeded actual (%)
1975	1.0	2.0	1.0	2.9	95.5
1976	3.5	7.0	3.5	7.7	3.4
1977	4.3	5.6	1.3	2.6	8.0
1978	2.5	2.3	0.2	0.9	65.4
1979	2.1	−1.8	−3.9	19.4	95.5
1980	−1.2	−7.8	−9.0	54.5	100.0
1981	−2.1	−5.9	−8.0	22.1	90.6
1982	−1.6	−4.7	−6.3	26.9	78.9
1983	−0.8	−0.8	0.0	8.0	56.4
1984	2.3	4.2	1.9	8.1	14.3

Sources: Texas Railroad Commission (column 1), US Department of Energy (column 2),
calculations by the author.

1975 to 1984. There we show the mean of projection increase, the actual percent increase, the forecast error, and the mean squared percentage error, and the percent of company forecasts that were too optimistic.

Table 7 highlights the increase in uncertainty with respect to the level of supply and demand in the United States during the years after collapse of the Shah. Similar errors were probably observable in short run forecasts of Free World consumption made by major oil companies.

2.1.5 The Increase in the Volatility of Prices

The final major structural change that has caused the petroleum market to evolve into a commodity market is the increase in price volatility. As Hieronymus notes, "When supply and demand are large, and both uncertain and subject to wide fluctuations from season to season or year to year, a condition exists where the forces of supply and demand on free markets is constantly changing. This interplay of uncertain economic forces produces the constant fluctuations in price which must exist in any successful futures market" (Hieronymus, 1982, p. 21). Hieronymus could also note that the same conditions are necessary for the successful formation of a cash commodity market.

A comparison of data on the fluctuation of prices during the period from 1960 to 1972 and 1979 to 1984 indicates that the volatility in prices has increased substantially. Here again, *The World Petroleum Market* provides an absolutely essential input into the analysis. Appendixes IV-B, IV-E, and IV-I

Table 8

Comparison of mean and variance in product prices in northwest Europe for three periods

	1960–1967	1967–1971	1978–1984
Gasoline			
Mean (cents per gallon)	5.95	6.33	85.64
Standard Deviation	0.67	0.99	17.76
Ratio	8.88	6.39	4.82
Gas oil			
Mean (cents per gallon)	7.20	7.91	82.64
Standard Deviation	1.22	1.62	20.30
Ratio	5.90	4.88	4.07
Heavy fuel oil			
Mean (dollars per barrel)	4.28	5.24	23.14
Standard Deviation	0.23	0.55	5.87
Ratio	18.39	9.53	3.94

Sources: Adelman (1972), appendix IV-B; *Petroleum Intelligence Weekly*.

provide tabulations of free market prices of product and crude for the 1960 to 1971 period when such information was almost impossible to collect.[7]

The analysis of volatility in prices is made by comparing the average price level to the standard deviation in prices. Volatility was analyzed for three periods: 1960 to May 1967, 1968 to 1971, and 1978 to 1984. Data for the first two periods were taken directly from *The World Petroleum Market* with the last seven months of 1967 excluded due to the transitory impact of the Middle East crisis that year. The measure of volatility used here is the ratio of the mean of the price series to its standard deviation. These measures could be criticized because they fail to correct for an underlying trend in prices. However, the data for the early period exhibit no trends, and the trend in prices between 1978 and 1984 has been decidedly erratic—indeed the uncertainty as to the trend has contributed to the change in the industry. Results are shown in table 8.

The increase in the variance of heavy fuel oil since 1971 is particularly noteworthy since heavy fuel oil accounted for the largest share of product sales in Europe prior to the 1973 embargo, and because a high portion of residual fuel oil was sold at spot related prices.[8] The increase in the variance of gasoline prices is also noteworthy.

It is more difficult to perform these calculations for spot crude prices because data on crude oil transactions were not published as regularly in the 1960s or even in the late 1970s. However, a rough estimate for the period from 1968 to July 1970 can be developed from Adelman's appendix VI-I. There information on reported transactions are reported for 22 crudes. (Adelman,

1972, p. 417, cautions that the data are taken from *Platts* and *PIW* and vary in scope "from spot offers to long-term contracts and from precise details of transactions to unconfirmed reports.") The average price for the crude reported most frequently—Iranian light 34 gravity crude—was $1.32 per barrel and the standard deviation was $0.09 per barrel for the 17 reported transactions. The ratio of the mean to the standard deviation was 14.7. For the period from 1978 to 1984 the mean of the spot price of Arab light 34 gravity crude was 27.2 while the standard deviation was 6.54. The ratio had declined to 4.16.

In summary, the volatility of crude and product prices increased substantially, particularly after 1979. At the same time refiners were forced to bring contract product prices more in line with spot product prices. Thus, the increase in volatility was spread to a larger portion of the barrel.

2.1.6 Summary: Oil Has Become a Commodity

The materials presented in the sections above show that the characteristics of petroleum markets have evolved toward those found in other, better known commodity markets. Control over the flow of the material to the market by the largest firms has been cut from more than 80% to less than 20%. Fluctuations in supply and demand have increased. Prices have become more volatile. Petroleum should continue to evolve into a more complete commodity unless these changes are reversed. In the next section we indicate that three changes in the structure of the market guarantee that the market will continue to progress toward a commodity market.

3 Changes in the Structure of the Industry That Will Perpetuate the Shift to Petroleum as a Commodity

The three changes in the oil market described in the previous section can be directly or indirectly traced to actions of the exporting countries. Nationalizations of company interests and reductions in the incentive to handle third party sales clearly caused the change in the flow of oil to shift. Increases in prices caused by exporting country mismanagement of supply contributed to economic recession, conservation, and fuel substitution, which made oil consumption more uncertain. Finally the inability of exporting countries to control production contributed to the volatility of prices. Each of these three actions is, in theory, reversible. However, the events of the "OPEC decade" have lead to other changes in the market, changes that are both difficult to reverse and make a return to the past almost impossible. The most dramatic of the changes concerns the approach to the taxation of resources in consuming countries and the creation of a futures market in crude oil.

3.1 Changes in Taxation of Resources in Consuming Countries

At the dawn of the "OPEC Decade" the oil industry in the United States operated under a system of taxation that was highly favorable to resource production. Producers of resources benefited from percentage depletion and from special regulations that permitted them to expense intangible drilling expenses. It was percentage depletion that directly affected the price of oil because the structure of the tax system encouraged producers to inflate the price of oil artificially to reduce tax liabilities.[9]

Tax reform legislation passed in 1976 repealed percentage depletion for the major oil companies and drastically limited the benefits received by independent producers. As a result of these changes, major producers should have become indifferent with respect to the source of profits because income earned at the lease was effectively taxed at the same rate as income earned at the refinery. The period of indifference should have been short, however, because further legislation enacted in 1980, the Windfall Profit Tax, created an incentive for the producer to minimize the wellhead value of crude oil because, under present law, income earned from resource production of oil is almost always taxed at a higher rate than income earned from refining.

Tax regimes adopted in the United Kingdom and Norway appear to offer private companies similar incentives to cut the price of oil.

Under the US Windfall Profit Tax the federal government takes approximately 85% of every incremental dollar when the price exceeds a certain base level (presently about $20 per barrel). Given the structure of the tax, after-tax receipts from the production of crude oil should be relatively constant even if there is a large variation in the pretax price of oil. Such an effect could be observed between 1981 and 1983 when pretax receipts per barrel for a group of ten companies declined 18% from $30.73 to $25.21 while after tax receipts declined only 3.3% from $22.38 per barrel to $21.64 (*PIW* 2, 11 February 1985).

The Windfall Tax appears to influence the current incentives faced by almost every firm operating in the United States. According to data released by the US Treasury Department almost 90% of all production is subject to the tax and approximately 40% is taxed at the highest, 70%, rate.

In theory, the Windfall Tax should encourage integrated producers to minimize the price of crude oil while maximizing the value added in refining because the incremental dollar per barrel output earned in production returns less than $0.10 after all taxes and royalties are deducted, while the incremental dollar in refining or marketing returns at least $0.54 per barrel. Accordingly, integrated companies should, except in special circumstances, want to lower the price set on crude oil. This incentive is precisely the reverse of the incentive offered in the 1960s under percentage depletion.

The British Petroleum Revenue Tax has had a similar impact on production incentives from the North Sea. Under the PRT, incremental revenue is taxed at a rate of 75% after deduction of expenses and an "oil allowance" of specified volumes that are free of tax. This leaves the producer with incentives little different from those offered in the United States. The system of taxes in the United Kingdom does, however, offer the producer a different set of incentives than are faced in the United States. Essentially, the PRT and other associated systems offer mechanisms that provide for rapid recovery of capital investment, particularly from small fields. Thus, the initial production from a successful field will enable a producer to recover expenditures for exploration and development quickly. This facet of the tax is, however, independent of the price of oil. Thus, once a firm has recovered its investment from a property, most, if not all, of the incremental revenue from higher prices will flow to the government, and not to the company.

An identical situation exists in Norway. Companies are permitted to recover funds invested in development projects over a six year period after production commences. The tax rate on incremental income after deduction for depreciation can be as high as 88%. Thus in Norway as in the United Kingdom and United States, the burden of price risk is absorbed by the state.[10]

Both the North Sea taxes and the Windfall Tax are taxes on economic rents. The high marginal per barrel rates in each tax leave producers with little interest in the absolute level of prices—precisely the desired effect of a tax on rent. Under this type of a regime a producer suffers a reduction in profits only if it delays its adjustments of prices. The effect, then, is to promote increased price volatility.

3.2 The Creation of the Futures Market

The second major change in structure has occurred with the introduction of a futures market in crude oil. Trading in futures in crude oil began in March 1983 on the New York Mercantile Exchange (NYMEX). The NYMEX contract calls for delivery of 1,000 barrels of West Texas Intermediate crude oil (or one of nine alternative types of crude) to Cushing, Oklahoma, a landlocked location in the middle of the United States whose only justification is that it is located at the intersection of several major crude pipelines.

In theory, commencement of trading in a futures contract on a domestic US crude with delivery in a US location should have no impact on the world oil market for two reasons. First, the delivery point is isolated from ports and the transportation costs would make exportation prohibitively expensive even if it were legally possible to export domestic crudes. Second, the US crude oil market has always been isolated from the world market. In fact, there is only one reference to West Texas crude in *The World Petroleum Market* and that relates to the period when the United States still exported crude to Europe (Adelman, 1972, p. 134). However, crude oil futures have had an impact on the world oil market by undercutting the stability of the traditional system of crude postings.

The increased impact of domestic US crudes on world oil prices (even if only temporary) was noted by the editors of *PIW*, who suggest that "highly visible price quotes on the New York futures market account for much of the leadership role enjoyed by WTI, even though it is technically a poor proxy for the international market." They argue that the prominence of WTI is especially surprising because "physical supplies are largely landlocked in US mid-continent pipeline systems, and non-exportable" (*PIW*, 21 January 1985).

This skepticism shown toward the futures market is not isolated. Most of those individuals involved in the oil industry have tended to view the development of the futures market with skepticism and outright hostility. Some petroleum economists appear to have had the same feelings. In reality, however, trading in futures represents the natural market response to the breakdown in control over the market and increase in uncertainty. As risks become larger it is to be expected that economic agents will attempt to find methods that permit them to transfer some portion of the risk to others. What is surprising, however, is that the development of this mechanism has become a further agent of change in the market.

The creation of a futures market in crude oil would appear to have had two impacts on the world oil market, both of which undermine price stability and enhance the commodity characteristics of petroleum. First, the futures market has permitted independent refiners in the United States to break away from the system of posted crude oil prices that historically prevented them from setting widely divergent prices. Second, the market has contributed to a drastic reduction in the cost and risk of speculation against oil prices.

3.2.1 The End of the Posting System
The system of posting crude oil prices can be traced to the 1920s. McDonald notes that oil was marketed in the field at prices "posted by the principal buyers, who were nearly always refining companies or their affiliates"

(McDonald, 1971, p. 25). The buyer then paid gathering and transportation costs to move the crude to a refining center. Both McDonald and Hamilton (1958) observe that crude postings tend to change infrequently. Further, postings have tended to be identical across companies in those fields where several firms are capable of buying crude oil. This commonality of prices was enforced by government regulation of prices during the 1970s. In theory, equality of postings should continue to be enforced by the market as long as the United States remains a significant importer of crude oil. In these circumstances, any firm proposal to cut its posting would risk seeing its crude oil captured by another refiner, who would not lower its posting.

Postings did behave as theory would predict from 1981 to late 1984. In one instance a firm did attempt to cut postings but was forced to rescind its cut within two weeks when other companies did not follow suit. In that case, Citgo Petroleum, the independent refining company created by Occidental Petroleum's sale of the refining and marketing arm of Cities Service Petroleum, cut its posting for WTI by $1.50 per barrel in mid-December 1983 and was followed in a few days by a second independent refiner, Ashland Oil. Both companies were forced to rescind their cuts within two weeks because other firms failed to follow. Citgo's and Ashland's actions suggest that market conditions were such that the supply of crude at a $1.50 discount was inadequate for their needs.

The situation was different, however, in the fall of 1984. Cuts in postings of $1.00 per barrel were initiated by four independent refiners in mid-October and then followed by others in early November. Further cuts were made in December and early January. By the end of the first week of January Citgo had posted a price of $25.90 per barrel and several other independents had set prices at between $26.50 and $27.00. Meanwhile, the major refiners held their postings at $29.00 per barrel. Thus in late 1984 and early 1985 the independent refiners had been able to break away from other refiners, whereas they had been forced to conform a year earlier. One explanation for the change in behavior may be found in the futures market. The futures market had developed into a viable alternative source of crude in the twelve months between December 1983 and December 1984. By December 1984, US refiners were obtaining approximately 4% of their crude supplies either directly or indirectly through the futures market. Volume obtained through the futures market grew from 2.1 Mb/d in June 1983 to 370 Mb/d in February 1985.

Thus, one effect of the introduction of trading in crude oil futures has been to offer a viable source of supply to independent refiners. This change has, in turn, enabled them to cut their crude postings more freely.

3.2.2 Reduction of the Cost of Speculation

Introduction of trading in crude oil futures has also contributed to a reduction in the cost of speculation in crude oil by lowering two serious barriers to entry into the crude market. Prior to the creation of the crude futures market, entry by smaller speculators was barred by the large size of the average traded lot and the unwillingness of traditional buyers to do business with unknown and presumably undercapitalized firms.

The size of the average tradable lot was probably the greatest impediment to entry into the crude market in the past. On the international market the average lot was generally thought to be a VLCC or ULCC cargo of crude—600,000 barrels of oil or more. The cost of such a cargo would have ranged from $6 million to $20 million. In the US market the average lot still represented a considerable expense although they were smaller—10,000 barrels to 50,000 barels. As a consequence both markets were illiquid. Further, entry was difficult because most oil companies were extremely reluctant to buy from an unknown supplier (trader). Thus, an individual or firm desiring to speculate in crude oil prices first needed to establish a record as a proven and dependable trader before it could presumably speculate in crude by selling oil that it had not yet acquired.

The creation of a successful futures market has substantially cut the cost of speculation against crude prices by increasing liquidity of the market, reducing the size of the tradable lot to 1,000 barrels, and removing the need to establish a reputation as a proven, dependable trader. Entry to the futures market is controlled by the commodity brokers, who only require that potential speculators make adequate deposits of cash or securities to guarantee their financial performance. The value of these deposits can be as low as $5,000.00, a much smaller entry fee.

Data collected by the US Commodity Futures Trading Commission suggest that speculators took advantage of the lowered cost of entry to speculate against crude oil in the fall of 1984. These data, which are summarized in table 9, show that open interest[11] in crude futures increased from 37.6 million barrels at the end of October 1984 to 49.2 million barrels at the end of December. Further, the share of the short side of the market held by speculators increased from 53% to 68%, while the share of the long side of the market held by commercial firms increased 72% to 82%. Essentially, speculators sold and oil companies bought during this period of time.

The net short position of speculators increased by 14,734 contracts (14,734 million barrels of oil). Translated to a barrels per day basis this amounts to between 250 and 400 thousand barrels a day.[12] These sales had the effect of increasing the apparent supply of crude oil by non-OPEC producers, neutraliz-

Table 9

Open interest and position of hedgers and speculators in the crude oil futures contract[a]

Date	Open interest[b]	Market shares speculators (%)		Hedgers (%)	
		Long	Short	Long	Short
July 1983	5,140	73.9	63.5	26.1	36.5
August 1983	6,742	51.5	58.4	48.5	41.6
September 1983	10,314	47.8	53.7	52.2	46.3
October 1983	11,786	44.3	43.1	55.6	56.9
November 1983	19,351	32.7	38.8	67.3	61.2
December 1983	21,554	40.5	48.1	59.5	51.9
January 1984	23,168	22.4	34.4	77.5	65.6
February 1984	27,650	31.8	40.7	68.2	59.3
March 1984	28,142	26.3	36.5	73.7	63.5
April 1984	26,647	31.2	45.8	68.8	54.2
May 1984	23,970	43.5	22.9	56.5	77.1
June 1984	28,635	22.8	36.8	77.2	63.2
July 1984	37,349	16.8	47.9	83.2	52.1
August 1984	32,245	26.9	37.3	73.1	62.7
September 1984	37,613	30.0	45.4	70.0	54.6
October 1984	37,613	27.1	52.7	72.9	47.2
November 1984	39,896	28.9	55.9	71.1	44.1
December 1984	49,201	18.3	67.8	81.7	32.1

Source: CFTC, *Commitments of Traders.*

a. CFTC data distinguish positions in three categories. These are commercial positions, non-commercial positions, and nonreportable positions (traders holding less than 50 positions). Here speculators are defined as nonreportable and noncommercial positions.

b. Open interest in contracts. One contract represents 1,000 barrels.

ing in part cutbacks in production announced by members of OPEC on 31 October 1984. Prices then declined because OPEC did not make further compensating cuts in production.

4 Conclusion

The world petroleum market has gone through a series of transformations since 1972. Oil has emerged as a commodity. The process began when exporting countries took control of their own resources. It was then furthered when the multinational oil companies elected (or were denied) the opportunity to be the marketing agents for the exporting countries. Then, discoveries in non-OPEC areas reduced OPEC's control over the flow of oil to the market. Finally, the price increases of 1979 and 1973 changed the relationship between oil consumption and economic activity, causing supply and demand to become more volatile. Simultaneously, the adoption of new tax systems in Britain and the United States reduced producer interest in stable prices, effectively increasing price volatility. Last, the creation of a futures market in petroleum created a mechanism that opened the oil market to a much larger number of participants.

The consequence of these changes is a much more open and transparent oil market. Prices change daily and are duly reported in many different sources. Control appears to have passed from a few organizations to the market. It is difficult to determine whether price movements in the long run will be wider. However, it is clear that price changes will be more frequent than they were when Morry wrote his classic work.

Short of nuclear war, the transformation of the industry could be reversed in only two possible ways: a return to the system of preferential agreements between the multinational companies and the producing countries, which existed prior to 1972, or the complete downstream integration by producing countries. Since a return to past regimes seems out of the question, the only real possible solution for producers would seem to be to become fully integrated from the wellhead to the pump. Some countries, such as Kuwait, have started down this road. Many officials of OPEC countries seem to think that this type of downstream integration will prove to be the cartel's salvation. However, the conclusions to be drawn from Morry Adelman's seminal analysis of the market as of 1972 would lead me to a different conclusion. Downstream integration is not enough. Instead, the market stability that existed in the 1950s and 1960s resulted from the maintenance of sufficient surplus capacity to meet any unexpected surge in demand. At the same time, the joint production agreements provided multinational companies with the ability to exert control over total output both among themselves and within exporting countries.

To achieve a return to the market stability of the past, producers need to exert control over output in a fashion that will achieve the effect of the market structure that existed in 1972. Both prices and consumption need to be stabilized. Uncertainty must be eliminated. Oil will not be "decommoditized" simply by ending the current glut because the return to a tight market will not eliminate uncertainty. Instead, prices will once again spiral upward. Oil can only be removed from the list of economic commodities through the establishment of joint producing agreements and maintenance of sufficient surplus capacity in producing countries. This is an outcome that seems beyond the ability of the members of OPEC. Thus, I am led to two conclusions. First, the oil market has permanently evolved as a commodity market. Second, the explanation for the permanence of the change can be found in chapter 3 of *The World Petroleum Market*. The first conclusion is surprising; the second should have been expected.

Notes

1. It may be noted that a successful market in products had flourished in northwest Europe after 1950. The data on transactions in this "Rotterdam" market formed the basis for many of the calculations in *The World Petroleum Market*. However, the Rotterdam market was a unique institution in oil until the late 1970s or early 1980s.

2. *Petroleum Intelligence Weekly* 18(2):4, 19 March 1979.

3. This calculation is not exactly comparable to the one reported by Vernon. According to data shown in the individual company annual reports, the seven majors indicate that they distributed 13 million barrels per day (MMb/d) of products through their affiliates. Their total market amounted to 17 MMb/d including third party sales. Of course, some of the crude required to supply the 13 MMb/d of products distributed was purchased from other oil companies including producing country companies.

4. The process was originally noted in Adelman (1980) and formalized in Jacoby and Paddock (1980) and then quantified by Verleger (1982). The empirical results in Verleger indicate that the official price of Saudi light is changed by approximately $0.30 in the current quarter for each $1.00 difference between netbacks and official prices in the prior quarter.

5. The experience of many companies during the spring of 1979 provides an excellent example. As the first episode of price increases came to an end in March Libya, Algeria, and Indonesia notified term customers that liftings would be reduced by 15 to 18% (*PIW*, 12 March 1979). Then in April, *PIW* reported that Saudi Arabia had arbitrarily directed volumes of crude away from the Aramco customers in order to increase government to government sales. The amount of the cut was estimated to be 400 thousand barrels per day (*PIW*, 14 May 1979).

6. Each year in January or February the Texas Railroad Commission has collected projections of total petroleum consumption for that year from the major companies operating in Texas. Prior to 1973 these forecasts were used to assist in setting allowables for the year. The practice continued until 1984 despite the fact that no production had been shut in for years. The forecasts were published with company identification in the Commission's March statistical report.

7. Estimation of arms length prices for transactions in crude in 1960–1971 is quite difficult because the number of deals was few and the interest of secrecy great. Thus I would guess that Adelman and his assistants were forced to comb through over 2,000 separate issues of *Platt's Oil Price Service* and *Petroleum Intelligence Weekly* looking for the occasional reference to a transaction price. These estimates then had to be put on a common footing by correcting for differences in transportation costs and gravity. Today, the academic economist can obtain the same information from a simple table in *Platt's*.

8. See Adelman (1972, p. 367) for market shares. Roeber (1979a, 1979b, 1979c) documents the importance of *Platt's* prices to prices charged to consumers of heavy fuel oil.

9. McDonald (1971, p. 192) notes the following: "In fields or market areas where buyers produce about 80 percent or more of the oil they buy, it is profitable for such buyers to transfer net income from transportation and refining to production by overpricing

crude oil relative to products. This increases the benefits of percentage depletion, which is based on the wellhead value of oil, and thus reduces the effective tax rate on aggregate income." It turns out that the breakeven percentage is closer to 30% for many oil companies because few firms paid a marginal tax rate of 50%.

10. The best description of North Sea petroleum taxes are to be found in the works of Kemp and Rose (1983).

11. Open interest refers to the number of contracts outstanding at the end of a trading day. Arthur (1971, p. 376) offers the following definitions: *Open contracts*—contracts in the futures market that have been bought or sold without the transaction having been completed by subsequent sale or repurchase, or actual delivery or receipt of commodity. "In any futures market, at any given time, the number of futures contracts bought by all customers exactly equals the number sold by the same or other customers. Thus, published figures representing *Open interest* always mean either the total of *Long* contracts or the total number of *Short* contracts, never the sum of the two."

12. This calculation assumes that the 14 million barrels represented a commitment to deliver during a period of 40–60 days. Of course few if any of the speculators ever intended to deliver oil. Instead, the commitments would repurchased later. However, the sales have the same impact on the market as a promise to make forward physical delivery if the futures prices and cash prices converge at the expiration of trading.

8 Cartel Theory and Cartel Experience in International Minerals Markets

Jeffrey K. MacKie-Mason
Robert S. Pindyck

1 Introduction

Until the ascendance of OPEC and the 1973–1974 oil shock, the economics literature paid much more attention to *implicit* rather than *explicit* behavior as a model of oligopolistic behavior. Most oligopoly models were outgrowths of the "Prisoners' Dilemma," i.e., the agents could not talk to each other directly (although they might devise means of "signaling"). The oil-exporting countries, on the other hand, could and did talk to each other directly. That greatly reduced the severity of the prisoners' dilemma. It did not completely eliminate the dilemma, however, because participants could not enforce agreed upon constraints.

The 1973–1974 oil shock set off debate about the stability and durability of cartel agreements, as well as the likelihood of a proliferation of cartels. (History, of course, records a plethora of formal and informal attempts at cartelization, most of which were failures, well before OPEC.) The oil shock stimulated both theoretical and empirical research on cartels specifically, and cooperative pricing and production behavior in general. Beginning with work by M. A. Adelman, the oil cartel became one of the better studied examples.[1] As a result, the past decade has also seen exhaustible resource theory incorporated into more traditional models of cartel behavior.

When the cartelized commodity is an exhaustible resource, optimal cartel behavior can become much more complicated to determine. This is particularly true if consumers have rational expectations (i.e., use all available information to make dynamically optimal decisions), and if marginal extraction cost is not constant. Even if the cartel operates as a perfect monopolist—

This work was supported by the Center for Energy Policy Research of the MIT Energy Laboratory, and that support is gratefully acknowledged.

i.e., there are no problems with respect to internal organization and adherence to the cartel agreement—its optimal policy is complicated by the intertemporal trade-off associated with depletion. For example, the finite resource constraint will reduce any potential monopoly power, but in a way that depends critically on the structure of cost and demand, the presence of uncertainty, etc.[2]

·Many of the commodities whose markets have been subject to (successful or unsuccessful) cartel attempts are indeed exhaustible resources. However, for any of the commodities that we are aware of—including oil—Hotelling rent (or "user cost") is small as a fraction of price, particularly in cases where cartelization has been successful.[3] In other words, resource depletion has not been a quantitatively important factor in determining cartel success, or cartel pricing behavior. Much more important are short-run and long-run demand and competitive supply elasticities. It therefore makes sense to ignore resource depletion in an attempt to determine the relative importance of other factors for cartel success in a broad spectrum of commodity markets.[4]

Much of cartel theory stresses organization, i.e., the *internal* problems of reaching an agreement and then detecting and deterring cheating. Much less emphasis has been placed on *external* factors, i.e., the *potential for monopoly power* as determined by demand, market share, costs, and potential entry. One could argue, however, that if minimal conditions of concentration have been met and if the potential gains from cartelization are large enough, the internal problems can and will be sorted out—not perfectly, and not for an indefinite period of time, but well enough and for long enough to make the endeavor very worthwhile. On the other hand, if the potential gains are small, the internal problems are unlikely to be resolved, and even if a cartel organization is formed, it will have little impact on the market.

This view was suggested and tested against cartel experience in the oil, bauxite, and copper markets in Pindyck (1977, 1978). Here we examine cartel experience in the markets for two other internationally traded mineral resources, mercury and sulfur. The markets for both of these commodities have been successfully cartelized. As we shall see, factors relating to external market structure were the main determinants of cartel success and cartel behavior.

In the next section we briefly summarize some of the theoretical issues relating to cartel stability and success, and we argue (heuristically) for the relative importance of external factors. We then test this view in the succeeding sections by reviewing cartel experience in the world markets for mercury and sulfur.

2 Cartel Theory

As Paul Eckbo (1976) noted in a historical survey of international cartels, there have been attempts to cartelize the markets for most of the major internationally traded commodities. A few of these cartel attempts were successful, but most were not. Why is it that most attempts at cartelization failed, with the organization dissolving after a short period of time, or else remaining in force officially, but having no significant impact on prices and member revenues?[5]

The usual argument is that because cartel agreements are not enforceable, cartel members face a prisoners' dilemma that is unresolvable, so that competitive warfare eventually breaks out, and the agreement collapses. D. K. Osborne (1976) has argued that this prisoners' dilemma *can* be resolved if the cartel members can locate the contract surface, and if cheating can be detected. The two remaining internal problems—determining production quotas, i.e., a point on the contract surface, and deterring cheating—can then be solved jointly through the use of a production *rule* for each member (as opposed to a fixed production level). Letting q_i^* be the assigned output quota of member i, s_i member i's share of total production, and Δq_j the amount by which member j's output deviates from his quota, consider the following production rule for member i:

$$\text{Produce } \max\{q_i^*, q_i^* + (s_i/s_j)\,\Delta q_j\}. \tag{1}$$

Osborne shows that if each member adopts a production rule of this form, it provides a sufficient threat of retaliation to deter cheating, and the cartel agreement will be stable.[6]

This production rule is in fact one of many that will deter cheating *in the sense of making it unprofitable for any one member to cheat if the other members indeed follow the rule*. Such rules correspond to particular sets of conjectural variations in a Cournot-Nash framework. However, those conjectural variations need not (and generally will not) be *consistent*. In other words, it may not be in the interest of each member to actually follow the rule once it becomes clear that the *threat* of following the rule has failed to deter the delinquent member.[7]

To see this, consider the following simple model in which N identical firms form an explicit or implicit production agreement.[8] Assume costs are zero, and market demand is given by $Q = 2 - P$. Clearly joint profits are then maximized when $Q^* = 1$, so that each firm has a production allocation of $1/N$. Now consider a Cournot-Nash equilibrium. If each firm sets output to maximize its own profits, it will follow the production rule (i.e., reaction function) given by

$$Q_i^* = \left(2 - \sum_{j \neq i} Q_j\right) \bigg/ \left(2 + \sum_{j \neq i} v_{ji}\right), \qquad i = 1, \dots, N, \tag{2}$$

where v_{ji} is the set of conjectural variations, i.e., $v_{ji} = dQ_j/dQ_i$. Given that the firms are identical, we can assume these conjectural variations are all equal to some value v.

Now we can ask what value of v will induce all firms to adhere to their production allocations, i.e., to produce only $1/N$? From (2) it is easy to see that that value is just $v^* = 1$. In other words, if each firm *threatens* to follow a production rule of one-for-one retaliatory response (so that a 1-unit increase above quota by the delinquent firm is met by an additional N-1 units from the other N-1 firms), *and if the threat is believed* by each firm, there will be no deviations from quota.

The problem is that the conjectural variation $v^* = 1$ is not consistent, and therefore may not be credible. To see this, observe from (2) that each firm's profit-maximizing response, *assuming that other firms follow the deterrence rule* $dQ_j/dQ_i = 1$, is given by

$$\partial Q_i^*/\partial Q_j = -1/(N + 1). \tag{3}$$

Thus the *deterrence* production rule is quite different from and inconsistent with the *profit-maximizing* production rule, and it only makes sense to follow if all firms are convinced that it will work. Once some firms begin to think that other firms have lost that conviction, the agreement will break down. (In fact in this example the only consistent conjectural variations lead to a *competitive* output and price.)

This does *not* mean that cartel agreements are doomed to failure. Although the "tit for tat" retaliatory strategy discussed above may be at variance with the rational expectations hypothesis, it might be the one that is most easily and successfully adhered to. (There is no evidence that conjectures by and large *are* consistent.) As Heiner (1983) recently pointed out, in the presence of uncertainty rigid behavior may dominate flexible behavior, given the limits to computational ability. For example, in experiments in which the basic prisoners' dilemma is sequentially replicated, "round robin competition found the simplest strategy (tit for tat) as dominant over all others.... Moreover, the worst performance came from the strategy that specified the most 'sophisticated' learning and probability adjustment process to guide its behavior." Simple retaliatory strategies may therefore provide a reasonable model for cartel behavior.[9]

If cheating can easily be detected, retaliatory threats can remain credible, at least for some time. This is especially the case if the potential gains from cartelization are large. As seen above, adherence to a deterrence rule involves the risk of reduced profits in the short run. That risk is more likely to be worth taking if potential monopoly profits are large. We see that potential monopoly power is likely to be the dominating factor for cartel success.

What about the problems of locating the contract surface and detecting cheating? The first problem would seem to be a formidable one, given differences over costs, discount rates, etc., that are likely to exist among the members of any actual or potential cartel. As Fog (1976) has pointed out, determining the contract surface may be complicated by differences in opinion over the characteristics of demand and competitive supply, the existence of substitutes, etc. And, what is more important in some cases, cartel members may operate under different constraints (for example, reserve levels in the case of mineral resources), and/or have different time preferences.

On the other hand it would be a mistake to think that the contract surface must be located with precision, and that an *exact* point on that surface must be agreed upon by cartel members. As with deterrence, if the potential monopoly power is large—as it must be for the cartel to be successful—there can be room for imperfect agreement over the contract surface. In fact, the differences among cartel members might be such that an agreement based on a "fuzzy" or imprecise contract surface may be easier to arrive at and enforce than an agreement based on a more precisely defined contract surface.

This last point can be seen in the model of OPEC production and pricing developed in Hnyilicza and Pindyck (1976). There OPEC consists of two groups of producers with different reserves and discount rates; "saver" countries like Saudi Arabia have large reserves and a low discount rate, and "spender" countries like Venezuela have low reserves and a higher discount rate. Resource depletion imposes intertemporal production rules on any cartel agreement, and a price that changes over time. With reasonable parameter values, the Nash cooperative solution for the cartel can be such that at first only "spender" countries produce until their reserves are exhausted, and then the "saver" countries produce. As a result, the production rule of equation (2) will not apply. Furthermore, given each producer's uncertainty over the reserves of the other producers, this Nash cooperative solution will be much more than one can expect from an actual oil cartel. Instead, a cartel agreement is much more likely to hold if it is based on a contract surface that approximates away at least part of these differences in reserves and discount rates. Thus as a practical matter, locating the contract surface need not be a serious problem.

The detection of cheating also need not be a serious problem, especially if the cartel produces a good that is fairly homogeneous (like oil or other mineral resources), or if sales can to some degree be centralized. At least part of the success of the iodine cartel, the longest-lived in Eckbo's survey, can be attributed to the fact that all sales were made through a central office in London.

In some cases consuming countries can take steps to make the detection of cheating more difficult, as was noted by Adelman with respect to OPEC. He proposed (1976) an import ticket plan in which tickets give the holders the right to import oil. These tickets would be sold in an anonymous auction, and would be freely transferable. The system would encourage cheating by permitting OPEC countries to establish brokers who would bid for and purchase tickets (at a premium) in the United States, thereby secretly discounting the price of their oil in exchange for assured sales. This plan was never adopted, and we can only speculate as to how effective it might have been. In any case, the detection problem does not seem to have been a major hindrance for most cartels.[10]

There is no general answer to the question of whether cartels' internal problems can be solved. A cartel agreement imposes costs on the participants— costs associated with the rationalization of output and revenues, political costs that may result when output is reduced, and costs associated with the risk of being undercut by other cartel members. Also, the agreement may require adherence to rigid rules (i.e., a behavioral mode that might be viewed as "irrational"). But these costs are easier to bear if they are small relative to potential monopoly profits.

Cartel success is therefore more likely to depend on external factors, and in particular the potential for monopoly power that the market offers. Large potential profits make the solution of internal problems just one more cost of doing business. Of course potential monopoly power must be viewed in a dynamic context. International commodity markets are inherently dynamic in structure, and depending on the time required for demand and competitive supply to adjust to price changes, there may be large short-run profits available to a cartel that has little potential for long-run gains. In the following sections we examine the relative importance of these external factors in the context of historical cartel experience in the international markets for mercury and sulfur.

3 Cartel Experience in the World Mercury Market

Of all mineral resources, mercury has one of the longest continuous histories of cartel activity. A long period of successful two-country cartelization

(1928–1972) was followed by years of unsuccessful many-country attempts at price fixing. After briefly reviewing the history of the industry, we shall show how cartel success and the pattern of price movement was largely determined by evolving external market conditions.

3.1 The Industry

Historical production and price data for the mercury market are shown in table 1. Because of their low production costs, Spain and Italy have been the dominant producers.[11] Their market shares, in terms of both production and exports, are shown in table 2. The potential for cartelization was enhanced by the small number of firms in the major producing countries, and by the role of governments in concentrating control. There are only one or two mines in most major countries, and the mines were wholly or partly state owned or controlled in Spain, Italy, Yugoslavia, and Algeria.

The mercury cartel began in 1928 with the formation of Mercurio Europeo by Spain and Italy. These two producers then controlled more than 80% of world production. Supplemented by an implicit agreement with Mexican producers,[12] the cartel began as an effective monopoly facing an inelastic market demand. Potential profits from cartelization were large, and the cartel operated stably and successfully until 1950.[13]

The cartel agreement included a geographical division of markets; Spain supplied the United States, and Italy supplied Europe. The agreement was *formally* terminated by Spain in January 1950, after Monte Amiata, the largest Italian mine, sold 80,000 flasks of mercury to the US government stockpile in late 1949. (Italy claimed the sale was in accord with the cartel agreement.) But after an initial (retaliatory) price cut by Spain, *informal* cartel pricing continued, the price rose sharply in 1950, and a formal cartel was secretly reestablished in 1954.[14] Although prices declined in real terms from 1955–1963, monopoly profits remained high, and the cartel prices and production levels behaved as one would have predicted based on market conditions.

The most dramatic price increases occurred during 1963–1965. The Italians increased the price by $13, and the Spaniards announced a temporary withdrawal from the market (although they did not in fact lower their actual output). Following a second Italian price increase, noncartel producers were induced tacitly to collude in demanding higher prices for their mercury. Anticipating a shortage, consumers rapidly expanded inventories, so that demand shifted up simultaneously. Despite a near tripling of the real price from 1963 to 1965, Spanish and Italian production and exports increased dramatically.

Table 1
World price and production of mercury (1972 $/flask of 76 lb, and 1,000 flasks)

Year	Price	Spain	Italy	USSR	Mexico	US	China[a]	Yugoslavia	Algeria	Total
1941		86.5	94.2	NA	23.1	44.9	6.6	[b]	0.0	275.0
1942		72.3	75.9	NA	32.4	50.8	4.7	[b]	0.0	260.0
1943		47.8	58.0	NA	28.3	51.9	3.1	[b]	0.0	236.0
1944		34.3	28.7	NA	26.1	37.7	3.5	[b]	0.0	163.0
1945		40.7	25.4	NA	16.4	30.8	1.8	[b]	0.0	131.0
1946		41.8	50.8	NA	11.7	25.3	1.2	8.9	0.0	154.0
1947	168.49	55.6	54.0	NA	9.7	23.2	.3	9.5	0.0	168.0
1948	143.97	22.7	38.2	NA	4.8	14.4	.3	10.9	0.0	107.0
1949	151.09	32.3	44.5	NA	5.3	9.9	.3	12.8	0.0	121.0
1950	151.49	51.8	53.3	11.6	3.8	4.5	1.5	14.4	0.0	143.3
1951	368.07	44.5	53.8	11.6	8.1	7.3	4.0	14.6	0.0	146.7
1952	343.75	39.1	55.9	11.6	8.7	12.5	4.0	14.6	0.0	150.5
1953	328.17	43.5	51.7	12.3	11.6	14.3	5.0	14.3	0.0	159.7
1954	443.98	43.1	54.5	12.3	14.8	18.5	10.0	14.4	0.0	179.3
1955	477.24	36.2	53.5	12.3	29.9	19.0	11.5	14.6	0.0	185.1
1956	413.95	55.4	62.3	22.0	19.5	24.2	17.0	13.2	0.0	228.1
1957	380.38	51.7	62.2	25.0	21.1	34.6	17.0	12.3	0.0	243.2
1958	333.22	56.0[c]	58.7	25.0	22.6	38.1	17.0	12.3	0.0	251.9
1959	336.51	51.7	45.8	25.0	16.4	31.3	23.0	13.3	0.0	223.3
1960	306.78	53.4	55.5	25.0	20.1	33.2	23.0	14.0	0.0	241.7
1961	285.03	51.2	55.4	25.0	18.1	31.7	26.0	16.0	0.0	239.7
1962	270.80	52.8	54.5	35.0	18.9	26.3	26.0	16.3	0.0	244.6
1963	264.34	57.0	54.4	35.0	17.2	19.1	26.0	15.8	0.0	239.7
1964	432.58	78.3	57.0	35.0	12.6	14.1	26.0	17.3	0.0	255.0
1965	767.55	74.7	57.3	40.0	19.2	19.6	26.0	16.4	0.0	267.7

1966	575.46	70.1	53.5	40.0	22.1	22.0	26.0	15.9	0.0	265.0
1967	618.97	49.2	48.0	45.0	23.9	23.9	20.0	15.9	0.0	241.3
1968	651.43	56.9	53.2	45.0	17.2	28.9	20.0	14.8	0.0	259.7
1969	587.51	65.0	48.7	47.0	22.5	29.6	20.0	14.3	0.0	290.0
1970	457.23	45.4	44.6	48.0	30.3	27.3	20.0	15.5	0.0	284.0
1971	315.54	50.8	42.6	50.0	35.4	17.9	26.0	16.6	7.1	298.6
1972	226.76	54.0	41.8	50.0	22.5	7.3	26.0	16.4	13.4	279.0
1973	275.59	60.1	32.7	52.0	28.0	2.2	26.0	15.6	13.3	262.3
1974	253.70	54.4	26.0	54.0	NA	2.2	26.0	NA	14.0	257.5
1975	132.86	44.0	31.7	55.0	NA	7.4	26.0	NA	28.0	252.4
1976	94.05	42.7	22.3	56.0	NA	23.1	26.0	NA	30.9	234.6
1977	99.91	26.9	0.4	58.0	NA	28.2	20.0	NA	30.4	190.7
1978	102.34	29.6	0.1	60.0	NA	24.2	20.0	NA	30.6	181.4
1979	177.54	33.3	0.0	61.0	NA	29.5	20.0	NA	30.0	190.0
1980	223.57	33.0	0.0	62.0	NA	30.7	20.0	NA	30.0	191.1
1981[c]	176.82	33.0	0.0	62.0	NA	28.0	20.0	NA	30.0	190.4

Sources: (prices) 1951–1980, Commodity Research Bureau, *1981 Commodity Yearbook*; 1981, US Bureau of Mines, *Mineral Commodity Summaries 1982*; (quantities) US Bureau of Mines, *Minerals Yearbook* (various years).

a. Data for China are estimates for 1949–1967.

b. Output of Idria mine (Yugoslavia) included with Italy through 1945.

c. Estimate.

Table 2
Mercury market shares, 1941–1981 (percentage of total world production)

Year	Production			Exports		
	Spain	Italy	Combined	Spain	Italy	Combined
1941	31.5	34.3	65.8			
1942	27.8	29.2	57.0			
1943	20.3	24.6	44.9			
1944	21.0	17.6	38.6			
1945	31.1	19.4	50.5			
1946	27.1	33.0	60.1			
1947	33.1	32.1	65.2			
1948	21.2	35.7	56.9			
1949	26.7	36.8	63.5			
1950	36.1	37.2	73.3	69.4	57.4	126.8
1951	30.3	36.7	67.0	33.1	18.7	51.8
1952	26.0	37.1	63.1	29.4	22.5	51.9
1953	27.2	32.4	59.7	27.4	34.6	62.0
1954	24.0	30.4	54.4	24.3	34.5	58.8
1955	19.6	28.9	48.5	17.4	15.1	32.5
1956	24.3	27.3	51.6	17.8	32.9	50.7
1957	21.3	25.6	46.9	19.1	11.8	30.9
1958	22.2	23.3	45.5	20.1	4.6	24.7
1959	23.2	20.5	43.7	19.3	15.7	35.0
1960	22.1	23.0	45.1	21.8	21.9	43.7
1961	21.4	23.1	44.5	20.1	13.6	33.7
1962	21.6	22.3	43.9	18.8	14.6	33.4
1963	23.8	22.7	46.5	20.5	31.6	52.1
1964	30.7	22.4	53.1	27.7	32.7	60.4
1965	27.9	21.4	48.3	24.2	19.3	43.5
1966	26.5	20.2	46.7			
1967	20.4	19.9	40.3			
1968	21.9	20.5	42.4			
1969	22.4	16.8	39.2			
1970	16.0	15.7	31.7			
1971	17.0	14.3	31.3			
1972	19.4	15.0	34.4			
1973	22.9	12.5	35.4			
1974	21.1	12.7	33.8			
1975	17.4	12.6	30.0			
1976	18.2	9.5	27.7			
1977	14.1	0.2	14.3			
1978	16.3	0.1	16.4			
1979	17.5	0.0	17.5			
1980	17.3	0.0	17.3			
1981	17.3	0.0	17.3			

Sources: Production shares calculated from table 1. Exports from Charles River Associates, *Economic Analysis of the Mercury Industry*, March 1968.

Prices peaked in 1965 as the US government began a program of stockpile sales, and as high prices induced increased noncartel production. The cartel's market share fell from 53% in 1964 to only 32% in 1970, by which time its effectiveness had largely ended. Not only had the Spanish-Italian market share eroded, but the mercury poisoning incident in Japan and emerging environmental concerns in the United States initiated a long period of declining demand. Real prices declined 86% from 1968 to 1976.

From 1972 to the present, several producers, including Spain, Italy, and at various times Mexico, Algeria, Yugoslavia, Peru, and Turkey, met more or less frequently. These countries (less Mexico) signed a formal cartel agreement in 1975, forming Assimer, which covered 60–80% of world production. This new cartel was unsuccessful for several years, largely due to continued downward shifts in demand. Prices again rose when demand stabilized in the late 1970s, as the cartel took advantage of favorable market conditions.

We have argued that once minimal conditions of market concentration have been met, the controlling factors in cartel success or failure are not the internal problems of organization, but the external constraints posed by the market. We now sketch out the conditions in the mercury market since World War II, and show how they can explain mercury price movements over the last three decades, price movements that cannot be explained by (and in fact often run counter to) changes in internal cartel organization.

3.2 Market Conditions

A cartel's potential for success is determined by its costs and its net demand function, where the latter is the difference between the world demand function and the fringe (noncartel) supply function. Estimates of mercury demand and supply elasticities, calculated at mean prices and quantities, are shown in tables 3 and 4. As table 3 shows, the demand for mercury has been extremely inelastic. DeBartolo's (1976) estimate of the short-run (1 year) world demand elasticity is −0.065; even in the most elastic submarket (US other) it is only −0.21. Table 4 shows a slightly different picture. Again, short-run elasticities are low. However the long-run supply elasticity estimated for 1960–1972 by DeBartolo is large, at 2.36. In particular, US primary supply appears quite elastic in the long run (5.29), which will be of significance in explaining price behavior over time.

Table 5 shows estimates of production costs. Noncartel costs are shown per short ton of ore because of wide grade variations across time and location. Spanish and Italian costs are given in 1972 dollars per 76 lb flask because their grade did not vary much during the 1950s and 1960s.[15] The CRA (Charles River Associates) estimate for underground production in the United States,

Table 3
Estimates of the mercury price elasticity of demand

		Short-run	Long-run	Static	Average consumption flasks
I.	*Rohlfs* (US)				
	a. Chlorine and caustic Soda Prep.			0.0	5,200
	b. Electrical apparatus			−0.13	10,300
	c. Other end uses			−0.48	42,100
	d. Weighted average, 1948–1967			−0.29	
II.	*DeBartolo/CRA*				
A.	US (1960–1972)				
	a. Chlorine preparation			−0.35	11,431
	b. Batteries			−0.16	14,769
	c. Instruments	−0.07	−0.64		5,962
	d. Dental	−0.13	−0.60		2,366
	e. Other	−0.21	−0.34		1,979
	f. Weighted average, 1960–1972	−0.21	−0.34		36,507
B.	Japan (1960–1972)				
	a. Chlorine preparation			0.0	16,148
	b. Catalysts	−0.106	−2.53		9,879
	c. Other	−0.079	−2.01		14,829
	d. Weighted average 1960–1972	−0.054	−1.34		40,856
C.	ROW (excluding US, Japan, Spain Italy)[a]	−0.039	−0.232		184,637
D.	Weighted average Total world	−0.065	−0.420		

Sources: Rohlfs (1969); DeBartolo (1976).
a. Calculated using average world production minus average US and Japanese consumption.

which was based on a 0.25% ore grade, yields a cost of \$334/flask (all values in 1972 dollars). Also, it appears that there have been no significant changes in production costs per ton of ore since World War II. This is supported for the later years by the CRA estimates of Spanish and Italian costs.

We shall use a simple cartel-fringe firms model with linear demand and supply functions to describe short- and long-run mercury market conditions. World demand in this model excludes domestic demand in Spain and Italy, and fringe supply includes all countries other than Spain and Italy.

We calculated linear supply and demand functions using DeBartolo's elasticity estimates, together with available data on supplies and prices. For a short-run elasticity of −0.065, a mean price of \$443, and mean consumption of 262,000 flasks, the inverse world demand function is

$$P = 7342 - 26.3QT. \tag{4}$$

Table 4
Some estimates of price elasticities of supply

		Short-run	Long-run	Static	Average production
I.	*Rohlfs* (1969)				
	(a) US secondary 1947–1967			0.29	
	(b) World primary except Spain, Italy, USSR, 1949–1967	0.09	0.53		
II.	*DeBartolo* (1976), 1960–1972 averages				
	(a) Noncommunist except Spain, Italy, US, Mexico	0.082	1.4		43.75
	(b) US primary	0.645	5.29		23.14
	(c) Mexican exports	0.43	1.14		20.80[b]
	(d) US secondary			0.6	NA
	(e) Weighted average[a]	0.22	2.36		

a. Average of (a), (b), and (c).
b. Average *production* for Mexico, so this is an overestimate of elasticity.

Table 5
Estimates of mercury production costs (1972$)

		Mining cost/ton[a]	Concentrating cost/ton	Roasting cost/ton	Total cost/ton	Total cost/76 lb flask
I.	*Roxburgh* (1980)					
	Underground	24.95		10.69	35.64	541.73[b]
	Open-pit	2.50		10.69	13.19	200.49[b]
II.	*Rohlfs* (1969)					
	1959 Abbot Mine, US				46.11	700.87[b]
	Circa 1960 New Idria Mine, US	44.38		4.63	49.01	744.95[b]
III.	*CRA* (1975)					
	Underground	13.20	3.91	4.88	21.99	334.25[b]
	Open-pit	3.92	3.91	4.88	12.71	193.19[b]
IV.	*CRA/EFA* (1974)					
	1969 Spain					51–76
	1969 Italy					129

a. Equals short ton.
b. Calculated assuming 5 lb mercury per ton. Actual grades vary widely by location.

Given the noncartel short-run supply elasticity of 0.22, and mean noncartel supply of 152,000 flasks, the fringe supply function is

$$P = 1587 + 13.3QS. \tag{5}$$

The net demand function facing the cartel is just $D = QT - QS$. The cartel's average revenue (inverse demand) function is thus

$$P = 1415 - 8.8D. \tag{6}$$

The cartel's short-run marginal revenue function is therefore given by

$$MR = 1415 - 17.6D. \tag{7}$$

   Long-run market conditions can be described in the same way. Again using DeBartolo's elasticities, evaluated at the same mean quantities and prices, we construct the following functions:

$$P = 1500 - 4.03QT^*, \tag{8}$$

$$P = 256 + 1.23QS^*, \tag{9}$$

$$P = 547 - 0.945D^*, \tag{10}$$

$$MR^* = 547 - 1.890D^*, \tag{11}$$

where * denotes long-run equilibrium.

   The short-run and long-run elasticities of the cartel's *net demand*, again calculated at the mean price and quantity, are -0.46 and -4.26, respectively. The much larger long-run elasticities reflect substitution in uses of mercury and shifts away from mercury-using products, as well as increased production from higher-cost producers and entrants.

   We are reluctant to put too much weight on DeBartolo's point estimates of long-run parameters, since his sample covered only 13 years, which included the rather dramatic disequilibrium period of 1964–1965 (see table 1), and possibly other disequilibrium periods as discussed below. Equations (8)–(11) are not intended to pinpoint the long-run equilibrium; instead they provide a yardstick for measuring the severity of market constraints facing the cartel as demand and supply adjust to new prices. Our concern is with the implicit adjustment path between the short run and the long run.[16]

3.3 Explaining the Price Pattern

We now turn to the central question. How can one explain observed cartel behavior and mercury price patterns over time? In particular, can the cartel's internal problems (e.g., the cheating, retaliation, and reconciliation episode of 1950–1954) explain prices and profits, or are they better explained by changing external market conditions? We shall see that external, not internal, conditions determined the behavior and success of the mercury cartel.

The Italian cheating incident of late 1949 and the subsequent turmoil in 1950 provide the most dramatic example of internal cartel problems prior to the early 1970s. Italy's sale to the US government stockpile was two-thirds as large as the entire world output of mercury in 1949. The Mercurio Europeo agreement was terminated, and for about ten months Spain tried to retaliate by undercutting Italy's price.[17] Spain offered mercury to the market at $120 (1972 dollars), approximately equal to Italy's cost of production.

One might think that this apparent collapse of the cartel would lead to depressed, competitive pricing. In fact prices began to rise during the summer of 1950. Spain stopped undercutting, and increased price to $385 in January 1951. Prices and profits reached historical highs, just one year after the cartel's "demise." The average price for 1951 was $368, and it stayed near that level through 1953.

The high prices of the early 1950s were the result of the extremely low short-run elasticities of supply and demand.[18] When Spain tried to undercut Italy in 1950, its production capacity, combined with that of fringe suppliers, was too constrained in the short run to fulfill demand at the low ($120) price. Italy was able to sell at higher prices in the disequilibrium market; demand held strong as Italy gradually raised the price. As long as the market was unresponsive, it was in Spain's interest to raise its price, which it did, and Italy followed suit. Thus any internal problems the cartel faced were irrelevant to its success in exploiting market power to obtain excess profits. None of the internal problems were overcome; Spain and Italy did not reach a new agreement until 1954,[19] cheating was not deterred, and retaliation was unsuccessful. If anything, these events made the cartel more aware of its strength.

In 1954, mercury prices jumped again. One might think this was a result of the new cartel agreement reached that year. But in fact, the 1954–1955 price jump was also the result of external market conditions. Prices had declined only slightly from 1951–1953, and elasticities of demand and fringe supply were not high enough to erode cartel profits. Also, demand increased during the years 1953–1957. World output rose during this period of rising prices from 160,000 flasks to 243,000.[20]

From 1955 to 1963, real mercury prices steadily declined. This was the result of a transition from short-run to long-run equilibrium. Equations (8)–(11) imply a long-run net cartel demand elasticity of −4.26 at average price and quantity. (Compare this with the short-run elasticity of -0.46.) If the cartel fully exploited its market power in the short run, as it appeared to in 1954–1955, its optimal price would fall in later years as the market adjusted and its net demand curve became more elastic. Consistent with this, the price decline in mercury was accompanied by a declining share for the cartel. The combined Spain-Italy share peaked in 1953–1955, after which it fell until 1963 (see table 2). Cyclical price behavior in the 1950s was thus the result of very inelastic short-run supply and demand, becoming much more elastic in the long run.

This price pattern was repeated in the 1960s. As mentioned earlier, the cartel pushed prices from \$264/flask in late 1963 to a peak of \$768 in 1965. The only change in internal cartel organization around this time would have predicted increased competition and lower prices: in 1963 Mercurio Italiano was disbanded in response to new and stiffer EEC antitrust regulations. Again, we must look at the constraints of the external market.

In terms of our short-run model of equations (4)–(7), a \$768 price implies output of 73,000 flasks, at a marginal revenue of \$130 per flask. Actual cartel exports were significantly higher, at 117,000 flasks, but as we explained earlier, the price run-up changed consumers' expectations of availability, inducing inventory accumulation and shifting the excess demand and marginal revenue curves outward. Without knowing the extent of this expectations-induced shift, we can still estimate the cartel's potential for short-run profits before the price increases of 1964–1965. Assuming a constant marginal cost (equal to marginal revenue) of \$130,[21] the Italians would have been earning about \$638/flask in 1965, and the Spaniards as much as \$720, with the Lerner index of monopoly power equal to 0.83, an astounding number. If the price-cost margin held over total exports for the year, then the joint cartel excess profit would have been about \$75 million on total sales of \$90 million.

We would like to see external conditions predict the timing of price jumps, as well as the magnitude. The pattern of market shares is instructive. The cartel's market share dropped considerably between 1955 and 1962 (see table 2). But, in 1963, the share leapt back up to 52%. At the same time, US production began rapidly falling off (table 1). (Recall that US supply was the most price elastic sector in DeBartolo's model; see table 4.) One interpretation is straightforward. Spain and Italy had a dramatic and unassailable cost advantage in mercury production, because of high ore grades.[22] By the end of 1962, the 1955–1963 price decline had begun to drive fringe suppliers out of the market. Having reached an effective limit-pricing point, lowering the short-run supply elasticity by putting marginal producers in the position of facing new sunk costs to reopen mining operations, the external conditions were ripe for a new price surge. These conditions were enhanced by another apparent upward shift in demand beginning about 1964 (see table 1).

The price gradually fell from $768. By 1966 the average price was about $600, around which it fluctuated for four years, and then steeply declined. There were no known internal disagreements during these years of declining price, at least until 1971 or 1972. However, the long-run demand and non-cartel supply elasticities indicate why large price surges are necessarily a short-run phenomenon in the mercury market. Again assuming constant marginal cost at $130, (11) implies that the cartel should have been selling about 220,000 flasks, at a price of $339. This is roughly how far the price indeed declined by 1971.[23] (Afterward demand began shifting downward, forcing price down further.) Again, mercury prices can be plausibly explained by profit-maximizing subject to the dynamic external constraints of the market.

Finally, let us briefly discuss the mercury market of the 1970s. In 1972, the cartel's share of world production had reached an all-time low, and price had fallen to $227, its lowest level since 1950, and a number well below our estimate of the long-run equilibrium price. After 1975, prices approached the cartel's marginal cost.

This cannot be explained in terms of internal organization. As mentioned earlier, several other producers who had become major sellers during the late 1960s began meeting regularly with Spain and Italy to fix prices. These producers accounted for 60–80% of world production and in 1975 they signed a formal agreement establishing a new international cartel. But this did not increase monopoly power in the mercury market—the 1970s were dominated by the drastic and continuing downward shift in demand. Using production figures as a proxy for demand, table 1 shows that output fell from an historical high of 299,000 flasks in 1971 to 181,000 in 1978. The overriding importance of demand is highlighted by the price rise from 1978 to 1980. Output and demand turned around in 1978, and the price quickly began to rise as cartel members again restricted output to take advantage of improved external conditions.[24]

4 Cartel Experience in the World Sulfur Market

As an industrial raw material, sulfur is used in two forms: elemental (pure molecular) and nonelemental. Some consumers can use only elemental sulfur, or sulfuric acid manufactured from pure sulfur (for medicinal and other scientific purposes). But about 75% of sulfur demand (in 1970) was to produce industrial sulfuric acid, which can be made from either elemental or nonelemental sulfur.[25] Elemental sulfur is produced from US Gulf Coast salt domes and other deep deposits by the Frasch process, from pure ("brimstone") deposits, and by recovery from "sour" oil and natural gas and pollution control systems. Nonelemental sulfur comes from pyrites (metal sulfides) and as by-product acid from other primary metals production. Here we examine the elemental sulfur industry, which was first a monopoly and then effectively cartelized from 1833 until the 1960s.

The sulfur cartel, for reasons we discuss below, separated the world into two markets: the United States and elsewhere. In the non-US market, the cartel was explicit, with detailed contracts and strict operating procedures. In the United States no formal cartel existed, but producers acted as though they had an established organization, and maintained monopoly prices. Since the same US producers made up the Sulexco export cartel, it is easy to imagine how tacit collusion in the domestic market could be as effective as formal cartelization. We shall refer throughout to "the cartel" because of this pattern of cooperative conduct.

Following a brief industry history, we shall examine a few aspects of conduct between 1922 and the 1960s (the years of dominant US participation in the cartel). Because of favorable supply and demand conditions, the cartel was very successful and stable until the 1950s. Then, changing external constraints altered the market, causing the cartel's power to decline. At no time during this century were problems of internal cartel organization central to the determination of sulfur prices.

4.1 The Industry

Sicily had a monopoly on sulfur during the nineteenth century, producing from its brimstone mines.[26] The Italian government established Consorzio, a cartel, in 1906. In 1907, Union Sulfur Co. began commercial production from US salt domes using the new Frasch process. That year, Union and Consorzio signed an agreement dividing the world market (except the United States and Italy), one-third to Union and two-thirds to Consorzio. The cartel set a minimum price, which remained unchanged (in nominal terms) until 1916.[27]

After the original Frasch patents ran out, two large US firms entered: Freeport (1912), and Texas Gulf (1919). In 1922, the three US producers established Sulexco, an export cartel allowed by the Webb-Pomerene Act of 1918. One of Sulexco's first acts was to sign a new agreement with Consorzio, renewable every four years, which this time divided the world (except home markets) as 75% to Sulexco, and 25% to Consorzio.[28] By 1925, the Union Co. had depleted its reserves and left the market. In 1928 and 1932, respectively,

Duval and Jefferson Lake entered the market as small, US Frasch producers. These two companies did not join Sulexco, but exported most of their output at cartel prices. From 1925 to 1966, Freeport and Texas Gulf controlled about 90% of elemental sulfur production in the United States.

The sulfur market was very stable until the 1950s, when the growth of the natural gas industry made recovery of elemental sulfur from "sour" gas feasible. Spurred by high prices during the Korean War supply shortage, this source rapidly grew in Canada and France, and new Frasch production was begun in Mexico. A price war broke out in 1956–1957, and pricing changed from f.o.b. to a delivered basis, with freight contributions and discounts used to compete for contracts.[29] To strengthen their position, the two small US Frasch producers joined Sulexco in 1958. The turbulent 1950s closed with the conversion of most US and some European shipments to liquid form.

By the 1970s Frasch native and recovered elemental sulfur was being produced in many countries. In 1968, the United States was only producing 28% of the world's sulfur. Even in North America recovered sulfur has greatly weakened the Frasch producers; Freeport, Texas Gulf, and Duval had only a 45.5% share in 1977.[30] Though production is still concentrated and Sulexco continues to operate, there is no longer a successsful dominant cartel controlling the sulfur market. Rather, the market has been responding to conditions in oil and gas markets (the primary source of by-product recovered sulfur), exogenous demand shocks, and political turmoil (the Iranian revolution, Polish political crises, and the Iran-Iraq War, which all involved major producing contries).

4.2 External Conditions and the Sulfur Cartel

The dominant role of external market conditions on cartel behavior was clear during the years between the world wars. Even without a formal cartel organization, potential monopoly profits were large enough for Frasch producers to behave cooperatively in the US market.

Frasch producers had cost advantages over pyrites in the US market in both production and transportation. In the early 1920s, when the posted price was only $32, Frasch captured nearly the entire US sulfur market, which demonstrates the absolute cost advantage.[31] In addition, since pyrites are only about 45% sulfur by weight, elemental sulfur has a significant freight advantage for inland markets. At prices above $32, the Frasch market share was lower in coastal markets than in the interior.

Sulfur was usually used in fixed proportions in production, implying a rapidly declining marginal physical product. In addition, sulfur inputs were only a small fraction of total cost. Both facts suggest a low elasticity of demand. On the other hand, there were few unique uses for sulfur, and at higher prices many sources became available. We conclude that the demand for Frasch sulfur was very inelastic up to the cost of substitutes (primarily pyrites), at which point it became very elastic.[32]

Based on a 1939 study, we can roughly estimate the elasticity of excess demand facing the Frasch producers before World War II. Morrison (1939) estimated that domestic consumption was 1.6 million tons of Frasch sulfur when the price was $32 per ton (1923–1926). When price rose to $42, consumption fell to 1.4 million tons. Further, at $46/ton, Morrison calculated that inland markets would begin shifting to pyrites, and demand would fall to 1.1 million. The implied arc elasticity of excess demand between $32 and $42 is −0.53; between $42 and $46 it is −2.28. We assume a point elasticity of −1.7 at $42, which was the posted price in the United States from 1927 to 1939.

If producers were maximizing profits at $42, marginal revenue would have been equated to marginal cost, and the usual relationship indicates a marginal cost of $17/ton. Hazleton (1970) develops engineering cost estimates that range from $5.19 to $23.76 per ton in 1970. Jefferson Lake reported costs of $11–$13 at its largest mine during 1961–1963.[33] Production costs from a given mine do not appear to have changed much (in real terms) over the years. Though the estimates vary, it is reasonable to assume that marginal cost was about $17 before World War II. Based on this, the Lerner index for the cartel would have been about 0.60 at the $42 price.

During the 1922–1927 period, external conditions also led the cartel to establish firmly the export price discrimination that would characterize the sulfur market for many decades. In 1928 the average value of exports was $9.50 greater than the average value of domestic sales. Sulexco and Consorzio chose to sell only to consumers who required elemental sulfur, a submarket with a lower elasticity of demand than the market that could also be supplied by pyrite producers. The price differential was thus the result of market conditions, conditions that were actually manipulated by the cartel, first by isolating a low-elasticity submarket, and then by dividing this submarket, so that Sulexco and Consorzio each separately faced steeper demand curves.[34]

The export differential illustrates in another way the importance of external conditions to the cartel and the relative ease with which it handled internal coordination, even without formal agreements. During the late 1920s, the price differential led American purchasers to act as middlemen, reselling to the export market. Sulexco developed a plan to forbid member firms from selling more than domestic requirements to domestic consumers, but the FTC disallowed this contract amendment as a restraint of domestic trade. However, having agreed upon the plan already, Sulexco did not need a formal contract provision. Middleman marketing was not a major force thereafter, and the price differential was stable and persistent (see table 6).

Following the cartel's adjustment to profit-maximizing price levels in the domestic and export markets, sulfur prices remained remarkably stable until World War II. The average nominal value of all US shipments from 1927 to 1946 only twice varied from the posted price by more than $0.11, and was within $0.04 for 15 of those years. This stability, so different from the wide fluctuations seen in mercury prices, is understandable given sulfur market conditions. Remember that the Frasch producers faced an approximately kinked excess demand curve, with the arc elasticity jumping from -0.53 ($32–$42) to -2.28 ($42–$46). After a certain price level had been reached, the elasticity of demand facing the cartel rose rapidly, so the potential returns to short-run, sharp price jumps were small. In the export market, it is probable that the elasticity of fringe supply rose fairly rapidly even for elemental sulfur, because of the incentives a high price differential would create for US purchasers to get around Sulexco's system of preventing middleman trading.

After World War II changing external conditions, and in particular growing fringe supply of *elemental* sulfur, led to the eventual (effective) demise of the sulfur cartel. In 1954, Frasch production was begun in Mexico, and recovery from "sour" gas became important in Canada and France as the natural gas industry grew. When the elasticity of fringe supply increases, the elasticity of excess demand facing the cartel also increases, lowering potential profits. Shortly after Mexican Frasch became available in the European market, prices began to decline. The average value of US export shipments declined steadily from $41 in 1954 to $25 in 1964. By 1958, pricing had become more typical of a competitive market as the f.o.b. posted price system was dropped in favor of delivered pricing with widespread freight contributions and discounts.

One Sulexco response to new competition was an investment program to change the US distribution system from dry to liquid shipments. This would eliminate a Mexican freight advantage by requiring all producers to use special liquid sulfur tankers. By 1963, 90% of sulfur shipments in the United States were in liquid form, and the cartel had lowered the elasticity of demand it faced by increasing the relative cost of fringe supply.[35] Through price cutting and conversion to liquid shipments, the cartel was able to slow the growth of Mexican imports to the United States, but it no longer dominated the world sulfur industry.[36]

By the mid-1960s the cartel probably had little or no independent influ-

Table 6
Value of shipments and posted prices for frasch sulfur (1972$/ton)

| Year | Shipments value | | | Posted price |
	All	Exports	Domestic	
1906	64.59	77.17	74.48	82.74
1907	62.03	72.49	60.65	76.21
1908	66.53	74.00	65.14	80.17
1909	63.31	67.90	62.63	75.29
1910	59.06	59.03	59.16	72.18
1911	63.99	69.01	63.46	78.21
1912	57.88	62.36	56.91	73.60
1913	58.23	59.32	57.76	72.78
1914	61.76	62.47	61.31	74.65
1915	56.07	64.43	54.74	72.99
1916	43.21	52.56	41.21	84.69
1917	42.06	45.05	41.61	85.16
1918	38.70	48.66	37.56	50.35
1919	25.15	46.89	35.28	46.64
1920	29.89	28.15	30.17	35.64
1921	42.15	37.48	44.18	61.09
1922	39.14	34.87	41.46	33.61
1923	36.95	34.51	37.82	32.13
1924	38.37	38.04	38.39	33.00
1925	34.79	38.99	32.67	32.76
1926	41.55	43.67	40.72	42.05
1927	44.74	49.84	41.27	43.57
1928	42.96	49.98	39.52	42.96
1929	43.59	49.99	40.12	43.66
1930	48.15	56.02	44.80	48.18
1931	57.08	68.67	52.17	57.02
1932	64.33	72.60	60.44	64.19
1933	63.12	66.21	61.65	63.05
1934	55.26	56.99	54.46	55.54
1935	51.68	56.26	50.26	51.91
1936	51.35	52.95	49.10	51.41
1937	48.07	48.18	48.04	48.18
1938	49.29	52.70	47.40	51.49
1939	47.67	51.48	46.20	48.00
1940	46.99	51.37	45.20	47.05
1941	42.23	45.32	41.38	42.25
1942	37.46	45.07	35.78	37.44
1943	35.84	42.65	33.89	25.82
1944	35.55	41.60	34.17	35.55

Table 6 (continued)

Year	Shipments value			Posted price
	All	Exports	Domestic	
1945	34.88	39.53	33.42	34.90
1946	30.56	34.66	28.90	30.54
1947	27.48	30.42	26.39	25.70
1948	25.89	30.49	24.32	25.89
1949	27.24	32.25	25.11	27.24
1950	27.65	31.27	26.18	27.69
1951	28.12	32.24	26.68	28.77
1952	29.03	34.59	27.14	29.62
1953	36.84	37.97	36.48	33.75
1954	36.27	41.68	33.87	36.07
1955	37.90	41.26	36.63	35.95
1956	34.78	38.41	33.30	34.80
1957	31.16	35.54	29.17	32.56
1958	29.62	31.52	28.64	29.59
1959	29.33	31.19	28.50	29.55
1960	28.98	28.89	29.02	29.49
1961	29.23	28.12	29.74	29.62
1962	27.35	29.01	26.61	29.52
1963	24.98	26.35	24.34	29.62
1964	25.17	25.96	24.79	30.81
1965	28.00	30.19	26.74	31.44
1966	31.11	40.41	27.10	31.92
1967	39.02	47.53	35.94	39.90
1968	45.17	NA	NA	NA
1969	30.25	41.48	NA	NA
1970	24.96	24.99	NA	NA
1971	18.27	19.00	NA	NA
1972	17.03	17.55	NA	NA
1973	16.87	18.28	NA	NA
1974	25.13	31.21	NA	NA
1975	35.55	40.97	NA	NA
1976	35.16	35.90	NA	NA
1977	31.24	33.72	NA	NA
1978	29.63	27.49	NA	NA
1979	33.70	44.03	NA	NA
1980	49.40	61.63	NA	NA
1981	56.65	68.42	NA	NA

Sources: Hazelton (1970); US Bureau of Mines, *Minerals Yearbook* (various years).

ence on price. A sudden and unexpected upward shift in demand from 1962 to 1966—following years of falling prices and low investment—caused a shortage similar to the Korean War years.[37] The price jumped from 1964 to 1968, but then fell to its lowest level ever in 1973. As expected, high prices brought forth a large supply response in the late 1960s. Noncommunist world production increased from 20 to 28 million long tons between 1964 and 1969. By 1973, the cartel probably earned no profit on the marginal unit of production, though its members still garnered economic rents from older, low-cost mines.[38]

Before the Korean War, the sulfur cartel enjoyed a long period of profitability at prices it fixed to maximize profits. Up to a point, the elasticity of excess demand was low, providing a significant potential return to successful cartelization. Beginning in the early 1950s, external conditions were rapidly changing, and prices fluctuated in response. The cartel was fortuitously profitable for several years due to exogenous, unexpected demand shocks. But fringe supply was also increasing, and although Sulexco survives to this day, its monopoly power has been largely eroded. By 1977, recovered sulfur accounted for 57.9% of world elemental production, and even within North America the three large Frasch producers had only a 45.5% share. Clearly external market conditions and not problems of internal organization determined the cartel's early success, and its eventual loss of market power.

5 Market Structure and Cartel Behavior

We have seen that the performance of the world mercury and sulfur cartels over time was largely the result of evolving market structure. In both cases the cartels had the high degree of monopoly power that made success feasible. Minimal conditions of market concentration were, of course, necessary, but those conditions have also been met in markets where cartelization was unsuccessful. In the mercury and sulfur markets concentration was accompanied by an inelastic demand and an inelastic competitive (noncartel) supply. Of course market structure was changing over time in the mercury and sulfur markets (as demand changed, elasticities varied, etc.), and it is those changes that explain most of the historical variation in prices, not changes in internal cartel organization.

There are numerous examples of attempts of cartelizaton that were completely or nearly completely unsuccessful, in that prices remained close to competitive levels. In every case that we are aware of, the lack of success was due largely to the constraints of external market structure. Two examples— the lead and copper markets—might be instructive.

An international lead cartel was formed in 1964 under the leadership of Rio Tinto Zinc, a company also involved in cartel activity in the zinc and uranium markets. The cartel operated secretly, but information discovered in the mid-1970s indicated that it controlled virtually all primary production outside the United States.[39] In 1965 the cartel produced about 55% of the world's lead; 37% came from secondary (recycled) production, and the rest from US mine production.[40] A series of *Metals Week* articles during the mid-1970s detailed the cartel's activities in manipulating the London Metal Exchange price. But although it fixed prices, it did so with little gain. During the life of the cartel (1964–1976), real lead prices were below those of the mid-1950s. The problem was the size and price responsiveness of competitive fringe supply. Noncartel production accounted for close to half the market, and most of that came from a very competitive secondary supply industry. Secondary supply was in turn highly price elastic, particularly in the short run. This is what put a limit on the cartel's monopoly power.[41]

CIPEC, the world copper cartel, whose members include Chile, Peru, Zambia, and Zaire, has operated openly. But it too has been a cartel on paper only, and has had no significant impact on copper prices. Again, the problem has been a large and highly elastic competitive supply, much of which is secondary supply. (Unlike the case with lead, demand is also fairly elastic.) Pindyck (1978) calculated an optimal cartel price trajectory for CIPEC and found it to be very close to the series of prices that would prevail under competition.

These examples are consistent with our heuristic argument that external market factors, and not problems of internal cartel organization, should dominate in determining cartel success or failure. Of course we have not attempted to do an exhaustive historical study of cartel experience, and there may be examples that are contradictory. However, until such examples are brought to light, research on cartels might be more fruitful if directed at the relationship between market structure and cartel behavior. This in turn will require the detailed study of the evolution of market structure and cartel experience in individual industries—a difficult task.

Notes

1. Adelman began studying OPEC and the world oil market in general well before it became fashionable after the 1973–1974 oil shock. His book on *The World Petroleum Market* and his *Foreign Policy* article (1972–73) are among the more widely cited publications in this area.

2. Stiglitz (1976) has shown that with zero extraction cost and isoelastic demand, the price and production trajectories for a monopolist are the same as under competition.

Even if extraction cost is positive, resource depletion will reduce monopoly power (i.e., bring the monopolist's production closer to the competitive level), but uncertainty over the reserve level will restore some of this lost monopoly power. See Pindyck (1983).

3. Estimates of Hotelling rent as a fraction of price in the case of oil can be found in Pindyck (1978, 1979a). For bauxite and copper see Pindyck (1977, 1978). For the case of nickel see Stollery (1983).

4. In Pindyck (1977, 1978, 1979a), the gains from cartelization were measured by comparing the present discounted value of the flow of profits under cartelization (beginning at the time the cartel forms) with that for a competitive market, assuming in both cases that production decisions are made in a dynamically optimal manner. While this explicitly treats resource depletion, it requires the computation of numerical solutions to a nonlinear optimal control problem.

5. Eckbo documented over fifty formal cartel organizations, and of these only nineteen could be considered successful in the sense of maintaining a price significantly higher than would have been the case under competitive conditions. But even the successful cartels were limited in their durability. According to Eckbo's study, the average lifetime of the formal agreements was about five years, and only five of the nineteen cartels lasted ten years or longer.

6. A similar deterrence strategy is given by Orr and MacAvoy (1965).

7. For a discussion of consistent conjectures in models of oligopoly, see Bresnahan (1981).

8. This example should also help make it clear why the distinction between explicit collusion and implicit collusion is often an artificial one.

9. In addition, variations of the "tit for tat" strategy might characterize a rational expectations equilibrium in the context of a *repeated* game, i.e., if the cartel operates with a long time horizon and cartel members develop "reputations."

10. Rather than adopting measures to exacerbate cartels' internal problems, consuming countries seem to favor policies for commodity market intervention that would only assist cartels in solving their problems. Any measure that has the effect of centralizing or disseminating information on transactions and prices works to help solve the detection problem. This is why buffer stocks, marketing arrangements, and national or international purchasing agencies would work so much to the disadvantage of the consuming countries.

11. See, e.g., Roxburgh (1980) and Charles River Associates (1975).

12. See Hexner (1946).

13. Although price data are generally available, we have been able to find little evidence of production costs before 1950. Eckbo (1976) asserts that the cartel maintained price at levels at least 200% of marginal cost. This is not an unreasonable estimate, at least for Spain, since prices ranged from $214 to $447 (in constant 1972 dollars), while 1969 production costs were estimated for Spain at $44 per flask, and for Italy at $112 per flask (Charles River Associates, 1975). Production technology did

not change dramatically over this period, but ore grades were probably twice as high before World War II as in 1970; if anything, production costs were probably lower during the early cartel years.

14. Although an international cartel was never explicitly reestablished after 1950, all industry observers agreed that Spain and Italy reached a new, secret agreement by late 1954: e.g., "In market circles here it is generally held that the cartel has been operative ever since differences over the 1950 deal were settled earlier this year" (*Engineering and Mining Journal*, 30 September 1954, p. 1). The two Italian firms formally cartelized in 1958, only officially to disband in 1963 in response to new EEC antitrust regulations. Even after 1963, however, market observers concluded the international cartel was functioning. See, e.g., Burrows (1974) and Rohlfs (1969).

15. Rohlfs (1969), pp. 151, 158.

16. Pindyck (1978) sets up the nonlinear optimal control problem for a cartel maximizing profits given short- and long-run conditions, then obtains a numerical solution for the optimal path. For our backward-looking analysis, we found it sufficient to consider only the nature of the implied adjustment path.

17. Rohlfs (1969) has a good discussion of this episode.

18. Our supply and demand curves pertain to 1960s quantities, but it is reasonable to assume that elasticities did not change much. Note, for instance, that Rohlf's (1969) 1947–1967 estimates of supply and demand elasticities fall in between DeBartolo's (1976) estimates.

19. *Engineering and Mining Journal* (1954).

20. While some of this output might have gone into inventories, the new level was sustained and eventually increased in the 1960s, clearly indicating increasing consumption.

21. Charles River Associates (1975) estimated the 1969 cost per flask for Spanish production at $51–$76, and for Italian production at $129 (both in 1972 dollars). While we cannot make too much of the agreement between the CRA cost estimate and our calculation of marginal revenue at $130, the evidence is heartening.

22. See Roxburgh (1980), p. 125, for some historical comparisons.

23. The cartel never produced anywhere near 220,000 flasks, and it is probably not true that marginal costs were constant up to such a high output. Spain produced all of its mercury from just one mine; Italy from just two. Though a mine can be expanded, beyond some scale of operation, costs would necessarily significantly rise.

24. US Bureau of Mines, *Minerals Yearbook, 1982*.

25. Hazleton (1970). For a good description of sulfur forms and uses see US Bureau of Mines, *Minerals Yearbook*, "Sulfur" chapter, any year.

26. In 1838 the King of Sicily granted a full monopoly license to one commercial firm, which promptly raised the price from $25/ton to $75 (nominal dollars). This action was reversed by what has variously been referred to as "British diplomacy" (US Bureau of Mines, *Mineral Facts and Problems, 1960*), and "British gunboats" (Mikdashi, 1976).

27. US Congress (1939), pp. 2219–2226.

28. Under the agreement, prices, terms, and conditions of sale were fixed. Monthly statements to the cartel furnished member shipments, sales, deliveries, destinations, prices, freight rates, and other information. A penalty of two tons of sulfur was mandated for every ton sold in violation. See US Congress (1939), pp. 2214–2217.

29. Hazleton (1970).

30. Rogers (1977).

31. Again, all prices and costs are in 1972 dollars. In addition to possible production cost advantages, Frasch had some cost advantages in use. The capital investment in a sulfuric acid plant is about 30–60% more when pyrites are the feedstock (Faith, Keyes, and Clark, 1957). Total factory costs are also greater (*Chemical Week*, 1967).

32. The demand curve thus has the same shape as the demand for bauxite, another successfully cartelized commodity. See Pindyck (1977).

33. Hazleton (1970), p. 41. Hazleton had deducted royalties from the reported costs, arguing correctly that they should be considered part of economic profit.

34. The Frasch producers probably were not interested in a similar strategy in the domestic market for several reasons. First, the total demand they would face would then have been quite small. In fact, because of World War I shortages, the producers had greatly expanded their capacity, and would have had to leave much of it idle if they had not competed in the general US market. Also, Webb-Pomerene organizations are not allowed to affect US markets, and such blatant price fixing probably would have been prevented by the FTC or Justice Department.

35. Hazleton (1970) discusses the conversion from dry to liquid shipments at length. The various effects on cost are complicated, but it appears that the net result was to stabilize long-run demand for the cartel, by limiting the inroads made by Mexican imports, without necessarily increasing its market power.

36. US Bureau of Mines, *Minerals Yearbook*, various years.

37. *Engineering and Mining Journal*, February issue, various years. The new demand was attributed to a boom in the world fertilizer industry; see US Bureau of Mines, *Mineral Facts and Problems, 1965*.

38. Recall that Hazleton's estimate for a high cost mine was about $23.76. The 1973 price was $16.61.

39. Documents were found detailing cartel operations. See, for example, *Metals Week*, 28 October 1974 , Clarfield et al. (1975), and the Australian *National Times*, 13–18 June 1977.

40. Metallgesellschaft Aktiengesellschaft, *Metal Statistics*, 1966.

41. See Clarfield et al. (1975), and Stubbs (1982).

9

Worldwide Petroleum Taxation: The Pressure for Revision

Paul Leo Eckbo

1 Introduction

Over the last decade, fiscal regimes have evolved in line with the rising price of oil and with the prevalent price expectations of government policymakers and company executives. In the mid-1970s perception of scarcity changed the bargaining power in favor of governments controlling the resource base. Companies accepted dramatic jumps in fiscal costs with the equally dramatic jumps in prices. The price increases produced pressure for immediate fiscal measures. These pressures, in turn, coupled with the complicated politics of capturing a larger portion of rents from the oil industry, produced ad hoc fiscal measures that proved workable only within a narrowly defined price and cost environment. Often there was not enough time to develop robust fiscal regimes, that is, regimes that would work under a range of industry and market environments.

The incentive structures of many of today's fiscal regimes reflect these ad hoc measures of yesterday. These systems are not particularly suited to the current market environment. Although market conditions began to change drastically in 1982, the tax regimes have not yet been properly revised. Adelman has expressed it as follows: "Governments were quick to believe and slow to abandon the powerful legend that oil and gas prices could only go up, up, and away. With such enormous profits in store they thought they could wait, especially because they could not bear the terrible accusation of being soft on foreign oil companies" (Adelman, 1985, p. 19).

I shall review the incentive structures of four fiscal regimes and compare them along a common set of dimensions of profitability and risk exposure. The discussion will highlight the pressure for change in these regimes and its

The author is grateful for the collaboration of James L. Smith and Panos Cavoulacos in many and lengthy discussions on fiscal analysis. Henry D. Jacoby has provided valuable guidance that has improved this paper's clarity and form. Thomas Gochenour and Arlie G. Sterling have provided editorial comments. Responsibility for the final result remains with the author.

likely direction. Because the price of oil today has dropped to about half of what it was in 1980 in real dollar terms, the industry is operating in a price environment for which these systems were not designed. Governments are competing for scarce exploration and development capital in an attempt to attract new investment, or at the very least to maintain activity levels in the petroleum sector. The current perception of downside risk in the oil industry, and the increased competition among governments, should force fiscal reforms of current regimes so that they will become better balanced with respect to profitability and risk exposure.

Project risk is discussed in terms of a company's exposure to several different factors, as represented by alternative price, cost, and geologic success scenarios. Our comparison of scenario-specific exposure between countries is from the perspective of an investor choosing between alternative petroleum exploration and development projects. The focus is on the behavior of a decision maker attempting to maximize his wealth while minimizing his exposure to unfavorable events. The article by Blitzer et al. (1985) expands on the financial concepts of risk in extraction contracts.

In this discussion, the term "fiscal regimes" refers not only to tax rules but to concession terms and the participation terms for the national oil company (NOC). Thus the examination includes all the provisions that affect the distribution of risk and returns between the host government and the multinational oil company (MOC). Concession terms might include, for example, work program provisions, signature bonuses, and the participation level of the NOC, all of which are usually specified through some process of negotiation. Compared to the tax rules, these negotiated terms have more often accurately reflected current industry expectations for the oil market and country specific investment opportunities. Governmental tax rules and petroleum legislation have changed less frequently, and have been less sensitive to market realities.

2 The Period 1973–1985

2.1 Overall Trends

Governments have pursued several objectives as they have attempted to manage the petroleum sector in the 1970s:

1. control of where and when petroleum reservoirs were explored for and developed, and by whom;

2. capture of rent and excess profits, particularly those resulting from sudden price increases;

3. encouragement of the development of high cost reservoirs;

4. provision of incentives for cost efficiency;

5. the evaluation of a country's total resource base;

6. administrative simplicity;

7. local participation and transfer of technology.

Designing a fiscal regime to meet these often contradictory objectives, given rapidly changing market conditions, a heterogeneous resource base, and disagreement over internal political issues, has turned out to be an exceedingly complex task. The resulting regimes often have been poorly designed and unstable. It seemed impossible to identify a robust fiscal regime, that is, a fiscal regime that could perform satisfactorily under a wide range of market environments.

The ill-defined nature of the resulting systems, and the rapid rate of change of the rules of the game, made it very difficult for companies to allocate their resources to achieve a "healthy" return consistent with a "reasonable" level of risk. Furthermore, the discretionary system of allocation of concessions in many countries implied an additional aspect of political risk. Regulatory regimes prevented the free flow of capital between regions. However, overriding concerns about oil resource scarcity and security of supply led companies to expect to make money in every region if they could only get access to acreage. The key issue confronting company executives was one of "access" rather than a thorough assessment of the risk-return outlook for each region.

Over the last decade, the major fiscal developments have followed the major market developments:

1973–1975: Introduction of special taxes in addition to general corporate taxes, to capture the rent resulting from higher oil prices. Nationalization of many company holdings.

1975–1979: The participation of NOCs and other domestic entities are increased through revised concession terms to maintain the level of local activity in a market with stagnating oil prices and volumes.

1980–1981: Further increases in the tax rates and participation levels following the second price explosion. Concerns for cost consciousness emerge as geologic depletion becomes a concern (Norwegian Ministry of Petroleum and Energy, 1980). Development of smaller, higher cost reservoirs, and reservoirs in more hostile environments, are emphasized.

1982–1985: The high cost areas opened up by the 1973 price explosions are maturing with declining discovery trends. Oil prices are sliding downward. Fiscal regimes are under pressure to support better a "stable" activity level in a world of declining and volatile oil prices.

2.2 The British Experience

To illustrate how the evolution of fiscal regimes of the period 1973 to 1984 was reflected in individual countries we might review the history of Britain, which has had one of the more market-sensitive oil policies.[1]

Prior to 1975, the only special provision in the British tax system affecting the oil and gas sector was a 12.5% royalty. Higher oil prices in 1973–1974 led to substantially higher profit expectations from the anticipated exploitation of North Sea oil fields. The government favored appropriation of this newly created economic rent through a profits-related levy. The Oil Taxation Act of 1975 established a new fiscal system and the rate of the new Petroleum Revenue Tax (PRT) was set at 44%. Because the government wanted to generate tax revenue immediately, the PRT was levied on a field-by-field basis, so that new development expenditures could not be deducted from tax liabilities associated with existing production. The British government was concerned that the UK subsidiaries of foreign companies would shift North Sea profits to their parent companies in the form of interaffiliate interest payments, and it therefore disallowed interest deductions for PRT determination.

In response to oil company criticism that the development of smaller, less profitable fields would be hindered by this additional taxation, an "oil allowance" equal to 1 million tons per year for 10 years was permitted, a maximum PRT liability level was set, and a safeguard provision was drafted that stipulated that, if gross profits were less than a 30% treshold, PRT would fall to zero.

Beginning in 1979, a series of further changes were made to the fiscal system. These changes coincided with the doubling of world oil prices in 1979–1980. The changes were

1. the rate of PRT was raised to 60% in 1979 and to 70% in 1980,

2. the oil allowance was reduced to 0.5 million tons per year,

3. the uplift allowance on capital expenditures was reduced from 75% to 35%.[2]

A new tax was introduced in the 1981 budget in a move to increase government revenue further. The Supplemental Petroleum Duty (SPD) was set at a rate of 20% on the basis of gross revenue less an oil allowance of 1 million tons per year. The absence of any capital allowance meant that revenue would accrue immediately. SPD also was levied on a field-by-field basis. However, SPD was repayable up to the amount lost if a field ceased production before costs were recovered. Other changes in the 1981 budget included restrictions on "uplift" and of the safeguard provision. These changes were made to avoid "goldplating" incentives that occurred when incremental investments reduced PRT by an amount greater than the expenditure.

The imposition of SPD resulted in a slackening of interest in exploration investment and a postponment of some scheduled development projects. Combined with the royalty, the SPD rendered many high-cost fields uneconomic. In response to industry recommendations, the government abolished the SPD in January 1983. In its place the Advance Petroleum Revenue Tax (APRT) was instituted. APRT was levied at the same rate as SPD but was creditable against "normal" PRT. At the same time, the PRT rate was raised to 75%.

In the March 1983 budget, however, it was decided to phase out APRT. The changes in the 1983 budget were not enough to restore North Sea activity in the face of falling oil prices. The government subsequently adjusted fiscal terms to make the system more profit-related. Royalties were abolished on new fields in the Northern Basin (i.e., those approved for development after April 1982). The oil allowance for PRT was doubled to 1 million tons per year. Appraisal drilling costs could be deducted from any field's PRT income. These changes were estimated to have amounted to $1.2 billion in tax relief for oil companies operating in the British Sector of the North Sea.

Changes introduced in the 1984 budget, to reduce general corporate tax rates in general in exchange for slower depreciation deductions, also affected the oil sector. The corporation tax rate was scheduled to fall from 52% to 50% in 1983, 45% in 1984, 40% in 1985, and 35% thereafter. However, capital allowances for plant and machinery were to be reduced from a 100% first year basis to 25% on the declining balance basis.

The evolution of British tax terms reflects expectations for the profitability of North Sea exploration and development activities and the national need for offshore activity, as well as the interaction between special tax regimes for the petroleum sector and the general corporate tax environment. This evolution also reflects the difficulty of designing one stable tax regime for a sector as heterogeneous as petroleum. The British government has relied upon annual adjustments of the tax regime to meet its own objectives and the industry's concerns. It is obvious that the process of making annual revisions is costly because of the resources committed to the debate over the required revisions, and because of the uncertainty it creates. Viewed from another angle, the fact that the British government has demonstrated a willingness to adjust tax terms both downward as well as upward has given the industry some confidence that, if the market environment should change dramatically, the British tax regime would not add to its short term problems by remaining rigid.[3]

Over the period 1973–1984 there were parallel developments in a number of countries. Because oil companies seemed willing to accept substantial downside risks so long as they got some limited upside potential, bargaining power shifted almost entirely to the hands of governments. Accordingly competition for investment between countries was very limited. Such competition between countries surfaced for a short period in 1977–1978 but disappeared again with the price explosion of 1979. However, today there is substantial competition between countries and the investigation of the relative attractiveness of the fiscal regimes of individual countries has become essential. Below we shall examine how a fiscal regime determines the division of returns and risks between government and foreign oil companies, using four countries to illustrate the wide range of different circumstances.

3 Characteristics of Country Cases

The four countries selected to illustrate the range of petroleum fiscal regimes are the United States, the United Kingdom, Indonesia, and China. The US Gulf of Mexico is a substantial and mature area that relies totally on a cash bonus bidding system. The UK North Sea represents a substantial and mature non-OPEC region where activity began on a grand scale only after the price explosion of 1973–1974. The United Kingdom is the economic base for many of the larger MOCs in the oil industry and it has suffered less from an "us versus them" mentality than from the general politics of oil versus industry (Barker and Brailowsky, 1982).

Indonesia represents a second-rank OPEC country and as such has to cope with the politics of cartel production quotas and allocation decisions. Of the four here chosen, Indonesia also represents the extreme case in terms of its dependence on the petroleum sector. Oil accounts for about two-thirds of its export revenue and about 13% of its GNP. With a large population, a large foreign debt, and great dependence on the petroleum sector, Indonesia's compliance with OPEC-designed prorationing output quotas is nearly intolerable. However, it is also the case that Indonesia cannot afford to see oil prices fall. Its primary concern then is to extract as much revenue as possible from slowly expanding oil exports without further upsetting the oil market.

In terms of profitability China represents the other extreme in our sample. The Chinese fiscal regime was established in 1982. It has therefore developed during a period when there were expectations of ever increasing oil prices and initial estimates of substantial geologic potential in China. The first bidding round in China was completed in December 1983.

The tax terms of a particular country typically consist of a large body of fixed terms and a number of negotiable terms. Furthermore some terms are subject to administrative judgment and revisions that make it difficult to describe the risk/return implications of the rules. With the obvious risk of oversimplification, I have attempted in table 1 to summarize some of the distinguishing characteristics of the four regimes. The table shows the type of contract in use and the terms that govern the relationship between the host government and the MOC.

The table illustrates the heterogeneous and complex nature of fiscal regimes. We may highlight each regime in a simplified format as follows.

The regime applicable to the US Gulf is characterized by heavy reliance on a competitive auction system that allocates offshore leases among interested parties. Two entirely different sets of leasing rules (production royalty versus net profit sharing) have been used selectively by the government during recent years. Under the traditional cash bonus lease a 16.6% royalty is paid as indicated in column (3) of table 1. The United States has added taxation of "windfall profits" by a mechanism that applies to the oil industry alone, and that is universally recognized as a poorly disguised excise tax. The form of the windfall profits tax is indicated in column (12).

The UK regime after the changes introduced by the 1984 Finance Act still consists of a discretionary system of concession allocation under which cash bonus bids have been solicited for selected blocks. The tax system relies heavily on special taxes on petroleum activity added to the body of corporate taxation. In the United Kingdom there is no participation by the public sector in petroleum activity, except for marketing of crude oil via the British National Oil Company (BNOC, which was terminated in March 1985). The management of the incentives for additional investments is illustrated in the royalty column, column (3), which indicates that there is no royalty for new fields but 12.5% for fields developed 1976–1983.

In Indonesia a general tax reform was enacted in December 1983. Its fiscal regime has the following characteristics. The tax system is based on corporate income tax but no special taxes on petroleum activity. Indonesia has a discretionary system of concession allocation with negotiable signature and production bonuses. The generic contract is, as indicated in column (1) of table 1, a production-sharing contract whereby the contractor undertakes exploration at his own risk, and if commercially exploitable hydrocarbons are discovered, is compensated with a share of production after cost recovery. The contract permits recovery of the contractor's exploration, development, and production costs from gross annual production before production sharing with Pertamina, the national oil company.

The terms of the fiscal regime of the People's Republic of China are to be revised in connection with the concessions to be allocated in 1985. The following key characteristics are expected to remain the same. It is a discretionary system of concession allocation, with companies bidding on a production-

Table 1
Country fiscal terms

Country and national oil company	(1) Generic contract type for offshore	(2) Government or NOC participation (% carried or not)	(3) Royalty (%)	(4) Corporate income tax (%)	(5) Deductions from corporate tax	(6) Cost recovery: exploration
China, (People's Republic), CNOOC	Production sharing	Optional, up to 51% carried through discovery, full cost participation through development	17.5%	Sliding scale: 20–40% + 10% local surtax	Costs, expenses, losses	Expensed out of cost oil = 50% of gross production after recovery of operating expenses
Indonesia, Pertamina	Production sharing, some joint ventures	Optional 10% participation of Indonesian company reimburses contractor	20% of after-tax profits	35% of net profits	Operating costs, bonuses, interest, survey and IDC, 20% investment allowance	Cost oil allowances expensed
United Kingdom, BNOC	Invited exploration and production licenses		None for new fields, 12.5% on production of fields developed 1976–1983	45% for 1984–1985, 40% in 1985–1986, 35% thereafter	Royalty, operating costs, interest, depreciation, exploration costs, and PRT	Usually expensed from corporate tax or carried forward
United States	Leases acquired under cash-bonus bidding		16.6% of gross production values on lease holds	46%	Expensed IDC, depreciation, percent depletion allowance, windfall profits tax, net profit sharing payments	Intangible exploration costs expensed immediately

(7) Cost recovery development operations	(8) Risk-service payments or reimbursement	(9) Production-sharing (% split, HG/company)	(10) Signature, discovery, and production bonuses	(11) Domestic sales requirements	(12) Special taxes, windfall profits, supplemental taxes	(13) Other features or tax instruments
Capitalized, recovered after operating and exploration costs + 9% annual compound interest		Composite sliding scale X-factors schedules linked to production levels, negotiated in advance CNOOC takes pro rata share as partner and as representative of China's percentage take	$1 million			
		Profit oil split 65.9–34.1% for effective 85–15% split	Negotiable	34.1% of 25% of gross annual production at full market price for first 5 years		Investment tax credit 20% of development expenditures if Pertamina's share + 56% of company's share exceeds 49% of cumulative production
100% first year capital allowance, can be carried forward, IDC expensed					Petroleum Revenue Tax (PRT) 75% of assessable profits base less losses, royalty, and oil allowance	Oil allowance provides tax relief from marginal fields, uplift = 35% of qualifying capital expenditures
IDC expensed tangible development costs depreciated over 5 years			Competitive auction for bonuses		Windfall Profits Tax, sliding scale tax on difference between current sales price and adjusted base price, 20% 1985	Net profit sharing leases usually taxed at 30%, no royalty, investment tax credits of 10% of acquisition costs of tangible investments

sharing schedule as indicated in column (9) of table 1, a work program, and other contributions such as technology transfer. Under the production sharing contract, under which CNOOC (the national oil company) has 51% participation in development, and is carried through exploration, the annual production is split between the private operator and CNOOC via a production-sharing schedule linked to the level of production. The Chinese contract permits recovery of the private operator's share of production, exploration, and development costs from 50% of production. The Chinese tax system is based on royalties and corporate income taxes on petroleum activity as indicated in columns (3) and (4) of table 1.

For those interested in a more extensive description of fiscal regimes, consult Barrows (1983).

The fiscal and contracting regimes of these four countries differ substantially. In the following we shall attempt to compare these regimes as to the attractiveness of their incentive structures. To undertake such a comparison, we need to introduce some common assumptions and dimensions.

4 Comparative Analysis of Countries

4.1 Assumed Project Characteristics

Most fiscal regimes reflect the level of rent anticipated in the individual petroleum sectors. They also tend to reflect the anticipated composition of the reservoirs to be discovered. A tax regime designed to provide incentives to develop many small high cost reservoirs will differ from one for which a few large reservoirs are expected. Before attempting to compare the incentive structures of these tax regimes, we should therefore define our assumptions with respect to the *pretax* economics of exploration and development activities in the respective regions. The first four columns of table 2 summarize the assumptions with respect to the geologic prospectivity and the exploration and development costs of each region as well as the total pretax rent or profits that the project offers.

We have defined an "expected" discovery size in each country. The expected discovery was determined according to "consensus" estimates of median, future expected discoveries for each country. The expected discoveries were assigned to water depths where future acreage would likely be offered. For instance, in Indonesia, the expected discovery size for evaluating the tax regime is a 50 million barrel (MMb) field in 200 feet of water.

Based on a review of published costs around the world and private communications with operating companies,[4] an estimate was made of exploration, development, and production costs as a means of giving a reasonable, relative

Table 2
Indicators of costs and profitability

	(1) Expected discovery (MMB)	(2) Exploration costs ($/B)	(3) Development costs ($/B)	(4) Total rent ($/B)	(5) Private rent ($/B)	(6) Profit index
United States Gulf of Mexico	50	2.4	4.5	20	0	0
United Kingdom	100	4.1	7.8	14	11	0.9
Indonesia	50	2.10	3.9	21	3	0.5
PRC: South China Sea	100	3.6	5.4	17	2	0.2

picture of cost levels. Costs are adjusted according to water depth and the harshness of the offshore region. Cost estimates are based upon review of a large number of projects in different regions of the world, with the largest number of these projects having taken place in the Gulf of Mexico and the North Sea.

For presentation in table 2 exploration and development costs per barrel ($/b) have been calculated. This is done by dividing the present value of exploration and development costs by a similarily discounted value of the production profile for the expected discovery. Discounting of the production profile represents a rough correction for the different lengths of the production profiles in the various regions. The analysis furthermore assumes a 10% probability of discovery, that is, a success rate of 1 out of 10 wildcat wells.

To facilitate comparisons I have used a common set of economic and financial assumptions to evaluate each country's expected discovery. The analysis was performed with a $29 per barrel price of oil (in 1984 real dollars), and a discount factor of 10%. Exogenous production profiles were assumed, and these data plus the cost assumptions were input to a simple reservoir simulation model that can calculate present value of the pretax project, or of the project with the different tax regimes in effect. Because project finance has some influence on tax obligations, a 40% debt financing was assumed. An annual inflation rate was set at 8%. By ignoring foreign tax credits and bilateral tax treaties the resulting analysis is a meaningful assessment of one country's incentive structure versus another's.

4.2 Expected Profitability

The before-tax profitability of the projects by regime is shown as the per-barrel rent in column (4) of table 2. The per-barrel rent is defined as the present value of the net cash flow divided by the discounted value of the production profile for the expected discovery. No leverage of the project is assumed, and as noted earlier a discount factor of 10% is applied to net project cash flow.

The private rent, shown in column (5), was calculated by including a detailed representation of how the fiscal regimes allocate revenue and costs between the host government (including the NOC) and the foreign MOC. The tax takes differ depending on a company's existing income base in the country. It is assumed that the MOC has an established income base in the United States, the United Kingdom, and Indonesia, but not China. This assumption is very significant in the case of the United Kingdom, where an "old-timer" with established North Sea income receives a subsidy of $85 million to develop a 50 MMb field, which would increase the projected value to company from $60 million to $145 million, whereas a "newcomer" pays taxes of $48 million. The same assumption does not significantly affect operations in the United States and Indonesia. An old-timer enjoys an advantage over a newcomer measured in terms of a higher net present value of the expected discovery of almost 40% in the South China Sea.

The last column of table 2 is an index of the projected level of profitability associated with making the expected discovery in each region. It has been calculated by dividing column (5) by the sum of columns (2) and (3).

It should be noticed that the competitive cash bonus system of the United States has been presumed to result in the government receiving all of the rent of field exploration and development in that region. There is strong empirical evidence suggesting that the US bonus bidding system will absorb all the rent,[5] although relying on such empirical evidence "on average" and ignoring the "winner's curse" represent an oversimplification. Projected profitability is substantial before the bonus bid in the Gulf of Mexico. Oil companies are thus chasing substantial rents in that area. The division of rent between the government and the oil companies is the result of the collective behavior of the companies at the auction. It is possible that a low bid would by chance win a concession that turned out to contain the expected discovery size. There is therefore a chance of earning a profit substantially higher than the average. However, when comparing one region average with other region averages, the fact that the cash bonus bid on average captures 100% of the rent for the government has to be reflected in the comparison. Oilmen that are better than the average at assessing prospects will earn returns that are better than this zero rent level.

There are substantial differences in the level of after-tax profitability between the four countries in table 2. The United Kingdom stands out with a margin of $11.00 per barrel. Indonesia and China have margins of $3.00 and

$2.00, respectively, although the investment requirements in Indonesia are substantially lower and the return on investment therefore substantially higher than in China.

Risk differences not accounted for in the calculations might explain the differences in profitability levels. We would like to know whether the incentive structure of the fiscal regimes properly balances risk and returns and thus could remain unchanged under the economic environments expected to dominate the next ten years.

In table 2, it is apparent that there is little correlation between the profitability of the expected discovery before and after tax. The obvious implication is that it is essential to review the details of the tax regimes to assess the economic attractiveness of country investments. Table 2 furthermore indicates that emerging competition between countries is likely to change the fiscal regimes dramatically so that they will properly reflect the required balancing of ex ante risk and returns. Balancing of ex ante risks includes nonquantifiable factors such as the low sovereign risk of investing in the United States. Risks and opportunities also include the probability that a company might find a giant oil field off China's shore.

It should be observed that if table 2 where to be corrected for differences in exploration risk between the various regions, the United Kingdom and Indonesia are the two regions offering high and well established rates of success, whereas the new areas licensed in the Gulf of Mexico and in China are substantially more uncertain from the point of view of exploration success rates. The success rate of the UK North Sea has averaged almost 25% over the last two years, whereas success rates commonly being referred to for the new acreage in the Gulf of Mexico vary between 7% and 12%.

From my own interaction with corporate decision makers in the period 1979–1981 I got the distinct impression that decision making focused on access to acreage and on security of supply more than on efficient allocation of capital in the face of substantial downside price risk. Feeling confident that oil prices could go nowhere but up, companies were willing to accept a modest upside potential in return for a substantial downside risk if oil prices were to collapse. Concession negotiations did not seem to focus on the likelihood of large oil price declines nor on how the relative position of countries would change if that should happen. Because oil companies have so far applied only limited pressure, this imbalanced incentive structure in many fiscal regimes has survived. This incentive structure continues to be inconsistent with a competitive market for exploration capital.

However, before we make strong conclusions about the incentive structures of the country cases, we should investigate to what extent differences in risk

Table 3
MOC exposure and profitability[a]

	Percent decrease in NPV			
	(1) Price	(2) Development cost	(3) Exploration cost	Profit index
United States	35	9	21	0
United Kingdom	31	5	4	0.9
Indonesia	34	4	19	0.5
China	70	16	133	0.2

a. Exposure is measured by percentage decline in base case net present value as a result of the above unfavorable scenarios. (1), 25% price drop from \$29/b to \$21.75/b. (2), 25% cost overrun. (3), probability of success drops from 1 in 10 to 1 in 25 wildcats.

exposure might explain the apparent wide discrepancies between marginal returns across the world.

4.3 Dimensions of Risk

As mentioned in the introduction, the downside risk associated with the incentive structure of each country can be compared by investigating the relative change in the net present value of corporate cash flow that would result from a set of unfavorable price, cost, and geologic developments. In table 3, the percentage declines in the projected net present value of net corporate cash flow that would result from a 25% drop in the price of oil, a 25% increase in development and operating costs, and a 150% increase in exploration costs (from 10 to 25 wells) have been calculated. In table 3 the fourth column repeats the profit index based on expected cash flows for the regions from table 2.

The United Kingdom and Indonesia dominate the United States and China to an even greater extent when these dimensions of risk are included in the analysis. The profit level of China seems insufficient to compensate companies for the dramatic impact of potential unfavorable price or cost developments. If it were necessary to drill 25 rather than 10 wells to make the expected discovery of 100 MMb, the whole exploration and development program would turn unprofitable. Exposure to price fluctuations is almost as dramatic. A 25% price drop would produce a 70% drop in projected profits in China.

The general conclusion to be drawn from table 3 is that a company's exposure to unfavorable events varies widely under different fiscal regimes. The incentive structure of individual tax regimes seems to reflect a distorted market for exploration capital when risk is incorporated in the analysis. Low returns are not in general associated with lower risks; on the contrary—low returns are found to be most frequently associated with high levels of risks imposed by the fiscal regimes. Yet MOCs have continued to invest in regions like the US Gulf of Mexico when they are clearly dominated by other regions from the point of view of these measures of risk and return. From table 3 it is also apparent that some countries may have unintentionally offered better terms than has been otherwise necessary to attract capital, and other countries are going to see investment in exploration and development activities decline as MOCs turn away from countries with an unacceptable balance of risks and return. The picture that emerges from the current international situation implies that a country like the United Kingdom may decide to tighten its fiscal terms because it no longer feels such generous tax incentives are needed to attract the desired capital investment and activity levels.

Over the last decade, geology may have played a more important role than economics in the decision to accept concession terms for new acreage. Earlier geologic expectations of field size much greater than the discovery size we have used in table 2 seem to have been the only explanation for why China has managed to attract exploration dollars. Disappointing exploration results to date are the pressure point for revision of the Chinese fiscal regime.

The prevalence of discretionary systems of allocation of concessions around the world and the emphasis on noneconomic criteria do not provide a mechanism for efficient worldwide allocation of exploration capital. Furthermore, discriminatory fiscal treatment dependent on income status and nationality creates additional market imperfections. I expect that today's keener competition for investment capital will break down many of the barriers between countries and produce an international incentive structure that would more closely align itself with a "reasonable" trade-off profile between risk and return.

5 Directions for Improvement

By removing elements of taxation that are unrelated to profits, countries can improve the incentive structures of their fiscal regimes. The significance of nonprofit related elements of taxation may be illustrated by a set of "distortion ratios." The ratios are calculated by considering how a project breakeven level (i.e., zero projected NPV) is affected by changes in one particular factor before and after tax calculations. For example, if the cost characteristics of a region imply that a 28 MMb field could be discovered and developed in a world of $29 oil before tax payments, while in the same region a field no smaller than

Table 4
Distortion ratios

	Price	Size	Development cost	Exploration cost
United States	1.18	1.3	1.20	1.50
United Kingdom	0.73	0.48	0.84	0.22
Indonesia	1.22	1.38	1.03	1.72
China	1.54	1.96	1.17	3.40

55 MMb could be profitably developed after taxes to the host government are paid, then the distortion ratio is 55/28, or about 2. If the tax regime were neutral, the distortion ratio would be 1.[6] When the distortion ratio is above 1 it indicates that some level of activity that would otherwise benefit the government and the MOC is being forgone. If below 1, the government could win by the introduction of a less distortive tax regime.

The "distortion" columns of table 4 have been calculated by dividing the breakeven level before taxes by the outcome or answers to the following questions:

Column (1): What is the lowest oil price at which a company could explore for and develop the expected discovery size?

Column (2): What is the minimum economic field size that can be explored for and developed with an oil price of $29 per barrel?

Column (3): What are the highest development costs that can be spent to develop the expected discovery if the oil price is $29 per barrel?

Column (4): What is the maximum number of exploration wells that can be drilled to find the expected discovery?

The United States relies on cash bonus bids—"up-front rent capturing"— and relatively lower marginal taxes than other countries in the sample. This means that the MOC will experience a substantially higher capital exposure during the exploration stage than under a discretionary system but that it stands to gain if prices move higher than expected at the time of the auction. Furthermore, if prices decline, the MOC will lose money, but it will maintain activity as its tax payments or cash bonus payment represents sunk costs.

The US tax regime is distortive in terms of exploration risk even when we disregard the up-front cash bonus risk. According to the distortion ratios, a company can afford to drill 50% more exploration wells before taxes than it can under the current tax regime in the United States, that is, the level of activity permitted by the current tax regime relative to the tax-free level of activity.

The British, on the other hand, are willing to "buy" activity by subsidizing offshore exploration and development. A company can afford to drill almost five times as many exploration wells under the current tax regime as compared to the no-tax case, as indicated by the distortion ratio of 0.22. An MOC can also profitably look for and develop a discovery half the size of the minimum field in a tax-free environment.

The Chinese seem to have designed a tax regime unsuited to its needs. The distortion ratio for exploration costs indicate that 71 wells could be drilled to discover the expected field size in a tax-free environment, while only 21 wells are affordable under current Chinese terms. The current minimum economic reservoir size is almost twice as large as in the no-tax case, namely, 55 MMB versus 28 MMB in the no-tax case. This is an unfortunate distortion to be imposed on a region before its geologic potential has been clearly established. It should be noted that China was initially considered a potential "elephant" country, i.e., field sizes of 500–1,000 MMb were anticipated. The tax regime was accordingly designed to capture the "substantial rent" from giant fields rather than to facilitate the discovery and development of smaller and marginal fields.

Indonesia is highly dependent on its petroleum sector. In addition, Indonesia has a fiscal regime with a marginal tax rate with respect to the oil price of 86%. The government thus picks up 86% of a drop in revenue. No effort seems to have been devoted to protecting Indonesia's poorly diversified economy from declining oil prices.

If tax neutrality is the most desirable approach to improving the incentive structure of a country's fiscal regime, such regimes have already been discussed extensively in the literature (Garnaut and Clunies-Ross, 1979). Australia has implemented a fiscal regime based upon a resource rent tax concept.[7] The distortion ratios for the Australian tax regime are all between 1 and 1.15.

A more neutral tax regime would permit profitable exploration and development of smaller, higher costs reservoirs at a lower oil price. They thus increase the attractiveness of a region. According to distortion ratios, China has the greatest potential of the countries in this survey for improving its international competitiveness through redesign of its fiscal regime.

6 Conclusions

The level of taxation and the distortive nature of fiscal regimes increased along with the oil price over the period 1973–1981. Administrators were unable to design, and have politicians approve, fiscal regimes that would capture rent in a neutral fashion from the heterogeneous resource base of the petroleum sector. They were unable to do so even though the technology for achieving such objectives had been developed as indicated by Clunies-Ross (1983). Throughout the 1970s and early 1980s administrators focused primarily on capturing the windfalls resulting from ever increasing prices. Fiscal regimes were not designed to limit the impact of falling oil prices, and as it happened, they unintentionally magnified the impact of falling prices. An extensive worldwide study of petroleum regimes, with which I have been involved, has shown that a resource rent tax combined with cash bonus bidding would capture rent in a tax neutral fashion and behave robustly.

Oil companies in the 1970s and early 1980s were equally optimistic about future oil prices. The psychology of scarcity in those years gave all the bargaining power to governments. Companies accepted a wide range of high-risk concession terms because every region looked attractive as long as oil prices escalated rapidly. As a result governments designed and companies accepted fiscal regimes with incentive structures that did not reflect a balanced risk-return picture internationally.

With stiffer competition for scarce exploration capital between countries and more realistic investor expectations for returns on oil-related investments, the incentive structure of the world's fiscal regimes is likely to reshape itself to reflect a more equitable balance between risks and returns. The first step in that direction is likely to be the removal of nonprofit related elements of taxation. Such reforms will contribute to more neutral and, if properly done, more progressive fiscal regimes. China, for example, may substantially improve its fiscal incentives by removing distortive elements imposed by its tax regime. The United Kingdom would have to tighten its fiscal terms to produce a neutral regime. Furthermore it is questionable whether the UK Treasury can sustain a tax regime that subsidizes the North Sea development.

It is not clear how quickly the world will move toward the adoption of rent capturing regimes. Cash bonus bidding systems capture rent in an efficient manner. The politics of rent capturing is, however, rather complex. Oil companies have no incentive to push such regimes unless they believe that a more stable industry environment will also result. However, the US system is accepted. It gives every oilman an opportunity to demonstrate that he is better than the average.

The residual rents left after taxes are a key source of power for administrators. Many countries emphasize "control" rather than "efficiency" and thus prefer a more discretionary system rather than a market-related system. Furthermore, the existence of residual rents and an unwillingness to rely upon cash bonus bidding are major reasons for the existence of NOCs. Control rather than efficiency was foremost in the minds of politicians when NOCs were first established, although a minimum level of expertise on the part of the host government is also required to ensure efficiency. Information, expertise, financial strength, and residual rent are the power base of NOCs. Neither NOCs, MOCs, nor administrators seem to have a strong incentive to introduce cash bonus bidding systems in countries with a tradition of discretionary concessions allocation. The recent cash bidding experiment being discussed in Australia partially refutes this statement.

However, the major tendency seems to favor reducing the level of distortions without increasing the efficiency of the rent capturing mechanisms. This tendency is the natural response to the pressing need to maintain stable activity levels in the petroleum sector in the face of declining oil prices and increased competition among countries.

Notes

1. The British experience is also one of the most extensively discussed cases in the literature, as exemplified by Barker and Brailowsky (1982), Bohren and Schilbred (1980), Dam (1976), Institute for Fiscal Studies (1981), Kemp (1975, 1976) and Kemp and Rose (1982, 1983), and Mitchell (1982).

2. Uplift is the percentage by which actual investments are increased when creating the basis for depreciation.

3. It is important to notice the difference between changes in the tax regime that are general and retroactive and changes in the concession terms that might be changed from round to round to create the appropriate incentive for additional investments but are not retroactive.

4. Sources include Adelman and Ward (1980), Norwegian Ministry of Petroleum and Energy (1980), Eckbo Jacoby and Smith (1978), Smith and Paddock (1983), Mannsveldt-Beck and Wiig (1977), and internal papers of Wood Mackenzie Stockbrokers.

5. Mead, Moseidjord, and Sorenson (1983) analyzed 1223 OCS oil and gas leases in the Gulf of Mexico issued from 1954 through 1969 and found that "rates of return to the investors in oil and gas leases are normal or subnormal."

6. For a discussion of tax neutrality see Anders et al. (1980), Church (1981), The Institute for Fiscal Studies (1981), Summer (1978), and Swan, (1976, 1979).

7. The concept is discussed by Clunies-Ross (1983) and Garnaut and Clunies-Ross (1979).

10   Oil Tanker Markets: Continuity amidst Change

Zenon S. Zannetos

1 A Mysterious Market

It was twenty-eight years ago when I was introduced to the topic of oil transportation by Morry Adelman. I was a student in his class when at the end of one of the sessions he explained that he was looking for someone to carry forward the work of Professor Koopmans (1939). His gentle encouragement helped overcome my fears of this difficult topic, and what followed has had a profound effect on my professional orientation. It is still a fascinating part of my academic life.

As Professor Koopmans warned me at the time, the road has not been easy. In the years that followed there was ample cause to reflect on his discouraging advice, and on the admonition of another famous oil economist, Dr. Walter Levy, who said, "Many people have tried to do what you are planning to do, but failed. I feel sorry for you because you will probably spend a lot of time on this subject and end up not having a thesis. Take my advice and try something else. It is a very complex and difficult subject. No one can unravel it." Ultimately the dissertation was finished but this does not mean that Dr. Levy was completely wrong! Three decades later part of the mystery still remains, but so does the allure.

Koopmans (1939), in his classic study of freight rates, and Tinbergen (1934) before him, had identified a cyclical price behavior in the tanker-freight and tankship-building markets without seeing much evidence of any cyclical demand. Koopmans tried to explain the price cyclicality in both the tanker-transportation and shipbuilding markets in terms of the replacement cycle of vessels. He hypothesized that tanker owners, independents as well as oil companies, being in business to provide transportation services, will

I wish to thank Hyundai Heavy Industries for partial support of this research, the editors of this volume, especially Professor Jacoby, for valuable comments, and those of my students who over the years researched the field of ocean transportation.

automatically scrap and reinvest when their vessels become old.[1] Spot freight rates and orders for new vessels were seen, as a result, to be dynamically interdependent, causing price cyclicality because of the replacement cycle, even with demand constant.

The notion that capital investment decisions are made independently of expectations regarding future returns, and the implicit assumption that scrapping and replacement will take place irrespective of the current level of freight rates, provided a challenge for me to find a more satisfactory explanation of the freight-rate and shipbuilding cycles. The task was to penetrate the symptoms in order to understand the causes of cyclicality.

What followed was an incredible view of an exciting world. On the theoretical side, the thought that something mysterious and even possibly contrary to traditional economic theory was happening in the tanker markets led to the development of a theory of price-elastic expectations[2] and the proof that prices are not explosive; i.e., they do not necessarily increase or decrease indefinitely. Even under price-elastic expectations, I have shown that the range of price fluctuations is definitely bounded. Within this range, therefore, prices must converge toward temporary equilibria, which the developed theory delineates. If, furthermore, the price fluctuations were looked at in a time frame and coupled with the consequences of price-elastic expectations on the supply side, one could obtain cyclical prices without the necessity of cyclical demand. The theoretical developments opened up a number of corollaries and consequences, which, together with the theory itself, needed empirical testing.

After many unsuccessful attempts to gain access to data, and to decision makers from oil companies and independent tanker operators, and having come close to giving up as Dr. Levy advised, finally some doors were opened.

The experience was indeed amazing. "Proprietary information" came to mean tanker brokers' reports collecting dust in vaults. "Unique decision-making models" evaporated in thin air after the conversants got to know each other. People were protecting "secret weapons" not because there were any but because they were afraid to say they had none.

Yet the tanker markets were not normal markets. There was either feast or famine. Some tanker owners were thriving and coexisting with others who could not make ends meet. It was the almost unanimous opinion of oil-company employees involved in tanker operations that "this is a bad business, an ancillary evil for us." When asked to explain the success of some independents, the answer was, "we do not know how they make it . . . they must have a lot of money to throw around." The illogic of the statements did not sink in for they were confused, and if I may say so, shell-shocked, for

Table 1
Commercial fleet as of 1 January 1959, vessels of 6,000 DWT and over[a]

	Number of vessels	T-2 equivalent[b]	DWT in thousands	% of total
Oil Companies	906	1,038	17,060	32.6
Independents	1,713	1,066	34,191	65.2
Government commercial	84	64	1,158	2.2
Total	2,703	3,167	52,409	100.0

Source: Zannetos (1966), pp. 66–67.
a. Average size of vessel: oil companies, 18,830 DWT; independents, 19,960 DWT; world fleet, 19,390 DWT.
b. A T-2 equivalent is the carrying capacity of a tanker of approximately 16,542 DWT traveling at a speed of 14.5 knots.

they had made disastrous decisions during the 1956–1957 period. In a four-month period between February and June 1957, they saw rates drop to 14%, or one-seventh, of their peak of February 1957. One oil company could have saved at least $1.25 *billion* had it waited six months to place its orders. The only excuse was, "When you get into a stampede you do not stop to ask questions." And the only consolation: "We did not do any worse than our competitors."

2 Characteristics of the Industry in the Late 1950s

The above gives some idea of the confusion, turmoil, fear, and suspicion that existed at the time I began research on the industry. In the paragraphs that follow I shall present a brief summary of some of my findings in the late 1950s, in order to establish a basis for a comparison with the present state of the markets. The order in which points are presented does not necessarily imply a ranking of significance. Also some of the findings are interdependent and may be derived from others, but are listed separately for expositional purposes. Readers interested in details and the full rationale may wish to consult the original sources (Zannetos, 1959, 1966), as well as the classic studies of Professors Tinbergen (1934) and Koopmans (1939).

2.1 Competitive Markets

One of the most striking aspects of the tanker markets in the late 1950s is that they operated in a manner approximating perfect competition. The concentration of ownership of tanker capacity that is being traded in the relevant market—the spot market[3]—was found to be too low to affect the efficiency of the markets. In January 1959, as table 1 shows, the fleet consisted of 2,703 vessels of over 6,000 dead weight tons (DWT) each, for a total of 52.4 million DWT, and an average size of a vessel of 19,000 DWT. Of this total, the oil companies controlled 32.6% and the independents 65.2%. The rest, 2.2%, belonged to governments, but operated commercially. The five largest owners of tankers among the oil companies controlled only 22.2% of the total fleet. The five largest independents controlled 12.3% (Zannetos, 1966, p. 175). At no time did anyone control even 1% of the capacity traded in the *spot* market. The tonnage controlled by the oil companies, being well below their average needs, did not appear in the charter markets, unless under extremely depressed market conditions. And even then, the mathematics and the economics underlying oil-company decisions were such that the odds of any one oil-company vessel appearing in the spot market were insignificant.

2.2 Economies of Scale

Vessels were subject to economies of scale. However, because of (1) the large number of vessels needed to satisfy the demand, even if these vessels were of the largest size, (2) the constraints imposed by geography, canals, channels, harbors, refinery locations, storage capacities, and the size of markets, and (3) the risks associated with investment decisions, disruption of schedules, satisfaction of contracts, and unemployment as well as underemployment of vessels, the market forces encouraged efficiency and equalization of average rates of return by vessel class and market segment, both in terms of geography and by type of charter.

The realization of extensive economies of scale was found to encourage surplus capacity, and mitigate the risk of unemployment for large vessels, as these could effectively bypass some of the constraints described above, by being able to operate effectively at less than full capacity and/or unload offshore to shuttles. Therefore, I concluded, innovation leading to the construction of larger tankers would continue and coexist with the more-or-less perfect competitive operations of the tanker markets.

2.3 Freight Rates and Delivered Oil

The imbalance between crude oil production and refining capacity at consuming and producing centers placed transportation in a critical role. In order to equalize the price at the marketplace, the oil companies sold oil on a delivered basis. This almost perfect complementarity between producer plans and transportation needs, and the fact that the demand for oil in the short run was very inelastic, caused negative covariations in the demand for transportation capacity among the oil companies. As a result, the operations of the independent tankship markets made an important contribution to the long-run minimization of transportation costs.

Another consequence of the critical role of transportation in oil transactions and of the different transportation intensities of various crudes and products was the impact of freight rates on the net backs. To guarantee constant delivered prices, net backs were allowed to float and freight absorption was a common secret among oil companies. Given that the marginal cost of oil at various producing centers was such a small part of the delivered price, the extensive fluctuations in freight rates were reflected in the net backs.

2.4 Mobility of Capital

Unlike most capital investments, the purchase of tankers does not fix the capital in a specific geographic location. This mobility of capital facilitates the entry and exit of vessels from the various geographic markets, and contributes to a faster global equalization of supply and demand for transportation services. In turn this reduces the cost of exit from the industry. The ex ante risk facing potential tanker owners, therefore, is mitigated because of the mobility of capital, which encourages entry into the industry, and enhances competition.

2.5 The Vessel Is the Firm

Given that (1) the economies of scale accruing with an increase in the vessel size are far more significant than those realized by increasing the size of a fleet, (2) capital investment in tankers is mobile, (3) entry into and exit from markets and the industry are rather easy, and (4) effective managerial control from a distance is not feasible, the vessel for all practical purposes becomes the firm. There are many implications of this fact, all of which explain the more-or-less perfectly competitive nature of the tanker markets. Rather than repeat arguments made elsewhere (Zannetos, 1959, 1966, pp. 182–183), I shall only mention here the consequences for the financing of a vessel if it is viewed as a firm.

The normal way of financing vessels built by independents during the late 1950s was to mortgage a charter given by an oil company. As a result, many banks loaned as much as 90% of the cost of the vessel over a five-year period. The risk associated with most of these loans was minimal, as the charters guaranteed the repayment of the loan. In effect, the oil companies assumed the risk. The net result for the independent was a lower cost of capital, a high debt-equity ratio, a lower cost function, and higher returns, if freight rates were to reflect the long-term average cost of vessels owned by the oil companies.

If the oil companies were to invest funds in tankers and followed the *normal method of financing their normal activities*, their cost of capital would be dominated by the high risk associated with exploration and production. Related to this risk was a debt-equity ratio far lower than that achieved by many independents. The net result was that in capital budgeting decisions oil companies imposed hurdle rates (the same rates of return demanded of their normal operations) too high for a low-risk and low-return operation such as tankers—hence, an investment in tankers by oil companies well below the optimum level.[4]

The above findings encouraged me to identify the normal risks facing the industry, to distinguish these from those facing the firm, and those facing the vessel,[5] and to measure the effects on freight rates of shifting the risks of unemployment and underemployment from the owner to the charterer.[6] The conceptual framework and methodology thus developed and used in the late 1950s to determine the long-term rate was not unlike what later came to be called the capital-asset pricing model (CAPM), but was more complex, because of the presence of vessel economies of scale, objective savings associated with long-term contracts, and the various dimensions of risk (Zannetos, 1959, volume II, chapter X).

2.6 Price-Elastic Expectations

One of the most exciting results of this research was the development of a theory of price-elastic expectations, and the proof of the hypothesis that the behavior of tanker markets was governed by such expectations.

The opinion of the experts at the time was that price-elastic expectations did not exist, because one did not observe continuously exploding prices either upward or downward. Only in the case where expectations were assumed to be "extrapolative" (Enthoven and Arrow, 1956; Arrow and McManus, 1958) or "adaptive" (Arrow and Nerlove, 1958) were they found not to destabilize an otherwise stable system.

By assuming that price-elastic expectations cause interperiod substitutions, and by analyzing the consequences on demand of these substitutions and of the income effects, a convergence toward stable equilibria could be obtained. As a result, it was shown that

1. The demand for tanker transportation was composed of five segments, as shown in figure 1, alternating between negative *and positive* slope. Under

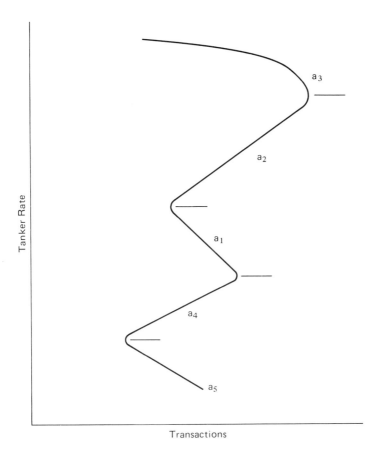

Figure 1
Demand schedule for oil tanker services. Areas a_1, a_3, and a_5 contain stable equilibria.

price-elastic expectations and in the absence of substitutes in the short run, the income-compensated substitution effect of the Slutsky-Hicks formulations represents interperiod substitutions exclusively. In the normal case the income-compensated substitution effect is negative. In the case of interperiod substitutions, however:

$$(\partial Q/\partial P)_{u=\text{constant}} = (\partial Q/\partial P_f)(\partial P_f/\partial P) = E_b E_{D,P_f} Q/P$$

and is positive. The price-elasticity of demand E_D then becomes

$$E_D = (E_b E_{D,P_f}) - (PE_{D,M})Q/M,$$

where

E_b = the elasticity of expectations of buyers,

E_{D,P_f} = the elasticity of demand with respect to future prices,

P = "present" price,

$E_{D,M}$ = the income elasticity of demand,

Q = the quantity demanded,

M = the income or money available.

Both E_{D,P_f} and $E_{D,M}$ are mathematically well behaved, positive and finite. Therefore, for certain values of P and Q, even with $E_b > 1$, we obtain $E_D < 0$. So prices are bounded and the demand schedule assumes a shape as shown in figure 1.

2. Interperiod substitution effects were causing an increase in the number of transactions as freight rates increased (region a_2 in figure 1) and reducing the quantity demanded as the rates decreased (region a_4). Region a_1 was found to be associated with the full cost of the "marginal vessels."

3. Opposing the interperiod-substitution effect was the income effect. So the slope of the demand schedule was determined by the net effect of the two.

4. The interperiod-substitution effect (income-compensated) was far more significant than the income effect up until either the high freight rates caused all the budgets to be exhausted (close to "bankruptcy" for buyers, region a_3) or the rates fell to such precipitously low levels (close to bankruptcy for sellers, region a_5) as to encourage the oil companies to "slow steam," use chartered vessels and tie up or scrap some of their own vessels, or use tankers for floating storage.

5. Freight rates were bounded on the upper side by the "opportunity value" of the cargo (region a_3), the latter being the short-run contribution margin plus the opportunity cost of losing long-term contracts. On the low side the rates were bounded by the withdrawal rate of vessels reduced by the expected cost of tie-up and recomissioning (region a_5). The above resulted in freight rates on the upper side where the total value of the cargo "plus something" was paid for transportation, and on the low side, rates that were below the out-of-pocket cost of vessels.

6. "Feast or famine" conditions were the norm in the tanker markets and not the exception. Price equilibria would rarely be observed in the range of the long-run break-even cost of the marginal vessel (region a_1). It was more likely that equilibria at very high and very low rate levels be observed, because of the shape of the demand schedule and the hockey-stick shape of the short-term supply schedule.

7. The price range above the hypothetical long-run cost of tanker services was up to twenty times greater than the range below, for good economic reasons mostly implied in item 5 above.

8. Price-elastic expectations in the tanker transportation markets caused orders for vessels to be placed with a manifested time lag of six to eight months, bringing about a lumpiness in investment and deliveries of vessels during depressed market conditions, further prolonging the recovery.

9. The more-or-less predetermined physical life of tankers and the huge lumpiness in investment set the conditions for a lumpiness in withdrawal and the beginning of another freight rate and shipbuilding cycle. Thus, price-elastic expectations were found to cause cyclical price behavior without the necessity of cyclical demand.[7]

10. Cobweblike behavior at very low levels of freight rates caused fluctuations in the rates as vessels came in and went out of markets.

11. Price-elastic expectations also affected the shipbuilding markets, with the quantity of orders being determined by two interperiod substitution effects (both positive) and two income effects that opposed each other. The income effect associated with the change in freight rates, and the size of the tonnage in one's control, was found to be positive, while that associated with the orders budgeted for the period and the change in shipbuilding cost was negative. So feast and famine patterns were also observed in the shipbuilding markets, and a cyclicality that could be explained in terms of the theory of price-elastic expectations.

12. The orders placed at the peak of the rate cycle were about equal to the total fleet at the time. This, and the speed with which price-elastic expectations take hold, led us to infer that the "famine" part of the rate cycle would be much longer than that of the "feast."[8]

3 The Ensuing Decades

3.1 Crude Oil

Many significant events have taken place in the field of oil economics during the last 25 years, but their impact on the fundamental determinants of freight rates and on general tanker-market behavior has been negligible. OPEC, which was established in 1960 ostensibly to bring some stability to the flow of oil revenues to the oil-producing countries, has tried to maximize revenues and in the process unleashed expenditure patterns that destabilized the economies of member nations and plunged the world into an economic disarray.

In the very early 1970s, oil consumption was projected to increase at a compounded rate of 5% per year in the United States, 7% in the rest of the Western World and 8.5% in the developing countries. This was at a time when the posted price of oil was still at $1.80 per barrel and the net revenue going to the producing countries was $1.025 per barrel. Then came the events of 1973, with the early spring demands by the Shah for $7.00 per barrel for Iran, which, according to the formula used at the time, necessitated a posted price of $11.65 per barrel. The latter became the official OPEC price in October 1973, and the price for participation oil was set between 93 and 94% of posted prices.[9]

For about five years after 1973, the posted prices remained relatively under control, rising by about $2.00 per barrel on the average. The inflow of funds to the OPEC countries, however, increased 13-fold between 1970 and 1978. This flow of money, and the stupor of the newly discovered power of riches, changed the expenditure patterns and even the nature of most of the OPEC countries irrevocably. Imports of the OPEC countries increased 26-fold between 1972 and 1978, and 4-fold in one year, between 1977 and 1978, reducing their current account surpluses to an estimated $18 billion in 1978 and foretelling the deficits that were to follow.

The insatiable appetite of the oil-producing countries for more revenues— often approaching the vengeful—and the unwitting encouragement by those who claimed that oil was underpriced and that we would run out of it in a decade combined to bring about the 1979–1981 price increases of over $23 per barrel and the onset of another major economic crisis.[10] Of course, some may claim that it was the Iranian oil field strikes and the subsequent political problems in that country that caused the price increases by reducing the available supply of oil. No doubt, the Iranian situation had its psychological impact, but the objective evidence vindicates Adelman (and very few others), who have claimed all along that there was a surplus of oil.

By the end of 1980, the new round of price increases by Libya, Indonesia, and Venezuela, all effective 1 January 1981, raised the OPEC ceiling price from $37 per barrel to $41, although the official benchmark price for marker crude was still set at $34. However, with the possible exception of Saudi Arabia, which held to a price of $32, no one paid attention to official prices. The game was to see who would succeed in charging more by adding surcharges. All in all, it was a chaotic situation, with prices floating all over the place.

Meantime, the law of supply and demand, even under these strained conditions, was working amazingly well, admittedly with the help of some political muscle flexing by Saudi Arabia. Inventories were piling up, and by early May the oil glut was such that it encouraged talks within OPEC aimed at unity at $34 per barrel. The efforts failed, because Saudi Arabia insisted on a price of $32 per barrel and a clear delineation of price differentials, while the "hawks" demanded price increases and control of output.

On 29 May 1981, is an unprecedented move, the oil companies demanded a cut of $6 per barrel. On 4 June 1981, Mexico cut its prices by $4 per barrel, to be followed ten days later by Great Britain with a $4.25 per barrel reduction. By this time spot prices for crude dropped as low as $32.15 per barrel and one could get the products of a barrel of crude at even lower prices.

For about a year, several behind-the-scenes attempts were made for a unification, but resulted in no viable plans. Then on 28 April 1982 it was announced that Iran, in order to increase its sales above the ceiling of 1.2 million barrels per day (MMb/d) "allowed" by OPEC (they wanted to produce 2.1 million barrels), cut its price to $28 per barrel.

Attempts to control output and prop up prices were not very successful. In January and February 1983, further cuts were announced, so at the quarterly meeting of OPEC, held on 14 March 1983, a historical step was taken to reduce the OPEC official benchmark price by $5 per barrel, to $29. The spot price of crude at this time was around $27.50 per barrel.

The significance of the price reductions must not be underestimated for it showed the weakening fiber of OPEC. In fact, it could be that the signing of the agreement effecting the price reduction does not indicate "strength in unity," but, instead, evidence of its lack of importance. If the OPEC members have no intention of obeying it and there are no sanctions if it is violated, why fuss about it? It did not, for example, keep Iran from cutting its prices reportedly to $26 per barrel to Japan, and to $25 per barrel to Syria less than two months later (*Wall Street Journal*, 5 May 1983, p. 38). On the other hand, we have had a lot of evidence of the flexibility of the OPEC countries when it comes to serving their own interests. So OPEC, although extensively weakened, should not be counted out, at least not yet. However, more pressures on the OPEC structure for price reductions and further erosion of their ability to control output should be expected.

The net effect of the escalation of crude oil prices was the reduction in worldwide oil consumption, from 55 MMb/d in 1973 to 52 MMb/d in 1983.[11] Although this reduction may appear insignificant, it must be contrasted with a level of over 110 MMb/d had the projected 6.5% average growth in world oil consumption materialized. This discrepancy proved to be very critical for the tanker markets, as we shall now show.

3.2 Tankers

The reduction in oil consumption left its unmistakable imprint on the demand for transportation. However, unlike the case of oil, where excess capacity can

Table 2
World seaborne trade, 1972–1983 (in billions of ton-miles)[a]

Year	Crude oil	Oil products
1972	7,720	930
1973	9,207	1,010
1974	9,661	960
1975	8,885	845
1976	10,233	950
1977	10,472	995
1978	9,661	985
1979	9,614	1,045
1980	8,385	1,020
1981	7,731	1,000
1982	5,412	1,070
1983 (est.)	5,200	1,050

Source: *Fearnley's* (1983).

a. Estimates for 1983 are based on statistics for the first nine to eleven months of the year for the most important countries as regards the specified commodities, supplemented with data from international associations.

be shut in to be used later, albeit at a cost, the burden of idle tonnage is very heavy because idle capacity cannot be preserved for later use. There is a more definitive physical life (average 20 years) for a tanker than for an oil well. Moreover, the variable costs associated with tie-up and temporary idleness, and the readiness of the owners to enter into the market with slight improvements in rates, keep the latter, during periods of surplus tonnage, at levels that do not even cover the out-of-pocket cost of operation for most vessels.

The oil production data, previously mentioned, do not reveal the total impact of falling demand on oil transportation because they do not indicate seaborne trade and the transportation intensity of such. According to *Fearnley's* (1983, p. 24), the seaborne trade of crude oil and products in 1972 was 1,446 million metric tons, reached a peak of 1,817 in 1979, and dropped to 1,292 in 1983, registering an 11% drop for the eleven-year period. More significantly, the total ton-miles of oil delivered decreased from 8,650 billion in 1972 to 6,250 billion in 1983, or by 28%, and from the peak of 1977 by 45.5% (see table 2).[12]

Taking the above statistics and applying them to the average fleet of 1973, we arrive at a requirement of only 122 million DWT for the 1983 seaborne trade.[13] This figure is almost identical to what one may derive by looking at the supply side from data provided by *World Tanker Fleet Review* (1983, p. 42). As can be seen in table 3, the total surplus under all categories as of 31

Table 3
Idle oil tanker capacity, 31 December 1983

	DWT in millions
Laid-up tankers and combined carriers (proportion)	55.9
Slow steaming VLCC tonnage	29.5
Slow steaming smaller tonnage (40–160,000 tons)	28.5
Excess port time	10.8
Delays waiting cargo, etc.	4.0
Part cargo incidence	17.6
Tonnage acting as temporary storage	2.7
Overall gross surplus as of 31 December 1983	149.0
Total fleet	272.0

Source: *World Tanker Fleet Review* (1983, p. 42).

December 1983, was estimated at 149 million DWT out of a fleet of 272 million DWT, indicating a requirement of only 123 million DWT.

The price increases by OPEC, as a result, extracted a heavy toll on the value of the capital invested in oil transportation. In addition to the permanent loss of capacity, extensive investment is required to bring ships out of lay-up and back to the operating stage. The size of the expenditure for recommissioning tankers depends on the length of idleness and the care taken of the vessel while in lay-up. Most of the large tankers in lay-up have been idle for so long that it is very doubtful that they will be recommissioned. It could be that the owners are holding on to them for investment purposes, expecting improvement in scrap values.

To the extent that tanker rates influence orders for vessels, it is not surprising to find that shipyards are now begging for business and that the prices quoted for the very large vessels are *in nominal* dollars what these were back in 1976 (*Fearnley's*, 1983, p. 32).

I shall now examine the various characteristics of the tanker markets in order to identify significant recent changes.

3.2.1 Market Structure

I have found no evidence to suggest that the structure of the industry has changed during the last twenty-five years. The distribution of ownership between oil companies and independents followed the pattern of old, fluctuating between 30% and 40% of total, with the independents controlling the rest. As in the late 1950s, the percentage oil company ownership reaches the low point during periods of high tanker rates and the high point during the bottom of the depression. In 1974 the relevant figures were 32% for the oil companies and 68% for the independents, but by the end of December 1983 were close to 40% and 60%, respectively.

The ownership of the five largest oil companies dropped significantly, from 22.% of the total fleet on 1 January 1959 to 15% twenty-five years later. Ownership by the five largest independents remained almost unchanged at 12.3% on 1 January 1959 versus 12.4% on 1 January 1984. During this period only one change occurred in the ranks of the top five oil companies, with Mobil replacing Gulf, but in the case of the independents a complete transformation occurred. In 1959 there were four Greek companies and one American among the top five, but by 1984 all were replaced by Far Eastern corporations and one Norwegian.[14]

So the nature of the tanker markets remains the same; close to perfect competition. The oil-producing countries have attempted to move into transportation "in order to control the delivered price of oil," but as I had predicted (Zannetos, 1973, pp. 108–114), they failed on both counts.[15] Chartering "on private terms" so as to hide freight absorption does occur, as it always did, and it will continue. But this does not appear to threaten the competitive nature of the tanker markets because of the low concentration of ownership and the other characteristic factors of the markets to which I shall soon turn. In fact, there are still over 1,100 owners of vessels, and with the reduction in the degree of concentration in the oil industry, brought about to a great extent by the birth of the national oil companies, the competitive nature of the independent tanker markets is more or less guaranteed.

3.2.2 Economies of Scale

The drive toward larger vessels continued in the 1960s and 1970s because of compelling economic reasons. The largest vessel in operation increased from 105,000 DWT in 1959 to 546,000 DWT in 1979, and no one should be surprised to see this tendency continued. As pointed out elsewhere (Zannetos, 1973, p. 44), however, ancillary technologies must be developed to allow for these economies of scale to be realized and still mitigate the risk of unemployment and underemployment of large vessels. The size of markets served is also critical; that is why one would not expect to find a preponderant number of these huge vessels in the world fleet.

If we look at the scale curves of the industry, we find that in 1958 the economic long-run average cost of tankers "flattened" at 75,000 DWT, in 1966 at 250,000 DWT, and in 1979 at 475,000 DWT (Zannetos, 1966, p. 235; 1973a, p. 44; Serghiou and Zannetos, 1982, p. 43). This is mostly due to progress in the ancillary technologies of welding, propulsion, loading and unloading, navigation, and safety, as well as the size of refineries, markets served, stor-

Table 4
Tanker rates and posted prices for crude, Persian Gulf-US basis[a]

December 1972			June 1984		
World Scale[b]		% of posted prices	World Scale[b]		% of posted prices
%	$/b[c]		%	$/b[c]	
30	.38	15.57	30	1.11	3.8
100	1.28	51.88	100	3.70	12.76
250	3.20	129.71	250	9.25	31.89
450	5.76	233.48	450	16.65	57.41

a. Assumptions: (1) crude prices: Iranian Light $2.467 for December 1972 and $29.00 for June 1984; (2) for 34° API we assume 7.5 barrels per ton.
b. World Scale is an index that at 100% is supposed to represent the "full cost" of transporting one ton of oil on a very small vessel for the specified run.
c. $/b = dollars per barrel.

age facilities, canals, channels, and harbors. As a result the long-run cost of transporting oil today in a 475,000 DWT vessel is only 41% of that of 75,000 DWT (the "optimal" vessel of 1958), and only 23% of the cost of a 30,000 DWT vessel.

Given the extensive economies of scale that accrue with the size of the vessel and the reduction in the transportation intensity of crude oil, we would expect some reduction in the number of vessels in the world fleet, especially in the years to come.

3.2.3 Freight Rates and Delivered Oil

Because of the escalation in the price of crude oil and the fact that shipbuilding costs have not increased in proportion to the oil prices, transportation is not as important now in the delivered price of oil as it was in the past. As table 4 shows, at the present levels of freight rates for VLCCs of World Scale 30, the cost of transporting oil from the Persian Gulf to the United States is less than 4% of posted prices, or about 24.4% of what it was in December 1972.[16]

There is another consequence, however, of this relative diminution of transportation cost in oil pricing, which relates to the market structure and the fluctuations of the spot rates. The oil companies, as well as the oil producing countries, will now pay even less attention to tankers, which in the long run will reduce concentration even further. Finally, in times of "crises" the charterers who own their sources of crude, and particularly the national oil companies, will, in all likelihood, be willing to pay rates that, in terms of world scale, will be even higher than what they paid in the past for the marginal capacity required to preserve long-term oil contracts—and this because the spread between delivered prices and the marginal cost of oil is much greater now than before.

3.2.4 Mobility of Capital
The technology of transporting oil and its products has not changed over the years to challenge the workings of the tanker markets. The invested capital in tankers is still mobile, and with the increase in the number of relevant markets, the importance of this factor in bringing about an equilibrium between markets has been increasing over the years.

3.2.5 The Vessel Is the Firm
It was pointed out that the realizable economies of large vessels have increased over the years. Also in the area of financing vessels, shipyards as well as countries provide 80–90% of the capital and charter the vessel back to the owner, bare boat, with a considerable subsidy. As a result the vessel is regarded as a "venture," and the emphasis placed on "the vessel as the firm" back in the late 1950s has continued and even increased.

There are not many economies that accrue with the size of the fleet, and even those of which I can find evidence are insignificant as compared to the economies of size realized by the vessel. Discussions with independent tanker owners indicate that the function is not monotonic. As one increases the size of the fleet, diseconomies are realized before any economies start to manifest themselves. The overhead of small tanker operators is not greater than $100–$150 per day per vessel, but for larger fleets, say twenty vessels, the cost rises to over $250—and this mostly because of the information and control systems.

3.2.6 Price-Elastic Expectations
In the years following my initial study, I had two opportunities, one in 1970 and one in 1973, to test the theory of price-elastic expectations. In both cases, the evidence fully supported the existence of price-elastic expectations and a cyclicality in freight rates and shipbuilding prices that is not caused by a cyclical demand. Table 5 presents a comparison of the impact of tanker rates on shipbuilding activity for the periods 1956–1959 and 1973–1983.

Tanker rates reached their peak in November 1956 and, as table 5 indicates, they generated such an avalanche of orders for new ships that the shipyard backlog rose from almost nothing to 79% of the total fleet in operation as of 1 January 1957 and to 106% nine months later. What ensued was a prolonged period of depression in the tanker markets, with some cancellations, but no new orders of any significance. The depression continued up until the growth

Table 5
Tanker fleet and backlog[a]

	Fleet			Backlog		
Date	Number	DWT (thousands)	T-2 equivalent	Number	DWT	T-2
1/1/57	2,094	39,642	2,397	966	29,229	1,898
10/1/57	2,278	42,979	2,538	1,211	44,535	2,693
1/1/74	3,458	215,593	14,801	1,171	197,631	13,668
4/1/74	3,480	219,460	15,077	1,260	213,876	14,792
7/1/74	3,550	234,180	16,039	1,202	194,637	13,463
1/1/84	2,989	272,018	18.742	206	10,395	711

Source: *World Tanker Fleet Review* (semiannual issues).
a. A T-2 equivalent is the carrying capacity of a tanker approximately 16,540 DWT traveling at a speed of 14.5 knots. Largest size on order in 1958 was 106,000 DWT. Largest size on order in 1974 was 477,000 DWT. Before 1966 vessels of 6,000 DWT and over were included in the fleet. From 1966 and on the vessels were 10,000 DWT and over. On 1/7/74, there was also a fleet of combined carriers of 39,463,575 DWT and 8,926,700 on order. Largest vessel in backlog on 1/1/78 was 541,000 DWT, scheduled for 1979 delivery. It was delivered in 1979 as a 546,210 DWT vessel and as of 1984 it is the largest vessel afloat. A vessel of 230,000 DWT sold in February 1978 for $22 per DWT. It was six years old. A similar vessel in the first half of 1974 was sold for $187 per DWT, and a smaller vessel (85,000) went for $259 per DWT in 1974. Backlog as % of fleet—106% as of 10/1/57; 92% as of 1/1/74. On 4/1/74, the backlog was 98% of the total fleet. The fleet figures for 7/1/83 and 1/1/84 exclude 11.76 and 9.54 million DWT, respectively, which represent vessels committed to "permanent" storage.

in transportation requirements and, more important, the retirement of the vessels built as a result of the World War II effort absorbed the surplus tonnage. The lumpiness in investment in early 1957 caused lumpiness in deliveries between 1957 and 1959 that in turn caused the lumpiness in the retirements of 1978. The scrapping of vessels, the lay-up of an additional 11 million DWT, and the absorption of 25% of the total capacity in slow steaming, excess port time, and port cargo brought about the minisurge in rates in the latter part of 1978. As rates improved, idle vessels were attracted into the markets (the tonnage in lay-up decreased from over 40 million DWT on 30 June 1978 to 21 million six months later), to depress freight rates once again.

The movement of vessels in and out of the markets caused cobweb oscillation and fluctuations in rates. In the last part of 1979 there was another moderate increase in rates, but it was short-lived because 34% of all the capacity was surplus at the time.

In 1973 and before the October events, retirements of vessels built during the 1950–1952 freight-rate peaks started causing tightness in the supply of transportation capacity. As a result freight rates started rising fast and by

October 1973 they reached World Scale 450, causing orders of over 200 million DWT (table 5). As in the case of 1956–1957 the orders placed created a backlog of 13,668 T-2 equivalents by 1 January 1974, which rose further to 14,792 T-2 equivalents by 1 April 1974, almost equal to the total tonnage in operation. *One month* after rates reached a peak of World Scale 450, they dropped precipitously, reaching World Scale 55 by the end of November 1973. This, however, did not deter oil companies and independents from placing orders for the period of December 1973 to May 1974.[17] Subsequently, orders for new vessels dried up and the shipyards entered a prolonged period of depression. So history again repeated itself and set the foundation for the next cycle, like the rate cycles before that.

To conclude, then, price-elastic expectations have continued to influence the behavior of those who operate in the tanker markets.

3.2.7 *Structure versus Level of Rates*
The extensive economies of scale combined with the risk of unemployment and underemployment (which also increase with size) determine a structure of rates.

For spot rates, the "normal rate" is the short-run cost of the then marginal capacity. A vessel that is smaller or less efficient than the then marginal capacity, in order to be drawn into the market, must obtain a rate that is higher than the "normal" rate. Larger and more efficient vessels exchange part of their economies of scale for mitigating the risk of short-run unemployment and mainly underemployment. Thus a structure of rates is formed.

In the case of period or time-charter rates, we have another structure, spread around the long-run economic cost of the vessel itself (certainty equivalent). This range of rates is a function of the spot rate and the duration of the time charter. Again these two factors, spot rates and time-charter duration, affect the ex ante probability of underemployment and unemployment of the vessel.

The change in the size composition of the fleet and the increase in the range of sizes of tankers brought about an increase in the range of the structure of rates. This, however, does not imply that the tendency of the markets toward perfect competition is destroyed. On the contrary, it is an indication that the market mechanism of apportioning risks and returns indeed works.[18]

4 What Will the Future Hold?

To summarize, the rise of the OPEC cartel caused a change in oil consumption patterns, changed its transportation intensity, accentuated the surplus of tankers, but did little to affect, thus far, the basic nature of the tanker markets.

That much is clear, but will this structure continue? I shall now say a few words about the future, fully realizing the vagaries of such an effort.

As already mentioned, the oil-producing countries have attempted to move downstream by obtaining tankers,[19] building refineries on their own soil, and in some cases entering into the distribution network of some consuming countries. Although these involvements have not been big enough to effect meaningful changes in the market structure for tankers, the building of more refineries at the producing centers will require, other things being equal, the seaborne movement of more products and less crude oil. As a result, we expect that the average size of tankers will continue to decrease. According to *World Tanker Fleet Review* (1983, p. 7), the average size of the fleet on 31 December 1983 was 91,006 DWT, and of the vessels on order 50,463 DWT. More significantly, however, on 31 December 1983, the average size of vessels on order to be delivered in 1984 was 53,160 DWT, for the 1985 deliveries it was 48,886 DWT, for 1986 it was 40,068 DWT, and for 1987 it was 30,900 DWT.[20] Also for the same reasons, I do not expect to see a push for more and larger ULCCs because of the high expected cost (risk) of unemployment and underemployment for these vessels.

Given that the oil companies are now producing a lower percentage of the oil they are distributing as compared to the preexpropriation era, they will, in all likelihood, reduce their share of ownership of tankers in the future. This will increase the importance of the independent tanker owners and of the free markets. As for the oil-producing countries, I expect that they will make further investments in tankers, but their efforts will not completely offset the impact of the oil-company actions. Therefore, the separation of the ownership of the oil-producing assets from the control of the distribution network for a significant percentage of the total oil consumption, especially of the oil that is most transportation intensive, will make the oil industry (and in particular the international oil companies) more dependent on the *spot* segment of the tanker markets.[21] Furthermore, even with the reduction in oil prices that I foresee, the significance of tanker rates in the delivered price of oil will never be what it used to be. Any rational oil producer and/or distributor, as a result, would not devote as many financial and *planning* resources on tanker transportation as in years past—hence, more spot chartering and less time chartering and building vessels.

Another change that I see in the future relates to the oil/ore carriers. The relative importance of these vessels will increase, because of the flexibility they provide, but again, I do not expect that the role of pure tankers will be threatened.

The behavior of those who will operate in the tanker markets is not expected to change and will continue to be governed by price-elastic expectations—and this because of the absolutely necessary role transportation plays in the oil arena. As in the days of old, when the oil companies were trying to protect their share of the market, the OPEC and other oil-producing countries will try to prevent others from eroding their position. They will, therefore, absorb transportation during periods of high tanker rates and guarantee a delivered price to protect their customer base. If they continue to bypass the oil companies in order to increase their share of the *end*-user market, and most probably they will, the fluctuations in tanker rates, from peak to trough, will be even greater in the future than these were in the past. And this will happen because for the oil that is sold directly by the oil-producing countries, the difference between the delivered price and the out-of-pocket cost of production is so much greater now than before. Ironically, had the oil-producing countries decided to market their oil exclusively through the international oil companies, the rate fluctuations would have been dampened in spite of price-elastic expectations. Thus the oil-producing countries would have derived more net revenue, and on top of that the oil companies would have been left responsible for the collections of receivables and for absorbing the bad debts.

If we now look at the supply schedule for tankers, the economies of scale will cause certain changes to its slope. As Mr. Hettena, President of Maritime Overseas Corporation, pointed out at a speech before the MIT Shipping Club about a year ago, the fundamental economies realized by large vessels that allow them to accept part cargo (underemployment) and the economics of slowdown and speedup create more elasticity in the supply schedule above the effective full-capacity level for the industry and inelasticity below. This implies that the cobweb iterations and the range of equilibria during depressed market conditions will widen and become more volatile. For the same reason, the fall in spot rates from their highest level reached will be more precipitous and the feast more short-lived than in the past. Finally, the student of tanker rates in the future must monitor not only tie-ups but also the amount of underemployment, both actual and potential, associated with part cargo and slowdowns, because of its impact on the supply schedule.

5 Epilogue

As we stand at the threshold of a new era, those of us who have been privileged to be associated with the work of Morry Adelman and whose professional lives have been touched by the intense excitement with which he views the world are happy that the challenges in the field of oil economics and oil transportation are still there for future generations.

He has been a good mentor, a good colleague, and a great friend. We hope that we may be able to reach a small measure of his accomplishments and that as educators we may enjoy hearing from our students the words that come naturally to our lips from the depths of our hearts: "Thank you for all these years, and for the life long challenge, but above all, many thanks for what you are."

Notes

1. Koopman's hypothesis assumed implicitly that the ex ante and ex post investment horizons for vessels are identical, and would have precluded tonnage being traded in the second-hand markets.

2. The price-elasticity of expectations E is defined as $E = (\partial P_f/\partial P)(P/P_f)$, where P_f stands for the future price level and P for the present price. Under price-elastic expectations we have $E > 1$; therefore with each price increase buyers *accelerate* purchases and sellers *accelerate input but postpone output*. As a result, prices increase, confirming expectations that fuel further price increases. A similar type of analysis follows price decreases.

3. In the terminology of tanker chartering, "spot" refers to contracting for one round trip. Other types of contracts are for "consecutive voyages" and "period" or "time" charters. Although in reality there is only one organized market, where all transactions take place internationally, brokers as well as charterers often refer to "markets" as if these are distinct by type of transaction and world trading center. The most important of these "markets" is the spot market because of the *number* of spot transactions and because spot freight rates indicate, at any moment, the marginal cost of transporting oil by a given vessel size for a given run. In terms of *capacity* only about 15% of the total tonnage has been historically traded in the spot market.

4. Another consequence of this asymmetry between independent tanker owners and most oil companies was the treatment of oil-tanker operations as a "loss center" and an ancillary evil.

5. As far as the independents were concerned, the *vessel* was the firm, but for the oil companies the *total legal entity* was the firm. The independent multivessel owner would intuitively use portfolio management techniques to achieve an acceptable risk-return balance in operations, viewing the vessels as independent, and truly zero-covariated entities, especially on an ex ante basis. For the oil companies, on the other hand, the concern was the risk of not being able to deliver crude oil and oil products. Their portfolio of vessels was "balanced" between owned, time-chartered, and spot-chartered vessels with this risk in mind, in order to protect the high returns obtained from the contracts associated with the cargo.

6. The risk of unemployment is greatest for vessels operating in the spot market and decreases with the duration of the time charter, reaching zero when the contract

extends to the total life of the vessel. The risk of underemployment increases with the size of the vessel and applies to both spot and time charters alike.

7. Professor Koopmans was to a certain extent right in associating the retirement of vessels with a shipbuilding cycle, especially at the symptomatic level. However, we found that there was no "one-to-one correspondence" between retirements and replacement decisions. The investment horizons associated with these decisions were proven to be different and were not necessarily made by the same decision makers.

8. The lead time to delivery of vessels, which under pressure could be shortened to eight months, guarantees that enough tonnage can be delivered and shift the supply schedule far enough to the right to bring about a precipitous drop in prices. So, even if spot rates were not to drop before new orders dried up, the feast could not last more than a few months. The famine period, however, may last for years, until growth in demand and retirement of vessels combine to bring about a scarcity.

9. Participation oil is that produced by the oil companies but owned by the nation. Normally the producing company bought this oil at the country-determined price.

10. The 1979 price increases brought forth the two-tier price for crude oil, with Saudi Arabia holding at first to an $18 per barrel price while others charged between $24 and $27 per barrel. Finally, in 1980, in two successive increases, the official lower bounds were set at $32 per barrel for Saudi Arabia and $34 for the majority of OPEC countries.

11. The data represent production rather than consumption and were obtained from the Energy Information Administration, *Monthly Energy Review* 108–109 (March 1984).

12. The reason for this reduction in the transportation intensity of oil was mainly the increase in production of oil in areas closer to the main consumption centers, such as Alaska, Mexico, and the North Sea.

13. The mid-1973 fleet we estimate at 200 million DWT. The decrease in the ton-miles of oil delivered between 1973 and 1983 was 39% according to *Fearnley's*. I chose mid-1973 as the base period because there was a semblance of a balance between supply and demand for transportation at the time.

14. My sincere thanks to my student Costas Bardjis for collecting the data included in this paragraph.

15. Furthermore, with the current account deficits and the many demands on the budgets of the OPEC countries, it is inconceivable how any one country (and "doubly inconceivable" as a cartel) can allocate the necessary funds to change the structure of the tanker markets.

16. World Scale is an "index" used as a base for quoting freight rates, and at 100% is supposed to represent the "full cost" of carrying one ton of oil on a very small vessel for a specified run. One must be careful in making intertemporal comparisons in terms of World Scale levels. Ever since the cost of bunkers became the most significant factor in the short-run cost of transportation, yearly adjustments in the scale reflect changes in the short-run operating costs only. The capital costs have not been changed for many years. As a result, at, say, World Scale 30, the relationship between revenue and cost for a tanker in 1972 is not identical to that of 1984.

17. As we have pointed out, expectations and orders placed for building tankers follow those in the freight markets with a lag of six to eight months. It is not possible to determine exactly the lag because of the administrative delays in consummating and reporting shipbuilding contracts. Ideally one would like to identify the date of the decision.

18. All the above factors were analyzed and an attempt was made to measure the part of the economies of scale that remains with the owners versus the part that goes to the charterers under various market conditions and given the size of the relevant marginal vessel. In the case of spot rates, the most recent results of our research are included in Serghiou and Zannetos (1982). As for time-charter rates, the basic theoretical details of the model used may be found in Zannetos (1965), and for the most recent application of the model the interested reader may wish to refer to Zannetos et al. (1981).

19. In the top thirty flags of registry there were five OPEC countries represented as of 31 December 1983: Saudi Arabia, Kuwait, Iraq, Iran, and Lybia. Their combined ownership was 4.41% of total (Jacobs, 1983, p. 52). We realize that the data refer to the flag of registry, but for the OPEC countries the tonnage owned is more or less identical to that registered under their flags.

20. It should be realized, of course, that under depressed market conditions the backlog is very small and does not fully represent the size composition of the future fleet. Special purpose or handy size vessels may be influencing the average size, but the trend, in our estimation, is clear.

21. I expect that the national oil companies will also depend relatively more on the spot market for oil and oil products.

11

Oil and Gas Resource and Supply Assessment

Gordon M. Kaufman

1 Introduction

"According to delicate Chinese proverb, prediction is difficult art—especially with regard to future." This oft quoted proverb is particularly apt if applied to primary energy mineral resource and supply assessments, exercises whose history is littered with the wreckage of now nonsensical but once rigidly held hypotheses about prices, costs, mineral deposition, and occurrence, and in particular about where a particular mineral *cannot* be found. Destruction of favorite but false beliefs and replacement of them by new beliefs based on new facts, new interpretation of old facts, and new ideas is a natural progression in science. We learn principally from experience.

What has the experience of the past decade taught us about primary energy mineral resource and supply assessment? More particularly, what have we learned about how to assess petroleum resources and supplies since the Arab oil embargo of 1974? The latter, more narrowly focused question guides this essay. Even though the nature of the data, the methods of exploration and production, and the relative ease with which a mineral can be found and exploited differs from one primary energy mineral to the next, the broad lessons learned about petroleum are more generally applicable.

Well done primary energy mineral resource and supply projections play at least two important but different roles in our society: they provide firms with information about when and where to explore for and develop a mineral resource, and they enhance our ability to analyze both public and private sector policy issues. The fortunes of an exploration oriented petroleum firm depend on how well it can predict how much petroleum is in the ground, in what form, and what fraction of it is recoverable at what cost—in each of

For Morry, my friend and fellow coauthor. Long ago he awakened my respect for good data and earned my admiration for his ability to squeeze out meaning from facts and numbers.

many locations. Only by being armed with such information can a firm sort out desirable from undesirable exploration alternatives. Resource and supply projections are centerpieces of the real world microeconomics of mineral exploration and development. They are the stuff of which marginal cost curves are constructed, which in turn help guide choices among exploration and development projects. At a state and national level, a complete and continuing record of mineral resource and supply statistics and projections is essential for reasoned analysis of controversial energy related public policy issues—deregulation of field markets for natural gas, offshore drilling in Georges Bank and the Santa Barbara channel, and the nature of our preparation for possible imported oil supply disruptions, for example—and requires historical energy resource and supply data coupled with projections of the future time path of mineral reserves and production.

A paradigm for oil and gas resource and supply assessment might begin with a four legged stool analogy. Four disciplines must be combined to do such assessments well: geology, petroleum engineering, economics, and statistics. Exclusive reliance on one or two of these disciplines may possibly result in an assessment that ignores critical features of the physical, engineering, and economic systems by which petroleum is discovered and produced. The result is an assessment that, like a four legged stool with legs of different lengths, is tipped over by a small change in circumstances. Significant changes in levels of rates of change of variables or in the structure the system may then be ignored or incorrectly represented and the resulting assessment may become grossly inaccurate.

Most current approaches to appraisals of future supply of petroleum from undiscovered resources are like unbalanced stools, but some are more unbalanced than others. This endemic weakness is not wholly attributable to lack of insight as to how really good, really useful resource analysis should be done. It is partly due to a continuing undercurrent of scientific parochialism. Examples are some geologists' distaste for analytical methods that do not exploit their penchant for detailed nonquantitative descriptive analysis of resource deposition with particular emphasis on exceptions to observed patterns, and some economists' adherence to traditional economic paradigms that do not conform to how the oil and gas supply system actually works. It is also partly due to lack of easily accessible disaggregated data describing attributes of individual mineral deposits and exploration and production costs in sufficient detail to permit meaningful large scale testing of the relative merits of alternative approaches to resource and supply assessment.

The experiences of the past decade have provided some valuable lessons and highlighted

- the importance of a credible, accessible *individual oil and gas field* data base of national scope,

- the importance of attaching measures of uncertainty to resource and supply projections,

- the need for a close working relationship between federal government agencies responsible for gathering resource and reserve data and petroleum firms so as to promote a flow of useful data without compromising the competitive positions of these firms.

We have

- improved our ability to incorporate uncertainty into resource and supply forecasts using subjective probabilities and objective statistical methods,

- discovered that traditional forms of econometric supply and demand modeling and predictions are not robust, do not predict well, and do not usually yield information that addresses detailed policy issues,

- advanced to a second generation of disaggregated physical models of mineral deposition and extraction that would allow regional and national assessments of supply to be composed by blending these models with the microeconomics of exploration and production and then aggregating directly discovery and production projections generated by them—if the right data were in place.

Unfortunately, the right data are not yet in place.

2 Data Needs

All interested parties pay homage to the desirability of a continuing complete nationwide record of individual oil and gas field physical properties, production, and associated exploration, drilling, and production costs. Such a record is useful for analysis of some public policy issues and is essential for analysis of others. Fields are units at the focal point of exploration and development decisions made by petroleum firms. Consequently, data gathered at the field level are pitched at the right level of disaggregation for study and analysis of decision making by petroleum firms as well as for a robust analysis of petroleum supply and demand. The character of a field file suitable for microanalytical analysis of petroleum supply has been succinctly described by Nehring (1981, pp. 5–6) in his report describing significant US oil and gas fields:

The analysis of field size distributions and discovery patterns requires an appropriate data base. Such a data base should ideally be comprehensive or near-comprehensive, well-organized, consistently constructed according to a common set of defining characteristics, and detailed enough to permit sophisticated analysis.

. . . the basic unit of data and analysis is the petroleum field. The field data are organized by region and state or statistical area and by field size. We also give information necessary to organize the field data by geologic province. Because we developed the data base to provide a means of analyzing discovery patterns and of assessing the potential for future discoveries, we included several basic items of information that are relevant to the discovery process:

(1) the year in which the field was discovered; (2) the methods used to discover the field; (3) the general and specific type of trap; (4) the major system and series of the reservoir rocks; (5) the major reservoir lithologies in the field; and (6) the spatial location and dimensions of the field (the depth to the top of major reservoirs, the average net reservoir thickness, and the productive acreage of the field). These variables provide a means of answering questions about the discovery of significant fields: When?, How?, in Which circumstances?, and Where?[1]

A principal purpose of Nehring's work is to provide a data base that would allow study of discovery patterns and serve as a basis for predicting future discoveries.

The time rate of future discoveries is dependent on the physical attributes of undiscovered deposits *and* on future values of economic variables such as predrilling exploratory costs, exploratory and development drilling and completion costs, operating costs, and prices as well. Thus, projections of the response of petroleum supply to economic incentives, such as prices and costs, and to regulatory externalities should ideally rest on *disaggregated economic data collected in a form compatible with physical field data.*

Analysts currently may study a region or petroleum province and find access to adequate field data, but inadequately disaggregated economic data, or the converse. Then we are reminded of one of Morry Adelman's favorite Oriental aphorisms: "What is the sound of one hand clapping?"

In order to model petroleum exploration and development as a dynamic system—whose responses to incentives and disincentives to explore, develop, and produce oil and gas reflect how this industry actually works—the analyst requires data describing each of the major physical and economic functions that firms perform: geological and geophysical data acquisition and analysis, lease acquisition, exploratory development drilling, construction of gathering lines, and liquid extraction and purification. How far have we progressed or retrogressed in assembling data that address this specific set of needs?

The quick answer is that data of national scope fit to this set of needs are neither publicly nor, with high probability, privately available. However, data sets that address pieces of the system are available for some but not all

US petroleum provinces. In addition, many current and historical oil and gas data are too aggregated to allow rigorous examination of changes in the nation-wide marginal cost of reserve additions over time. Nonuniform levels of aggregation of physical and economic data coupled with significant data gaps severely limit our ability to construct models for analysis of the impact of alternative policy choices on petroleum supply and demand. Sustained effort to improve the quality of petroleum sector data would sharpen the quality of analyses of fundamental issues that have sparked controversy since the founding of the US petroleum industry: wealth transfer, the presence or absence of competition in field, pipeline, and end use markets, and the impact of federal and state intervention in these markets on efficiencies of extraction and use of petroleum.

A thorough review of available data sets and major data gaps is beyond the scope of this short essay, but some insight is provided by a recently completed National Academy of Sciences study (*Natural Gas Data Needs in a Changing Regulatory Environment*, 1985). Table 2 in chapter IV of this study displays sources of currently available natural gas and oil data, together with comments on strengths and weaknesses of each. Tables 1A and 1B recast the aforemen-tioned table, listing data sources by level of aggregation. The wide variation in levels is not surprising given that no uniform criteria for data use have been shared by the government agencies and private organizations that collect, analyze, and disseminate these data. Even where there might be agreement that public reporting of summary statistics is not sufficiently disaggregated to permit useful analysis of public policy issues, US oil and gas firms' concern with confidentiality forces the level of aggregation upward. Whether or not publication, after a suitable time lag, of disaggregated field and well data does in fact diminish competitive advantages in exploration is an open question.[2]

If an analyst's interest is focused on a single basin or province, he will have to turn to data sources other than public data like that cited in tables 1A and 1B. In addition to Nehring's study of significant oil and gas fields (Nehring, 1981), other major sources of field level data are the Petroleum Data System (PDS) at the University of Oklahoma and Petroleum Information Inc. (PI). PDS is plagued with incompleteness: individual field attributes are often missing. Access to PI data is expensive and the quality of coverage varies; midcontinent basin data in particular are of good quality, and well data for more than 2,300,000 wells are present in the PI well file.

An obvious tactic for improving the completeness of individual data files describing identical attributes of petroleum fields is to interface them. While this tactic is appealing in principal, formidable problems confront the analyst

Table 1A
Publicly available data sources by level of disaggregation

	Physical attribute data				
	Field	Basin or province	State	Larger region	National
Resource appraisal		USGS Circular 860 (1981)		Potential supply of natural gas in the United States (1982) (interbasinal regions)[a]	
Seismic line-miles and crews				Society of Exploration Geophysicists (*On-shore– Off-shore Monthly Energy Review*)[b]	
Rigs in operation			Hughes Tool Co.		
Wells drilled and footage					*API Monthly Drilling Report*
Discoveries					
Reserves	The discovery of significant oil and gas fields in the United States[c]		EIA Annual Report: US crude oil, natural gas, and natural gas liquid reserves[d]		
Production	PDS				

a. Potential Gas Committee.
b. Also in annual report published in *Geophysics and Leading Edge*.
c. Rand Corp. Report R-2654/1-USGS/DOE.
d. DOE/EIA-0216 Annual Report. Subdivisions of CA, LA, NM, and TX reported.

Table 1B
Cost and price data

	Field	Basin or province	State	Larger region	National
Geological and geophysical expenditures					
Exploratory well drilling					Joint Association Survey[a]
Development well drilling					Joint Association Survey[a]
Current operating costs					Annual Survey of Oil and Gas[b]

a. API, AAPG, and M CO GA. As of 1984 IPA individual well ticket redesigned to add well spud date and rig removal date.
b. US Census MA-13K. Recently discontinued.

who employs it. Disparate field files do not have unique common names for fields or unique common identifiers. Errors in field names and codes and possibly different assignments of values to the same attribute for a given field in different files make truly accurate field file matching difficult. While a large literature describing objective matching techniques exists (cf. Winkler, 1984, for example), little work on their application to petroleum field and well files has been done. Effective matching of descriptively complex files will most likely require either intensive human intervention or a well constructed "expert system" that represents acceptable variations in description, not at the string level, but at the content level.

An excellent example of the data analytical minuet that must be performed to provide useful information about a particular policy issue is afforded by a recent EIA study of drilling activity and production for "post-Natural Gas Policy Act" gas; i.e., gas regulated under Title I of this act (US DOE/EIA, 1984b). EIA is in a privileged position. No private sector entity has an equivalent degree of access to confidential data. Even so, a large effort was necessary to convert available data into a form amenable to analysis, to validate them, to fill in missing items, and to merge disparate files. The basic data source used was form FERC-121, "Application for Determination of Maximum Lawful Price under the Natural Gas Policy Act." This source was merged with API well ticket data, Dwight's Oil and Gas Well Data, Dwight's Oil and Gas Field Data, and EIA's Crude Oil and Natural Gas Resource Evaluation

System (CONGRES). The latter system provides *field level data*. It is not available to the general public.

A careful statement of the methods employed to merge and analyze these data sources is provided in appendix A of this EIA report. Appendix A offers a fine description of a host of problems that plague the data analyst who wishes to study oil and gas data at a level of disaggregation that provides useful information for policy analysis. This particular study is a good example of data analytic detective work by a large organization with privileged access to disaggregated data.

3 Methodological Progress

The principal paradigms underlying methods currently employed to project undiscovered oil and gas resources and future supply do not differ much from those employed ten to fifteen years ago. Then we could loosely classify a model of how data were generated and the corresponding method for estimating model parameters and projecting or for projecting amounts of petroleum remaining to be discovered as falling within one of six broad categories: geologic-volumetric, life cycle, rate of effort, subjective probability, econometric, and discovery process. We still can. There have been, however, some innovative attempts to elide two or more of the approaches suggested by the above broad categories of methods. Experience has alerted us to pitfalls and sharpened our ability to avoid them. A monograph by Adelman et al. (1983) affords a detailed review and discussion of several applications of each of these approaches to resource and supply prediction and serves well as a background for some general observations about what we have learned about methods of resource and supply estimation since the early 1970s.

We have at last begun a process of intellectual cross-fertilization by arousing significant interest in problems of resource and supply estimation among professional statisticians. Before the early 1970s few projections of petroleum resources and supply incorporated explicit measures of uncertainty; point estimates abounded, as did arguments about who was "right." Practitioners of oil and gas resource and supply assessment have long been sensitive to the dominant role of uncertainty in this domain, yet only in the past decade have logically defensible measures of uncertainty appeared in published petroleum resource appraisals.

Some appraisals of the future of petroleum supply made over the past decade exhibit what cognitive psychologists call "anchoring"—a failure to account properly for the likelihood of future events that differ from a current state. Psychologists view "anchoring" as a heuristic that can lead to bias in subjective probability appraisals of uncertain events, and the analogy with a weakness of geologic-volumetric, rate of effort, econometric, and life cycle models of petroleum supply and demand is close: parameters of these models are traditionally estimated (anchored) on past data. If there is a change in the structure of the system generating past data, inferences based on these data will not reflect the nature of the change. If structure does not change, but absolute and relative magnitudes of economic quantities—prices and costs—change by large amounts, the reliability of projections may decrease significantly. These weaknesses are endemic in any approach based on extrapolation of technological and economic activity by use of a model with static structure.

The implication is that we should build and validate dynamic models that can adapt to real world changes in the economic and technical environment. While a desirable goal in principle, both our lack of knowledge of the character of future states of the technological and economic environments in which our oil and gas discovery system functions, and lack of the right kind of data, render this an elusive goal at all but the most abstract and aggregate level.

Improvements in methods will likely continue at a more modest rate, along lines established during the past decade:

• Introduction of increasingly sophisticated yet useful techniques of inference about model parameter estimation and of prediction that were absent in early studies.

• More emphasis on structural and predictive validation of models.

• Increasing elision of approaches to modeling oil and gas resource discovery and supply. For example, the logistic function adopted by Hubbert (1962, 1967, 1974) as a model of production and discovery over time was combined by Dietzman et al. (1979) with a geologic-volumetric model to provide a projection of petroleum production and discovery in Nigeria. Such apparently different probabilistic characterizations of discovery as Arps and Roberts' exponential model of number of fields discovered by an increment of exploratory wells and successive sampling share a common conceptual origin (cf. L. Gordon, 1983a, and Kaufman, 1985).

To set the stage for examination of the evolution of resource analysis methodology, figure 1 classifies oil and gas resource estimation methodological work into each of the earlier mentioned categories. Methods that combine two approaches, subjective probability and discovery process modeling, for example, are schematically displayed as intersections of categories of methods.

Life cycle models of production or of discovery rest on the assumption that, as a function of time, the rate of extraction of the aggregate mineral

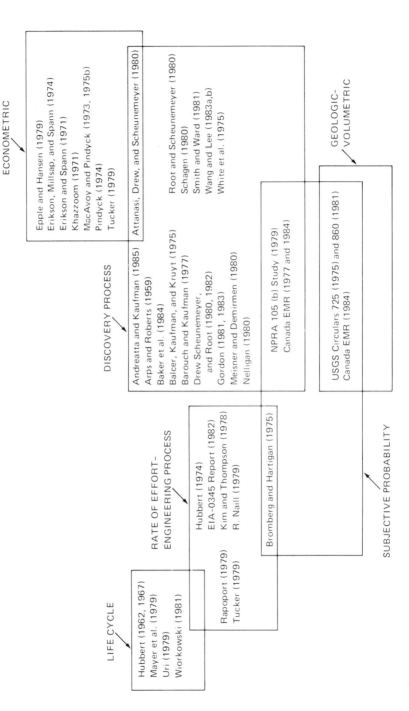

Figure 1
Resource analysis methods.

endowment of a large geographic area first rises to a peak value and then declines. For example, a time series beginning at year t_0 of aggregate US production of petroleum $Q(t)$ in year t might be assumed to be of the form $Q(t) = Q(\infty)[1 + \alpha \exp\{-\beta(t - t_0)\}]^{-1}$, a "logistic function." Here α, β, and $Q(\infty)$ are model parameters to be estimated by use of a historical time series $Q(t_0)$, $Q(t_0 + 1)$, of annual US production.

Life cycle methods, pioneered by Hubbert (1962, 1967, 1974), were challenged by Ryan (1965) for the ad hoc fashion in which Hubbert fitted to data the logistic function he adopted as a model. Wiorkowski (1981) was the first to use rigorous statistical methods to examine the quality of fit. Mayer et al. (1979) and Uri (1979) subsequently employed up-to-date statistical methods to test the fit of Hubbert's model to aggregate production and discovery data. All three found that the fit was quite good for production data to 1976, silencing the earlier debate. However, the time series of annual amounts of oil and of natural gas compiled by the American Petroleum Institute until 1978, when the EIA assumed responsibility for this time series, does not adequately mirror the aggregate magnitude of actual discoveries made in each reported year. Year-to-year variations in the API-AGA time series of new reserves "discovered" are nearly independent of actual amounts discovered (cf. Adelman et al., 1983 pp. 45–46, for a detailed explanation).

The trend toward use of more rigorous statistical methods to validate ad hoc attempts at fitting models to data is also manifest in the evolution of discovery process models that, in contrast to life cycle models, are based on explicit assumptions about how the process of petroleum exploration works. In their pioneering effort to model discovery in a petroleum basin, Arps and Roberts (1959) proposed a simple exponential model for the number $N(w, A)$ of discoveries of a given fixed magnitude A as a function of the number w of exploratory wells drilled: $N(w, A) = N(\infty, A)[1 - \exp\{-cAw/B\}]$. In the first application of their model, $N(\infty, A)$ denotes the number of fields of area A present in the Denver-Julesberg Basin, B the basinal area, and c an efficiency parameter equal to one if drilling is "random" and greater than one if predrilling exploration is able to discriminate field locations from unproductive acreage. As with Hubbert, their procedure for fitting the model to data was ad hoc, but their insight was excellent: the functional form of their model can be rigorously justified as an approximation to unbiased estimators for model parameters when sampling a finite population of deposits without replacement and proportional to magnitude. This sampling scheme is called "successive sampling" in the statistical literature. Connections between successive sampling and Arps and Roberts' model are discussed by L. Gordon (1983b) and Kaufman (1985).

Successive sampling was first proposed as a model for the order of discovery of petroleum deposits by Balcer, Kaufman, and Kruyt (1975). The heuristic underlying this model can be visualized by imagining exploratory wells as darts thrown onto a dartboard in such a fashion that the dart has an equally likely chance of hitting within any small rectangle of area irrespective of the rectangle's location on the board. Fields of arbitrary shape are drawn on the board and labeled 1, 2, ..., N. Corresponding areas are $A_1, ..., A_N$. If a dart hits within the area of a field, this field is "discovered" and its area recorded. Ignoring "dry holes"—dart throws that hit no field—and repeats—darts that fall within the area of a field discovered by an earlier throw—the probability that all fields are observed in a particular order, say, 1, 2, ..., N is $\prod_{j=1}^{N} A_j/(A_j + \cdots + A_N)$. The probability model implied by this reasoning about the order of observation of fields is called "successive sampling." Balcer, Kaufman, and Kruyt assumed in addition that the magnitudes $A_1, ..., A_N$ are uncertain quantities characterized by a log-normal probability law and used the model for the order of observation of fields discovered implied by attaching a superpopulation model to successive sampling in a study of petroleum plays in Alberta, Canada. Barouch and Kaufman (1977) and Nelligan (1980) investigated this model further.

At that time there was no apparent connection between Arps and Roberts' type estimators and successive sampling, which has a long history in the sample survey and finite population sampling literature. Gordon (1983) noticed the connection and developed moment type estimators that are similar in form to those suggested by Arps and Roberts. If the basinal area B and the efficiency of discovery c are both known, and if w wells have discovered $N(w, A)$ fields of area A, the form of the Arps-Roberts model suggests $N(w, A)/(1 - \exp\{-cAw/B\})$ as an estimator of the number $N(\infty, A)$ of fields of area A in the basin. The moment type estimator investigated by Gordon is of this form but differs in two respects; first, successive sampling models the order of discovery of fields and does not depend on the number of exploratory wells drilled; second, all elements of the complete sample of discovery are used jointly to form the estimator, in contrast to the estimator implied by the Arps-Roberts model, which treats each of a predetermined number of magnitude classes independently. The price paid in return for squeezing joint information from all elements of the sample is that a recondite pair of transcendental equations must be solved (Barouch et al., 1985).

Independently, Andreatta and Kaufman (1985) studied successive sampling estimators of the Arps-Roberts type that are anchored on knowledge of a parameter of the finite population of deposits in a play or basin. Smith and Ward's (1981) maximum likelihood estimates of number of North sea fields remaining to be discovered in seven discrete magnitude classes are closely replicated by these anchored estimators. Smith and Ward generated their estimates by a seven dimensional grid search. Approximately unbiased estimates of the form suggested by Andreatta and Kaufman can be calculated on a hand calculator.

In a different vein, Root and Scheunemeyer (1980) provided a rigorous probabilistic generalization of Arps and Robert's original model using the cumulative area exhausted by drilling in place of the number of exploratory wells drilled as a measure of exploratory effort, and in a companion paper, Drew, Scheunemeyer, and Root (1980) analyze Denver-Julesberg Basin data using the approach developed by Root and Scheunemeyer. Up to 1954, the results are not strikingly different from those of Arps and Roberts' original study of this basin.

Yet a different approach is studied by Meisner and Demirmen (1980). They combine proportional-to-size (size-biased) sampling of deposits with a model of well drilling successes and failures. Their drilling model can be interpreted as a "parameter" that is sequentially modified by drilling history. This "parameter" modulates the shape of a superpopulation probability law like that adopted by Balcer, Kaufman and Kruyt, and so influences the probability distribution, given a well history, of the "next" discovery. The fit of their model to an unspecified segment of North Sea data is examined in several ways.

Wang and Lee (1983a,b) couple a superpopulation model for deposit magnitudes with a probablistic model for the number of prospects and the number of deposits in a petroleum play to produce a distribution of the rth largest deposit in the play, conditional on the total sum of magnitudes of all deposits. They use this distribution together with a similarly conditioned distribution of the number of deposits in the play to impute deposit magnitudes "missing" from the empirical distribution of magnitudes of discovered deposits, and illustrate their method by applying it to an east coast of Canada play. This is an objective probability model that incorporates many of the features of the Canadian Geological Survey's subjective probability play evaluation system, entitled the Hydrocarbon Assessment System Processor (HASP).

An interesting application of random field theory (here "field" has a specific mathematical meaning unrelated to the concept of petroleum field) to the problem of predicting the number of and magnitudes of oil and gas deposits is given by Schagen (1980). He examines projective areas of British North Sea discoveries. Using map coordinates of contours delineating boundaries of discovered fields as data, he projects the number of fields remaining to be found per unit of basinal area and the average area of these fields. For application of Schagen's model to yield meaningful projections, highly disaggregated geologic map data must be available, and the region examined must be partially explored.

All of the aforementioned recent studies meet standards of analytical rigor required for publication in professional statistical journals.

In contrast to this suite of highly disaggregated modeling of physical variables, nationwide econometric modeling of oil and gas supply and demand rested on the notion that linear and/or log-linear specification of structural equations, which work reasonably well for many other sectors of the economy, would also work for petroleum supply. This notion was false. Projections made by such models in the late 1960s and the decade of 1970–1980 have fared poorly. Changes in the structure of the industry induced by order of magnitude changes in costs, prices, and regulatory regimes, and lack of sufficiently disaggregated data of good quality, contributed to poor predictive performance over all but short-term time periods. Aside from very aggregate sectoral models of oil and gas supply designed to be components of nationwide econometric macromodels, interest in building detailed econometric models of oil and gas supply like those of Khazzoom (1971), Erikson and Spann (1971), MacAvoy and Pindyck (1973, 1975b), and Pindyck (1974) has waned.

Epple and Hansen criticize these studies for their reliance on "intuitive judgments about the appropriateness of a particular set of explanatory variables" and suggest that econometric mineral supply models should possess three features (1981, p. 104):

1. The econometric supply equations should be explicitly derived from maximization of the objective function of suppliers.

2. The derivation of the econometric equations should include an explicit treatment of the sources of uncertainty or unobservability of variables that give rise to the residuals in the supply equations.

3. If future values of exogenous variables are uncertain, the model should incorporate a specification of how producers' expectation of those variables are determined.

They present an econometric model in which parameters of producers' probability distributions for future values of exogenous variables, such as prices, appear in equations describing supply. In this setting, revealed prices and supply can modify producers' forecasts of future exogenous variables (i.e., change producers' expectations) and thus influence current optimal drilling decisions. This model is truly dynamic. In spite of its intuitive appeal, beyond Epple and Hansen's (1979) application to aggregate US oil and gas data, their approach has not been vigorously pursued by others.

The fifth study by the Stanford Energy Modeling Forum dealt with US oil and gas supply. As part of this study, Clark, Coene, and Logan (1981) compared and contrasted nationwide and one worldwide oil and gas supply and demand models, each loosely classified as engineering process (rate of effort) or econometric. Table 2, from Ball et al. (1981), summarizes gross characteristics of each model. Two central messages emerge: "multiple, inconsistent sources for current and historical information and (an) inability to validate those statistics that do exist" frustrate comparisons of model predictions (Ball et al., 1981, p. 145). In addition, none of the models reviewed were disaggregated enough to address usefully a number of specific policy issues at the forefront of public interest at the time the comparisons were made, e.g., the impact of alternative specifications of a windfall profit tax on oil and gas producers.

At the microlevel of a single petroleum basin a different style of econometric modeling was studied by Attanasi, Drew, and Scheunemeyer (1980). Their key idea is to use a physical model—that of Arps and Roberts—to generate expectations of returns to exploratory effort. These expectations are interfaced with a variety of traditional (autoregressive) models of key exploratory economic variables and the hybrid models used to project the time rate of future discoveries. In spite of moderate to large relative mean square errors of prediction, projections of discoveries over time mimic actual patterns of discoveries with more accuracy than would be expected from the use of econometric models that do not explicitly incorporate a model of physical variables that stands on its own. This form of hybrid modeling holds considerable promise.

Studies of the microeconomics of exploration and production by Uhler (1979) and Ramsey (1981) carry foward our understanding of how geology, engineering, and microeconomics can be interfaced to create models that, like Attanansi, Drew, and Scheunemyer's model, mirror industry exploration and production behavior more accurately than either the highly aggregated models mentioned earlier or industry level engineering process models that "reduce exploration behavior to mechanical rules, assuming for example, that firms' exploration expenditures are a certain percent of the previous period's net profit" (Attanassi, Drew, and Scheunemeyer, 1980, p. C2). Models of this type have been employed by the National Petroleum Council (1972) and the US Federal Energy Administration in its *Project Independence Report* (1974).

The Energy Information Administration's PROLOG model is an ambitious attempt to project production and reserve additions by blending costs, prices, and individual well production with constraints on rig availability and footage that can be drilled. Annual levels of exploratory and development drilling in

Table 2
A catalog of oil and gas supply models

Name	Builders	Users (funders)	Dates	Ancestors	Resources	Geography	Methodology	Modes of operation	Integrated
Epple-Hansen	Epple, D. (Carnegie-Mellon)	—	1975–1979	—	Oil and gas	Lower 48 on- and offshore	Econometric	Simulation	No
E-M-S	Erickson, E. (NCSU) Spann, R. (UPI) Millsaps, S. (ASU)	Brookings Institution	1974	—	Oil	Lower 48 on- and offshore	Econometric	Simulation	No
FOSSIL2	Naill,R. (Dartmouth-DOE)	DOE	1976–1979	—	Oil, gas, and others	All United States	Engineering process	Simulation	Yes
GEMS	Marshalla, R. (DFI) Nesbitt, D. (DFI)	EIA/DFI	1977–1978	SRI/Gulf	Oil, gas, and others	All United States	Engineering process	Intertemporal optimization	Yes
K-T	Kim, Y. (U of Houston) Thompson, R. (U of Houston)	TEAC	1977–1978	NPC	Oil and gas	Lower 48 onshore	Engineering process	Optimization	No
Lorendas	Rapoport, L. (VPI)	VPI/NSF	1975–1979	—	Oil, gas, and others	All United States	Engineering process	Intertemporal optimization	Yes
MIT-WOP	Adelman, M. A. (MIT) Paddock, J. (MIT) Jacoby, H. D. (MIT)	MIT/NSF	1976–1979	—	Oil	World	Engineering process	Simulation	No

EIA/ICF								
MOGSMS	Stitt, W. (ICF)	NPC/FEA		Oil and gas	Lower 48 on- and offshore	Engineering process	Simulation	Yes
AHM	Everett, C. (EIA)			Oil and gas	Alaska		Intertemporal optimization	
EOR				Oil only	Lower 48 on- and offshore		Simulation	
Rice	Rice, P. (ORNL)	—	1975–1979	Oil and gas	Lower 48 on- and offshore	Econometric	Simulation	Yes
TERA								
Onshore	Tucker, L. (AGA)	AGA	1971–1979	Oil and gas	Lower 48 onshore	Econometric	Simulation	No
Offshore		—			Lower 48 offshore	Engineering process	Optimization	No

Source: Ball et al. (1981).

six onshore regions are generated by a linear program that determines drilling levels which maximize the present value of profits from drilling. Projections of additions to reserves from new discoveries are exogenous and based on either expert judgment or independent modeling and projection of the timing and amounts of petroleum discovered. As a consequence, any but the shortest term projections of these additions will directly mirror assumptions made about aggregate magnitudes of amounts remaining to be discovered and about the shape of the empirical distribution of deposit magnitudes. This is a possible point of intersection with disaggregated analysis of supply via a geologic-volumetric discovery process and subjective probability models. Some initial work aimed at providing input to the PROLOG model using successive sampling as a model for deposit magnitudes in order of discovery appears in an as yet unpublished study by EIA of "near-deep" gas.

It is reasonable to suppose that a coupling of an explicit physical model of returns to exploratory effort with microeconomic models of exploratory and development well drilling would be more robust than econometric models designed to this end in the 1970s; i.e., projections of the time rate of drilling and returns to this effort will respond more accurately to changes in the structure of the economic environment and to large changes in costs and prices.

Applications of subjective probability to petroleum resource assessment have grown steadily along two different tracks since first being introduced in the early 1960s. The early work of Grayson (1960) and Kaufman (1962) on use of decision theory to analyze individual exploratory drilling decisions—whether or not to drill a single exploratory well—was followed by more elaborate subjective probability modeling of drilling and discovery in plays and basins. Prominent among these exercises in assessment of expert judgment is the work of the Canadian Department of Energy, Mines and Resources (EMR) as presented in "Oil and Gas Resources of Canada—1976" (1977) and more recently in an update entitled "Oil and Natural Gas Resources of Canada—1983" (1984). Components of an objective discovery process model are present in their approach, the essential distinction being that all uncertain quantities are assessed by experts—the "expert" is the information and inference processing mechanism. Further refinements are incorporated in the EMR's HASP system cited earlier. This system is in active use: EMR uses it to assess possible additions to reserves from partially explored Canadian petroleum provinces.

The Exxon group, led by David White, uses a similar, but geologically more detailed, approach to assess play potential, presumably as a guide to deciding *where* to drill (White et al., 1975; White, 1980). Baker et al. (1984) give an excellent review of play analysis methods. They outline steps in the assessment of key uncertain quantities and describe how Monte Carlo simulation can be used to generate a probability distribution for total hydrocarbons in a play. Three possible ways of generating a field size distribution are mentioned: (1) geologic analogy—use of the empirical field size distribution of a "look-alike" (geologically similar) play, (2) probabilistic combination of assessments (subjective or by analogy) of individual reservoir parameters, such as area, fill fraction, average pay thickness, and recovery factor, and (3) point assessment of representative play prospects as a guide to creating a field size distribution. Cross-validation of a field size distribution for a partially explored play is in principle possible by employing *all three* methods.

An example is the assessment of the petroleum potential of the National Petroleum Reserve in Alaska (NPRA) by the Department of Interior's Office of Minerals Policy and Research Analysis (1979). This large scale study brought together geophysicists, geologists, petroleum engineers, and economists in a two year review of known geologic features of the NPRA and a subjective probability assessment of variables that determine the existence of and amounts of hydrocarbons in prospective plays. As of December 1979 the 24 million acre reserve had been drilled by only about 50 test wells, 36 of them before 1953. Most wells were in the northeast. In order to analyze the economic viability of developing the NPRA and to address a wide range of detailed policy options, the NPRA was divided into fifteen subregions and geologists were asked to assess probability distributions for both numbers of and types of prospective petroleum plays within each region. For each prospective play, probability distributions for the number of prospects, number of deposits, and distribution of deposit magnitude were also assessed. This level of assessment detail was necessary because of the complex, detailed character of the policy options examined:

1. What are the economic effects on oil and gas development of alternative land management approaches that could be applied in NPRA? If specific areas of NPRA are excluded from petroleum production and development and/or transportation to afford maximum protection to nonpetroleum values, what will be the consequences of such designations on NPRA petroleum production and economic values?

2. Which leasing system or systems and terms should be used if titles to NPRA petroleum resources are transferred from the public to the private sector?

3. How will the State of Alaska be affected by NPRA development? NPRA petroleum development could result in additional jobs, higher incomes, large tax revenues, and increased population for Alaska, but development could also place burdens on state and local public finances.

4. When and at what rate and geographical sequence should NPRA be developed? The timing of development, both when it begins and how fast it proceeds, will determine how soon NPRA's resources will become available to the nation and how development will affect Alaska.

In addition to applications of subjective probability methods to assessment of attributes of individual plays, expert judgment in the form of personal probabilities appeared in 1975 in a geologic-volumetric appraisal of US petroleum resources. All earlier published US geologic-volumetric appraisals were point estimates. "Geological Estimates of Undiscovered Recoverable Oil and Gas Resources in the United States" (US Department of Interior, USGS Circular 725, 1975) was the first of its kind. Assessments composed by aggregating individual geologists' probability judgments were made for each of over one hundred individual petroleum basins. To create probability distributions for larger regions basinal probability distributions were convolved by Monte Carlo simulation. USGS Circular 860 (US Department of Interior, 1982) is a 1981 update of Circular 725. The Canadian EMR assessments of unexplored or sparsely explored frontier areas are done in a similar way (cf. EMR, 1977, for example). Probability appraisals of this type are now common.

A warning is warranted. It is difficult, if not impossible, to ascertain how the experts queried in the conduct of these studies coped with and adjusted for cognitive biases that afflict probability assessments of uncertain events. There is much experimental evidence documenting the assertion that all humans (experts among them!) employ heuristics that can significantly bias personal probability judgments. (Tversky and Kahneman's seminal article in *Science*, 1974, offers many examples and some experimental evidence. It spurred much experimentation, most of which supports their findings.)

The preceding discussion of methods of projecting additions to oil and gas reserves from new discoveries focuses on one approach at a time. Possible approaches are so different in character that one might reasonably expect that considerable effort has been devoted to the comparative study of the predictive accuracy of alternative approaches. However, beyond the Energy Modeling Forum comparative study of large scale models cited earlier and Pindyck's comparison of three econometric models (Pindyck, 1974), there are few published studies of this type. A notable example is the recent comparison of geologically based (expert evaluation of all information sources) petroleum resource projections with statistically based (model plus objective field and well data) projections for Nigeria, North Africa, and world offshore by the World Energy Resources Program at the USGS. Many more such studies are needed to further our understanding of the merits and deficiences of alternative approaches.

4 Conclusions

The recent history of development of analytical approaches to oil and gas supply analysis reinforces our earlier statement of lessons learned about data needs and also estimates of the predictive performance of several types of modeling. It also suggests how resource analysis methodology might evolve in the near future.

The microeconomics of petroleum supply and both subjective probability and (objective probability) discovery process models are currently more proactive areas of current research than highly aggregated econometric or rate of effort models. This is a natural response to the poor predictive performance of the latter types of modeling. Increased focus on the physical and engineering processes by which petroleum is found and produced is the *only* route to enhancement of our capacity to build robust models that predict more accurately than their predecessors.

My personal view is that we shall not see any dramatic conceptual innovations in primary energy mineral resource analysis in the next decade, but shall see

1. steady improvement in the quality of statistical analysis of resource data,

2. a parallel improvement in the predictive quality of disaggregated approaches to modeling oil and gas exploration, development, and production,

3. new types of models (e.g., construction of hybrid models that incorporate features of several of the approaches reviewed earlier),

4. attempts to cross-validate alternative methods of projecting petroleum supply, done in accordance with good statistical practice,

5. continued use of subjective probability methods in resource appraisal,

6. failure to train earth scientists in sufficient depth about subjective probability judgments to avoid cognitive biases that creep into such judgments and taint them.

Finally, as drilling evidence mounts, we should be able to narrow current bands of uncertainty about recoverable resources in frontier and partially explored basins.

In perspective, these projected incremental improvements in conventional oil and gas data and in approaches to resource appraisal currently in vogue may be overshadowed by enhanced understanding of properties of unconventional petroleum resources, such as geopressured zones and Western tight sands, along with new recovery technologies. With the advent of economically efficient recovery technologies, these sources could contribute to order of magnitude increases in economically recoverable natural gas in the United States and elsewhere. New technology has always rescued us in the past, and it is reasonable to predict that as stocks of undiscovered conventional oil and gas decline, need will spur inventiveness. If this comes to pass, future generations of resource analysts will have to adapt what we have learned about forecasting conventional oil and gas discovery and supply to a new oil and gas industry that functions differently from the old.

Notes

1. A record of the year of discovery of a field is too imprecise to be particularly useful; a record of the date of spudding of the initial discovery well would be a very significant improvement. However, a demand for this degree of temporal precision creates a host of definitional and measurement problems.

2. Canada is a good test case. Individual well data are by law filed with Energy, Mines, and Resources after the elapse of a prespecified time period during which the operator retains exclusive control. Has this requirement diminished competitiveness in the market for Canadian exploration ventures? This is an open question that, to my knowledge, has not been addressed by oil and gas economists.

12 Cost and Output Analysis in Mineral and Petroleum Production

Paul G. Bradley

The 1970s saw a resurgence of interest in the economics of natural resources. This was the result of widespread concern that resource scarcity would constrain economic growth. At a more disaggregate level, which is the setting of this paper, attention was directed toward the imminence of shortages of particular minerals, seen as the inevitable result of depletion. The mood has shifted in the 1980s. Most minerals, including petroleum, are in over supply on world markets at current prices, and not much is heard about "running out."

This paper is devoted to the economic analysis of the supply of minerals, defined broadly enough to include the fossil fuels, in particular, petroleum. Consideration will be given to types of analysis that are applied, the assumptions that are made, and the problems that must be dealt with. The themes to be considered are drawn from a remarkable paper by Professor Adelman, published in 1970 and titled "Economics of Exploration for Petroleum and Other Minerals." It appeared in a journal not regularly read by economists, *Geoexploration*. The various sections of this paper are introduced by quotations from Professor Adelman's paper.

The topics addressed in the major sections of the present paper are these:

1. supply analysis for minerals and petroleum;

2. specification of incremental cost curves;

3. supply depiction and uncertainty;

4. a geostatistical approach to supply analysis.

In connection with the last of these topics, research results are reported that relate to the cost and occurrence of natural gas in the Province of Alberta, Canada.

1 Supply Analysis for Minerals and Petroleum

"Perhaps the very concept of exhaustible resources ought to be discarded as wrong or irrelevant."

It will be useful to consider the application of an Alchian (1959) cost-output function to mineral production:

$$C = f(x, V, T), \tag{1}$$

where total cost (C) depends upon the rate of output (x), the ultimate volume of production (V), and the time before initial delivery (T). Alchian, who was analyzing costs and outputs for manufactured products, criticized the attention paid to rate of output (x) as a cost determinant to the exclusion of the other variables in the equation. When costs and outputs are analyzed for resource commodities—specifically, minerals and petroleum—the variables V and T assume even greater relative importance.

In Alchian's description of the production of manufactured goods, great stress is laid upon the volume of planned production as a determinant of total cost. While this may be appropriate in many manufacturing industries, for most the volume effect seems to be adequately captured by the x term, as suggested in Hirshleifer's response (1962) to the Alchian paper. For mineral production, however, volume must be regarded in its own right as an important constraint on the production plan. The orebody to be mined or the petroleum reservoir to be tapped is a "given" for the mineral developer.

Although the nature of a particular ore body or petroleum reservoir is fixed, thereby imposing a constraint on production, it does not follow that the ultimate volume of production is predetermined. It will depend upon expenditure, and, in general, larger expenditure (C) will yield more total expected output (V). Postponing an explicit cost analysis until the next section, beyond some point the incremental cost of output (V) must increase, the rate of output (x) being held constant. The rate at which the cost of extra units of output can be expected to increase will depend upon the resource. If the deposit is a base metal ore body or one of several types of crude oil reservoir, there may be a substantial range of increasing V over which the rate of increase of incremental cost is modest. With certain types of gold lode or natural gas reservoirs, an increase in V may be obtained only at a very large increase in cost.

The individual ore body or reservoir is a basic unit in mineral production. It typically corresponds to the plant or establishment in manufacturing, although in some cases one mine may work several ore bodies. The broader picture of output potential in mining, as in manufacturing, requires examination of firms and the industry. At the industry level there are a number of sources of additional output beside higher recovery from individual ore bodies or reservoirs. In this perspective, five sources of additional output can be identified:[1]

1. higher recovery from existing, producing deposits;

2. development of known, previously nonproducting deposits;

3. discovery and development of new deposits in established formations;

4. discovery and development of new deposits in new formations;

5. creation of new technology that enhances the possibilities of any of the sources 1–4.

As the successive sources of extra output on this list are included, supply will become more price elastic. At the same time, as the list is organized, successive sources are generally available only with a greater time lag. They might conveniently be indexed by the variable T in equation (1) to indicate this, as well as implicitly to indicate increasing uncertainty.

In order to analyze supply additions from the various sources that have been listed it is necessary to inquire into the nature of the specific factor, resources in the ground. Consequently, the geology of resource occurrence must be taken into account, and the uncertainty of resource availability must be dealt with explicitly. This is the realm of the mineral economist. Again with reference to equation (1), the rate of output (x) is assumed to be constant while attention is directed to additions to stock (V). By contrast, "mainstream" economists have shown greater interest in flow questions, which entail holding stock (V) in (1) constant, or ignoring it, while examining variation in output (x). This constitutes the economics of "exhaustible resources."

2 Specification of Incremental Cost Curves

"Exploration is never for minerals as such, always for cheaper minerals."

Later sections of this paper will be concerned with methods for analyzing mineral supply where cost is related to potential volume of output, that is, the stock variable (V). Whether supply is being examined with reference to incremental stocks or incremental flows, cost is the crucial consideration. In this section a closer look will be taken at the analysis of cost as it pertains to mineral supply, and the Alchian formulation will be a convenient point of departure.

The development of new productive capacity, and the corresponding creation of new stocks of proved reserves, is a form of investment. A project entails
a series of expenditures, perhaps very large in the preproduction stage,
together with an anticipated flow of output. Cost comparison of projects must
thus be carried out in the common currency of present value dollars. In this
regard the Alchian specification of cost (C) in present worth, or "equity,"
terms is appropriate.

Alchian developed his theory of costs for manufacturing industry by
formulating a series of propositions about the nature of the total cost (C) of a
project. These were expressed in terms of the first and second partial deriva-
tives of the cost function of equation (1). The analysis here will be limited to
the incremental cost of additional total output (V) and the incremental cost of
higher rates of output (x). The unit for analysis is the individual ore body or
petroleum reservoir.

Conjectures about the shape of these curves will be aided by a very simple
model in which a uniform stream of output is obtained over the life of a
resource project. To achieve this an initial investment outlay is required,
followed by a stream of operating expenditures based on the assumption of
constant unit cost. Thus the basic model is

$$C = I(V, x) + akx, \tag{2}$$

where

I = initial investment,

a = the annuity factor, $(1 - e^{-rT})/r$,

T = production period, V/x,

r = discount rate,

k = unit operating cost.

Figure 1 depicts the likely shape of an incremental cost curve when total
expected output from an ore body or a reservoir is increased, rate of output
remaining constant. With the constant output model, it would represent the
equation

$$(\partial C/\partial V)_{x=\bar{x}} = (\partial I/\partial V) + kv, \tag{3}$$

where

v = the discount factor, e^{-rT}.

The two components of the incremental cost curve, the terms on the right of
(3), are also shown in figure 1.

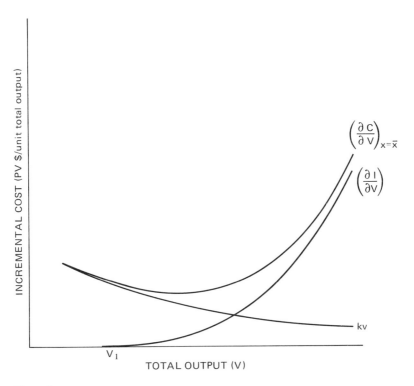

Figure 1
Incremental cost related to total volume of output. Symbols as defined in equation (3).

Incremental capital expenditure $(\partial I/\partial V)$ is depicted in figure 1 as negligible initially, but eventually rising rather steeply. This could be the situation, for example, in offshore crude oil production where a platform and a number of development wells are required to achieve the output rate $\bar{x}$. Little additional investment is required until recoveries greater than V_1 are sought, but these higher volumes can only be obtained with investment in increasingly costly recovery schemes. The incremental present value of operating cost diminishes with higher volumes of output, since the additional expenditures are subject to progressively greater discounting.

The resultant incremental cost curve with respect to total output $(\partial C/\partial V)$ shown in figure 1 falls slightly at first but eventually rises at an increasing rate. Initially the decline in incremental operating cost shows up, but this is soon dominated by steeply rising incremental investment. This shape contrasts with the downward sloping curve posited by Alchian for manufacturing industry. The underlying assumptions are quite different in the two cases. The Alchian analysis places emphasis on the availability of different pro-

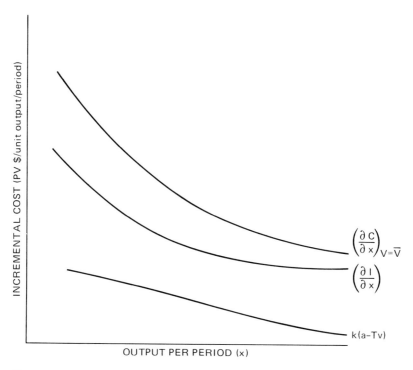

Figure 2
Incremental cost related to rate of output. Symbols as defined in equation (4).

duction methods, whereas it seems more appropriate to assume that there is not a great degree of flexibility in mining or petroleum production technology. The difference between manufacturing and mineral production that is highlighted here, however, is that for minerals the natural endowment, an ore body or reservoir, restricts the increase in total output in a way that has no counterpart for a manufacturing project.

Figure 2 depicts the incremental cost of higher rates of output, ultimate output remaining constant. With reference again to the constant output model, its equation is

$$(\partial C/\partial x)_{V=\overline{V}} = (\partial I/\partial x) + k(a - Tv). \tag{4}$$

Again the components of the incremental cost curve are shown.

Both the incremental cost of investment and the incremental present value of operating expenditures are depicted in figure 2 as declining with higher rates of output. Using an offshore petroleum reservoir for illustration, large capital expenditures are required for the platform and initial production well. Subsequent increase in capacity can be obtained by drilling additional development wells and expanding the capacity of processing equipment. Economies of scale of the conventional sort (for example, the changing ratio of cross section area to perimeter in processing equipment) cause incremental capacity expenditure to fall over a substantial range of rising output rates. The decline in the incremental present value of operating cost with higher rates of output reflects two offsetting forces. Additional expenditure is required for the extra unit flow of output, but, since total output is fixed, expenditure is eliminated as the production period is shortened.

In figure 2 the resultant incremental cost curve with respect to rate of output falls over the entire range of outputs. This is also in contrast with the Alchian hypothesis for manufacturing industries. The difference again involves underlying assumptions. Here the analysis posits a particular extraction technique that requires a significant amount of fixed—that is, non-recoverable—investment. This fixed capital gives rise to what have been termed conventional economies of scale. It also raises a disturbing matter with regard to the incremental cost measure. Because volume of output is held constant, extra increments of initial investment in capacity are utilized for progressively shorter periods. This effect is not revealed in the cost measure.

The two incremental cost curves just described related, respectively, to the present value cost of another unit of ultimate production and the present value cost of a one unit increase in rate of output, following Alchian in both instances. They would therefore be compared to the corresponding incremental increase in the developed value of the particular resource deposit in order to predict whether additional reserves or output would be forthcoming from that source. While this comparison is consistent with the procedure that would be followed in planning the resource project, it does not accord with the traditional analytical separation between supply and demand. This requires that the cost of additional supply be related to the corresponding additional units of output.

This situation is rectified by relating incremental cost to the appropriately measured incremental increase in output, either with respect to ultimate volume or to rate. Since the incremental cost is measured in present value terms, so must be the incremental increase in output. This leads to an alternative pair of definitions of incremental cost:

$$MC_V = \frac{(\partial C/\partial V)}{(\partial [PV(V)]/\partial V)_{x=\bar{x}}}, \tag{5}$$

$$MC_x = \frac{(\partial C/\partial x)}{(\partial [PV(V)]/\partial x)_{V=\bar{V}}}. \tag{6}$$

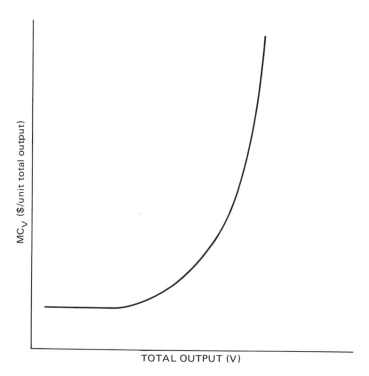

Figure 3
Total output (reserves) supply curve.

The denominator in (5), for example, represents the incremental increase in present valued total output from the deposit, given the investment that created one additional unit of reserves. Thus the incremental cost measure MC_V represents the cost of an increase in total output per additional unit of present valued output. It is expressed in dollars per output unit.

The particular utility of these incremental cost measures is that they can be compared with expected price in order to forecast increase in output. Such comparison requires the assumption of a uniform price level. This appears restrictive, but recognition of price dependence in this manner is probably the most that can be expected in the analysis of mineral supplies.[2]

Relating incremental cost to the commensurate unit of output, as in equations (5) and (6), significantly alters the shape of the resulting curves. Figure 3 shows MC_V, the incremental cost with respect to total output, as a function of total output. This is a reserves supply curve for the given deposit. After an initial flat portion, the curve slopes upward, very steeply in comparison with $(\partial C/\partial V)$ in figure 1. The constant output model provides some insight.

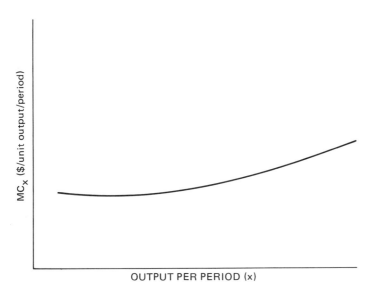

y-axis: MC$_x$ ($/unit output/period)

x-axis: OUTPUT PER PERIOD (x)

Figure 4
Rate of output supply curve.

The denominator in equation (5), the present value of the extra unit of output, is the present value factor ($v = e^{-rT}$) for the final date of production, which is when the extra output is obtained. This value diminishes, becoming very small at high volumes of output, since output rate is constant ($T = V/\bar{x}$). This analysis suggests that initial investment to increase total output is likely to be unattractive unless the rate of output is simultaneously increased.

The cost of an increase in rate of output per additional unit of present valued output, MC$_x$, is depicted as a function of rate of output in figure 4. This corresponds to a conventional supply curve for the deposit. Whereas the curve for ($\partial C/\partial x$) in figure 2 was downward sloping, the curve for MC$_x$ falls slightly, then rises. For the constant output model, the denominator of equation (6) is the term ($a - Tv$), which diminishes as output rate increases (with higher rates of output as T approaches zero, this term also approaches zero). This confirms that it will only be profitable to increase output rates from a particular deposit up to a price determined limit; that is, there is a stable production equilibrium.

Although the simulations that have been used to establish the shapes of the curves shown in figures 3 and 4 were based on the constant output model, it seems reasonable to conjecture that both these incremental cost curves will generally be upward sloping. In practice, incremental investment may often both increase ultimate output from a deposit and increase the rate of output.

Increasing output from individual deposits is but one means for augmenting resource supply, and I next turn to the more general analysis that embraces other items from the list in section 1.

3 Supply Depiction and Uncertainty

"We deplete the small economic portion, a quantity approximately estimated, of a very much larger resource, of which our knowledge trails off rapidly."

Discussion of resource stocks has generally been organized in the manner proposed by McKelvey (1975). This system recognizes two dimensions of stock description, cost ("degree of economic feasibility") and certainty ("degree of geologic assurance").[3] A version of the McKelvey system is shown in figure 5. It is designed to facilitate quantitative approaches to supply estimation.

The key feature of figure 5 is the depiction of quantity in the vertical dimension of a three dimensional figure. Sections of the diagram taken along the cost axis (for example, section AA') show the quantities of a resource available at corresponding levels of unit cost. If quantities were cumulated, beginning with the lowest cost, the information given in an AA' section of figure 5 could be presented in a more familiar supply curve format. This result would differ from conventional supply curves, however, in that it relates to available quantity (V) rather than to rate of output (x). Movement upward along the curve would indicate the incremental increase in reserves that would become available with higher unit production costs.

The second dimension in the horizontal plane of figure 5 relates to the likelihood assigned to the existence of a particular quantity of the resource. Cumulative probability is measured along this axis (for example, section BB'). Successive points along a curve in BB' therefore indicate the probability assigned to the existence of increasing quantities of the resource that could be produced at unit cost B. The use of cumulative probability to define the certainty dimension follows the procedure used by McKay and Taylor (1979) to describe the potential of certain Australian oil fields. McKay and Taylor relate the cumulative probability measures to a McKelvey type classification by requiring a 0.95 cumulative probability for the classification proved reserves and 0.50 for proved plus probable reserves.

The possible usefulness of the scheme shown in figure 5 depends on the extent to which analysis can delineate the quantity surface. By way of illustration, consider practice in the petroleum industry. Attaining the 0.95 certainty required for the proved reserves classification requires that a re-

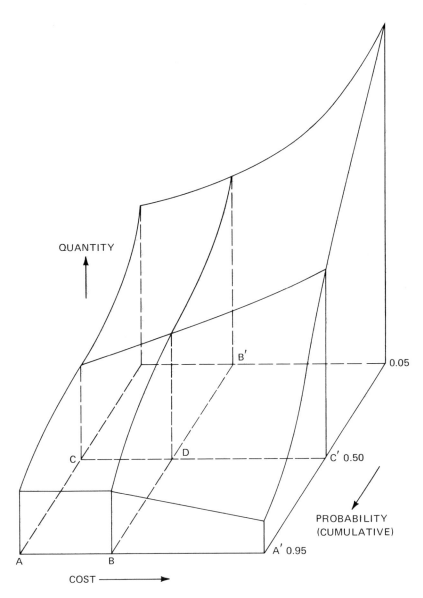

Figure 5
Quantity of reserves by cost and certainty.

servoir be delineated by drilling. This is not economic unless it is expected that the wells will be used for production, and indeed the classification requires that the reserves be economical to produce. At higher cost levels than B, therefore, we would expect the quantity of reserves shown on the curve of section AA' to decrease, even if reserves at these cost levels do exist in the particular basin.

In the work reported by McKay and Taylor, the reserves potential of a field is assessed. This is done by obtaining subjective probability estimates of the physical parameters that determine the quantity of reserves. These are combined using Monte Carlo simulation to yield the probability distribution that underlies a section of figure 5 such as BB'. To relate McKay and Taylor's work to the scheme set out in figure 5 it must be assumed that the reserves of the field can be produced at a specified unit cost.

A good example of the estimation of supply potential along a section representing a lower degree of certainty (say 0.50) is provided by the work of Zimmerman (1977) in regard to coal. He hypothesized that the distribution of coal deposits according to seam thickness could be represented by the lognormal probability distribution. This was substantiated with the use of estimates from well explored areas of the tonnage of coal existing in seams of various thickness. The hypothesis was then applied in less explored areas. However, a curve in a section such as CC' of figure 5 also requires cost information. Zimmerman provided this by establishing that seam thickness was the prime determinant of unit cost and then estimating the relationship. The result was a set of estimates of tonnage available at increasing levels of unit cost, precisely the information required for a curve in section CC'.

Zimmerman's analysis of geologic variables was restricted to seam thickness, since his data related tonnage to this variable. In general, the cost of producing a resource will depend on other physical variables besides the quantity of reserves in the deposit. In the next section this type of analysis is extended to the situation where more than one physical variable must be considered when specifying a reserves supply curve.

4 A Geostatistical Approach to Supply Analysis

"We still have almost everything to learn about the formation and incidence, therefore about the cost, of the minerals on which our lives depend."

In the preceding sections I have been concerned with certain distinctive features of supply analysis as applied to minerals and petroleum. Emphasis was placed on cost in relation to volume of output rather than to the rate of output. In this context, measurement of cost in terms of present value dollars per unit of present valued output offers significant advantages. Because natural resource endowment is the crucial factor in output availability, analysis of supply potential in the longer term draws on geological knowledge. When this is done it becomes necessary to describe the degree of certainty associated with reserves estimates. Supply specification is incomplete unless both cost and certainty dimensions are reported.

In this section some research results are reported in order to illustrate possibilities for developing mineral supply analysis. The work is concerned with the supply of natural gas in the western Canadian sedimentary basin. The nature of the task can be seen with reference to figure 5. Reported proved reserves of natural gas represent the summation of quantities over the line segment AB. Proved reserves must be established with a high degree of certainty, as indicated by the cumulative probability value 0.95 of section AA'. In practice, other information may be reported, such as proved plus probable reserves. Following McKay and Taylor, this figure could be interpreted as representing the summation of quantities over the line segment CD. More detailed reporting would obviously be desirable.

Extending the scope of reserves estimates beyond the quantities that have been proved requires reliance on geological information. Models based on hypotheses about mineral occurrence, whether formal or informal, can generate estimates of reserves quantities, that is, can be applied to specify curves such as that of section BB', as previously illustrated by the work of McKay and Taylor. Models have also been used to examine costs, as was illustrated by the work of Zimmerman, although this is a more unusual application. In order to formulate a complete supply specification for an area such as the western Canadian sedimentary basin, it would be desirable to consider the capabilities of various models and how the information they generate could be assembled along the lines suggested by figure 5. That task is beyond the scope of this paper, but the work to be reported does indicate the issues involved.

Models that apply geostatistics must be related to a geologically homogeneous sample. With respect to petroleum, the largest such unit is generally designated a formation, although formations are sometimes combined into a larger grouping, the horizon. Probability distributions have frequently been used to describe the occurrence of reservoirs, or traps, in a formation.[4] When a model based on a distribution is applied to an established but incompletely explored formation, available information is used to estimate distribution parameters. Then the model provides a basis for predicting the quantity of petroleum remaining to be found.

If the formation is the appropriate unit for geostatistical analysis, what can be said about the pattern of extraction costs for reservoirs, or pools, within the formation? The variables that determine reservoir size are assumed to display statistical regularity, and it seems reasonable to investigate the validity of similar assumptions about other variables that determine cost of production. If costs do display a pattern, then the nature of that pattern will have to be taken into account in assembling formation data to generate a figure 5 supply picture for the larger unit (here the western Canadian sedimentary basin). Two extreme situations might be visualized. Quantities of reserves might be uniformly distributed by cost; that is, the proportion of total formation reserves available at a cost between $0.50 and $1.00 might be the same as the proportion of reserves between $1.00 and $1.50. On the other hand, it could be that costs are quite similar within a formation.

Of the two extreme situations, the first would afford a very optimistic supply outlook, since field price increases would lead to substantial supply additions from established formations. Large reservoirs, previously discovered but uneconomic to develop, would be a major source of new reserves (item 2 in the list of supply sources in section 1). Furthermore, it is likely that discovery process models would have understated the potential of established formations. This would occur where the reserves potential of large pools was unreported, since at the time of discovery they were uneconomic. Distribution parameters would have been estimated from biased data. In this event, discovery and development of new pools in an established formation would be a more important source of new reserves than previously realized (item 3 of the list in section 1).

In contrast to this situation, if extraction costs were relatively similar for pools in a formation, the potential of the formation would be substantially realized at an early stage. Large reservoirs, accounting for a disproportionate share of the reserves in a formation, tend to be discovered early in the play. Subsequent increases in field price would not lead to major reserves additions of the sort contemplated where extraction costs vary over a significant range.

The study of the cost of extracting natural gas in the western Canadian sedimentary basin proceeded in two stages. The first phase consisted of an empirical investigation of the pattern of costs by pool for the major formations. It entailed estimation of supply curves describing the volumes of natural gas (specifically, initial recoverable reserves) available at various cost levels. The second phase sought to provide a model, based on geostatistics, to explain the observed cost patterns.[5] This work will be briefly described, and the results related to a strategy for comprehensive supply analysis.

The empirical analysis required data describing the physical parameters of the gas pools and information about the expenditures required to establish production. Data describing the pools (in particular, formation depth, initial recoverable reserves, and the absolute open flow potential of wells) were provided by the Alberta Energy Resources Conservation Board (AERCB). Pools were grouped by formation, to achieve geologic homogeneity, as previously discussed. A total of 21 formations was analyzed; this required consideration of over 1,800 pools and represented coverage of over 70% of the booked natural gas reserves in Alberta.

Unit production cost for each pool was computed by first estimating total required expenditure, then relating this figure to total expected output. Production cost comprises development and operating costs; it does not include any overhead allocation relating to exploration programs. The procedure that was used can be represented by two summary equations.

The first equation gives the present value, by pool, of expenditures, and hence is of the same form as equation (2):

$$C = W[K(d,g) + m(d,g)a], \tag{7}$$

where

W = number of wells required for production,

K = capital expenditure per well (drilling and equipping), a function of depth (d) and location (g),

m = yearly operating and maintenance cost per well, also a function of depth and location,

a = the annuity factor, as previously.

Equation (7) was implemented by the use of formulas that related well capital expenditure (K) and operating cost (m) to pool depth. Separate formulas were developed by econometric estimation for contractor drilling costs, noncontractor expenditures associated with pool development, and yearly operating and maintenance costs. For example, contractor drilling costs were represented by the product of a linear function in target depth for rig rental cost and a quadratic function in depth drilled for rig time.

For each pool the number of wells was selected to achieve a specified production profile. In line with industry rule of thumb for relating reserves to contract requirements, a ratio of initial daily production to marketable reserves of 1 : 7,300 was assumed. This level of output was projected for 10 years, followed by decline at 10% per year with output terminated after 20 years. The required number of production wells was calculated by dividing the initial pool output rate by estimated average initial well productivity and providing 25% excess capacity.

The second equation utilizes the present value of expenditures to calculate average (or unit) production cost (AC). This average cost measure corresponds to the measure of incremental cost defined earlier in equation (3). It is the quotient of the present value of expenditure and total present valued output, and is expressed in dollars per unit of output, the same units as price:

$$AC = C/x_0 b, \tag{8}$$

where

C = present value of expenditure, as defined in equation (7),

x_0 = initial pool output rate,

b = a factor that relates initial output to the present value of total physical output.

As previously noted, the initial pool production rate (x_0) was computed as a fixed fraction of recoverable reserves, and the remainder of the production profile followed a standard pattern. If output were constant over the pool's life, the factor b would be the annuity factor that appeared in the earlier cost examples. Here it converts the specified output stream (per unit of initial output) to present valued output.

It will be noted that in this formulation the prime determinants of unit cost are pool depth and average well deliverability (or productivity). Pool size, measured as recoverable reserves, is a factor in determining the number of wells, but it does not affect unit cost (AC), since it similarly determines initial output, the denominator of (8). Pool size would be expected to affect unit cost through scale economies in pool development, but this has not been taken into account. Also, although location is recognized in (7), and the pools are classified by location, it has not been possible in work to date to take account of this factor.

The assembled estimates of unit production cost and initial recoverable reserves made it possible to construct reserves supply curves for the various formations. These show cumulative reserves available at increasing levels of unit cost, and two examples are provided in figure 6. The curves for the different formations displayed this common shape. An initial flat portion indicated that the bulk of total reserves become available within a narrow cost range, for example, 20–40¢ per MCF. After the relatively flat portion of the curve, the right-hand tail rises steeply.

Space here does not permit a full discussion of the possible data bias that might influence these results. The crucial issue is whether economic conditions would have permitted the potential of pools in the cost ranges immediately above the flat portion of the curves to have been realized by

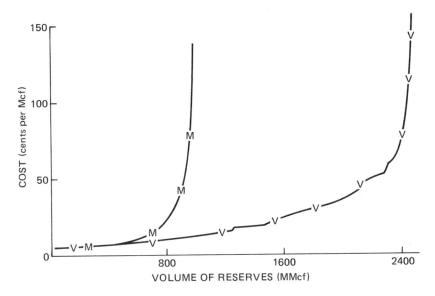

Figure 6
Estimated reserves supply curves: M, Mannville formation; V, Viking formation.

1981, the date of the reserves figures. If field prices were not high enough to make these pools economic, or if no market existed for the gas, no development activity would have been undertaken subsequent to discovery. This would have led to reporting error—reported estimates of initial recoverable reserves would understate the volumes in place in these higher cost ranges.

The likelihood of this reporting error was examined with reference to the wellhead value of natural gas. Using field price information, yearly estimates were made of average wellhead realization, that is, the amount available to producers to cover production costs. By 1975 this value had comfortably exceeded 60¢ (1980 dollars) per MCF. Reserves data for pools with higher unit cost were regarded as unreliable. Realizations were considerably higher in later years, but the lead time to develop reserves, coupled with the greater difficulty in marketing natural gas after 1975, dictated the lower figure. The steeply rising (low elasticity) ranges of the estimated reserves supply curves were typically observed in the cost range below the critical 60¢ figure. This lent support to the conclusions regarding the shape of formation supply curves.

The second phase of this research centered on the question of whether there might be an explanation for the observed cost-output relations. Specifically, the hypothesis examined was that the physical parameters that are the chief determinants of both quantity of reserves and production cost could be treated as random variables and that they might be jointly distributed according to a known probability distribution. This hypothesis found some support when the data were analyzed. To then demonstrate the possible usefulness of the hypothesis, supply curves where generated using a Monte Carlo procedure where parameter values were generated according to the posited distribution. These curves approximated in shape those that had been estimated directly from observed data.

The hypothesis that was investigated will be explained beginning with the more familiar proposition that the distribution of deposit sizes can be represented by a univariate probability distribution. If so, the cumulative distribution of reserves, in descending order of reservoir size, may be written

$$D(y_0) = -N \int_{\infty}^{y_0} yf(y)\,dy, \tag{9}$$

where

$y =$ reservoir size,

$N =$ number of reservoirs,

$f(y) =$ probability density function (probability of a reservoir of size y).

The information contained in (9) relates to availability of petroleum, but it does not necessarily relate to production cost; that is, it would not as it stands permit construction of a curve such as that in section CC' of figure 5. It could do this, however, if reservoir size was the principal determinant of cost, $C = C(y)$.

The more general case is one in which the principal determinant of cost is not deposit size, the measure of availability. With a mineral, for example, ore grade is a prime consideration, while for petroleum the productivity, or deliverability, of wells is crucial. This model could be written

$f(y, z) =$ probability density function for the joint distribution of
              variables y and z,

where

$y =$ a size measure,

$z =$ a cost-determining variable other than size (here average initial well productivity) such that $C = C(z)$.

Additional required notation is

$f(z) =$ the marginal distribution of z,

$g(y|z) =$ the conditional distribution of y, that is, $f(x, y)/f(z)$.

It is now possible to specify the quantity of resource that would be present by cost category. This is the information needed for the type of curve in section CC' of figure 5. The number of deposits for which production cost has a given value will be

$$N_C = N[C(z)]f(z). \tag{10}$$

Hence, the quantity of resource available at cost C is

$$Q[C(z)] = -N[C(z)]f(z) \int_{\infty}^{0} yg(y|z)\,dy. \tag{11}$$

A curve showing quantities available by cost category could be constructed from knowledge of the underlying distribution by evaluating (11) for successive categories, $a < z < b$.

Previous studies have provided substantial evidence that the marginal distribution of oil and gas pool size within a formation can be characterized as lognormal. The hypothesis that the marginal distribution of average well productivity is lognormal draws some support from evidence that pay thickness, a determinant of productivity, has been described as lognormal by researchers in this area. While lognormal marginal distributions are a necessary condition for joint lognormality, they are not sufficient. However, the data appeared to conform to the stronger conditions that are required.[6]

Proceeding on the hypotheses that the two variables are jointly lognormally distributed, the shape of the resulting supply curves will depend upon the correlation between them. The higher the correlation between pool size and productivity, the flatter the supply curve. Given the skewness of the lognormal distribution, if large pools on balance also are found to have highly productive wells, the bulk of the gas in the formation will be producible within a narrow range of unit costs. By contrast, as the correlation between size and deliverability weakens and grows negative, the supply curve will become more steeply sloped. Large pools will be less likely to have very productive wells, and hence can be produced only at higher levels of unit cost.

Based on the Alberta data, average well productivity and pool size are positively related. Correlation coefficients (between the variables $\log y$ and $\log z$) were positive for twelve of thirteen sets of data. For the thirteen samples, the median correlation coefficient was 0.325, with seven of the coefficients falling in the range 0.3–0.4.

If well productivity were the only factor affecting production cost, this positive correlation implies that supply curves for particular formations would tend to be quite flat over a wide quantity range. Large pools, which

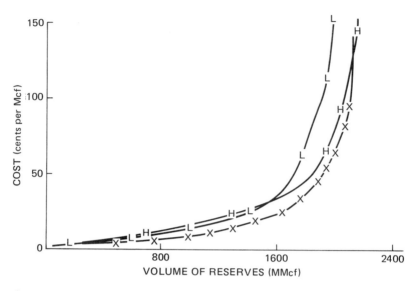

Figure 7

Comparison between simulated and estimated reserves supply curves. Mannville horizon (2,000–3,000 feet): X, observed; H, high simulation; L, low simulation.

account for the bulk of reserves, generally have the most productive wells and hence the lowest production costs. As smaller pools are exploited, unit costs tend to rise because of lower well productivity. However, these pools account for only a small share of total reserves in the formation, so the reserves supply curve rises only over a short range before sloping sharply upward. With reference to an initial flat portion of a formation supply curve, it appears to be unlikely that there will be subsequent plateaus, that is, further large volumes held in significantly higher cost pools.

To demonstrate the possibility of using sample data from a formation to establish a reserves supply curve, supply curves were simulated, using data generated from a bivariate lognormal distribution. This was done using a computer program that generated values for the random variables (y, z). The five parameters that characterize the bivariate lognormal distribution were first estimated using sample data for a particular formation. Then pairs of values (y, z) were generated, equaling in number the number of pools in the formation. The z value (deliverability) was used in the manner described previously to calculate unit cost figures corresponding to the y value (size).

Comparisons were made between "actual" supply curves—that is, those estimated as described in phase 1 of the research—and simulated supply curves. An example of one result is shown in figure 7. This relates to gas pools in the Mannville horizon, restricted to the 2,000–3,000 foot depth range for which data exist for 486 pools.[7] The high and low results of five simulation runs are compared with the supply curve as estimated directly. The degree of correspondence is representative, although in some instances there is wider divergence. The least correspondence occurs in formations where pools in the data set are large and fewer in number. Then the presence of a giant pool will greatly alter the comparison.

In the construction of figure 7, cost determinants other than well deliverability have been suppressed or ignored. Pool size, for example, will in itself be a cost-determining factor, because larger output will permit scale economies with respect to gathering lines and processing equipment. This will cause the supply curves to tend to rise more steeply after the relatively flat portion that contains the larger pools, but the effect seems unlikely to alter the typical curve shape. To summarize, at the formation level, output would appear to be highly elastic for a particular cost range, then quite inelastic for higher ranges.

The possible significance of this work in the context of mineral supply analysis can be considered with reference to figure 5. If the cost and reserves data were plotted in histogram form, rather than cumulatively, they would yield a curve in the plane of the CC' section. However, the empirical results indicate that for individual formations, the reserves-cost curves would not extend over a wide range. Rather, they would appear as fairly sharp peaks, with the bulk of reserves confined to a very limited cost range.

These results point toward the conclusion that for natural gas the formation may represent a useful unit for economic analysis because the contained pools exhibit relative cost uniformity. This should be comforting to researchers applying discovery process models. If pools accounting for substantial reserves occurred throughout a wide cost range, it is likely that available data would be severely biased. Pools in the uneconomic portion of the cost range would be subject to serious reporting error. As previously noted, this would raise doubt about the forecasting reliability of discovery process models.

If these results are correct, they should also encourage forecasts of the type described by McKay and Taylor. If such estimates were prepared by formation, the relative cost uniformity would support interpretation as a BB', or isocost, section of figure 5. This information could be accumulated for formations in a region or basin to yield a surface such as that shown in the figure. While there is theoretical as well as empirical support for the proposition that physical variables within a formation can be described by probability distributions, the notion of systematic behavior has not, to my knowledge, been extended beyond formations. Thus there is no basis for predicting the shape of a curve in the CC' section when a basin containing numerous formations is the unit of analysis.

For that portion of the western Canadian sedimentary basin within Alberta, 80% of booked reserves are in 30 formations. Another 20 formations account for an additional 10% of reserves. These numbers suggest that systematic supply appraisal, taking cost into account, would be feasible. Reserves estimates, defined in probability terms, would be prepared for approximately isocost sections—that is, by formation—then assembled in the manner of figure 5. The actual number of estimates would have to exceed the number of formations, since some formations would have to be subdivided according to depth and geographical location. It will be recalled that these two factors influence cost; figure 7, for example, represented a depth range. This increase in the required number of estimates would be offset to some extent by the possibility of combining some formations. Figure 7 again provides an example, since it comprises data from eleven Mannville horizon formations.

5 Summary

I have tried in this paper to describe some of the distinctive features of supply analysis as applied to minerals. One aspect is the importance of the cost of incremental volume. Supply curves relating to rate of output are necessary when analyzing current market price determination. However, in the longer term it is the development of new supply sources—hence, the cost of incremental volume—that is important.

The significance of incremental volume calls for a change of emphasis in cost analysis. The expected present value of resources in the ground determines incremental supply. In estimating this value, assumptions must be made regarding the most likely development plan. Following the logic of supply curve analysis, the further step is to relate the cost of incremental quantities to price (in this instance, to anticipated price levels).

The alternative means for adding to the supply of a mineral make it necessary to deal explicitly with timing and certainty. The time to initial production (T in the Alchian notation) becomes an important dimension of comparison, although no effort has been made here to develop this aspect of the analysis. The degree of certainty of incremental stocks has been recognized in various classification systems, including the McKelvey scheme. Although the significance of certainty as well as cost is acknowledged, this two dimensionality is not usually carried over to empirical analysis. To reiterate the example developed in the paper, if the geologic formation is the appropriate unit for analyzing potential petroleum reserves, is there empirical support for assuming a uniform level of cost among deposits in a formation? If so, formation reserves estimates can be assembled in the manner that has been described to present a complete supply picture. If not, a more complicated procedure is required.

The development of the probabilistic analysis required to specify certainty of supply has progressed considerably in recent years. The linking of this with geostatistical hypotheses about resource occurrence continues to provide an intriguing approach to mineral supply. It will be a useful extension if cost can be included as an integral part of this type of analysis. While deposit size is one factor that affects cost, it is not the only one, and it may not be the most important. The correlation of other cost-determining physical variables with size has an important bearing on the elasticity of mineral and petroleum supply.

To the reader of Professor Adelman's 1970 *Geoexploration* paper, this paper will have offered no novel insights. Indeed, the ideas examined here have been stressed elsewhere in his research and teaching. Gradually, and fortunately for progress in resource economics, their value is being appreciated.

Notes

1. This list, which relates to stock (V) increases, is adapted from Professor Adelman's classification in Adelman et al. (1983), pp. 8–9. That list contained output increases relating to both flows and stocks.

2. The use of cost measured per present value unit of output was pioneered by Professor Adelman in his early work on the economics of petroleum supply. See, for example, Adelman (1967), p. 67.

3. The utility of this two dimensional system was pointed out by Professor Adelman (1962). He illustrated it by describing the Soviet reserves classification system.

4. A recent example is Lee and Wang (1985); for a comprehensive survey see Kaufman in Adelman et al. (1983).

5. This empirical work is reported in greater detail in Bradley (1984). Another paper focusing on the analytical implications is in preparation (with A. Hanssen and A. Stedman).

6. Sufficient conditions are given by DeGroot (1975), p. 251. These results are discussed in the forthcoming paper cited in note 5.

7. The Mannville horizon sample comprises pooled data from eleven formations judged to be geologically similar. This larger data set permitted larger subsamples (for example, the 2,000–3,000 foot depth range).

13

Energy Price Shocks and Productivity Growth: A Survey

Ernst R. Berndt
David O. Wood

It will be difficult to come to terms with the impact of the OPEC cartel at an intellectual level until much time has passed. (Jorgenson, 1978, p. 23)

1 Introduction

In his long distinguished career, Morry Adelman has skillfully analyzed economic behavior in markets ranging from grocery food chains to petroleum. Morry's efforts to employ the insights of economic analysis have honed in him a skepticism of the "considered opinions" of well-intentioned politicians, judges, statesmen, and less analytical economists, an attitude typically expressed in uncommonly readable and enjoyable prose. This skepticism and characteristic style were evident in Morry's earliest work. For example, the final paragraph of his book on the A&P food company reads as follows (Adelman, 1959, pp. 529–530):

This book will have served some purpose if it helps make clear the essential unity of scientific method . . . . The method used, however haltingly, in this study, is the only way to observe the social as well as the physical world. It is compatible with many and various public policies or legal standards (since these depend also on certain preferences), but the method is totally irreconcilable—has nothing in common—with the warm assurance of those who *know* monopoly or competition on sight, *know* what needs to be done, and regard economic theory and statistical analysis not as imperfect tools but as barriers to results they *know* are right. Out of abundance of certainty comes a distaste for the concepts of economic theory, a preference for 'power,' 'strategic advantage,' 'intent,' and the like, to be verified by referring to an infallible source known as 'the opinion in the trade.'

Accordingly, in this Festschrift in Morry's honor, we consider ourselves

Research support from the Center for Energy Policy Research, MIT Energy Laboratory, is gratefully acknowledged, as are the helpful comments and suggestions of Richard Gordon, Henry D. Jacoby, John G. Myers, and G. Campbell Watkins.

excused from any excesses in mimicking this acknowledged master in scholarly skepticism and irreverence.

To energy analysts, Morry is best known for his seminal work on world oil markets, markets that have undergone dramatic changes in the last fifteen years. While nearly all of this work has focused on the cost and supply side of energy markets, Morry has often emphasized the importance of energy demand and energy-economy interactions in shaping the environment facing energy supplying companies and countries.[1] It is appropriate, therefore, that in this chapter we consider interactions among energy price shocks, energy demand, and measures of economic performance, particularly those involving productivity growth.

It is useful to review the "conventional wisdom." The oil price shocks of 1973–1974 coincided with sharp slowdowns in traditionally measured productivity growth, not only in the United States but throughout the industrialized world. Using traditional and time-honored measurement techniques, experts have found themselves unable to explain this slowdown. For example, Edward Denison, author of several widely cited productivity studies, concluded that energy had essentially no role in explaining the productivity slowdown and that "what happened is, to be blunt, a mystery" (1979a, p. 4).

Important intellectual puzzles typically attract a substantial amount of interest and analysis, and thus it is not surprising that a wide variety of new and not-so-new hypotheses have been advanced about energy and growth. Among the "thousand flowers that have bloomed" are hypotheses naming energy prices and energy conservation as the principal villains; others stating that energy could not be at fault given its small share in total costs; statements proposing that workers have simply become more idle, less cooperative, and less productive; arguments that the slowdown was essentially Keynesian and only indirectly related to energy price shocks; conjectures concerning the adverse effects of energy-capital complementarity and energy-labor substitutability; hypotheses concerning the biased nature of technical progress; postulates relating product mix changes to energy price increases; charges that decreased investment rates in plant-equipment or in research and development were at fault; and suggestions that a substantial portion of the slowdown was simply due to measurement errors.

Our purpose is to summarize and critique these various hypotheses, conjectures, and analyses. The outline of the chapter is as follows. In section 2, to protect ourselves from Adelman's First Fallacy of Public Policy Analysis ("The facts never had a chance," 1959, p. 415), we examine recent data from the 1958–1981 period in the context of longer time series that date back to the beginning of this century. This examination of US manufacturing data provides a framework for assessing the empirical credibility of a number of hypotheses mentioned above. For example, any hypothesis suggesting a significant relation between energy prices and productivity must explain how energy price changes induce sudden or abrupt breaks in productivity trends, when the equipment operating characteristics governing energy use change only gradually, and when the cost share of energy is so small.

Given this historical background, in section 3 we summarize and analyze a number of stages in the development of economic understanding of the energy-productivity relationship, and assess how each stage has fared in terms of its a priori plausibility and its consistency with recent empirical evidence.

In section 4 we advance our own hypothesis, demonstrate its plausibility and consistency with recent historical facts, and then assess quantitatively just how important it is. Our conclusion is that while energy price increases had a very important negative impact on measured productivity growth— much larger than many have heretofore believed—still a large proportion of the slowdown cannot be explained by energy-related matters. In section 5 we present concluding remarks and suggestions for further research.

2 A Look at the Recent Data in the Context of Longer Time Series

But the price effects work slowly. First there is advice: turn down the thermostats, turn off the lights, call off the trip. Then we get down to business: change the capital stock of energy-using equipment. First retrofitting: insulate buildings and machines; install heat exchangers, sensing devices and computer controls to save energy and increase its use only where and when and as it is needed; and so on. Even more important is to design and construct new buildings and equipment . . . . The half-life of the energy-saving process should approximate that of the capital stock, and be in the region of seven to ten years. (Adelman, 1979b, pp. 14–15)

We begin with a consideration of the behavior of energy prices and, in particular, evidence regarding energy price shocks. It is convenient to partition the recent data for US manufacturing into three periods, 1958–1973 (pre-OPEC), 1973–1978 (OPEC-I), and 1978–1981 (OPEC-II). In the pre-OPEC era, real energy prices (defined as nominal energy prices divided by the manufacturing gross output price deflator) were quite stable, falling slightly from 1958 to 1969, and then rising rather mildly from 1970 to 1973 (the price increases after 1969 were due primarily to coal and residual oil price rises). Sharp changes in this trend occurred during OPEC-I, when real energy prices suddenly rose 82%, and again during OPEC-II, when they rose another 76%. These three eras are shown in figure 1.

An important modeling issue concerns whether these OPEC price increases were consistent with widely held expectations, or whether they were "sur-

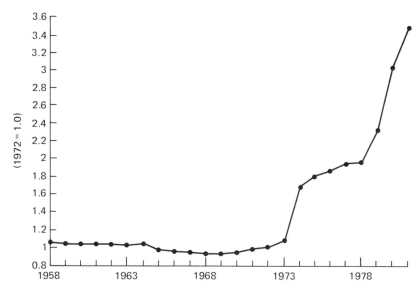

Figure 1
Real price of energy, US manufacturing.

prises.'' Activities in the spot markets for crude oil preceding OPEC-I suggest quite clearly that these price increases were unanticipated, i.e., that they were in fact price shocks; see Stanford Research Institute (1972) for typical pre-OPEC projections. But if these price increases were unexpected, what price trends were expected in the markets for crude oil and other types of energy? Was there any precedent for energy price shocks of this magnitude?

In an attempt to shed light on this issue, we have constructed an annual relative price index for aggregate energy in US manufacturing for the 75-year time span beginning in 1906.[2] This series was computed by dividing the nominal energy price by the price index for new equipment in US manufacturing, and then normalizing this relative energy price to unity in 1972.[3] The resulting price series is plotted in figure 2.

Although historical precedents exist for sudden increases in relative energy prices—see the years 1916–1921 and, to a limited extent, 1948—earlier energy price increases in the United States were considerably milder and less enduring than those of post-1973. Moreover, the long and sustained trend in falling relative energy prices from 1921 to 1969 surely contributed to expectations that future energy prices would continue to fall or at least would remain constant in real terms. The energy efficiency characteristics of the new long-lived equipment purchased during this era reflected such energy price expectations.

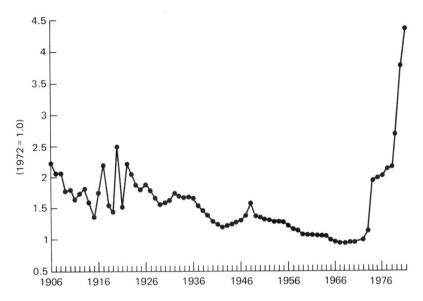

Figure 2
Relative energy prices, US manufacturing.

After the OPEC-I shock, and especially after OPEC-II, firms found themselves with vintages of capital equipment embodying energy efficiency that was no longer economically optimal given the new relative energy price expectations. Economic possibilities for energy-capital substitution were extremely limited with the existing capital stock, and since these stocks were relatively fixed in the short run, responses to the energy price shocks were initially constrained. Substantial improvements in energy efficiency could only be realized as older, energy-inefficient vintages of equipment were either retrofitted or replaced with more energy-efficient designs.

During this transition, however, firms attempted to reduce energy costs by altering utilization rates among their equipment vintages, shifting from the more- to the less-energy-using capital. Moreover, firms attempting to sell their energy-inefficient vintages found that prices in the secondhand market had fallen considerably. This accelerated economic depreciation occurred because the discounted shadow values of these vintages—their ability to reduce variable input costs and to increase expected net income—had been sharply reduced.[4]

To gain some quantitative insight into these qualitative arguments, it is useful to examine the response of manufacturing firms in the United States to the post-1973 energy price increases. Over the entire 1973–1981 period, the energy input-output coefficient (E/Y) dropped only 13%, while the real price

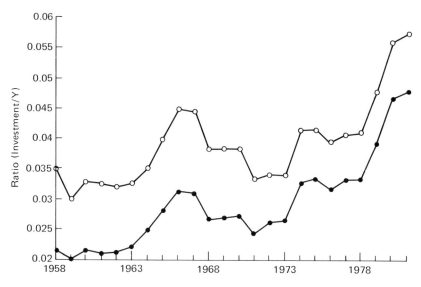

Figure 3
Ratio of real investment/output, US manufacturing: ●, equipment; ○, equipment and
structures.

of energy (P_E) rose 220%; if one performed a "back of the envelope" own-
price elasticity calculation as the ratio of these two percentage changes, the
result would be a rather meager own-price elasticity of only -0.06 over the
eight-year period.

More interesting, however, is the fact that during OPEC-I the E/Y coefficient
hardly changed at all; it dropped but 1% (real P_E increased 82%), while during
OPEC-II the E/Y coefficient decreased 12% (real P_E increased 76%). Hence
gains in energy conservation and energy efficiency, while negligible during
OPEC-I, accelerated substantially during OPEC-II.[5]

As noted earlier, the slow improvement in energy efficiency after the
OPEC-I price shock can be interpreted as being due to the fact that substantial
gains in energy efficiency tend to be possible only if investment in new plant
and equipment occurs, since economic possibilities for retrofitting are limited.
To the extent this interpretation is correct, one would expect substantial
reductions in the E/Y ratio to occur only after considerable investment in new
equipment had taken place.

In figure 3, therefore, we plot the ratio of total real investment—producers'
durable equipment plus nonresidential structures—to total real gross output
(the top curve), as well as the ratio of only the producers' durable equipment
component of total real investment to real gross output (the bottom curve)
over the period 1958–1981. Note first that if one looks only at 1958–1978 and

ignores the last three years, the total investment/gross output ratio (top curve) has considerable cyclical variability with a slight upward trend over time; the equipment component of this total investment also increases over time at a modest rate (bottom curve). However, sharp jumps in both these investment ratios occur beginning in 1978, with increases much higher than those observed even during the "Golden Age" of the mid-1960s.[6]

For our purposes, it is important to note that gains in energy conservation appear to be correlated with increases in the investment/output ratio. While more information on the composition of investment is necessary to establish this linkage, we see much of manufacturing investment since 1973 as an attempt to replace low quality, energy-inefficient fixed capital equipment with higher quality, more energy-efficient designs.[7] This raises the important measurement issue, however, of how much of this gross investment involves net increments to the capital stock, and how much should be attributed to replacement investment resulting from accelerated economic depreciation induced by the unexpected energy price increases. As will be discussed further in section 4, such changes in vintage-specific utilization rates are not properly incorporated in traditional procedures for computing aggregate capital stocks; these measures instead assume constant rates of utilization and deterioration and therefore indicate large increases in real capital input since 1973, increases that may overstate considerably net additions to economic capacity.

In the previous paragraphs we discussed data trends over the 1958–1981 period for energy prices, energy intensity, and gross investment in the US manufacturing sector. We now turn to the productivity performance of these manufacturing firms over the same period. While productivity growth can be measured in a variety of ways, here we focus on the two most often-used indices, namely, growth in average labor productivity (growth in output minus growth in labor input) and growth in multifactor productivity (growth in output minus growth in aggregate input, where the latter includes the inputs of capital, labor, energy, and nonenergy intermediate materials).[8] Since 1958 there have been significant differences in these two measures of productivity change.

We begin with labor productivity (LP) growth. In figure 4 we plot the level of average LP for the period 1958–1981. While the average annual growth rate (AAGR) in LP over the entire 1958–1981 period was 1.80%, considerable variation occurred year to year and in various subperiods. From 1958 to 1965, the AAGR in LP was a strong 2.58% per year; this impressive growth rate dropped sharply by about 30% to an AAGR of 1.76% during the 1965–1973 period (reflecting very low growth in 1965–1969, and high growth in 1969–

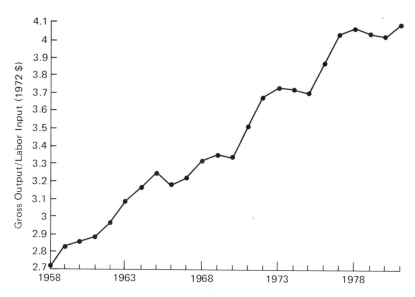

Figure 4
US manufacturing labor productivity.

1973), leveled off to an AAGR of 1.73% from 1973 to 1978, and then plummeted to 0.20% from 1978 to 1981.

Two points should be noted. First, a major slowdown in LP growth came prior to OPEC-I. LP growth in 1965–1973 (especially in 1965–1969) was considerably less than during 1958–1965, and while negative LP growth occurred simultaneously with OPEC-I in 1974–1975, over the entire period of OPEC-I to OPEC-II (1973–1978) the AAGR in LP growth was about the same as that from 1965 to 1973.[9] If in figure 4 one drew straight lines connecting the years 1958–1965 and 1966–1973, the slopes would be approximately the same. Second, subsequent decreases in LP growth coincided with both OPEC price shocks, and were of approximately equal magnitude. Again, a straight line connecting 1975–1978 has a slope similar to those for 1958–1965 and 1969–1973. Thus, although slopes are similar, figure 4 suggests that the intercepts shifted downward in 1966, 1974, and 1979, implying that sharp breaks in labor productivity growth (e.g., 1966) are not limited to years in which energy price shocks occurred.

Since labor is but one input in the production of output in US manufacturing (the labor cost share is on average about 25%), a more comprehensive measure of productivity performance would be one that compares output to the aggregate of all inputs, i.e., multifactor productivity (MFP) growth. In figure 5, therefore, we plot the annual level of traditionally measured MFP over the

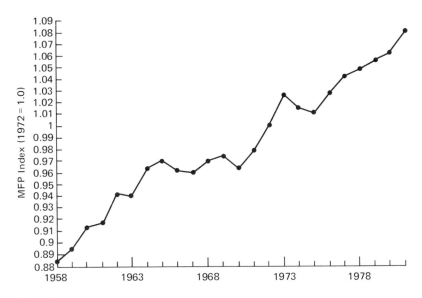

Figure 5
US manufacturing, traditional MFP.

1958–1981 interval.[10] The AAGR for the entire 1958–1981 time interval is 0.81%, while AAGRs for selected shorter time intervals are

1958–1965	1.26%
1965–1969	0.10%
1969–1973	1.27%
1973–1975	−0.68%
1975–1978	1.18%
1978–1981	0.77%

Year-to-year variations are again apparent. A number of points are also worth noting. First, as with LP, these MFP growth rate numbers indicate that the productivity growth slowdown had already begun in 1965. Second, MFP growth decelerated sharply in 1973–1975, as did LP growth; both measures then increased in the period 1975–1978. Third, however, MFP growth in the most recent 1978–1981 period was very respectable, although not as large as during the "Golden Ages" of 1958–1965 and 1969–1973; this contrasts with the behavior of LP growth, which dropped sharply from an AAGR of 3.27% (1975–1978) to 0.20% (1978–1981). Finally, it might be noted that actual drops in the level of MFP occurred in 1966–1967, 1970, and 1974–1975, while very low growth took place during 1979–1980.

The above figures and discussion clearly indicate that the slowdowns in MFP growth had a different timing than that for LP. As we now move on to consider a number of alternative hypotheses and stages in our thinking concerning "the" productivity growth slowdown, it will be useful to bear in mind this empirical distinction between MFP and LP movements. Recall also that while growth in MFP unambiguously represents outward shifts in production possibility frontiers (or downward shifts in average total cost curves) due to technical progress, changes in LP reflect the effects of both MFP and price-induced labor substitution.

3 The Energy-Productivity Connection: An Assessment

The problem is not of course that economists cannot provide explanations for the slowdown. Quite the reverse is true in fact. There are long lists of candidates; but for numerous reasons it is proving very difficult to find agreement on the main culprits or to identify their contribution to the overall slowdown. (Morris, 1983, p. 78)

This is not, however, an unfamiliar situation in any science: theory and facts do not seem to jibe, and either or both must give way. (Adelman, 1959, p. 9)

In the introduction it was stated that our purpose in this chapter is to summarize, examine, and critique a number of alternative hypotheses and stages in the development of our understanding of the links between energy price shocks and productivity growth changes. A variety of models will now be discussed, organized according to four different strands of thought: (1) energy conservation is the villain, (2) energy's cost share is small and therefore energy is not important enough to cause large slowdowns, (3) it's all Keynesian and cyclical anyway, and (4) energy is more important than its cost share indicates.

3.1 Energy Conservation Is the Villain

The hypothesis that responses to energy price shocks explain the post-OPEC productivity growth slowdown was put forward most decisively by Robert H. Rasche and John A. Tatom in articles appearing in the Federal Reserve Bank of St. Louis *Review*.[11] In the Rasche-Tatom framework, energy is highly substitutable with both capital and labor. Sharp rises in energy prices induce attempts to conserve energy. But because domestic capital and labor resources are fixed in the short run, conservation is achieved by reductions in optimal (capacity or potential) output. As a result, average labor productivity—

optimal output per unit of labor input—declines. In the longer run, according to Rasche-Tatom, capital-labor ratios will also decline, resulting in further reductions in growth of potential output.[12] Empirical implementation of this Rasche-Tatom framework involved use of parameter estimates of a Cobb-Douglas production function and was based on quarterly data for the entire US private business sector.

In examining the credibility of the Rasche-Tatom framework and conclusions, we make three observations. First, use of the Cobb-Douglas production function assumes that all Allen substitution elasticities—capital-labor, capital-energy, and energy-labor—are equal to unity. There is very little evidence in support of these Cobb-Douglas restrictions; see, for example, Jorgenson and Fraumeni (1981). In addition, use of this specification implies that the own-price elasticity for energy in the short run is on the order of -0.90, a very large number.[13]

Second, the data discussed in the previous section indicate very clearly that the large gains in energy conservation predicted by and absolutely necessary in the Rasche-Tatom framework simply did not occur in the manufacturing sector. Recall that over the entire 1973–1981 period, real energy prices increased 220%, while the energy input/output coefficient dropped only 13%, suggesting a "back of the envelope" energy own-price elasticity of -0.06, considerably less than that required by Rasche-Tatom. This limited energy conservation is certainly not sufficient to account for the slowdown in labor-productivity growth. Third and finally, even if such energy conservation had occurred, the Rasche-Tatom framework could only shed light on the slowdown in growth of labor productivity due to energy-labor substitution; it could not address the issue of what caused the slowdown in multifactor productivity growth.

Before leaving this "energy conservation is the villain" strand of thinking, we briefly consider a related debate concerning the effect of materials (not just energy) prices on productivity growth. Based on a framework with three factors of production (capital, labor, and aggregate materials—both raw and intermediate), Michael Bruno (1982, 1984) has argued that, apart from cyclical factors, the slowdown in US productivity growth in the manufacturing sector has resulted entirely from an increase in the price of material inputs to production. Bruno specifies a production function in which capital and labor are separable from materials, which implies that when materials prices increase, ceteris paribus, the capital-labor production possibility frontier for value-added shifts inward, i.e., productivity declines. An important component of Bruno's argument rests on the fact that, because double-deflation methods and fixed-weight price indexes are used to construct measures of value-added, the traditional measure of productivity growth derived from value-added is biased downward when material-saving substitution occurs, a condition that may have occurred post-1973.

Bruno's analysis has recently been considered by David Grubb (1986) and by Martin N. Baily (1984a). While both Grubb and Baily work within the context of Bruno's analytical framework, they call into question his empirical findings and his use of all intermediate goods as a proxy for raw materials. In particular, Grubb notes that the substantial substitution against materials that is necessary in Bruno's framework does not appear to have taken place since 1973. This empirical finding holds not only for energy, but also for a wide variety of other raw materials, in the United States and elsewhere. Moreover, Baily demonstrates empirically that the alleged downward bias in traditional productivity measurement due to use of inappropriate procedures is in fact very small for the United States. Both Grubb and Baily also note that raw materials are but a small component of total intermediate goods.

The conclusion that emerges from this Bruno-Baily-Grubb exchange is similar to that concerning the Rasche-Tatom hypothesis: the high substitution elasticities and substantial energy or raw material conservation required in order for energy/raw material price increases to have had a major impact on productivity growth simply do not appear to have taken place in the last decade.[14] In the absence of substantial conservation, the "energy/raw material conservation is the villain" hypothesis loses credibility. The mystery continues.

3.2 Energy Is Not Important Enough to Cause the Productivity Growth Slowdown

Macroeconomists paid little attention to "supply shocks" until the 1970s. Although after OPEC-I some models began to incorporate supply as well as traditional demand or Keynesian aspects into their equation structures, the reaction of many macroeconomists to supply side stories (such as that by Rasche and Tatom) was one of considerable skepticism.

A good example of this is provided by Arthur M. Okun (1974, 1975) and George L. Perry (1975a,b, 1977), who took issue with the Rasche-Tatom thinking. According to Rasche-Tatom, as a result of energy price increases, potential output had fallen considerably and current actual output was much closer to "capacity" than traditional capacity utilization numbers indicated. Such a conclusion was unwarranted, argued Okun and Perry, since energy has but a small cost share in total output, and thus changes in its availability could have only a limited impact, certainly much smaller than that implied by Rasche-Tatom.

Specifically, Okun (1974, p. 503) begins by assuming that energy and labor are perfect substitutes, implying an elasticity even higher than that assumed by Rasche-Tatom, and thus in this respect most favorable to their view. In such an environment, the response to an unexpected energy price increase would be virtually complete (and technologically impossible) energy conservation, so that every dollar that had been spent on energy inputs (or would be spent given higher energy prices) would instead be spent on employing additional labor. If this were to occur, average labor intensity per unit of output (L/Y) would increase, and therefore its reciprocal—average labor productivity (Y/L)—would decrease.

By how much would average labor productivity decrease? Based on data for the private US business sector, and average wage rates, Okun calculated that under the above assumptions (which are most favorable to Rasche-Tatom), the maximum possible increase in employment, and therefore the maximum possible decrease in average labor productivity growth, would be on the order of 0.2%. The clear implication that emerged from such a calculation was summarized by Perry as follows (Perry, 1977, p. 43): "I find it hard to see how high energy prices can affect productivity and output much. Energy is one input into production processes. Eventually some adjustment of production processes to conserve on energy is likely. But the effect on labor productivity can hardly be measurable."

The Okun-Perry analysis essentially poses a challenge to those relying on orthodox factor substitution analyses to identify and empirically measure new channels by which energy price shocks change factor utilization. The studies surveyed in section 3.4 in a sense represent responses to this challenge.

A somewhat different yet related approach has been taken by William W. Hogan and Alan S. Manne (1977), who have developed a stylized model of economic growth in which there are three factors of production (capital, labor, and energy), and labor input is exogenous. In this model even if energy has a small cost share, energy price increases can have a substantial adverse affect on economic growth if σ (the Allen substitution elasticity between energy and the capital-labor bundle) is greater than 0.5.

The assessment of the Hogan-Manne analysis in our context is affected considerably by two considerations: (i) while their story focuses on energy prices and growth in output, and while it does imply increased labor/output ratios (decreases in average labor productivity), it does not provide any predictions concerning the effects of energy price increases on multifactor productivity growth; (ii) the Hogan-Manne analysis highlights the fact that in order for energy price increases to affect labor productivity growth adversely, large energy-capital and energy-labor substitution elasticities are necessary. Since the empirical evidence summarized earlier casts doubt on the possibility of these elasticities being sufficiently large, especially in the short-to-medium run, the conclusions reached by Hogan-Manne are very much the same as those of Okun and Perry with respect to Rasche and Tatom. That is, energy price increases cannot be named the major villain in explaining the labor productivity growth slowdown. Energy is not sufficiently important, and energy-other input elasticities are too small.

3.3 It's All Keynesian and Cyclical Anyway

If one comes to the view that energy conservation is *not* the villain, it may be tempting to conclude that the extensive attention given to the direct effects of energy and raw materials prices was unwarranted. Traditional approaches to productivity trends might instead explain the phenomena of the last decade. Is there in fact a mystery?

One of the most sympathetic developers of such thinking is George Perry (1975a,b, 1977); other more recent advocates are noted in the survey by Assar Lindbeck (1983).[15] It is a well-established empirical regularity that multifactor and labor productivity growth have long tended to be procyclical.[16] If the OPEC energy price increases of 1973–1974 and 1979–1980 are viewed in the United States as equivalent to a domestic tax increase, then they also can be seen as tantamount to deflationary domestic fiscal policy. In such cases one might therefore expect that both average labor and multifactor productivity growth would be decreased. Energy price increases might therefore have had *indirect* adverse impacts on productivity growth, particularly if governmental policy failed to respond properly to the deflationary oil price increases.[17]

When one looks only at labor productivity growth, there is strong support for this hypothesis during both energy price shocks (see figure 4 and Okun, 1975); as noted in section 2, both in 1973–1975 and in 1978–1980 LP growth declined by slightly more than 3.0%. Thus both of the major LP growth slowdowns since 1973 coincided with deflationary energy price shocks that were approximately equal in magnitude.

A consideration of multifactor productivity, however, provides mixed evidence regarding the "it's all Keynesian" line of thinking. While support is again found in the 1973–1975 epoch when MFP growth declined almost 2.0%, during the 1978–1981 period the evidence is less conclusive since MFP growth declines only 0.4%.

Finally, the deflationary impact of higher energy prices during OPEC-II is not consistent with the coincident increased rate of investment in producers' durable equipment (see figure 3 and the discussion in section 2). Such increased investment could, however, be explained by firms replacing now energy inefficient vintages of capital in spite of deflationary macroeconomic conditions.

The bottom line assessment of this Keynesian argument is that it appears to have considerable empirical support regarding labor productivity, and mixed evidence concerning multifactor productivity growth and investment. What happened appears to have been more than simply a traditional Keynesian cyclical set of phenomena, although such cyclical effects are undoubtedly important. Energy-related events seem to have exerted influences in addition to traditional cyclical macroeconomic responses.

Denison is still unchallenged; the lowdown on the slowdown is that it is still a mystery.

3.4 Energy Is More Important Than Its Cost Share Indicates

In the next few pages, we consider four other lines of thinking that link energy price increases with productivity growth; they share the notion that energy may be more important than its cost share indicates. The four concepts to be considered are (1) energy-capital complementarity and energy-labor substitutability; (2) biased technical progress; (3) energy price-induced product mix changes; and (4) energy price-induced changes in real capital input and utilization.

3.4.1 Energy-Capital Complementarity and Energy-Labor Substitutability
One way by which energy effects could be more important than indicated simply by the energy cost share is through energy price-induced substitution with other inputs, especially durable capital. In a number of empirical studies, industries have been identified in which energy and capital were complementary rather than substitutable inputs; on the other hand, energy and labor were substitutable inputs.[18] Recall that with output given, when E and K are complements and E and L are substitutes, then, *ceteris paribus*, energy price increases would lead to increased labor intensity (decreased labor productivity) and reductions in the optimal capital-output intensity. In turn, since technical progress is often embodied in new plant and equipment, decreased captial formation might then lead to reduced rates of growth in multifactor productivity.

The Berndt-Jorgenson, Berndt-Wood, and Hudson-Jorgenson energy-capital complementarity analyses highlighted the special relationship between energy and capital, a relationship that will receive yet another interpretation later in this section. Considerable debate followed publication of these studies, much of it focusing on whether in fact energy and capital were complements,[19] and how energy-capital complementarity would relate to capital formation in a general equilibrium context.[20]

For our purposes here it is important to note that if energy-capital complementarity is to have an impact on multifactor productivity growth, it must be via the route of capital formation. Thus this hypothesis must be viewed in a long-run context involving gradual changes in investment behavior, and not in a short-run context involving, say, a one-to-five-year time span.

Although the years since 1973 and 1979–1980 do not yet constitute a sufficiently lengthy time series sample to examine long-run changes, it is of interest, nevertheless, to examine whether rates of capital formation increased or decreased after the energy price shocks of the 1970s. This apparently simple question actually raises important conceptual and measurement issues, and at times in the last decade has led to a confusing controversy. The answer to this deceptively simple question is ambiguous, depending critically upon how rates of capital formation are normalized for cyclical effects. For example, Thurow (1979, 1985) found that investment as a proportion of GNP increased from 9.5% in 1948–1965 to 10.2% during 1973–1978 and to 11.5% in 1977–1983, even as labor productivity fell and energy prices increased. Qualitatively similar results were noted by Berndt (1980) and Jorgenson (1984a) for the capital/output ratio, and by Denison (1980) for growth rates in both net and gross capital stocks. For the latter measure, however, quite different results were obtained when the capital stock measures were multiplied by the Federal Reserve Board capacity utilization index and the resulting product interpreted as capital input.[21] Since post-OPEC capacity utilization rates dropped substantially in almost all US industries due to the recessionary economic environment, the decrease in capacity utilization typically dominated the increase in traditionally measured capital stock, indicating a net decline in the growth rate of real capital input.

The above discussion makes clear that, in looking for early evidence concerning the energy-capital complementarity notion, the answer to the question of whether rates of capital formation after 1973 declined or increased depends in large part on the measure used.[22] While very strong reasons prevail in the productivity measurement context for favoring use of the capital-output ratio, and equally strong reasons can be cited for not employing the FRB capacity utilization-adjusted measure in measuring and weighting capital input,[23] such a discussion is only tangential to our concern here, namely, assessing the possible effects on productivity growth of energy-capital complementarity.[24]

Our overall assessment of the energy-capital complementarity hypothesis in helping to rationalize an "energy is more important than its cost share indicates" result is simply that it does not have much to say concerning events over the rather short periods 1973–1977 and 1978–1981. However, this hypothesis may be very important in the long run; that remains to be confirmed in a dynamic context using a longer time series of data, perhaps requiring data spanning several decades beyond 1973.[25] Moreover, decisive empirical confirmation of this energy-capital complementarity phenomenon will need to distinguish between net and replacement investment in the last decade, an important conceptual and measurement issue that we discuss further below.

3.4.2 Energy-Using Biased Technical Change

A second variant on the "energy is more important than its cost share indicates" theme is that of energy-using biased technical change, a hypothesis that has been put forward forcefully by Dale W. Jorgenson and Barbara Fraumeni.[26] The essence of this story is that since technical progress at the sectoral level has been found to be energy-using, increases in the price of energy, ceteris paribus, reduce the rate of multifactor productivity growth. Some background may be helpful for understanding this line of thinking.

In the translog model of production, cost-minimizing cost share equations for each input are specified to be functions of relative factor prices and time, the latter representing the effects of disembodied technical progress. (By disembodied is meant "manna from heaven"—technical progress that is costless, and improves the efficiency of all capital vintages and all other inputs as well.) The bias parameter of technical change is estimated as the coefficient on the time variable in the cost share equation for each input. This bias parameter is constant, which implies that the bias of technical change is exogenous and is not affected by, say, changes in factor prices. Technical change is said to be input i-using, i-neutral, or i-saving according as this coefficient on time in the ith factor cost share equation is positive, zero, or negative, respectively.

The interpretation of input i-using disembodied technical change is somewhat subtle, for technical progress frequently involves savings on the consumption of all inputs in producing a given level of output. It is often the case, however, that the derived demands for some inputs will be reduced more by technical progress than are those for other inputs. Those inputs whose derived demands are reduced most (or, more correctly, more than the weighted average of all inputs) are characterized as being subject to input-saving technical change, while those inputs whose derived demands are reduced less than the weighted average of all inputs are classified as being subject to input-using technical change. Hence this using-saving classification involves *relative* declines in consumption, not absolute savings.[27]

The relationship between biased technical progress and multifactor productivity growth is as follows. Consider the case where technical progress is of the form that exogenously augments the efficiency of the ith input at the constant rate λ_i; when the λ_i differ, technical change is nonneutral. It turns out that multifactor productivity growth is simply equal to $\sum s_i \lambda_i$, where s_i is the endogenous cost share of the ith input. An implication of this is that even though λ_i (the augmentation rate for the ith input) is constant and exogenous, since the cost shares s_i are price-responsive and endogenous, overall MFP (the share-weighted sum of the λ_i) is endogenous. Hence multifactor productivity growth is a function of share-weighted biased technical progress.

Using 1958–1974 annual data, Jorgenson-Fraumeni report that in almost all of the 36 sectors of the US economy, technical progress is energy-using. Further, when aggregate energy is decomposed into electric and nonelectric energy as in Jorgenson (1984b), technical change is found in most sectors to be both electric and nonelectric using, although the nonelectric bias parameter is typically larger than that for electric energy. This implies that at the sectoral level, growth in MFP is negatively related to increases in aggregate energy prices and to both its components—electric and nonelectric energy prices.

In assessing this biased technical progress line of thinking, we make the following observations. First, as was noted above, in this specification technical change is disembodied since the effects of technical progress do not depend, for example, on the vintage composition of the capital stock. In fact, however, much energy use depends critically on the time at which particular pieces of equipment were originally acquired—whether pre- or post-OPEC. When technical progress is restricted to be disembodied, the possibility of allowing new investment goods to be the carriers of technical progress is, unfortunately, explicitly ruled out.

Second, the Jorgenson framework is one in which inputs in each sector adjust instantaneously (within one year) to their long-run equilibrium levels. This implies that capital equipment is turned over and made optimally energy efficient within one year. As was noted in section 2, the energy consumption data are inconsistent with such a hypothesis; instead they suggest that energy conservation is a gradual process.[28] If one therefore thinks of technical progress in the US energy context as involving the gradual turnover of the capital stock where newer vintages embody greater energy efficiency, one cannot find such a mechanism within the Jorgenson one-year adjustment model.

Third, since the effects of energy price changes on MFP growth depend critically on the sign of the time coefficient in the energy cost share equation, evaluation of this biased technical change hypothesis should involve an examination of the robustness of this estimated parameter. As Berndt and Wood (1982) have reported, the values and even the signs of the estimated bias coefficients are sensitive to the time period of data used in the sample, as well as to slight changes in model specification. Hence the empirical foundations of this hypothesis are still to be validated.

Finally, as presented in Jorgenson-Fraumeni and elsewhere, discussion of biased technical progress typically addresses only the qualitative aspects, and not their quantitative magnitudes. In particular, to the best of our knowledge, results have not yet been presented that indicate the quantitative effect of energy price changes on MFP growth at the sectoral level. Because the cost share of energy is small, however, and because the absolute magnitudes of the energy bias coefficients are typically also very small,[29] there is reason to believe that the magnitude of the effect of an energy price increase on MFP growth at the sectoral level is modest at best. Even if energy price increases lead to a substantial change in the composition of output—a general equilibrium change in the sectoral composition of intermediate and final demand, which will be considered further in the next few pages—we therefore conjecture that it is very unlikely that energy price increases and biased technical change would play a major role in explaining the sudden economy-wide changes in MFP growth.[30]

We conclude, therefore, that the biased technical progress story, expanding the role of energy beyond its cost share and linking energy price increases to declines in MFP, is more of a long-run than a short-run hypothesis. Moreover, even if true, it can only explain a small portion of the sectoral slowdown in MFP growth.[31]

3.4.3 Productivity Growth with Energy Price-Induced Changes in Output Composition

The third variant on the theme ''energy is more important than its cost share indicates'' has been anticipated by the previous discussion, and involves the notion that energy price-induced changes in the composition of intermediate and final demand may have impacted productivity growth. It is useful to break down this line of thinking into its separate components: (i) What has been the effect of energy price changes on the composition of intermediate and final demand (and thereby on the demand for energy)? and (ii) What are the implications of this change for labor and multifactor productivity?

In the seminal article by Edward A. Hudson and Dale W. Jorgenson (1974), a general equilibrium model was specified for the US economy with nine producing sectors satisfying intermediate and final demands for goods and services. The model was simulated under a variety of scenarios, and implications for energy demand and economic growth were assessed. One of the most interesting simulations was of an increase in energy prices (all else constant). Of the total energy conservation in the long run, approximately three-quarters was due to energy price-induced changes in the composition of output, while only one-quarter was due to changes in production techniques. This suggests that energy price increases have their largest impact inducing changes in product mix, in large part through the price-sensitive demands of consumers.

Because the Hudson-Jorgenson production model was based on data ending in 1971, it is of interest to examine the more recent experience. Although the sectoral decomposition and data construction techniques differ from those of Hudson-Jorgenson, such a study has recently been published by Robert C. Marlay (1984). According to Marlay, aggregate energy demand was greatly affected by ".... unprecedented changes in the composition of industrial output away from industries that consume large amounts of energy" (p. 1277). More specifically, after examining 472 industries in US mining and manufacturing, Marlay concluded that about 55% of the total industrial energy conservation from 1973 to 1978 was due to increases in process efficiencies (movements along isoquants) and about 45% was due to changes in product mix.

While Marlay's 45–55 split is different from Hudson-Jorgenson's 75–25 decomposition,[32] broad agreement exists: energy price increases have a substantial impact on energy demand via the route of price-induced changes in product mix.

Not much attention has yet been devoted to the effects of these product mix changes on labor and multifactor productivity. It has long been known that *levels* of labor productivity vary considerably among sectors, being high in such industries as communications, finance, insurance, and real estate, and electric, gas, and water utilities, while being low in agriculture, construction, retail trade, and services. Changes in the overall composition of our national economy therefore bring about variations in the aggregate level of average labor productivity.[33]

Among others, Thurow (1979, 1980, 1985) has pointed out that product mix changes were favorable to aggregate labor productivity growth before 1973 (due in large part to the exodus of labor from the low labor-productive agriculture sector), but since then have been largely unfavorable. By 1977, product mix changes explained slightly less than 50% of the 1965–1972-to-1972–1977 slowdown in aggregate labor productivity growth. Thurow (1979) also notes, however, that there has been an almost universal decline in the growth rate of labor productivity industry by industry. In a related study, Martin N. Baily (1982) also finds that the productivity slowdown is virtually universal, and that only a trivial amount of the aggregate change is attributable to changes in industrial composition. Baily's results differ from Thurow (1979) in part because his data end in 1981 rather than in 1977. When Thurow (1980) employs data through 1978 rather than 1977, industry product mix shift effects account for only about one-quarter rather than slightly less than one-half of the slowdown in labor productivity growth.

In assessing these findings, we recall that the shift out of agriculture was virtually complete *before* the 1973–1974 energy price increases. And even if product mix changes since 1973 had some adverse affect on aggregate labor productivity, it is not clear how much of the shift to, for example, the service sectors was due to energy price increases. Finally, the almost universal decline in post-1973 and post-1977 labor productivity growth by industry suggests that something other than product mix is involved.

We now examine multifactor rather than labor productivity growth. The industry-specific story on multifactor productivity growth is very similar to that by Baily on labor productivity. According to Jorgenson (1984b) in 35 of the 36 US sectors analyzed, multifactor productivity growth dropped sharply post-1973. Hence at first sight the notion that product mix changes were a major influence does not appear promising.

As with labor productivity growth, however, variations among industries in the *level* of multifactor productivity can bring about changes in the *rate* of aggregate multifactor productivity growth when industrial product mixes occur. In principle, if one had a general equilibrium multisector model such as that constructed by Jorgenson and his associates, the effects of energy price increases on product mix and hence on aggregate multifactor productivity growth could be calculated. However, a major new problem arises. In order to undertake such a calculation, one would need to know the *level* of multi-factor productivity in each industry, not just its growth rate. To date no one has attempted the very difficult task of estimating such level differentials among industries, although some have conducted international interregional comparisons within the same industry.

We conclude, therefore, that while the energy price-induced change in product mix affected overall energy demand, its effects on labor productivity growth appear to be small, and its effects on multifactor productivity growth have not yet been calculated, and are unlikely to be calculated in the near future. The fact that the slowdown in the rate of multifactor productivity growth was virtually universal across industries, however, makes us doubt that the effect of energy-induced product mix changes on multifactor productivity will turn out to be substantial. This argument regarding a role for energy beyond its cost share does not, therefore, appear to be promising.

3.4.4 Energy Price-Induced Changes in Capital Utilization

A final argument in this series is based on the premise that measurement errors are important and that, in particular, traditional capital input measures fail to account properly for energy price-induced changes in capital utilization. Hence the effect of energy prices is not confined to energy input; it spills over to the measurement of real capital input. This line of thinking dates back at least to Lester Chandler (1951, pp. 234–235), and more recent variations have been put forward by Baily (1981a,b) and Berndt and Wood (1984).[34] We now briefly summarize this idea, and then expand on it in the next section.

According to this view, in the short run the available services from capital equipment are largely fixed, and so too are its operating characteristics. Although considerable energy-capital substitutability is possible ex ante, once capital is in place the ratio of energy consumption to capital services actually utilized is fixed; the relationship between energy and utilized capital services is one of putty-clay (malleable ex ante, fixed ex post). Dramatic changes in operating costs may, however, alter the pattern of utilization across differing vintages of capital embodying varying operating characteristics, decreasing in particular the utilization of energy-inefficient vintages relative to the more energy-efficient ones. As investment takes place and some of the energy-inefficient vintages are gradually replaced, the patterns of utilization across vintages adapt as well.

If this view is correct, then the energy price increases of the last decade altered vintage-specific utilization rates, and thus changed the relationship between the flow of capital services and the constant dollar measure of capital stock. Since the traditional procedure for measuring the flow of capital services in a given period involves first estimating the constant dollar capital stock and then assuming a fixed proportionality over time in the ratio of service flows to stocks, the conventional procedure cannot accommodate the effects of energy price-induced variations in the proportionality factor between service flows and capital stocks.

The implications of this measurement error problem for multifactor productivity measurement are as follows. Since MFP is computed as growth in output minus growth in aggregate input, where aggregate input is the share-weighted growth of the component inputs, it follows that if growth in real capital input were overstated since 1973 due to utilization reductions, then so too would be the growth of aggregate input; as a consequence, growth in the productivity residual would be understated.

An impressive feature of this hypothesis is that it is completely consistent with the slow and gradual improvement in energy efficiency since 1973, it is consistent with the sluggish turnover of energy-inefficient capital plant and equipment, which accelerated in particular during the OPEC-II epoch, and it may also be consistent with the dramatic changes that occurred in the post-OPEC valuation of capital in energy-using sectors such as manufacturing. Moreover, since it involves both capital and energy inputs, its effects on MFP growth are not constrained by the small cost share of energy.

There are, however, a number of potential problems. First, the utilization of capital typically cannot be measured directly, but instead must be inferred from the data. This implies that the econometric techniques used in implementing such a model must take into account either errors in variables or unobservable variables phenomena. Second, an economic framework must be developed that allows one to model the utilization of an input and simultaneously determine its shadow value. Third, once the above is accomplished, the quantitative magnitude of the effect of measurement error on MFP growth must be obtained and assessed. Fourth and finally, even if the effects of this measurement error were found to be substantial in "explaining" the post-1973 slowdown in MFP growth, there would still remain the problem of why productivity growth slowed down beginning already in 1965.

In the next section we elaborate on a model we have developed that accounts for embodied energy efficiencies that vary by vintage. Here, vintage-specific utilization rates are affected by energy price shocks, and the aggregation procedure over vintages using estimated shadow-value weights. Moreover, the implications of the model for MFP measurement errors are important.

4 Energy Price Shocks, Induced Variations in Capital Utilization, and the Productivity Growth Slowdown

The measurement of capital is one of the nastiest jobs that economists have set to statisticians. (Hicks, 1981, p. 204)

In this section we develop in more detail the notion that because of energy price changes, the relationship between aggregate utilized capital services and aggregate capital stock has been altered; in turn, this has implications for productivity measurement. Our discussion proceeds by focusing first on the capital aggregation and utilization issues, then on the implications for multifactor productivity measurement, and finally on the quantitative, empirical significance of this hypothesis (section 4.3).

4.1 On the Utilization and Aggregation of Capital Vintages

In virtually all research involving capital input in production or cost functions, it is assumed that the flow of capital services is proportional to the capital stock, and that this factor of proportionality is constant over time. Hence, it is not surprising that data construction procedures for capital input devote almost exclusive attention to the measurement of capital stock.

With traditional capital stock aggregation over vintages, it is assumed that capital physically deteriorates or "evaporates" at the constant rate δ. The significance of this assumption is that the relative marginal product at time t of a \$1 investment in each of the two periods $t - \tau$ and $t - \tau - v$ equals $(1 - \delta)^v$. More specifically, the marginal products at time t of period t, $t - \tau$, and $t - \tau - v$ investments of \$1 are 1, $(1 - \delta)^\tau$, and $(1 - \delta)^{\tau+v}$. In such a case of constant geometric deterioration, and only in such a case, the rate of economic depreciation is also constant and equal to δ.[35]

Thus, the implication of the "constant deterioration" assumption is that the relative prices of surviving vintages of capital are constant over time. Since relative prices are fixed, one can employ the Hicksian aggregation condition[36] and form an aggregate capital stock over vintages defined as

$$K_t = \sum_{\tau=0}^{T} S_\tau I_{t-\tau} = \sum_{\tau=0}^{T} K_{t,t-\tau}, \tag{1}$$

where S_τ is the physical survival rate, $S_\tau \equiv (1 - \delta)^\tau$, T is the physical lifetime of equipment, $I_{t-\tau}$ is the amount of real investment put in place at time $t - \tau$, and $K_{t,t-\tau}$ is the amount of $t - \tau$ investment physically surviving to period t. Note that the S_τ are precisely the proportionality factors that reflect relative marginal products.

It is useful to generalize this traditional treatment of capital aggregation over vintages to account for energy price-induced changes in vintage-specific rates of utilization. We now present a framework that permits us to construct an aggregate measure of utilized capital, denoted K_t^*, computed as

$$K_t^* = \sum_{\tau=0}^{T} e_{t,t-\tau} S_\tau I_{t-\tau} = \sum_{\tau=0}^{T} e_{t,t-\tau} K_{t,t-\tau}, \tag{2}$$

where the $e_{t,t-\tau}$ are relative vintage-specific utilization rates of the physically surviving $t - \tau$ investment at time t. Notice that if $e_{t,t-\tau} = 1$ for all t, τ, then traditional (K) and "utilization-adjusted" (K^*) measures of capital coincide.

Our use of the term "utilization-adjusted" capital is very suggestive, but obviously needs to be made more precise. We are reminded here of Morry Adelman's irreverent attitude toward "vague" and "suggestive" abstractions. Adelman's students may well remember Adelman's Second Fallacy of Public Policy Analysis, which Morry summarized in his commentary on the alleged existence of administered prices (Adelman, 1980, p. 48): "But the devil sees deeper. As Mephistopheles advised the hopeful student, you most need a *word* when you have no *idea*." So let us now make more clear the notion of "utilization adjusted" measures of capital.

Suppose that when firms make investment decisions for new equipment, they first decide the amount of funds to be devoted to the sum of the amortized capital and operating (say, only energy) costs; this decision could be based on, for example, expectations concerning output demand, materials costs, wage rates, and operating rates. Second, having decided this, firms then choose the optimal split between capital and energy costs using expected life cycle costing procedures. Once the optimal energy efficiency is chosen in this second step, the capital utilization energy use relation is fixed in "clay," hence, while flexible and "putty" ex ante, the amount of energy consumed per unit of capital service utilized is immutable ex post.[37]

Assume further that with the second decision noted above, the relevant production function is the familiar CES function with Hicks-neutral disembodied technical change and constant returns to scale. Using the first order conditions for life cycle costing, this CES production function yields the optimal ex ante energy intensity at time t,

$$\ln(E/K)_t = \ln a - \sigma \ln(P_E^*/P_K^*)_t, \tag{3}$$

where $\ln a$ is a constant, σ is the ex ante substitution elasticity between energy and capital equipment, and P_E^* and P_K^* are values of discounted expected prices for energy and capital equipment, respectively.

If firms followed this decision criterion at all points in time—at t and $t - \tau$ for all t, τ—and if relative energy prices suddenly changed, the optimal relative utilization rates for the surviving $t - \tau$ vintages could differ significantly from those originally intended. Specifically, within the capital-energy bundle, total variable (energy) costs VC_t over all surviving vintages can be written, using (3), as

$$VC_t = P_{Et} \sum_{\tau=0}^{T} a \cdot \left[\frac{P_E^*}{P_K^*} \right]_{t-\tau}^{-\sigma} \cdot u_{t,t-\tau} K_{t,t-\tau}, \tag{4}$$

where $u_{t,t-\tau}$ is the utilization rate for the $t - \tau$ vintage surviving to time t. The shadow values of these surviving vintages, i.e., their ability to reduce variable (energy) costs given their embodied energy efficiency and energy prices prevailing at time t, is given by

$$-\frac{\partial \, \mathrm{VC}_t}{\partial K_{t,t}} = -P_{Et} \cdot a \cdot \left[\frac{P_E^*}{P_K^*}\right]_t^{-\sigma} \cdot u_{t,t} \tag{5}$$

for the most recent (period t) surviving capital, and by

$$-\frac{\partial \, \mathrm{VC}_t}{\partial K_{t,t-\tau}} = -P_{Et} \cdot a \cdot \left[\frac{P_E^*}{P_K^*}\right]_{t-\tau}^{-\sigma} \cdot u_{t,t-\tau} \tag{6}$$

for surviving vintage $t - \tau$ capital. Assume the efficient firm utilizes these various surviving vintages of capital so that their shadow values in production are equal. Equating the shadow values in (5) and (6) for all t, τ and rearranging, we obtain

$$-\frac{u_{t,t-\tau}}{u_{t,t}} = \left[\frac{P_{EK,t}^*}{P_{EK,t-\tau}^*}\right]^{\sigma}, \tag{7}$$

where $P_{EK,t}^*$ and $P_{EK,t-\tau}^*$ are the relative price terms in square brackets in equations (5) and (6), respectively.

An implication of (7) is that when these shadow values are equalized, vintage-specific utilization rates will adjust, with the magnitude of the adjustment depending on the size of the ex ante substitution elasticity σ and the change between time $t - \tau$ and t in the relative energy prices P_{EK}^*. In particular, if relative energy prices increase between $t - \tau$ and t, and if the ex ante energy-capital substitution elasticity equals zero (no substitution possibilities available ex ante), then by (3) the optimal ex ante energy intensities at t and $t - \tau$ would be identical in spite of energy price increases, and thus no utilization adjustment would occur among the surviving vintages. However, if σ were substantial—if significant energy-capital substitution possibilities were available ex ante—then according to (7) the relatively energy-inefficient vintages would be utilized less in production. On the other hand, if relative energy prices fell unexpectedly and if $\sigma > 0$, then the relatively energy-inefficient vintages would be used more in production; the ratio in (7) can be on either side of unity. In our judgment, this utilization adjustment response to energy price shocks is eminently plausible.

Having derived vintage-specific rates of utilization that depend on relative energy prices and the ex ante substitution elasticity, we now employ them in constructing an aggregate measure of utilized capital over vintages. Since equating shadow values preserves relative service prices of capital vintages, the Hicksian aggregation condition can again be employed in aggregating these vintages. Specifically, we set the relative vintage-specific utilization rates $e_{t,t-\tau}$ equal to the left-hand side of (7), i.e., set

$$e_{t,t-\tau} = \frac{u_{t,t-\tau}}{u_{t,t}}, \tag{8}$$

normalize by setting $u_{t,t} = 1$ for all t, and then substitute into (3), thereby obtaining K_t^*, a utilization-adjusted measure of capital services. Finally, the vintage-weighted aggregate rate of capital utilization, denoted by $B_{K,t}$, can then be computed as K_t^* divided by K_t, i.e.,

$$B_{K,t} \equiv K_t^*/K_t. \tag{9}$$

Note that the aggregate measure of capital utilization can be less than, equal to, or greater than unity.[38]

4.2 Implications for Multifactor Productivity Measurement

Growth accountants and productivity analysts typically measure the rate of multifactor productivity growth (r_{MFP}) as the growth rate in output (r_Y) minus the growth rate of aggregate input (r_X), where the latter is computed as a cost-share weighted growth in each of the N component inputs, i.e.,

$$r_{MFP_t} = r_{Y,t} - r_{X,t} = r_{Y,t} - \sum_{i=1}^{N} s_{i,t} \cdot r_{X_{i,t}}, \tag{10}$$

and where $s_{i,t}$ is the arithmetic mean of the cost share of the ith input in the total costs of all N inputs over periods t and $t - 1$.[39] Since (10) is the basic relation employed in most growth accounting analyses, improvements in data construction, as well as controversies amongst researchers, can often be described in terms of measurement issues involving output and input quantities (affecting the r_i) or involving value measurements (affecting the s_i).

To highlight the effects on MFP measurement of accounting for energy price-induced changes in capital utilization, we note first that any two measures of a given input may be related by a scalar, i.e.,

$$\beta_{i,t} \equiv \frac{X_{i,t}^*}{X_{i,t}}. \tag{11}$$

The growth rate in one measure of an input may be written as the sum of the growth rates of the other measure and the ratio of the two measures, i.e.,

$$r_{X_{i,t}}^* = r_{\beta_{i,t}} + r_{X_{i,t}}. \tag{12}$$

Substituting (12) into (10) and denoting the alternative measure of MFP growth as MFP*, we have

$$r_{\text{MFP}_t^*} = r_{Y,t} - \sum_{i=1}^{N} s_{i,t}(r_{\beta_{i,t}} + r_{X_{i,t}}). \tag{13}$$

Subtracting equation (10) from (13), we obtain the difference in MFP measures associated with the difference in input measures:

$$r_{\text{MFP}_t^*} - r_{\text{MFP}_t} = - \sum_{i=1}^{N} s_{i,t} \cdot r_{\beta_{i,t}}. \tag{14}$$

As is seen in (14), the effect on the multifactor productivity growth rate of the alternative measures is given by minus the sum of the share-weighted differences in growth rates of the scalar relating the alternative measures. Note that this interpretation applies whether the differences are interpreted as errors in measuring inputs or simply as differences without any normative implications.

In our case, however, there is ample reason to believe that the utilization-adjusted measure of capital input is preferable to the conventional measure, which takes no account of changes in the relationship between capital service flows and capital stock. The consequences for MFP measurement of incorrectly measuring capital input flows are clear from (14). If vintage-specific utilization rates fell after OPEC-I, then the $r_{\beta_{i,t}}$ term in (14) is negative, and the difference between the conventional and the new utilization-adjusted measure of MFP growth will be positive, i.e., growth in MFP* will be understated using the conventional accounting procedures. We now assess the quantitative significance of this measurement error problem.

4.3 Quantitative Evidence on the Importance of MFP Measurement Errors

Preliminary results are available based on the above framework and data from the US manufacturing sector, 1958–1981, including also investment and relative energy price data back to 1937. In Berndt and Wood (1984), firms were specified as minimizing short-run variable costs (labor plus energy plus nonenergy intermediate material costs) given output, the beginning-of-period capital stock, its vintage composition and embodied energy efficiency, and prices of the variable inputs. Since the long-run average total cost curve is the envelope of the short-run curves, it was possible simultaneously to estimate ex ante and short-run or ex post substitution elasticities. The crucial ex ante substitution elasticity between capital equipment and energy was estimated in a variety of ways and with alternative treatments of expectations

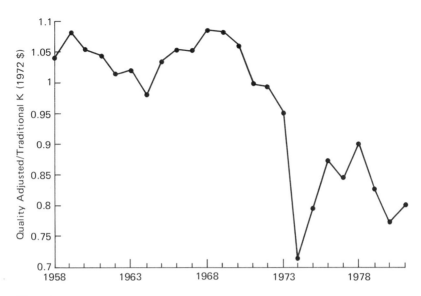

Figure 6
US manufacturing capital input (K^*/K).

concerning future relative energy prices. However, all estimates of σ fell in the range of 0.4 to slightly less than 1.0, the midrange estimate being about 0.65.

We have employed this $\sigma = 0.65$ value, first to calculate $B_{K,t}$, and then K_t^* as $K_t \cdot B_{K,t}$. In Figure 6, we plot the aggregate capital utilization rate $B_{K,t}$ for 1958–1981. A number of points are worth noting.

For most years prior to 1971, $B_{K,t} > 1$, which implies that it was economically attractive to utilize the capital stock greater than originally planned. As a result of relative energy price decreases prior to 1971, operating costs had become less than expected, and as a consequence it was optimal to utilize the now "too energy efficient" vintages more than originally planned. Note also that $B_{K,t}$ hit its maximum in 1969, precisely when the relative energy price attained its lowest level (sees figures 1 and 2).

Beginning in 1972 and especially during the 1973–1974 and 1978–1980 energy price shocks, the overall utilization rate $B_{K,t}$ fell sharply—about 25% in OPEC-I and 15% in OPEC-II. Its value at the end of the sample in 1981 was about 0.80, implying that, properly measured, the real flow of capital input was only about 80%, as large as that based on traditional capital accounting procedures.

Since capital service flows were measured with error over this period, so too were the growth rates of real capital input. In turn, since capital is one

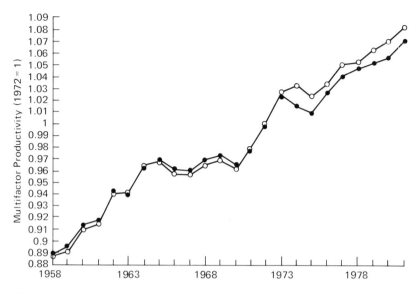

Figure 7
US manufacturing multifactor productivity: ●, MFP; ○, MFP*.

of the inputs comprising aggregate input, and since growth in multifactor productivity is computed as growth in output minus growth in aggregate input, MFP was also mismeasured. We now denote the level (not the growth rate) of traditionally measured multifactor productivity as MFP, and the level of multifactor productivity based on utilization-adjusted capital input as MFP*; both are plotted in figure 7. As might be expected, there is very little difference between the two series until 1973. After 1973, MFP* becomes larger than MFP, implying that traditional MFP growth has been understated due to the energy price shocks of OPEC-I and OPEC-II.

To assess the quantitative effect of this measurement error on MFP growth, we calculate average annual growth rates (AAGR) for MFP, MFP*, and LP during selected time intervals, based on the data underlying figures 4 and 5. Since significant variations occur from year to year in these productivity measures, averages can be affected by the choice of end points. AAGR over a number of time intervals are presented in table 1.

As the results show, relative movements between the multifactor and labor productivity measures are similar within and between the 1958–1973 and 1973–1981 periods. However, there is evidence of a productivity slowdown between the two periods in all three measures. Thus, LP slows from 2.14 to 1.15, slightly less than a 100% reduction. The slowdown in multifactor measures is somewhat less dramatic, 0.35% for the traditional measure (MFP)

Table 1
Average annual growth rates for MFP, MFP*, and LP US manufacturing (%)

Time interval	AAGR-MFP	AAGR-MFP*	AAGR-LP
1958–1965	1.34	1.29	2.58
1965–1969	0.10	0.01	0.81
1969–1973	1.30	1.45	2.73
1973–1975	−0.78	−0.27	−0.53
1975–1978	1.25	1.10	3.27
1978–1981	1.03	1.17	0.20
1958–1973	1.00	0.99	2.14
1973–1981	0.65	0.78	1.15
1958–1981	0.88	0.92	1.80

and 0.21% for the capital utilization adjusted measure (MFP*), indicating that the traditional measure overstates the slowdown by approximately 25%. Hence, while adjusting for capital utilization effects due to energy price shocks reduces estimates of the productivity slowdown, such adjustments alone do not fully account for the productivity slowdown since 1973.

Much greater heterogeneity in the measures reported in table 1 occurs within the two periods, 1958–1973 and 1973–1981. For example, while the overall MFP and MFP* rates for the period 1958–1973 are about the same (1.00% versus 0.99%), the growth rates for the two subperiods 1965–1969 (falling relative energy prices) and 1969–1973 (rising relative energy prices) begin to show divergence, with the traditional MFP measure slightly overstating productivity growth in the earlier subperiod, and understating growth in the latter period.

This pattern of bias caused by ignoring capital utilization adjustments is even more dramatic in the 1973–1981 period when relative energy price variations increased. Thus, in the three subperiods in the 1973–1981 period characterized by first sharply rising, then falling, and finally rising, relative energy prices (1973–1975, 1975–1978, and 1978–1981, respectively), the traditional measure (MFP) first understates productivity growth by 0.65% (0.78% vs. 0.27%), then overstates growth during the recovery by 0.14% (1.25% vs. 1.10%), and finally understates growth in the second OPEC price shock by 0.12% (1.03% vs. 1.17%). Adjusting for capital utilization due to energy price shocks results, therefore, in much more homogeneous productivity growth over the post-OPEC period, although, as noted above, these adjustments account for only about one-fourth of the traditionally measured slowdown between the 1958–1973 and 1973–1981 periods.

It is important to emphasize here that these results still imply that the post-1973 energy price increases had very substantial and adverse effects; firms did the best they could given the unexpected energy price increases, and once one accounts properly for their behavior in this changed environment, productivity performance, especially that for MFP*, is not as poor as commonly thought.

Finally, we note that unlike growth in MFP*, which dropped sharply during OPEC-I, but was unaffected by OPEC-II, LP growth was strongly affected by both OPEC-I and OPEC-II, with its AAGR falling 3.07% (3.27% − 0.20%) and 3.26% (2.73% versus −0.53%), respectively. Thus, an alternative way to envisage the effects of the post-1973 energy price shocks is to view them from the vantage of workers.[40] Especially in 1974 and 1979, production line workers suddenly found themselves with energy-inefficient capital whose optimal utilization rates had plummeted, and as a result their output was affected. These "capital decimation" shocks are reflected in figure 4 as downward shifts in the intercepts of labor productivity growth in 1974 and 1979.[41] This set of events brings to mind the Old Testament recording of a heated exchange between Pharaoh and an Israelite, an exchange that reflects the fact that labor productivity can be adversely affected by such reductions in nonlabor inputs (Exodus 5:15–18):

Then the foreman of the people of Israel came and cried to Pharaoh, "Why do you deal thus with your servants? No straw is given to your servants, yet they say to us, 'Make bricks!' And behold, your servants are beaten; but the fault is in your own people." But he said, "You are idle, you are idle; therefore you say, 'Let us go and sacrifice to the Lord.' Go now, and work; for no straw shall be given you, yet you shall deliver the same number of bricks."

5 Concluding Remarks

... But in the long run, presumably when we are all dead, there is at least a modest probability that the most significant economic reversal since the Great Depression of the 1930's will be seen to be the slowdown in economic growth brought about by the establishment of the OPEC cartel. (Jorgenson, 1978, p. 219)

It has been our purpose in this wide-ranging survey to summarize and evaluate the various hypotheses, conjectures, and analyses relating to the possible role of energy in accounting for the slowdown in productivity growth. While a number of hypotheses initially appeared promising, their credibility has declined as problems of consistency with common sense and empirical evidence have become apparent. The litmus test for any explanation is that it be able to explain how energy price changes can induce sudden or abrupt breaks in productivity trends when the characteristics governing energy use change only gradually, and especially when the cost share of energy is so small. On the basis of such a criterion, two hypotheses remain plausible—namely, the energy price-induced Keynesian deflationary effect with nonaccommodating government policy, and the adjustment by firms in the utilization of surviving capital. In this paper, we have concentrated on the latter hypothesis. In the paragraphs that follow, we summarize our principal findings and then suggest a research agenda.

In terms of MFP growth, it appears that the post-OPEC slowdown has been overstated by as much as 25%, due to errors in the measurement of real capital input. Moreover, if one adjusts for the energy price-induced changes in the utilization of capital equipment, on average the 1975–1981 MFP growth experience was about the same as that over the 1958–1973 era, with a sharp growth decline limited to the OPEC-I era (1973–1975). Of particular interest, the OPEC-II price shock had almost no effect upon capital utilization adjusted multifactor productivity growth, suggesting that US manufacturing industries may have substantially increased their resiliency between the first and second OPEC price shocks.

Yet another way to assess the link between energy price changes and productivity growth is to take advantage of the most recent data, particularly in the United States since 1981, when real energy prices have begun to fall. The various models considered in this paper, as well as the above quotation from Dale Jorgenson, all would seem to suggest that productivity growth should now be rebounding in the United States due to the recent decreases in energy prices. Whether this turnaround in productivity growth has recently occurred has not yet been established; the work of Baily (1984b) and Clark (1984) highlights difficulties in pinpointing changes in productivity growth and suggests that it may still take some time to assess the various energy-productivity hypotheses in light of the more recent price trends. Also of interest is that productivity growth acceleration since 1981 seems to have been larger in the manufacturing than in the nonmanufacturing sectors; whether this corresponds with recent trends in capital formation also needs to be established.

Clearly more work remains to be done. First, although we have referred to it rather casually, it is clear that rigorous analytical and empirical analysis is needed on the implications of changes in utilization for the valuation of durable assets—the present value of future quasi-rents. Changes in utilization rates undoubtedly imply variations in capital asset valuations that may well be consistent with the stock market behavior of US manufacturing firms during the last decade. This relationship between changes in capital stock valuations and capital service flows is of great potential importance.

Second, since energy prices and energy pricing policies have varied considerably among Europe, Asia, and North America, international comparisons of productivity growth must be reexamined in the context of the energy efficiency of the capital stock existing at the time OPEC-I occurred, and in the light of subsequent investment behavior. Energy-productivity links are likely to be better understood if advantage is taken of the wide cross-sectional and time series variation among countries in relative energy prices, energy intensities, capital formation, and productivity growth.

Third, once some consensus has been reached regarding sector-specific capital measurement, then it will be necessary to trace out the output effects of the price shocks, taking into account the capital utilization adjustment reflected in the capital measure. General equilibrium studies similar to the pioneering efforts of Hudson and Jorgenson will be required both to reconsider the distribution of changing energy consumption between input substitution and output mix, and to evaluate the combined effects of input substitution, technical change, capital utilization, and output mix on labor and multifactor productivity growth. As was noted in section 3.4, however, the thorny problem of relating and comparing industry multifactor productivity levels remains to be solved before such analyses can be conducted.[42]

Fourth, we have examined only the effects of energy price shocks on capital measurement and MFP growth. Price changes of other inputs, such as labor or nonenergy raw materials, might also be examined within our framework. What is crucial here, however, is not that the price of an input merely change (real wage rates have long been on an increasing path in many industries), but that the price change be unexpected and substantial.

Fifth, while not emphasized in this survey, it should be noted that other capital measurement issues will require increasing attention from economists and statisticians. Most important, the effects of the microelectronic and instrumentation revolution have significant implications for technical progress embodied in new capital goods. In fact, this effect is likely to be as important to capital measurement in coming decades as energy has been in the past decade.

Finally, the embodiment of advances in microelectronics in new capital goods will certainly have significant implications for energy use (in particular, electricity) through the changing economics governing the organization of production processes, both within existing plants and in new locational decisions. Hence, future research on energy demand will continue to deal with interactions among sudden changes in energy, capital, and/or productivity, although the shocks may now involve technological developments rather than OPEC-induced energy market turmoil.

These last two points implicitly involve judgmental forecasts on our part. We are, however, quite reluctant to tie ourselves to a specific prediction, particularly in a Festschrift in honor of Morry Adelman. The hazards are suggested by Morry's own experiences with world oil markets. Preparing for an early spring trip, including presentations to business executives in the Bahamas and to academics at the Norwegian School of Economics, Morry selected his materials with the usual care. Naturally then, as he trudged up the steps of the Nassau Hilton Hotel, cross-country skis were the most conspicuous item in his luggage. Whereupon an oil company executive, well informed on current "opinions in the trade," was overheard muttering to his colleagues, "Damn, another Adelman forecast."

Notes

1. See, for example, Adelman (1977, 1979a,b, 1982), Adelman and Friis (1975), and Adelman and Jacoby (1978).

2. The data employed in these and subsequent calculations in this and in section 4 are described in Berndt and Wood (1986). The series for 1947–1981 update and extend our earlier data series for capital, labor, energy, and intermediate materials input prices and quantities, as published in Berndt and Wood (1975).

3. We focus on the energy-equipment price ratio because of its importance in calculating equipment life cycle costs. In particular, it is the expected energy price relative to the current equipment purchase price that, along with the discount rate and planned utilization, determines the life cycle cost for equipment. In turn, expected equipment life cycle costs influence the firm's choice of the optimal energy efficiency characteristics for new equipment. The effects of differences between expected and realized prices upon the ex post, or shadow, value of equipment vintages, and upon relative ex post vintage utilization, are the subject of section 4.

4. For empirical evidence from the used automobile market, see Daly and Mayor (1983) and Ohta and Griliches (1986).

5. One reason for the small energy conservation response from 1973 to 1978 is that during this period a significant number of pollution abatement regulations went into effect. These regulations often increased energy consumption per unit of output. For a summary discussion of such issues, see John G. Myers and Leonard Nakamura (1978), p. 11.

6. Moreover, this sharp increase since 1978 in the gross investment-gross output ratio is not the result of the denominator falling, i.e., of lower output. Real annual investment in equipment averaged approximately 46% larger than that during 1974–1977, and 100% larger than the average during 1965–1973.

7. It is worth noting also that until recently, the computational procedures for calculating gross private domestic investment in the United States assumed that all imported goods were either consumer durables or nondurables, and in particular that

none of the imports were producers' durable equipment; see the 17 October 1983 *Business Week* article, "Why Economic Indicators Are Often Wrong," pp. 168–169. Considerable anecdotal evidence is available suggesting that US firms are importing a great deal of equipment (e.g., see *Business Week*, 4 March 1985), much of it more energy efficient than that available in the United States for similar prices. To the extent this is true, investment figures reported by the US Department of Commerce have been understated, especially in the last decade. The figures underlying figure 3 represent a preliminary attempt by Department of Commerce personnel to take imports properly into account.

8. The output measure employed here is gross output, not value-added, since the aggregate input measure includes intermediate inputs.

9. This leveling off of aggregate LP growth over the 1965–1978 time span masks substantial compositional changes, as production worker input fell and that of non-production workers increased. For a related discussion, see Berndt (1980) and Thurow (1985).

10. Discussion of MFP measures reflecting the possibility of vintage capital utilization is deferred to section 4.

11. See, for example, Rasche and Tatom (1977a,b) and Tatom (1979a,b, 1982).

12. Why this should occur in the long run is not clear, since with the Cobb-Douglas function the cross-price elasticities $\varepsilon_{KE} = \varepsilon_{LE} = \alpha_E$, where α_E is the cost share of energy. This implies that $\partial \ln(K/L)/\partial \ln P_E = 0$, i.e., the capital-labor ratio should be unaffected by changes in the price of energy.

13. With the Cobb-Douglas function, the own-price elasticity of demand for energy is equal to $\alpha_E - 1$, where α_E is the cost share of energy; in the Rasche-Tatom sample, this share was roughly about 0.1, which implies that $\alpha_E - 1 = -0.9$.

14. Similar empirical findings casting doubt on the extent of materials substitutability, and recent changes in materials-output coefficients have been reported by Zvi Griliches and Jacques Mairesse (1983).

15. Lindbeck's survey extends to most of the OECD countries, not just the United States. Moreover, he identifies resource misallocation due to sticky wages and prices and increasing government intervention in the marketplace as also being major components of the productivity growth slowdown. For further discussion, also see D. J. Morris (1983).

16. For a survey of this literature in the context of short-run labor productivity, see Morrison and Berndt (1981) and the references cited therein.

17. There is a vast literature on appropriate governmental policies toward energy price shocks, both in terms of energy-specific policies and in terms of appropriate monetary-fiscal responses. Useful discussions are found in George Perry (1975a,b), Knut Anton Mork and Robert E. Hall (1980a,b), Henry D. Jacoby and James C. Paddock (1983), Harry D. Saunders (1982), Brian D. Wright (1980), David W. Burgess (1984), and Robert S. Pindyck (1980).

18. See, for example, Berndt and Jorgenson (1973), Berndt and Wood (1975, 1979), and Hudson and Jorgenson (1974).

19. See, for example, Griffin and Gregory (1976), Griffin (1981a,b), Berndt and Wood (1979, 1981), Pindyck (1979a,b), and Gibbons (1983).

20. See, for example, John L. Solow (1979), William Hogan (1979), Stephen C. Peck and John L. Solow (1982), Graciela Chichilnisky and Geoffrey Heal (1983), and David W. Burgess (1984).

21. This procedure has been employed in studies by Clark (1978), Tatom (1979a), and Kopcke (1980). Disagreement also occurs if one uses growth rates in capital-labor ratios as a criterion or when one looks at the entire private business sector rather than at the manufacturing industries; see Thurow (1980) on Kendrick (1980), Thurow (1985), and J. Randolph Norsworthy, Michael S. Harper, and Kent Kunze (1979).

22. A related issue has been raised by, among others, Kendrick (1980), who points to decreases in research and development investment as a possible cause of the productivity growth slowdown. As Thurow (1980, 1985) notes, the empirical foundations for such an assertion concerning R&D investment are questionable, and even if they were true, one would not expect slowdowns in R&D spending in the early 1970s to manifest themselves in decreased productivity growth until much later, say, not until the 1980s or 1990s.

23. For a discussion of such issues, see Berndt (1980), Berndt and Fuss (1986), and Denison (1980).

24. Utilization issues, however, are important and will be discussed in further detail below.

25. Based on data up through 1971, long-run energy-capital complementarity has been established in the US manufacturing sector by Berndt, Morrison, and Watkins (1981), Kulatilaka (1985), Morrison and Berndt (1981), and Pindyck and Rotemberg (1983). Support for $E-K$ complementarity based on post-1973 data is reported for US manufacturing by Morrison (1985), and for Canadian manufacturing by Watkins (1985).

26. See Jorgenson and Fraumeni (1981) and Jorgenson (1984b).

27. Additional interpretation is given in Berndt and Wood (1982).

28. Further empirical support for and discussion of gradual energy demand adjustment to price changes is presented by William W. Hogan (1983).

29. The small estimated magnitudes may be due in part to the fact that much technical progress is in fact embodied, rather than disembodied, and the Jorgenson framework only incorporates disembodied technical change; for a discussion in a different context, see Otto Eckstein (1977), pp. 53, 60.

30. Some recent unpublished results of Jorgenson may, however, challenge our conjecture.

31. This brief analysis does not consider the intriguing hypothesis of Schurr (Schurr and Netschert, 1960, p. 189; Schurr, 1982) on the effects of electrification on average energy productivity, average labor productivity, and multifactor productivity. This hypothesis has only recently begun to receive econometric attention; see, for example, Richard B. Duboff (1966), Dale W. Jorgenson (1984b), Arthur G. Woolf (1984), and Ernst R. Berndt (1986).

32. Differences between Hudson-Jorgenson and Marlay could be due to a number of factors, including the more complete behavioral specification in Hudson-Jorgenson, and the shorter time span and more disaggregated data base used by Marlay.

33. For an earlier analysis of this phenomenon, see William D. Nordhaus (1972).

34. This notion is related to, yet distinct from, that of energy price-induced obsolescence of capital, for the latter involves valuation over the lifetime of the asset, while ours is primarily a flow notion within a single time period. On obsolescence, see, for example, Joel Gibbons (1984).

35. While economists are attracted to the geometric decay assumption in part because of its analytical convenience, economic statisticians have tended to employ other assumptions. Empirical evidence is mixed, but the important recent study of Hulten and Wykoff (1981) tends to support geometric decay for a wide variety of durable goods.

36. See Diewert (1978) for discussion of Hicksian aggregation.

37. In the framework adopted here, while the energy-capital service utilization relationship is clay, ex post substitutability may still be permitted between the capital-energy bundle and labor or material inputs.

38. While it would be preferable to impose the constraint that $B_{K,t}$ could never be negative and that its upper bound should be affected by the 24-hour-day and 365-days-a-year constraints, these are not imposed here. As a practical matter these constraints do not seem important since, as will be reported below, empirical estimates of $B_{K,t}$ all fall within a plausible range.

39. Because r_{MFP} is computed as a residual, it can capture the effects of all types of errors and omissions. This has led Moses Abramovitz (1956, p. 11) to call it a "measure of our ignorance."

40. For a nontraditional analysis of productivity growth changes including both the pre- and post-1973 eras, see Thomas Weisskopf, Samuel Bowles, and David Bordon (1983).

41. Recall that a similar shift also occurred in 1966, a year in which energy markets and energy price expectations were stable.

42. A related and more long-term general equilibrium research project of considerable importance would involve both points two and three, and would focus on the migration of industries and their capital to countries with favorable factor price conditions.

References

Abramovitz, Moses (1956), "Resource and Output Trends in the United States Since 1870," *American Economic Review*, Vol. 46, no. 2, May.

Ackerman, Bruce A., and William T. Hassler (1981), *Clean Coal/Dirty Air*, Yale University Press, New Haven, Connecticut.

Adelman, M. A. (1949), "Integration and Anti-Trust Policy," *Harvard Law Review*, Vol. 63, November.

Adelman, M. A. (1959), *A&P: A Study in Price-Cost Behavior and Public Policy*, Economic Studies No. 113, Harvard University Press, Cambridge, Massachusetts.

Adelman, M. A. (1962), *The Supply and Price of Natural Gas*, Basil Blackwell Press, Oxford, England.

Adelman, M. A. (1964), "Efficiency of Resource Use in Crude Petroleum," *Southern Economic Journal*, Vol. 31, October.

Adelman, M. A. (1966), "American Coal in Western Europe," *Journal of Industrial Economics*, Vol. 14.

Adelman, M. A. (1967), "Trends in Finding and Developing," *Essays in Petroleum Economics*, S. Gardner and S. Hanke (editors), University of Colorado Press, Denver, Colorado.

Adelman, M. A. (1970), "Economics of Exploration for Petroleum and Other Minerals." *Geoexploration*, Vol. 8, December.

Adelman, M. A. (1972), *The World Petroleum Market*, The Johns Hopkins University Press, Baltimore, Maryland.

Adelman, M. A. (1972–73), "Is the Oil Shortage Real? Oil Companies as OPEC Tax-Collectors," *Foreign Policy*, no. 9, Winter.

Adelman, M. A. (1976), "Oil Import Quota Options," *Challenge*, Vol. 18, January/February.

Adelman, M. A. (1977), "Producers, Consumers, and Multinationals: Problems in Analyzing a Noncompetitive Market," M.I.T. Energy Laboratory Working Paper No. MIT-EL 77-038WP, Cambridge, Massachusetts, October.

Adelman, M. A. (1979a), "Constraints on the World Monopoly Price," *Resources and Energy*, Vol. 1, no. 1, January.

Adelman, M. A. (1979b), "The Political Economy of the Middle East—Changes and Prospects since 1973," M.I.T. Energy Laboratory Working Paper No. MIT-EL 79-037WP, Cambridge, Massachusetts, June.

Adelman, M. A. (1979c), "The Case for Decontrol," *Challenge*, July/August.

Adelman, M. A. (1980), "The Clumsy Cartel," *The Energy Journal*, Vol. 1, no. 1, January.

Adelman, M. A. (1982), "OPEC as a Cartel," *OPEC Behavior and World Oil Prices*, Griffin and Teece (editors), George Allen and Unwin Publishing Company, Boston, Massachusetts.

Adelman, M. A. (1985), "An Unstable Oil Market," *The Energy Journal*, Vol. 6, No. 1, January.

Adelman, M. A., Paul G. Bradley, and Charles A. Norman (1971), *Alaskan Oil: Costs and Supply*, Praeger Publishers, New York, New York.

Adelman, M. A., and Soren Friis (1975), "Changing Monopolies and European Oil Supplies: The Shifting Balance of Economic and Political Power on the World Oil Scene," *Energy in the European Communities*, Frans A. M. Alting von Geusau (editor), A. W. Sijthoff Publishing Company, Leyden, Netherlands.

Adelman, M. A., John C. Houghton, Gordon K. Kaufman, and Martin B. Zimmerman (1983), *Energy Resources in an Uncertain Future: Coal, Gas, Oil, and Uranium Supply Forecasting*, Ballinger Publishing Company, Cambridge, Massachusetts.

Adelman, M. A., and Henry D. Jacoby (1978), "Oil Gaps, Prices, and Economic Growth," M.I.T. World Oil Project, M.I.T. Energy Laboratory Working Paper No. MIT-EL 78-008WP, Cambridge, Massachusetts, May.

Adelman, M. A., and Henry D. Jacoby (1979), "Alternative Methods of Oil Supply Forecasting," *Advances in the Economics of Energy and Resources*, Vol. II, R. S. Pindyck (editor), J.A.I. Press, Greenwich, Connecticut.

Adelman, M. A., and G. Ward (1980), "Estimation of Worldwide Production Costs for Oil and Gas," *Advances in the Economics of Energy and Resources*, Vol. III, J. Moroney (editor), J.A.I. Press, Greenwich, Connecticut.

Alchian, A. (1959), "Costs and Outputs," *The Allocation of Economic Resources: Essays in Honor of B. F. Haley*, M. Abramovitz (editor), Stanford University Press, Stanford, California.

Allen, Wendy (1977), *Nuclear Reactors for Generating Electricity: US Development from 1946 to 1963*, Rand Corporation Report No. R-2116-NSF, Santa Monica, California, June.

Alm, Alvin L., and Joan P. Curham (1984), *Coal Myths and Environmental Realities: Industrial Fuel-Use Decisions in a Time of Change*, Westview Press, Boulder, Colorado.

Altschuler, Alan (1979), *The Urban Transportation System*, The M.I.T. Press, Cambridge, Massachusetts.

American Enterprise Institute (1985), *Renewal of the Price-Anderson Act*, Washington, D.C.

Anders, G., W. P. Gramm, S. C. Maurice, and C. W. Smithson (1980), *The Economics of Mineral Extraction*, Praeger Publishers, New York, New York.

Anderson, R. J., Jr. (1979), "An Analysis of Alternative Policies for Attaining and Maintaining a Short-Term NO_2 Standard," Mathtech, Inc., Princeton, New Jersey.

Andreatta, G., and Gordon M. Kaufman (1986), "Estimation of Finite Population Properties When Sampling Is Without Replacement and Proportional to Magnitude," *Journal of the American Statistical Association*, September.

Arps, J. J., and T. G. Roberts (1959), "Economics of Drilling for Cretaceous Oil on East Flank of Denver-Julesburg Basin," American Association of Petroleum Geologists Bulletin, Vol. 42, no. 11.

Arrow, Kenneth J., and Maurice McManus (1958), "A Note on Dynamic Stability," *Econometrica*, Vol. 26, no. 3, July.

Arrow, Kenneth J., and Marc Nerlove (1958), "A Note on Expectations and Stability," *Econometrica*, Vol. 26, no. 2, April.

Arthur, Henry B. (1971), *Commodity Futures as a Business Management Tool*, Harvard University Press, Cambridge, Massachusetts.

Attanasi, E. D., L. J. Drew, and J. H. Scheunemeyer (1980), "An Application to Supply Modeling in Petroleum-Resource Appraisal and Discovery Rate Forecasting in Partially Explored Regions," U.S. Geological Survey Professional Paper 1138-A, B, C, U.S. Government Printing Office, Washington, D.C.

Baer, Julius B., and Olin Saxon (1948), *Commodity Exchanges and Futures Trading*, Harper Brothers, New York, New York.

Baily, Martin N. (1981a), "Productivity and the Services of Capital and Labor," *Brookings Papers on Economic Activity*, Vol. 1.

Baily, Martin N. (1981b), "The Productivity Growth Slowdown and Capital Accumulation," *American Economic Review*, Papers and Proceedings, Vol. 71, no. 2, May.

Baily, Martin N. (1982), "The Productivity Growth Slowdown by Industry," *Brookings Papers in Economic Activity*, Vol. 2.

Baily, Martin N. (1984a), "Productivity Growth and Materials Use in US Manufacturing," The Brookings Institution, Washington, D.C., May; forthcoming, *Quarterly Journal of Economics*.

Baily, Martin N. (1984b), "Will Productivity Growth Recover? Has It Done So Already?", *American Economic Review*, Papers and Proceedings, Vol. 74, no. 3.

Baker, R. A., H. M. Gehman, W. R. James, and D. A. White (1984), "Geologic Field Number and Size Assessments of Oil and Gas Plays," The American Association of Petroleum Geologists Bulletin, Vol. 68, no. 4, April.

Balcer, Y., Gordon M. Kaufman, and D. Kruyt (1975), "A Probabilistic Model of Oil and Gas Discovery," *Studies in Geology, No. 1—Methods of Estimating the Volume of*

Undiscovered Oil and Gas Resources, American Association of Petroleum Geologists, Tulsa, Oklahoma.

Ball, B. C., Jr., J. C. Houghton, J. L. Sweeney, and J. P. Weyant (1981), "U.S. Oil and Gas Supply," *The Economics of Exploration for Energy Resources*, J. B. Ramsey (editor), J.A.I. Press Inc., Greenwich, Connecticut.

Barker, T., and W. Brailowsky, editors (1982), *Oil versus Industry*, Cambridge University Press, Cambridge, England.

Barouch, E., and G. Kaufman (1977), "Estimation of Undiscovered Oil and Gas," *Proceedings of the Symposia in Applied Mathematics*, Vol. 21, American Mathematical Society, Providence, Rhode Island.

Barouch, E., G. M. Kaufman, S. Chow, and T. Wright (1985), "Properties of Successive Sample Moment Estimators," *Studies in Applied Mathematics*, Vol. 73.

Barrows, G. H. (1983), *Worldwide Concession Contracts and Petroleum Legislation*, PennWell Press, Tulsa, Oklahoma.

Baumol, William J., and David F. Bradford (1970), "Optimal Departures from Marginal Cost Pricing," *American Economic Review*, Vol. 60, June.

Beard, William (1941), *Regulation of Pipelines as Common Carriers*, Columbia University Press, New York, New York.

Berndt, Ernst R. (1980), "Energy Price Increases and the Productivity Slowdown in United States Manufacturing," *The Decline in Productivity Growth*, Proceedings of a Conference Held in June 1980, Conference Series No. 22, Federal Reserve Bank of Boston, Boston, Massachusetts.

Berndt, Ernst R. (1986), "Electrification, Embodied Technical Progress, and Labor Productivity Growth in US Manufacturing, 1889–1939," in *Productive Efficiency, and Economic Growth*, Sam Schurr and Sidney Sonenblum (editors), Electric Power Research Institute, Palo Alto, California.

Berndt, Ernst R., and Melvyn A. Fuss (1986), "Productivity Measurement Using Capital Asset Valuation to Adjust for Variations in Utilization," *Journal of Econometrics*, forthcoming.

Berndt, Ernst R., and Dale W. Jorgenson (1973), "Production Structure," *US Energy Resources and Economic Growth*, Dale W. Jorgenson et al. (editors), Final Report to the Ford Foundation Energy Policy Project, Washington, D.C.

Berndt, Ernst R., Catherine J. Morrison, and G. Campbell Watkins (1981), "Dynamic Models of Energy Demand: An Assessment and Comparison," *Modeling and Measuring Natural Resource Substitution*, Ernst R. Berndt and Barry C. Field (editors), M.I.T. Press, Cambridge, Massachusetts.

Berndt, Ernst R., and David O. Wood (1975), "Technology, Prices, and the Derived Demand for Energy," *Review of Economics and Statistics*, Vol. 56, No. 3, August.

Berndt, Ernst R., and David O. Wood (1979), "Engineering and Econometric Interpretations of Energy-Capital Complementarity," *American Economic Review*, Vol. 69, no. 3, September.

Berndt, Ernst R., and David O. Wood (1981), "Engineering and Econometric Interpretations of Energy-Capital Complementarity: Reply and Further Results," *American Economic Review*, Vol. 71, no. 5, December.

Berndt, Ernst R., and David O. Wood (1982), "The Specification and Measurement of Technical Change in US Manufacturing," *Advances in the Economics of Energy and Resources*, John R. Moroney (editor), Vol. 4, J.A.I. Press, Greenwich, Connecticut.

Berndt, Ernst R., and David O. Wood (1984), "Energy Price Changes and the Induced Revaluation of Durable Capital in US Manufacturing during the OPEC Decade," M.I.T. Energy Laboratory Report No. 84-003, Cambridge, Massachusetts.

Berndt, Ernst R., and David O. Wood (1986), "US Manufacturing Output and Factor Input Price and Quantity Series, 1906–1947 and 1947–1981," M.I.T. Energy Laboratory Working Paper No. 86-010WP, Cambridge, Massachusetts, April.

Bertrand, R. J. (1981), "The State of the Competition in the Canadian Petroleum Industry," Restrictive Trade Practices Commission, Ottawa, Canada, February.

Betancourt, Romulo (1979), *Venezuela: Oil and Politics*, Houghton Mifflin Publishing Company, Boston, Massachusetts.

Blitzer, Charles R., Panos E. Cavoulacos, Donald R. Lessard, and James L. Paddock (1985), "An Analysis of Fiscal and Financial Impediments to Oil and Gas Exploration in Developing Countries," *The Energy Journal*, Vol. 6, Special Tax Issue.

Bohn, Roger E. (1982), *Spot Pricing of Public Utility Services*, PhD Dissertation, M.I.T. Sloan School of Management, M.I.T. Energy Laboratory Report No. MIT-EL 82-031, Cambridge, Massachusetts, May.

Bohren, O., and C. Schilbred (1980), "North Sea Oil Taxes and the Sharing of Risk—a Comparative Case Study," *Energy Economics*, Vol. 2, no. 3, July.

Bradley, Paul G. (1984), "Costs and Supply of Natural Gas from Alberta: An Empirical Analysis," Economic Council of Canada, Discussion Paper No. 251, Ottawa, Canada.

Bradley, Paul G., and G. Campbell Watkins (1982), "Crude Oil Pricing in Canada," *The Canadian Oil Industry: An Analysis*, G. C. Watkins (editor), mimeo.

Bresnahan, Timothy (1981), "Duopoly Models with Consistent Conjectures," *American Economic Review*, Vol. 71, no. 5, December.

Breyer, Stephen, and Paul MacAvoy (1974), *Energy Regulation by the Federal Power Commission*, The Brookings Institution, Washington, D.C.

Broadman, Harry G., and Michael A. Toman (1983), "Non-Price Provisions in Long-Term Natural Gas Contracts," Report Prepared for Annual Meeting of the American Economics Association, December 30, 1983, Resources for the Future, Washington, D.C.

Bromberg, L., and J. A. Hartigan (1975), "U.S. Reserves of Oil and Gas," Report to the Federal Energy Administration, Department of Statistics, Yale University, New Haven, Connecticut, May.

Bruno, Michael (1982), "World Shocks, Macroeconomic Response, and the Productivity Puzzle," *Slower Growth in the Western World*, R. C. O. Matthews (editor), Heineman Publishing Company, London, England.

Bruno, Michael (1984), "Raw Materials, Profits, and the Productivity Slowdown," *Quarterly Journal of Economics*, Vol. 99, no. 1, February.

Bupp, Irving C., and Jean-Claude Derian (1981), *Light Water*, Basic Books, New York, New York.

The Bureau of National Affairs (1975), *The Environmental Reporter*, Vol. 18, Monograph No. 21, Washington, D.C.

Burgess, David W. (1984), "Energy Prices, Capital Formation, and Potential GNP," *Energy Journal*, Vol. 5, no. 2, April.

Burrows, James C. (1974), Testimony before the Subcommittee on Economic Growth of the Joint Economic Committee, 93rd Congress, 2nd Session, July 22.

Business Week (1983), "Why Economic Indicators Are Often Wrong," 17 October, pp. 168–169.

Business Week (1985), "The Bad News behind the Capital Investment Surge," 4 March, p. 20.

Canada Energy, Mines, and Resources (EMR) (1976), *An Energy Strategy for Canada, Policies for Self Reliance*, Ottawa, Canada.

Canada Energy, Mines, and Resources (EMR), Geological Survey of Canada (1977), "Oil and Gas Resources of Canada—1976," Calgary, Alberta.

Canada Energy, Mines, and Resources (EMR) (1980), *National Energy Program*, Ottawa, Canada.

Canada Energy, Mines, and Resources (EMR), Geological Survey of Canada (1984), "Oil and Gas Resources of Canada—1983," Calgary, Alberta.

Carpenter, Paul R. (1984), "Natural Gas Pipelines after Field Price Decontrol: A Study of Risk, Return, and Regulation," PhD Thesis, M.I.T. Sloan School of Management, M.I.T. Energy Lab Report No. MIT-EL 84-004, March.

Carpenter, Paul R., Henry D. Jacoby, and Arthur W. Wright (1983), "Natural Gas Pipeline Regulation after Field Price DeControl," Report Prepared for US Department of Energy, Office of Oil and Gas Policy, M.I.T. Energy Laboratory Working Paper No. MIT-EL 83-013WP, Cambridge, Massachusetts, March.

Chandler, Lester V. (1951), *Inflation in the United States, 1940–1948*, Harper Brothers Publishing Company, New York, New York.

Charles River Associates (1975), *Forecast and Analysis of the Mercury Market*, Report No. 223, Cambridge, Massachusetts.

Charles River Associates and Wharton Econometric Forecasting Associates (1974), *Forecasts and Analysis of the Mercury Market*, Cambridge, Massachusetts, August.

Chemical Week (1967), "Rethinking Rejected Routes," October 14.

Chichilnisky, Graciela, and Geoffrey Heal (1983), "Energy-Capital Substitution: A General Equilibrium Analysis," International Institute for Applied Systems Analysis Report No. CP-83-6, Laxenburg, Austria, February.

Church, A. M. (1981), *Taxation of Nonrenewable Resources*, Lexington Books, Lexington, Massachusetts.

Clarfield, Kenneth W., S. Jackson, J. Keeffe, M. A. Noble, and A. P. Ryan (1975), *Eight Mineral Cartels*, McGraw-Hill Publishing Company, *Metals Week*, New York, New York.

Clark, Peter K. (1978), "Capital Formation and the Recent Productivity Slowdown," *Journal of Finance*, Vol. 33, no. 3, June.

Clark, Peter K. (1984), "Productivity and Profits in the 1980s: Are They Really Improving?" *Brookings Papers on Economic Activity*, Vol. 1, The Brookings Institution, Washington, D.C.

Clark, Peter K., P. Coene, and D. Logan (1981), "A Comparison of Models in EMF 5," Stanford University Energy Modeling Forum Working Paper 5.1, Draft 5, October.

Clunies-Ross, A. (1983), *The Taxation of Mineral Rents*, Oxford University Press, Oxford, England.

Cohen, Bernard L. (1980), "Society's Valuation of Life Saving on Radiation Protection and Other Contexts," *Health Physics*, Vol. 28, no. 1, January.

Crandall, Robert W., Howard Gruenspect, Theodore E. Keeler, and Lester Lave (1986), *Regulating the Automobile*, The Brookings Institution, Washington, D.C.

Dagher, J. H. (1968), "Effect of the National Oil Policy on the Ontario Refining Industry," Unpublished PhD Thesis, McGill University, Montreal, Quebec, Canada.

Daly, George G., and Thomas H. Mayor (1983), "Reason and Rationality during Energy Crises," *Journal of Political Economy*, Vol. 91, no. 1, February.

Dam, K. W. (1971), "Implementation of Import Quotas: The Case of Oil," *Journal of Law and Economics*, Vol. XIV, no. 1.

Dam, K. W. (1976), *Oil Resources—Who Gets What How*, University of Chicago Press, Chicago, Illinois.

Deacon, Robert T., and Walter J. Mead (1985), "The Oil and Gas Industry: Regulation and Public Policy," in William A. Vogely, ed., *Economics of the Mineral Industries*, American Institute of Mining, Metallurgical and Petroleum Engineers, New York.

DeBartolo, Gilbert F. (1976), "Econometric Models of the World Molybdenum and Mercury Markets: The Roles of a Dominant Firm and a Competitive Fringe with an Exhaustible Resource," Unpublished PhD Thesis, Department of Economics, Massachusetts Institute of Technology, Cambridge, Massachusetts.

DeGroot, M. H. (1975), *Probability and Statistics*, Addison Wesley, Reading, Massachusetts.

Denison, Edward F. (1979a), *Accounting for Slower Economic Growth: The United States in the 1970's*, The Brookings Institution, Washington, D.C.

Denison, Edward F. (1979b), "Comment," *Brookings Papers on Current Economic Activity*, Vol. 2, The Brookings Institution, Washington, D.C.

Denison, Edward F. (1980), "Comment on Kopcke," *The Decline in Productivity Growth*, Federal Reserve Board of Boston Conference Series No. 22, Boston, Massachusetts.

Diebold, William, Jr. (1959), *The Schuman Plan: A Study in Economic Cooperation 1950–1959*, Frederick A. Praeger Press for the Council on Foreign Relations, New York, New York.

Dietzman, William D., Henry S. Weigel, and John H. Ubod (1979), "Nigeria—An Assessment of Crude Oil Potential," US Department of Energy, Energy Information Administration, DOE/EIA-0184/14, July 31.

Diewert, W. Erwin (1978), "Hicks' Aggregation Theorem and the Existence of a Real Value-Added Function," *Production Economics: A Dual Approach to Theory and Applications*, Vol. II, Melvyn Fuss and Daniel McFadden (editors), North-Holland Publishing Company, Amsterdam, Netherlands.

Drew, L. T., J. H. Schuenemeyer, and D. H. Root (1980), "An Application to the Denver Basin," *Petroleum-Resource Appraisal and Discovery Rate Forecasting in Partially Explored Regions*, U.S. Geological Survey Professional Paper 1138—Parts A, B, C, U.S. Department of the Interior.

Duboff, Richard B. (1966), "Electrification and Capital Productivity: A Suggested Approach," *Review of Economics and Statistics*, Vol. 48, no. 4, November.

Eckbo, Paul L. (1976), *The Future of World Oil*, Ballinger Publishing Company, Cambridge, Massachusetts.

Eckbo, Paul L., H. D. Jacoby, and J. L. Smith (1978), "Oil Supply Forecasting: A Disaggregated Process Approach," *The Bell Journal of Economics*, Vol. 9, no. 1, Spring.

Eckstein, Otto (1977), "Comment on Perry," *Brookings Papers on Economic Activity*, Vol. 1, The Brookings Institute, Washington, D.C.

Ellis, Randall P., and Martin B. Zimmerman (1983), "What Happened to Nuclear Power? A Discrete Choice Model of Technology Adoption," *The Review of Economics and Statistics*, August.

Energy Systems Research Group, Inc. (1982), *Testimony and Exhibits of Richard Rosen in Electric Rate Case of the Public Service of Indiana*, (Case No. 36818), Boston, Massachusetts.

Enthoven, Alain C., and Kenneth J. Arrow (1956), "A Theorem on Expectations and Stability of Equilibrium," *Econometrica*, Vol. 24, no. 3, July.

Epple, D., and L. P. Hansen (1979), "An Econometric Model of U.S. Petroleum Supply with Optimal Endogenous Depletion," Carnegie-Mellon University Working Paper, Pittsburgh, Pennsylvania.

Epple, D., and L. P. Hansen (1981), "An Econometric Framework for Modeling Exhaustible Resource Supply," *Contemporary Studies in Economic and Financial Analysis*, Vol. 26, J.A.I. Press, Greenwich, Connecticut.

Erikson, E. W., S. W. Millsap, and R. M. Spann (1974), "Oil Supply and Tax Incentives," Brookings Papers on Economic Activity, Vol. II, Washington, D.C.

Erikson, E., and R. Spann (1971), "Supply Response in the Regulated Industry: The Case of Natural Gas," The Bell Journal of Economics and Management Science, Vol. 2, no. 1, Spring.

European Economic Communities (EEC) Commission (1985), Memorandum on the Financial Aids Granted by the Member States to the Coal Industry in 1984 and on the Additional Financial Aids Granted by the Member States to the Coal Industry in 1983, Brussels.

Evans, Nigel, and Chris Hope (1984), Nuclear Power, Future Costs and Benefits, The Cambridge University Press, Cambridge, England.

Faith, W. L., Donald B. Keyes, and Ronald L. Clark (1957), Industrial Chemicals, 2nd edition, John Wiley and Sons, Inc., New York, New York.

Fama, Eugene F., Lawrence Fisher, Michael C. Jensen, and Richard Roll (1969), "The Adjustment of Stock Prices to New Information," International Economic Review, February.

Fearnley's Review 1983 (1983), Oslo, Norway.

Feldstein, Martin (1981), "Has the Rate of Investment Fallen?," National Bureau of Economic Research Working Paper No. 679, Cambridge, Massachusetts, May.

Fog, Bjarke (1976), "How Are Cartel Prices Determined?" Journal of Industrial Economics, Vol. 5, November.

Garnaut, R., and A. Clunies-Ross (1979), "The Neutrality of the Resource Rent Tax," Economic Record, June.

Gibbons, Joel C. (1983), "A Note on Capital-Energy Substitution in the Long Run," Energy Journal, Vol. 5, no. 2. April.

Gibbons, Joel C. (1984), "Energy Prices and Capital Obsolescence: Evidence from the Oil Embargo Period," The Energy Journal, Vol. 5, no. 1, January.

Goldberg, Victor P. (1976), "Regulation and Administered Contracts", The Bell Journal of Economics, Autumn.

Gordon, L. (1983a), "Estimation for Large Successive Samples with Unknown Inclusion Probabilities," US Department of Energy, Energy Information Administration, Washington, D.C.

Gordon, L. (1983b), "Successive Sampling in Large Finite Populations," Annals of Statistics, Vol. 11, No. 2.

Gordon, Richard L. (1966), "Conservation and the Theory of Exhaustible Resources," Canadian Journal of Economics and Political Science, Vol. 32, no. 3, August.

Gordon, Richard L. (1978a), "The Hobbling of Coal: Policy and Regulatory Uncertainties" Science, Vol. 200, April 14.

Gordon, Richard L. (1978b), "Hobbling Coal—or How to Serve Two Masters Poorly," Regulation, Vol. 2, no. 4, July/August.

Gordon, Richard L. (1981a), *An Economic Analysis of World Energy Problems*, The M.I.T. Press, Cambridge, Massachusetts.

Gordon, Richard L. (1981b), *Federal Coal Leasing Policy, Competition in the Energy Industries*, American Enterprise Institute for Public Policy Research, Washington, D.C.

Gordon, Richard L. (1982), *Reforming the Regulation of Electric Utilities*, Lexington Books, Lexington, Massachusetts.

Gordon, Richard L. (1985a), "Access to Federal Lands for Profit Making Purposes—an Economic Overview," *Materials and Society*, Vol. 8, no. 4.

Gordon, Richard L. (1985b), "The Production of Mineral Commodities," *The Economics of the Mineral Industries*, 4th edition, William A. Vogely (editor), American Institute of Mining, Metallurgical, and Petroleum Engineers, New York, New York.

Grayson, C. J. (1960), *Decisions under Uncertainty: Drilling Decisions by Oil and Gas Operators*, Harvard University, Division of Research, Graduate School of Business Administration, Boston, Massachusetts.

Griffin, James M. (1981a), "Engineering and Economic Interpretations of Energy-Capital Complementarity: Comment," *American Economic Review*, Vol. 71, no. 5, December.

Griffin, James M. (1981b), "The Energy-Capital Complementarity Controversy: A Progress Report on Reconciliation Attempts," *Modeling and Measuring Natural Resource Substitution*, Ernst R. Berndt and Barry C. Field (editors), The M.I.T. Press, Cambridge, Massachusetts.

Griffin, James M., and Paul R. Gregory (1976), "An Intercountry Translog Model of Energy Substitution Responses," *American Economic Review*, Vol. 66, no. 5, December.

Griliches, Zvi, and Jacques Mairesse (1983), "Comparing Productivity Growth: An Exploration of French and US Industrial and Firm Data," *European Economic Review*, Vol. 21, no. 1/2, March/April.

Grubb, David (1986), "Raw Materials and the Productivity Slowdown: Some Doubts," *Quarterly Journal of Economics*, August, Forthcoming.

Hamilton, Daniel C. (1958), *Competition in Oil, The Gulf Coast Refinery Market, 1925–1950*, Harvard University Press, Cambridge, Massachusetts.

Hazelton, Jared E. (1970), *The Economics of the Sulfur Industry*, The Johns Hopkins Press, Baltimore, Maryland.

Heiner, Ronald A. (1983), "The Origin of Predictable Behavior," *American Economic Review*, Vol. 73, September.

Hexner, Ervin (1946), *International Cartels*, Pittman Publishing Company, London, England.

Hicks, John (1981), *Wealth and Welfare: Collected Essays on Economic Theory*, Harvard University Press, Cambridge, Massachusetts.

Hieronymous, Thomas A. (1982), *Economics of Futures Trading*, Commodity Research Bureau, New York, New York.

Hill, Joanne, and Thomas Schneeweis (1983), "The Effect of Three Mile Island on Electric Utility Stock Prices: A Note," *The Journal of Finance*, Vol. 38, no. 4, September.

Hirshleifer, J. (1962), "The Firm's Cost Function: A Successful Reconstruction?" *The Journal of Business*, Vol. 35.

Hnyilicza, Esteban, and Robert S. Pindyck (1976), "Pricing Policies for a Two-Part Exhaustible Resource Cartel: The Case of OPEC," *European Economic Review*, Vol. 8, August.

Hoehn, W. E. (1967), "Nuclear Power Reactors for Power and Desalting," Rand Memorandum RM-5227-1-PR/ISA, Santa Monica, California, November.

Hogan, William W. (1979), "Capital-Energy Complementarity in Aggregate Economic Analysis," *Resources and Energy*, Vol. 2, no. 3, November.

Hogan, William W. (1983), "Patterns of Energy Use," Draft Report Prepared for the Energy Conservation Policy Project, Harvard University, John F. Kennedy School of Government, Energy and Environmental Policy Center, Cambridge, Massachusetts, October.

Hogan, William W., and Alan S. Manne (1977), "Energy-Economy Interactions: The Fable of the Elephant and the Rabbit?" *Modeling Energy-Economy Interactions, Five Approaches*, Charles J. Hitch (editor), Resources for the Future, Washington, D.C. A related version of this article with the same title is also found in *Advances in the Economics of Energy and Resources*, Vol. 1, Robert S. Pindyck (editor), 1979, J.A.I. Press, Greenwich, Connecticut.

Howland, R.D. (1966), "Canada's National Oil Policy," Address to the Annual Meeting of the Canadian Institute of Mining and Metallurgy, Quebec City, Quebec, Canada, April 25/27.

Hubbert, M. K. (1962), "Energy Resources: A Report to the Committee on Natural Resources: National Academy of Sciences," National Research Council Publication 1000-D, Washington, D.C.

Hubbert, M. K. (1967), "Degree of Advancement of Petroleum Exploration in the United States," American Association of Petroleum Geologists, Bulletin 51, No. 11, Tulsa, Oklahoma.

Hubbert, M. K. (1974), "U.S. Energy Resources, A Review as of 1972: A Background Paper," Serial No. 93-40 (92-75), Part I prepared at the request of H. M. Jackson, Chairman, Committee on Interior and Insular Affairs, U.S. Senate, U.S. Government Printing Office, Washington, D.C.

Hudson, Edward A., and Dale W. Jorgenson (1974), "US Energy Policy and Economic Growth, 1975–2000," *The Bell Journal of Economics and Management Science*, Vol. 5, no. 2, Autumn.

Hulten, Charles R., and Frank C. Wykoff (1981), "The Measurement of Economic Depreciation," *Depreciation, Inflation and the Taxation of Income from Capital*, C. R. Hulten (editor), The Urban Institute Press, Washington, D.C.

Institute for Fiscal Studies (1981), "The Taxation for North Sea Oil," Report of a Committee of the Institute for Fiscal Studies, London, England, December.

Interstate Natural Gas Association of America (INGAA) (1985), "1985 Price Effects of Decontrol: An Update on the Interstate Market," Washington, D.C., February.

Jacoby, Henry D., and James C. Paddock (1980), "Supply Instability and Oil Market Behavior," *Energy Systems and Policy*, Vol. 3, no. 4.

Jacoby, Henry D., and James C. Paddock (1983), "World Oil Prices and Economic Growth in the 1980's," *The Energy Journal*, Vol. 4, no. 2, April.

Jacoby, Henry D., and Arthur W. Wright (1982), "The Gordian Knot of Natural Gas Prices," *The Energy Journal*, Vol. 3, no. 4, October.

Joint Coal Board (annual), *Black Coal in Australia*, Joint Coal Board, Sydney, Australia.

Jorgenson, Dale W. (1978), "The Role of Energy in the US Economy," *National Tax Journal*, Vol. 31, No. 3, September.

Jorgenson, Dale W. (1984a), "The Great Transition: Energy and Economic Change," Harvard Institute for Economic Research Discussion Paper No. 1103, Harvard University, Cambridge, Massachusetts, December.

Jorgenson, Dale W. (1984b), "The Role of Energy in Productivity Growth," *The Energy Journal*, Vol. 5, no. 3, July.

Jorgenson, Dale W., and Barbara Fraumeni (1981), "Substitution and Technical Change in Production," *Modeling and Measuring Natural Resource Substitution*, Ernst R. Berndt and Barry C. Field (editors), The M.I.T. Press, Cambridge, Massachusetts.

Joskow, Paul, and Nancy L. Rose (1984), *The Effects of Technological Change, Experience and Environmental Regulation on the Construction Costs of Coal-Burning Generating Units*, Massachusetts Institute of Technology, Department of Economics Mimeograph, Cambridge, Massachusetts, March.

Joskow, Paul, and Joel Yellin (1980), "Siting Nuclear Power Plants," *Virginia Journal of Natural Resources Law*, Vol. 1, no. 1, Summer.

Julian, Louise Chandler (1982), "Evaluating the Impacts of the Coal Mine Health and Safety Act of 1969," *Materials and Society*, Vol. 6, no. 2.

Kalt, Joseph P. (1981), *The Economics and Politics of Oil Price Regulation*, The M.I.T. Press, Cambridge, Massachusetts.

Kalt, Joseph P., and Robert S. Stillman (1980), "The Role of Governmental Incentives in Energy Production: An Historical Overview," *The Annual Review of Energy*, Vol. 5.

Kaufman, G. (1962), *Statistical Decision and Related Techniques in Oil and Gas Exploration*, Prentice-Hall Publishing Company, New York, New York.

Kaufman, Gordon M. (1985), "Finite Population Sampling Methods for Oil and Gas Resource Estimation," Forthcoming American Association of Petroleum Geologists Special Publication: Oil and Gas Assessment: Methods and Applications, Tulsa, Oklahoma.

Keeler, Theodore E. (1971), "The Economics of Passenger Trains," *Journal of Business*, Vol. 44, April.

Keeler, Theodore E. Kenneth A. Small, and Associates, (1975), *The Full Costs of Urban Transport.* Volume III: *Automobile Costs and Final Intermodal Cost Comparisons*, Institute of Urban and Regional Development, Monograph 21, Berkeley, California.

Kemp, Alexander (1975), "Fiscal Policy and the Profitability of North Sea Oil Exploration," *Scottish Journal of Political Economy*, Vol. XXII, no. 3, November.

Kemp, Alexander (1976), *Taxation and the Profitability of North Sea Oil*, The Fraser of Allander Institute, Glasgow, Scotland, Research Monograph 4.

Kemp, Alexander, and David Rose (1982), "Tax Changes: A Lost Opportunity," *Petroleum Economist*, Vol. XLIX, April.

Kemp, Alexander, and David Rose (1983), *Petroleum Tax Analysis: North Sea*, Financial Times Business Information, London, England, June.

Kendrick, John W. (1980), "Survey of the Factors Contributing to the Decline in US Productivity Growth," *The Decline in Productivity Growth*, Federal Reserve Bank of Boston Conference Series No. 22, Boston, Massachusetts.

Khazzoom, J. D. (1971), "The FPC Staff's Econometric Model of Natural Gas Supply in the United States," *The Bell Journal of Economics and Management Science*, Vol. 2, no. 1, Spring.

Kim, Y. Y., and R. G. Thompson (1978), *New Oil and Gas Supplies in the Lower 48 States*, Gulf Publishing Co., Houston, Texas.

Kitch, Edmund W. (1968), "Regulation of the Field Market for Natural Gas by the Federal Power Commission," *Journal of Law and Economics*, Vol. 11, October.

Kneese, Allen V., and Charles L. Schultze (1975), *Pollution, Prices, and Public Policy*, The Brookings Institution, Washington, D.C.

Komonoff, Charles (1981), "Power Plant Cost Escalation," Komonoff Energy Associates, New York, New York.

Koopmans, Tjalling C. (1939), *Tanker Freight Rates and Tankship Building*, Haarlem Publishing Company, Amsterdam, Netherlands.

Kopcke, Richard W. (1980), "Capital Accumulation and Potential Growth," *The Decline in Productivity Growth*, Federal Reserve Board of Boston Conference Series No. 22, Boston, Massachusetts.

Kulatilaka, Nalin H. (1985), "Tests on the Validity of Static Equilibrium Models," *Journal of Econometrics*, Vol. 28, May.

Laslavic, Thomas J. (1981), *A Market Shock: The Effects of the Nuclear Accident at Three Mile Island upon the Prices of Electric Utility Securities*, Unpublished M.S. Thesis, Massachusetts Institute of Technology, Sloan School of Management, Cambridge, Massachusetts, June.

Lave, Charles (1976), "The Negative Energy Impact of Modern Rail Transit Systems," Department of Economics, University of California at Irvine. Cited in Altschuler [1979].

Lave, Lester B., and Eugene P. Seskin (1977), *Air Pollution and Human Health*, The Johns Hopkins University Press, Baltimore, Maryland.

Lee, P. J., and P. C. C. Wang (1985), "Prediction of Oil or Gas Pool Sizes When Discovery Record Is Available," *Mathematical Geology*, Vol. 17.

Lindbeck, Assar (1983), "The Recent Slowdown of Productivity Growth," *Economic Journal*, Vol. 93, no. 369, March.

Lister, Louis (1960), *Europe's Coal and Steel Community: An Experiment in Economic Union*, Twentieth Century Fund, New York, New York.

MacAvoy, Paul W., and Robert S. Pindyck (1973), "Alternative Regulatory Policies for Dealing with the Natural Gas Shortage," *The Bell Journal of Economics and Management Science*, Vol. 4, no. 2, Spring.

MacAvoy, Paul W., and Robert S. Pindyck (1975a), *Price Controls and the Natural Gas Shortage*, The American Enterprise Institute, Washington, D.C.

MacAvoy, Paul W., and Robert S. Pindyck (1975b), *The Economics of the Natural Gas Shortage (1960–1980)*, North-Holland Publishing Company, Amsterdam, Holland.

Mannsveldt-Beck, F., and K. Wiig (1977), *The Economics of Offshore Oil and Gas Supply*, Lexington Press, Lexington, Massachusetts.

Marlay, Robert C. (1984), "Trends in Industrial Use of Energy," *Science*, Vol. 226, no. 4680, December 14.

Mayer, L. S., B. Silverman, S. L. Zeger, and A. G. Bruce (1979), "Modelling the Rates of Domestic Crude Oil Discovery and Production," Resource Estimation and Validation Project, Departments of Statistics and Geology, Princeton University, Princeton, New Jersey, February.

McDonald, Stephen L. (1971), *Petroleum Conservation in the United States*, The Johns Hopkins Press for Resources for the Future, Baltimore, Maryland.

McDonald,Stephen L. (1979), *The Leasing of Federal Lands for Fossil Fuels Production*, The Johns Hopkins University Press, Baltimore, Maryland.

McGraw-Hill Publications Company (1981), *Historical Pollution Control Expenditures and Related Data*, April, Table 2.

McKay, B. G., and N. F. Taylor (1979), "Definition of Petroleum Reserves Using Probability Analysis," *The APEA Journal*, Vol. 19, Australian Petroleum Exploration Association, Australia.

McKelvey, V. E. (1975), "Concepts of Reserves and Resources," *Methods of Estimating the Volume of Undiscovered Oil and Gas Resources*, J. D. Haun (editor), American Association of Petroleum Geologists, Studies in Geology No. 1, Tulsa, Oklahoma.

McKie, J. (1975), "Review of Erickson and Waverman's *The Energy Question: An International Failure of Policy*," *Bell Journal of Economics*, Autumn.

Mead, W. J., A. Moseidjord, and P. E. Sorenson (1983), "Efficiency in Leasing," *International Energy Markets*, P. Tempest (editor), Oelgeschlager, Gunn, and Hain, Cambridge, Massachusetts.

Meisner, J., and Demirmen, F. (1980), "The Creaming Method: A Bayesian Procedure to Forecast Future Oil and Gas Discoveries in Mature Exploration Provinces," *Journal of the Royal Statistical Society*, Series A, Vol. 143.

Meyer, John R., and Jose A. Gomez-Ibanez (1981), *Autos, Transit and Cities*, Harvard University Press, Cambridge, Massachusetts.

Meyer, John R., John Kain, and Martin Wohl (1965), *The Urban Transport Problem*, Harvard University Press, Cambridge, Massachusetts.

Mikdashi, Zuhayr (1976), *The International Politics of Natural Resources*, Cornell University Press, Ithaca, New York.

Mills, Edwin S. (1978), *The Economics of Environmental Quality*, W.W. Norton and Company, New York, New York.

Mitchell, Edward J. (editor) (1983), *The Deregulation of Natural Gas*, The American Enterprise Institute, Washington, D.C.

Mitchell, John (1982), "Taxation of Oil and Gas Revenues of Four Countries—The United Kingdom," *The Energy Journal*, Vol. 3, no. 2.

Mooz, William E. (1978), *Cost Analysis of Light Water Reactor Power Plants*, The Rand Corporation, Report No. R-2304-DOE, Santa Monica, California, June.

Mork, Knut Anton, and Robert E. Hall (1980a), "Energy Prices and the US Economy in 1979–1981," *The Energy Journal*, Vol. 1, no. 2, April.

Mork, Knut Anton, and Robert E. Hall (1980b), "Energy Prices, Inflation, and Recession, 1974–1975," *The Energy Journal*, Vol. 1, no. 3, July.

Morris, D. J. (1983), "The Recent Slowdown of Productivity Growth: Comments on the Paper by Professor Lindbeck," *Economic Journal*, Vol. 93, no. 369.

Morrison, Catherine J. (1985), "The Impact of Quasi-Fixed Inputs in US and Japanese Manufacturing: A Development and Application of the Generalized Leontief Restricted Cost Function," Mimeograph, National Bureau of Economic Research, Cambridge, Massachusetts, June.

Morrison, Catherine J., and Ernst R. Berndt (1981), "Short-Run Labor Productivity in a Dynamic Model," *Journal of Econometrics*, Vol. 16, no. 4, December.

Morrison, Thurmond L. (1939), "The Economics of the Sulfur Industry," PhD Thesis, Department of Economics, University of Texas at Austin, Austin, Texas.

Myers, John G., and Leonard Nakamura (1978), *Saving Energy in Manufacturing: The Post-Embargo Record*, Ballinger Publishing Company, Cambridge, Massachusetts.

Nader, Ralph (1965), *Unsafe at Any Speed*, Grossman Press, New York, New York.

Naill, R. (1978), "A Review and Assessment of Fossil I Supply Structure," Thayer School of Engineering, Dartmouth College, DSD-125, September.

National Commission on Air Quality (1981), *To Breath Clean Air*, March.

National Energy Board (1974), *In the Matter of the Exportation of Oil*, Ottawa, Canada, October.

National Petroleum Council (1972), *US Energy Outlook: A Report of the National Petroleum Council's Committee on US Energy Outlook*, Washington, D.C., December.

National Safety Council (1982), *Accident Facts*.

Navarro, Peter (1980), "The Politics of Air Pollution," *The Public Interest*, no. 59, Spring.

Nehring, R. (1981), "The Discovery of Significant Oil and Gas Fields in the United States," The Rand Corporation Report R-2654/1-USGS/DOE, Santa Monica, California.

Nelligan, J. D. (1980), "Petroleum Resources Analysis within Geologically Homogeneous Classes," PhD Thesis, Department of Mathematics and Computer Sciences, Clarkson College of Technology, Potsdam, New York, June.

Nelson, Robert H. (1983), *The Making of Federal Coal Policy*, Duke University Press, Durham, North Carolina.

Niering, Frank, Jr. (1984), "Oil Industry's Changing Structure," *The Petroleum Economist*, Vol. 51, No. 1, January.

Nordhaus, William D. (1972), "The Recent Productivity Slowdown," *Brookings Papers in Economic Activity*, Vol. 3, The Brookings Institution, Washington, D.C.

Nordhaus, William D. (1980), "The Energy Crisis and Macroeconomic Policy," *The Energy Journal*, Vol. 1, no. 1, January.

Norsworthy, J. Randolph, Michael J. Harper, and Kent Kunze (1979), "The Slowdown in Productivity Growth: Analysis of Some Contributing Factors," *Brookings Papers on Economic Activity*, Vol. 2, The Brookings Institution, Washington, D.C.

Norwegian Ministry of Petroleum and Energy (1980), *Cost Study: Norwegian Continental Shelf*, Oslo, Norway.

Ohta, Makoto, and Zvi Griliches (1986), "Automobile Prices and Quality: Did the Gasoline Price Increase Change Consumer Tastes in the US?" *Journal of Business and Economic Statistics*, Vol. 4, No. 2, April.

Okun, Arthur M. (1974), "Unemployed and Output in 1974," *Brookings Papers on Economic Activity*, Vol. 2, The Brookings Institution, Washington, D.C.

Okun, Arthur M. (1975), "A Postmortem of the 1974 Recession," *Brookings Papers on Economic Activity*, Vol. 1, The Brookings Institution, Washington, D.C.

Orr, Daniel, and Paul W. MacAvoy (1965), "Price Strategies to Promote Cartel Stability" *Economica*, Vol. 32, May.

Osborne, D. K. (1976), "Cartel Problems," *American Economic Review*, Vol. 66, December.

Peck, Stephen C., and John L. Solow (1982), "Domestic Energy: A Forgotten Factor in Simple Energy-Economy Models," *Energy Journal*, Vol. 3, no. 3, July.

Peltzman, Sam (1975), "The Effects of Automobile Safety Regulation," *Journal of Political Economy*, Vol. 83, August.

Perry, George L. (1975a), "Policy Alternatives for 1974," *Brookings Papers on Economic Activity*, Vol. 1, The Brookings Institution, Washington, D.C.

Perry, George L. (1975b), "The United States," *Higher Oil Prices and the World Economy: The Adjustment Problem*, Edward R. Fried and Charles L. Schultze (editors), The Brookings Institution, Washington, D.C.

Perry, George L. (1977), "Potential Output and Productivity," *Brookings Paper on Economic Activity*, Vol. 1, The Brookings Institution, Washington, D.C.

Pindyck, Robert S. (1974), "The Regulatory Implications of Three Alternative Econometric Supply Models of Natural Gas," *The Bell Journal of Economics and Management Science*, Vol. 5, no. 2, Autumn.

Pindyck, Robert S. (1977), "Cartel Pricing and the Structure of the World Bauxite Market," *The Bell Journal of Economics*, Vol. 8, Autumn.

Pindyck, Robert S. (1978), "Gains to Producers from the Cartelization of Exhaustible Resources," *Review of Economics and Statistics*, Vol. 60, May.

Pindyck, Robert S. (1979a), "Some Long-Term Problems in OPEC Oil Pricing," *Journal of Energy and Development*, Vol. 4, Spring.

Pindyck, Robert S. (1979b), "The Cartelization of World Commodity Markets," *American Economic Review*, Vol. 69, May.

Pindyck, Robert S. (1979c), *The Structure of World Energy Demand*, The M.I.T. Press, Cambridge, Massachusetts.

Pindyck, Robert S. (1979d), "Interfuel Substitution and the Industrial Demand for Energy: An International Comparison," *Review of Economics and Statistics*, Vol. 61, no. 2, May.

Pindyck, Robert S. (1980), "Energy Price Increases and Macroeconomic Policy," *The Energy Journal*, Vol. 1, no. 4, October.

Pindyck, Robert S. (1983), "Competitive and Monopoly Resource Extraction with Stochastic Reserves," M.I.T. Energy Laboratory Working Paper No. MIT-EL 83-019WP, Cambridge, Massachusetts, July.

Pindyck, Robert S., and Julio J. Rotemberg (1983), "Dynamic Factor Demands, Energy Use, and the Effects of Energy Price Shocks," *American Economic Review*, Vol. 73, no. 5, December.

Portney, Paul R. (editor) (1978), *Current Issues in US Environmental Policy*, The Johns Hopkins University Press, Baltimore, Maryland.

Radlauer, Mary A., David S. Bauman, and Steven W. Chapel (1985), "Nuclear Construction Lead Times: Analysis of Past Trends and Outlook for the Future," *The Energy Journal*, Vol. 6, no. 1, January.

Ramsey, J. B. (1981), "The Economics of Oil Exploration: A Probability-of-Ruin Approach," *Energy Economics*, January.

Ramsay, William (1979), *Unpaid Costs of Electric Energy: Health and Environmental Impacts from Coal and Nuclear Power*, The Johns Hopkins University Press, Baltimore, Maryland.

Rapoport, A. (1979), *LORENDAS Model Documentation*. Vol. I: *Mathematical Concepts and Formulation*, Virginia Polytechnic Institute and State University, May.

Rasche, Robert H., and John A. Tatom (1977a), "The Effects of the New Energy Regime on Economic Capacity, Production, and Prices," *Federal Reserve Bank of St. Louis Review*, Vol. 59, no. 5, May.

Rasche, Robert H., and John A. Tatom (1977b), "Energy Resources and Potential GNP," Federal Reserve Bank of St. Louis *Review*, Vol. 59, no. 6, June.

Robinson, Bill (1984), "Economic Background to the Coal Dispute," *Economic Outlook 1984–1988*, Vol. 9, no. 1.

Roeber, Joe (1979a), "Oil Markets: Paradox and Platitude," *Petroleum Economist*, Vol. XLVI, no. 4, April.

Roeber, Joe (1979b), "The Dynamics of the Rotterdam Oil Market," *Petroleum Economist*, Vol. XLVI, no. 2, February.

Roeber, Joe (1979c), "The Wilder Shores of the Oil Trade, *Petroleum Economist*, Vol. XLVI, no. 3, March.

Rogers, Robert P. (1977), *Competition in the Sulfuric Acid Industry*, Federal Trade Commission Staff Report, US Government Printing Office, Washington, D.C., May.

Rohlfs, Jeffrey H. (1969), *Economic Analysis of the Mercury Industry*, Unpublished PhD Thesis, Department of Economics, Massachusetts Institute of Technology, Cambridge, Massachusetts.

Root, D. H., and J. H. Scheunemeyer (1980), "Mathematical Foundations," *Petroleum-Resource Appraisal and Discovery Rate Forecastng in Partially Explored Regions*, US Geological Survey Professional Paper 1138—Parts A, B, C, US Department of the Interior, Washington, D.C.

Roxburgh, Nigel (1980), *Policy Responses to Resource Depletion: The Case of Mercury*, J.A.I. Press, Greenwich, Connecticut.

Royal Commission on Energy (1959), *Second Report*, Ottawa, Canada, July.

Ryan, J. M. (1965), "National Academy of Sciences Report on Energy Resources: Discussion of Limitations of Logistic Projections," AAPG Bulletin 49, Washington, D.C.

Sanders, M. Elizabeth (1981), *The Regulation of Natural Gas: Policy and Politics, 1938–78*, Temple University Press, Philadelphia, Pennsylvania.

Saunders, Harry D. (1982), "Energy-Economy Interactions: Oil and the World Economy," Unpublished PhD Thesis, Department of Economics, Stanford University, Stanford, University.

Schagen, I. P. (1980), "A Stochastic Model for the Occurrence of Oilfields and Its Application to Some North Sea Data," *Applied Statistics*, Vol. 29, no. 3.

Schumpeter, Joseph A. (1950), *Capitalism, Socialism, and Democracy*, 3rd edition, Harper and Brothers, New York, New York.

Schurr, Sam H. (1982), "Energy Efficiency and Productive Efficiency: Some Thoughts Based on American Experience," *The Energy Journal*, Vol. 3, no. 3, July.

Schurr, Sam H., and Bruce Netschert (1960), *Energy in the American Economy, 1850–1975*, The Johns Hopkins Press for Resources for the Future, Baltimore, Maryland.

Schwing, Richard, et al. (1980), "Benefit-Cost Analysis of Automobile Emissions Reductions," *Journal of Environmental Economics and Management*, Vol. 7, March.

Serghiou, Serghios, and Zenon S. Zannetos (1982), "The Level and Structure of Single Voyage Freight Rates in the Short Run," *Transportation Science*, Vol. 16, February.

Shaffer, E. H. (1968), *The Oil Import Program of the United States*, Praeger Press, New York, New York.

Smith, James L., and James L. Paddock (1983), "Regional Modeling of Oil Discovery and Production," M.I.T. Energy Laboratory Working Paper No. MIT-EL 82-048WP, Cambridge, Massachusetts.

Smith James L., and G. L. Ward (1981), "Maximum Likelihood Estimates of the Size Distribution of North Sea Oil Fields," *Mathematical Geology*, Vol. 13, no. 5.

Solow, John (1979), "A General Equilibrium Approach to Aggregate Capital-Energy Complementarity," *Economics Letters*, Vol. 1, no. 2.

Sporn, Philip (1968), *Nuclear Power Economics 1962–67*, Joint Committee on Atomic Energy, 90th Congress, 2d Session.

Sporn, Philip (1970), *AEC Authorizing Legislation, Fiscal Year 1971*, Joint Committee on Atomic Energy, 91st Congress, 2d Session.

Stanford Research Institute (1972), "The Market Price for Natural Gas from Sources in Western Canada, 1972–1990," Volumes I and II, A Report Prepared for the Canadian Petroleum Association Submission to the Alberta Energy Resource Conservation Board, Menlo Park, California, June.

Statistik der Kohlenwirtschaft e.V. (semiannual), *Zahlen zur Kohlenwirtschaft*, Essen, West Germany.

Stiglitz, Joseph (1976), "Monopoly and the Rate of Extraction of Exhaustible Resources," *American Economic Review*, Vol. 66, no. 4, September.

Stollery, Kenneth R. (1983), "Mineral Depletion with Cost as the Extraction Limit: A Model Applied to the Behavior of Prices in the Nickel Industry," *Journal of Environmental Economics and Management*, Vol. 10, June.

Stubbs, R. L. (1982), "Lead and Zinc," *Mining Annual Review*, June.

Sumner, M. T. (1978), *Progressive Taxation of Natural Resources*, The Manchester School of Economics and Social Studies, Manchester, England, March.

Swan, P. L. (1976), "Income Taxes, Profit Taxes, and Neutrality of Optimizing Decisions," *The Economic Record*, Vol. 52, No. 138, June.

Swan, P. L. (1979), "Australian Mining Industry Taxation and the Industries Assistance Commission: An Appraisal of Two Reports," in Ben Smith (editor), *Taxation in the Mining Industry*, Centre for Resource and Environmental Studies, Australian National University, Report No. CRES R/GP 12.

Tatom, John A. (1979a), "Energy Prices and Capital Formation: 1972–1977," Federal Reserve Bank of St. Louis *Review*, Vol. 61, no. 5, May.

Tatom, John A. (1979b), "The Productivity Problem," Federal Reserve Bank of St. Louis *Review*, Vol. 61, no. 9, September.

Tatom, John A. (1982), "Potential Output and the Recent Productivity Decline," Federal Reserve Bank of St. Louis *Review*, Vol. 64, no. 1, January.

Thurow, Lester C. (1979), "The US Productivity Problem," *Data Resources US Review*, August.

Thurow, Lester C. (1980), "Comment on Kendrick," *The Decline in Productivity Growth*, Federal Reserve Bank of Boston Conference Series No. 22, Boston, Massachusetts.

Thurow, Lester C. (1985), "Slow Productivity Growth," Chapter 3 in Unpublished Book Manuscript, M.I.T. Sloan School of Management, Cambridge, Massachusetts, January.

Tinbergen, Jan (1934), "Tonnage and Freight," *De Nederlandsche Conjunctur*, reprinted in *Jan Tinbergen: Selected Papers*, L. H. Klaasen et al. (editors), 1959, North-Holland Publishing Company, Amsterdam, Holland.

Tucker, L. (1979), *TERA: Total Energy Resource Analysis Model, Technical Documentation*, AGA, Vol. II, Onshore Gas and Oil Supply Model.

Turner, Louis (1984), *Coal's Contribution to U.K. Self-Sufficiency*, Heinemann Educational Books, London, England.

Tussing, Arlon R., and Connie C. Barlow (1984), *The Natural Gas Industry: Evolution, Structure and Economics*, Ballinger Publishing Company, Cambridge, Massachusetts.

Tversky, A., and D. Kahneman (1974), "Judgment under Uncertainty: Heuristics and Biases," *Science*, Vol. 185, September.

Tyner, Wallace E., and Robert J. Kalter (1978), *Western Coal: Problems or Promise?*, Lexington Books, Lexington, Massachusetts.

Uhler, R. S. (1979), *Oil and Gas Finding Costs*, Canadian Energy Research Institute, Study No. 7, Calgary, Alberta, Canada.

United Kingdom, Monopolies and Merger Commission (1983), *National Coal Board Report on the Efficiency and Costs in the Development, Production and Supply of Coal by the NCB*, Her Majesty's Stationary Office, London, England.

Unternehmensverband Ruhrbergbau (1955 and 1961), *Die Kohlenwirtschaft der Welt in Zahlen*, Verlag Gluckauf GMBF, Essen, Germany.

Uri, N. D. (1979), "New Look at U.S. Reserves Shows Higher Potential," *World Oil*, February 1.

US Bureau of Labor Statistics (1980), "Guidelines for Adjustment of New Automobile and Truck Prices for Changes in Quality of Product," US Department of Labor, Washington, D.C., July 25.

US Bureau of Mines (various years), *Commodity Data Summaries*, US Government Printing Office, Washington, D.C.

US Bureau of Mines (various years), *Mineral Yearbook*, US Government Printing Office, Washington, D.C.

US Bureau of Mines (1960 and 1965), *Mineral Facts and Problems*, US Government Printing Office, Washington, D.C.

US Cabinet Task Force on Oil Import Control (1970), *The Oil Import Question*, US Government Printing Office, Washington, D.C., February.

US Commission on Fair Market Value Policy for Federal Coal Leasing (1984), *Report of the Commission*, US Government Printing Office, Washington, D.C.

US Comptroller General (1976), *Effectiveness, Benefits, and Costs of Federal Safety Standards of Protection of Passenger Car Occupants*, July 7.

US Congress (1939), *Hearings before the Temporary National Economic Committee*, 76th Congress, 1st Session, Part 5.

US Congress, Congressional Budget Office (1982), *The Clean Air Act, the Electric Utilities, and the Coal Market*, US Government Printing Office, Washington, D.C., April.

US Congress, House Select Committee on Small Business (1950), "Effects of Foreign Oil Imports on Independent Domestic Producers," US Government Printing Office, Washington, D.C.

US Congress, Office of Technology Assessment (1984), *Acid Rain and Transported Air Pollutants: Implications for Public Policy*, US Government Printing Office, Washington, D.C.

US Department of Energy (DOE), Energy Information Administration (EIA) (1980), *Nuclear Power Regulation*, DOE Report No. DOE/EIA-0201/10, Washington, D.C., May.

US Department of Energy (DOE), Energy Information Administration (EIA) (1982a), "Production of Onshore Lower-48 Oil and Gas-Model Methodology and Data Description, DOE/EIA-0345, June.

US Department of Energy (DOE), Energy Information Administration (EIA) (1982b), *Projected Costs of Electricity from Nuclear and Coal-Fired Power Plants*, Washington, D.C., November.

US Department of Energy (DOE), Energy Information Administration (EIA) (1983a), *Nuclear Plant Cancellations: Causes, Costs, and Consequences*, DOE Report No. DOE/EIA-0392, Washington, D.C., April.

US Department of Energy (DOE), Energy Information Administration (EIA) (1983b), *Structure and Trends in Natural Gas Wellhead Contracts*, DOE Report No. DOE/EIA 0419, Washington, D.C., November.

US Department of Energy (DOE), Energy Information Administration (EIA) (1984a), *A Study of Contracts between Interstate Pipelines and Their Customers*, DOE Report No. DOE/EIA-0449, July.

US Department of Energy (DOE), Energy Information Administration (EIA) (1984b), "Drilling and Production under Title I of the Natural Gas Policy Act," DOE Report No. DOE/EIA-0448, Washington, D.C., June.

US Department of Energy (DOE), Energy Information Administration (EIA) (monthly), *Monthly Energy Review*, US Government Printing Office, Washington, D.C.

US Department of Energy (DOE), Energy Information Administration (EIA), Office of Energy Markets and End Use (annual), *Annual Energy Review*, US Government Printing Office, Washington, D.C.

US Department of Energy (DOE), Energy Information Administration (EIA) (annual), *Annual Energy Outlook*, US Government Printing Office, Washington, D.C.

US Department of the Interior (1975), "Geological Estimates of Undiscovered Recoverable Oil and Gas Resources in the United States," Geological Survey Circular 725.

US Department of the Interior (1981), "Geological Estimates of Undiscovered Recoverable Oil and Gas Resources in the United States," Geological Survey Circular 860.

US Department of the Interior (1982), "Estimation of the Future Rates of Oil and Gas Discoveries in the Western Gulf of Mexico," Geological Survey Professional Paper 1252, US Government Printing Office, Washington, D.C.

US Department of the Interior, Office of Minerals Policy and Research Analysis (1979), "Final Report of the 105(b) Economic and Policy Analysis, NPRA," Washington, D.C., December 15.

US Environmental Protection Agency (EPA) (1979), *The Costs of Clean Air*, US Government Printing Office, Washington, D.C.

US Environmental Protection Agency (EPA), Office of Air and Waste Management, Office of Air Quality Planning and Standards (1977), *Compilation of Air Pollutant Emission Factors*, 3rd edition, August, pp. 1–2.

US Environmental Protection Agency (EPA), Office of Air Quality and Planning and Standards, Office of Air, Noise and Radiation (1978a), *National Air Pollutant Emissions Estimates, 1950–1976*, US Government Printing Office, Washington, D.C., July.

US Environmental Protection Agency (EPA), Office of Air Quality and Planning and Standards, Office of Air, Noise and Radiation (1978b), *National Air Quality, Monitoring, and Emissions Trends Report 1977*, US Government Printing Office, Washington, D.C., December.

US Environmental Protection Agency (EPA), Office of Air Quality and Planning and Standards, Office of Air, Noise and Radiation (1979), *Resources and Pollution Control*, US Government Printing Office, Washington, D.C., September.

US Environmental Protection Agency (EPA), Office of Air Quality and Planning and Standards, Office of Air, Noise and Radiation (1981a), *National Air Pollutant Emissions Estimates, 1970–1979*, US Government Printing Office, Washington, D.C., March.

US Environmental Protection Agency (EPA), Office of Air Quality and Planning and Standards, Office of Air, Noise and Radiation (1981b), *1980 Ambient Assessment—Air Portion*, US Government Printing Office, Washington, D.C., February.

US Environmental Protection Agency (EPA), Office of Air Quality and Planning and Standards, Office of Air, Noise and Radiation (1981c), *Appendices A and B to the 1980 Ambient Assessment Air Portion*, US Government Printing Office, Washington, D.C., February.

US Environmental Protection Agency (EPA), Office of Air Quality and Planning and Standards, Office of Air, Noise and Radiation (1982), *National Air Pollutant Emission Estimates, 1940–1980*, US Government Printing Office, Washington, D.C., January.

US Environmental Protection Agency (EPA), Office of Air Quality and Planning and

Standards, Office of Air, Noise and Radiation (1984), *National Air Pollutant Emission Estimates, 1940–1983*, US Government Printing Office, Washington, D.C., December.

US Environmental Protection Agency (EPA), Office of Enforcement (1981), *An Investigation of the Corrosion in Particulate Control Equipment*, February.

US Federal Energy Administration (1974), *Project Independence Report*, US Government Printing Office, Washington, D.C., November.

US General Accounting Office, Report by the Comptroller General of the United States (1982), *Cleaning Up the Environment: Progress Achieved but Major Unresolved Issues Remain*, Volumes 1 and 2, US Government Printing Office, Washington, D.C., July 21.

US House of Representatives, Select Committee on Small Business (1950), *Effects of Foreign Oil Imports on Independent Domestic Producers*, US Government Printing Office, Washington, D.C.

US National Academy of Sciences (1985), *Natural Gas Data Needs in a Changing Regulatory Environment*, Washington, D.C.

US National Highway Traffic Safety Administration (1983), *The Economic Cost to Society of Motor Vehicle Accidents*, US Government Printing Office, Washington, D.C., January.

US Senate (1936), "Federal Trade Commission Report on Utility Corporations," 70th Congress, 1st Session, Document No. 92, Part 84A.

US Senate (1969), *Hearings* before the Subcommittee on Antitrust and Monopoly, Committee on the Judiciary, 91st Congress, 1st Session, Senate Resolution 40, The Petroleum Industry, Part 1, March/April.

US Synfuels Interagency Task Force (1975), "Recommendations for a Synthetic Fuels Commercialization Program," Report Submitted to the President's Energy Resource Council, US Government Printing Office, Washington, D.C.

Verleger, Philip K., Jr. (1982), "The Determinants of Official OPEC Crude Prices," *The Review of Economics and Statistics*, Vol. LXVI, no. 2, May.

Vernon, Raymond (1983), *Two Hungry Giants*, Harvard University Press, Cambridge, Massachusetts.

Vickery, J., L. Cohen, and J. Cummins (1980), *Characteristication of Operation and Maintenance Problems with Air Pollution Control Equipment*, Report Prepared for the US Environmental Protection Agency, Office of Planning and Management, US Government Printing Office, Washington, D.C., July.

Wang, P. C. C., and P. J. Lee (1983a), "Conditional Analysis for Petroleum Resource Evaluations," *Mathematical Geology*, Vol. 15, no. 2.

Wang, P. C. C., and P. J. Lee (1983b), "Probabilistic Formulation of a Method for the Evaluation of Petroleum Resources," *Mathematical Geology*, Vol. 15, no. 1.

Watkins, G. Campbell (1977), "Conservation and Economic Efficiency, Alberta Oil Proration," *Journal of Environmental Economics and Management*, Vol. 4.

Watkins, G. Campbell (1981), "Living under a Shadow: The United States Oil Import Program and Canadian Oil Pricing," Paper Given to Energy Policy Seminar, Center for Energy Policy Research, Massachusetts Institute of Technology, Cambridge, Massachusetts, October.

Watkins, G. Campbell (1984), "Dynamic Models of Industrial Energy Demand," Mimeograph, Calgary, Alberta, Canada, September.

Watkins, G. Campbell, and Paul G. Bradley (1982), "Government Policy and the Canadian Crude Oil Supply Sector," *The Canadian Oil Industry: An Analysis*, G. Campbell Watkins (editor), mimeo.

Waverman, L., and G. Campbell Watkins (1985), "The Regulation of the Canadian Downstream Oil Industry: Nature, Impact and Remedies," University of Toronto, Policy Study No. 85-1, Toronto, Canada, January.

Weisskopf, Thomas E., Samuel Bowles, and David M. Gordon (1983), "Hearts and Minds: A Social Model of US Productivity," *Brookings Papers on Economic Activity*, Vol. 2, The Brookings Institution, Washington, D.C.

White, D. A. (1980), "Assessing Oil and Gas Plays in Facies-Cycle Wedges," *American Association of Petroleum Geologists Bulletin*, Vol. 64.

White, D. C., R. W. Garrett, Jr., G. P. Marsh, R. H. Baker, and H. M. Gehman (1975), "Assessing Regional Oil and Gas Potential," *AAPG Studies in Geology, No. 1: Methods of Estimating the Volume of Undiscovered Oil and Gas Reserves*, American Association of Petroleum Geologists, Tulsa, Oklahoma.

White, Lawrence J. (1982), *The Regulation of Air Pollution Emissions from Motor Vehicles*, American Enterprise Institute, Washington, D.C.

Williams, Stephen F. (1985), *The Natural Gas Revolution of 1985*, American Enterprise Institute, Washington, D.C.

Williamson, Oliver (1975), *Markets and Hierarchies: Analysis and Antitrust* Implications, Free Press, New York, New York.

Williamson, Oliver (1979), "Transaction Cost Economics: The Governance of Contractual Relations," *Journal of Law and Economics*, October.

Wilson, Richard, Steven D. Colame, John D. Spengler, and David Gordon Wilson (1980), *Health Effects of Fossil Fuel Burning, Assessment and Mitigation*, Ballinger Publishing Company, Cambridge, Massachusetts.

Winkler, W. E., (1984), "Exact Matching Using Elementary Techniques," *American Statistical Association Proceedings of the Section on Survey Research Methods*.

Wiorkowski, J. J. (1981), "Estimating Volumes of Remaining Fossil Fuel Resources: A Critical Review," *Journal of the American Statistical Association*, Vol. 76, no. 375, September.

Wood, William C. (1981), "Nuclear Liability after Three Mile Island," *The Journal of Risk and Insurance*, Vol. 48, September.

Wood, William C. (1983), *Nuclear Safety: Risks and Regulation*, American Enterprise Institute for Public Policy Research, Washington, D.C.

Woolf, Arthur G. (1984), "Electrification, Productivity, and Labor-Saving: American Manufacturing, 1900–1929," *Explorations in Economic History*, Vol. 21, April.

World Tanker Fleet Review (1983), John I. Jacobs, PLC, London, July–December.

Wright, Brian D. (1980), "The Cost of Tax-Induced Energy Conservation," *The Bell Journal of Economics*, Vol. 11, no. 1, Spring.

Yellin, Joel (1976), "The Nuclear Regulatory Commission's Reactor Safety Study," *The Bell Journal of Economics*, Vol. 7. no. 1, Spring.

Zannetos, Zenon S. (1959), "The Theory of Oil Tankership Rates, Vols. I and II," PhD Thesis, Department of Economics, Massachusetts Institute of Technology, Cambridge, Massachusetts, August 24.

Zannetos, Zenon S. (1965), "Theoretical Factors Affecting the Long-Term Charter Rate for Tankers in the Long Run and Suggestions for Measurement," Massachusetts Institute of Technology, Sloan School of Management Working Paper 118–65, Cambridge, Massachusetts.

Zannetos, Zenon S. (1966), *The Theory of Oil Tankship Rates: An Economic Analysis of Tankship Operations*, The M.I.T. Press, Cambridge, Massachusetts.

Zannetos, Zenon S. (1973a), "Market and Cost Structure in Shipping," *Shipping Management*, Lorange and Norman (editors), Institute for Shipping Research, Bergen, Norway.

Zannetos, Zenon S. (1973b), "Persistent Economic Misconceptions in the Transportation of Oil by Sea," *Maritime Studies Management*, Vol. 1.

Zannetos, Zenon S., et al. (1981), "Cost Structure and Period Rates for Oil Tankers," *Proceedings, Twenty-Second Annual Meeting*, Vol. XXII, no. 1, Transportation and Research Forum, San Francisco, California.

Zimmerman, Martin B. (1977), "Modeling Depletion in a Mineral Industry: The Case of Coal," *The Bell Journal of Economics*, Vol. 8.

Zimmerman, Martin B. (1978), "Estimating a Policy Model of US Coal Supply," *Materials and Society*, Vol. 2, no. 1.

Zimmerman, Martin B. (1981), *The US Coal Industry: The Economics of Policy Choice*, The M.I.T. Press, Cambridge, Massachusetts.

Zimmerman, Martin B. (1982), "Learning Effects and the Commercialization of New Energy Technologies," *The Bell Journal of Economics*, Vol. 13, no. 2, Autumn.

Zimmerman, Martin B. (1983), "The Valuation of Nuclear Power in the Post Three Mile Island Era," *The Energy Journal*, Vol. 4, no. 2, April.

Zimmerman, Martin B. (1985), "Regulatory Treatment of Abandoned Property: Incentive Effects and Policy Issues," Graduate School of Business Administration, University of Michigan, Ann Arbor, Michigan, Mimeo, January.

Index